KAGETORA
カゲトラ

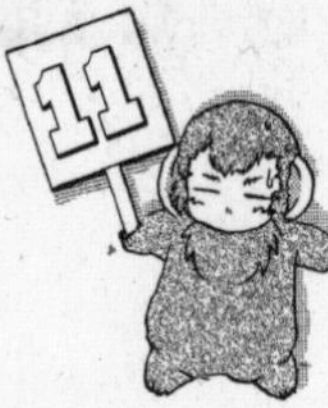
11

Akira Segami

TRANSLATED BY
Satsuki Yamashita

ADAPTED BY
Nunzio DeFilippis & Christina Weir

LETTERING AND RETOUCH BY
North Market Street Graphics

DEL REY

BALLANTINE BOOKS · NEW YORK

A Del Rey Manga/Kodansha Trade Paperback Original

Kagetora, volume 11 copyright © 2006 by Akira Segami
English translation copyright © 2008 by Akira Segami

Published in the United States by Del Rey Books, an imprint of The Random House Publishing Group, a division of Random House, Inc., New York.

DEL REY is a registered trademark and the Del Rey colophon is a trademark of Random House, Inc.

Publication rights arranged through Kodansha Ltd.

First published in Japan in 2006 by Kodansha Ltd., Tokyo.

ISBN 978-0-345-49898-4

Printed in the United States of America

www.delreymanga.com

9 8 7 6 5 4 3 2 1

Translator—Satsuki Yamashita
Adapters—Nunzio DeFilippis and Christina Weir
Lettering and retouch—North Market Street Graphics

Contents

KAGETORA

A Note from the Author

Emotional

Thankful Frog

Thank you everyone.
This is the final volume.
I feel I was able to draw
everything I wanted in
KAGETORA.
I just hope this manga
was satisfying for all
readers...

Segami

Honorifics Explained

Throughout the Del Rey Manga books, you will find Japanese honorifics left intact in the translations. For those not familiar with how the Japanese use honorifics and, more important, how they differ from American honorifics, we present this brief overview.

Politeness has always been a critical facet of Japanese culture. Ever since the feudal era, when Japan was a highly stratified society, use of honorifics—which can be defined as polite speech that indicates relationship or status—has played an essential role in the Japanese language. When you address someone in Japanese, an honorific usually takes the form of a suffix attached to one's name (example: "Asuna-san"), is used as a title at the end of one's name, or appears in place of the name itself (example: "Negi-sensei," or simply "Sensei!").

Honorifics can be expressions of respect or endearment. In the context of manga and anime, honorifics give insight into the nature of the relationship between characters. Many English translations leave out these important honorifics and therefore distort the feel of the original Japanese. Because Japanese honorifics contain nuances that English honorifics lack, it is our policy at Del Rey not to translate them. Here, instead, is a guide to some of the honorifics you may encounter in Del Rey Manga.

-san: This is the most common honorific and is equivalent to Mr., Miss, Ms., or Mrs. It is the all-purpose honorific and can be used in any situation where politeness is required.

-sama: This is one level higher than "-san" and is used to confer great respect.

-dono: This comes from the word "tono," which means "lord." It is an even higher level than "-sama" and confers utmost respect.

-kun: This suffix is used at the end of boys' names to express familiarity or endearment. It is also sometimes used by men among friends, or when addressing someone younger or of a lower station.

-chan: This is used to express endearment, mostly toward girls. It is also used for little boys, pets, and even among lovers. It gives a sense of childish cuteness.

Bozu: This is an informal way to refer to a boy, similar to the English terms "kid" and "squirt."

Sempai/
Senpai: This title suggests that the addressee is one's senior in a group or organization. It is most often used in a school setting, where underclassmen refer to their upperclassmen as "sempai." It can also be used in the workplace, such as when a newer employee addresses an employee who has seniority in the company.

Kohai: This is the opposite of "sempai" and is used toward underclassmen in school or newcomers in the workplace. It connotes that the addressee is of a lower station.

Sensei: Literally meaning "one who has come before," this title is used for teachers, doctors, or masters of any profession or art.

-[blank]: This is usually forgotten in these lists, but it is perhaps the most significant difference between Japanese and English. The lack of honorific means that the speaker has permission to address the person in a very intimate way. Usually, only family, spouses, or very close friends have this kind of permission. Known as *yobisute,* it can be gratifying when someone who has earned the intimacy starts to call one by one's name without an honorific. But when that intimacy hasn't been earned, it can be very insulting.

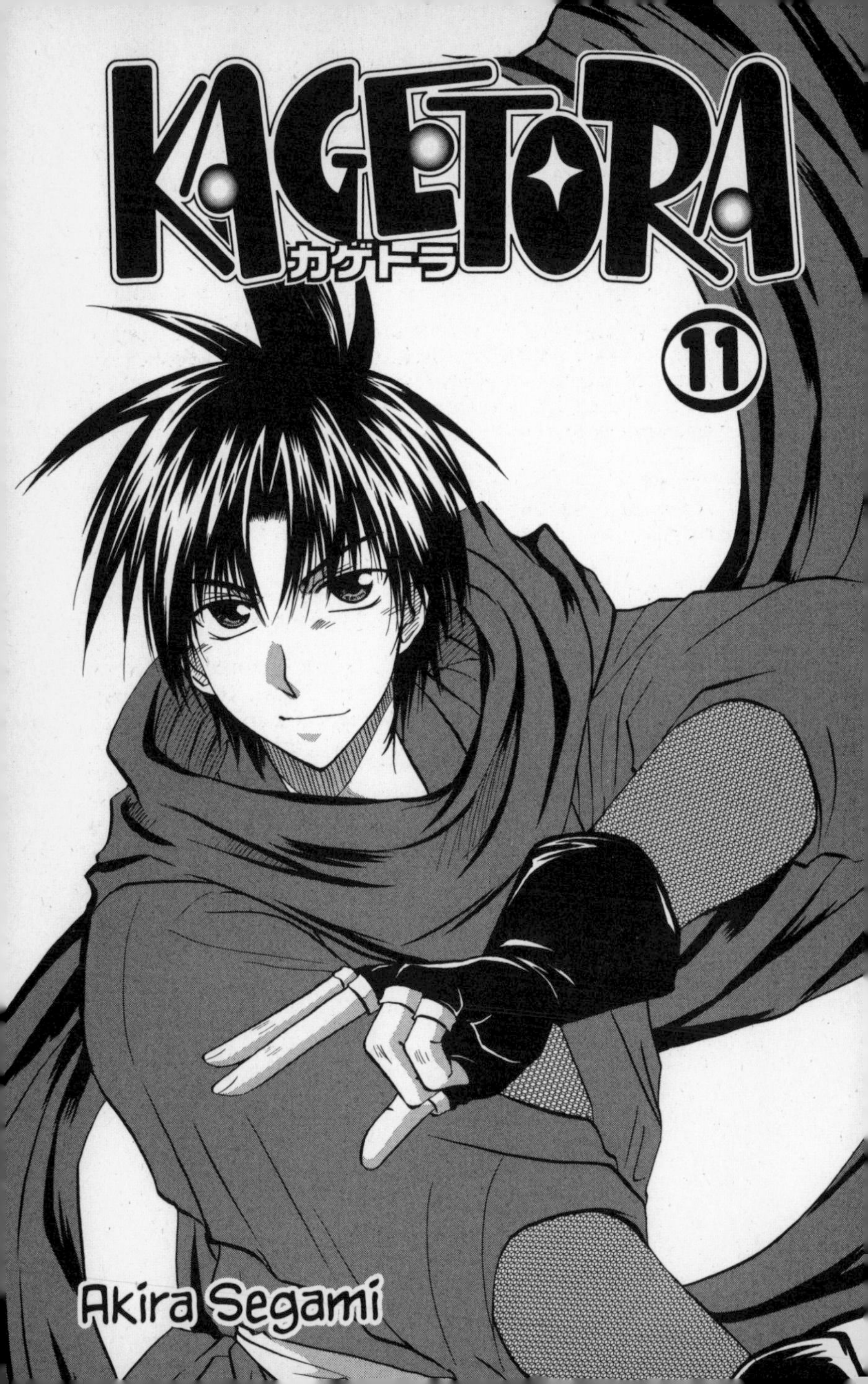
KAGETORA
カゲトラ
11
Akira Segami

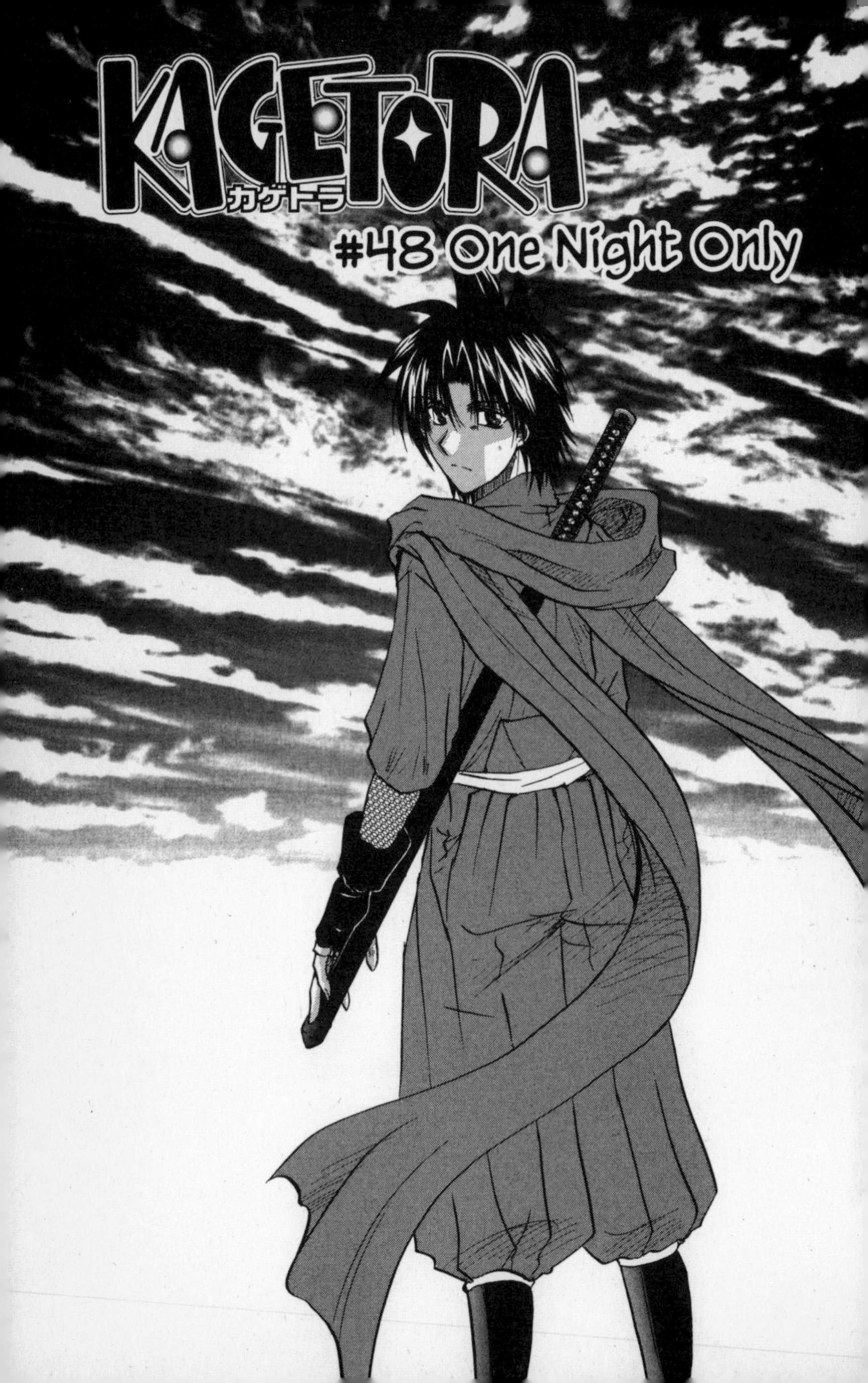
KAGETORA
カゲトラ
#48 One Night Only

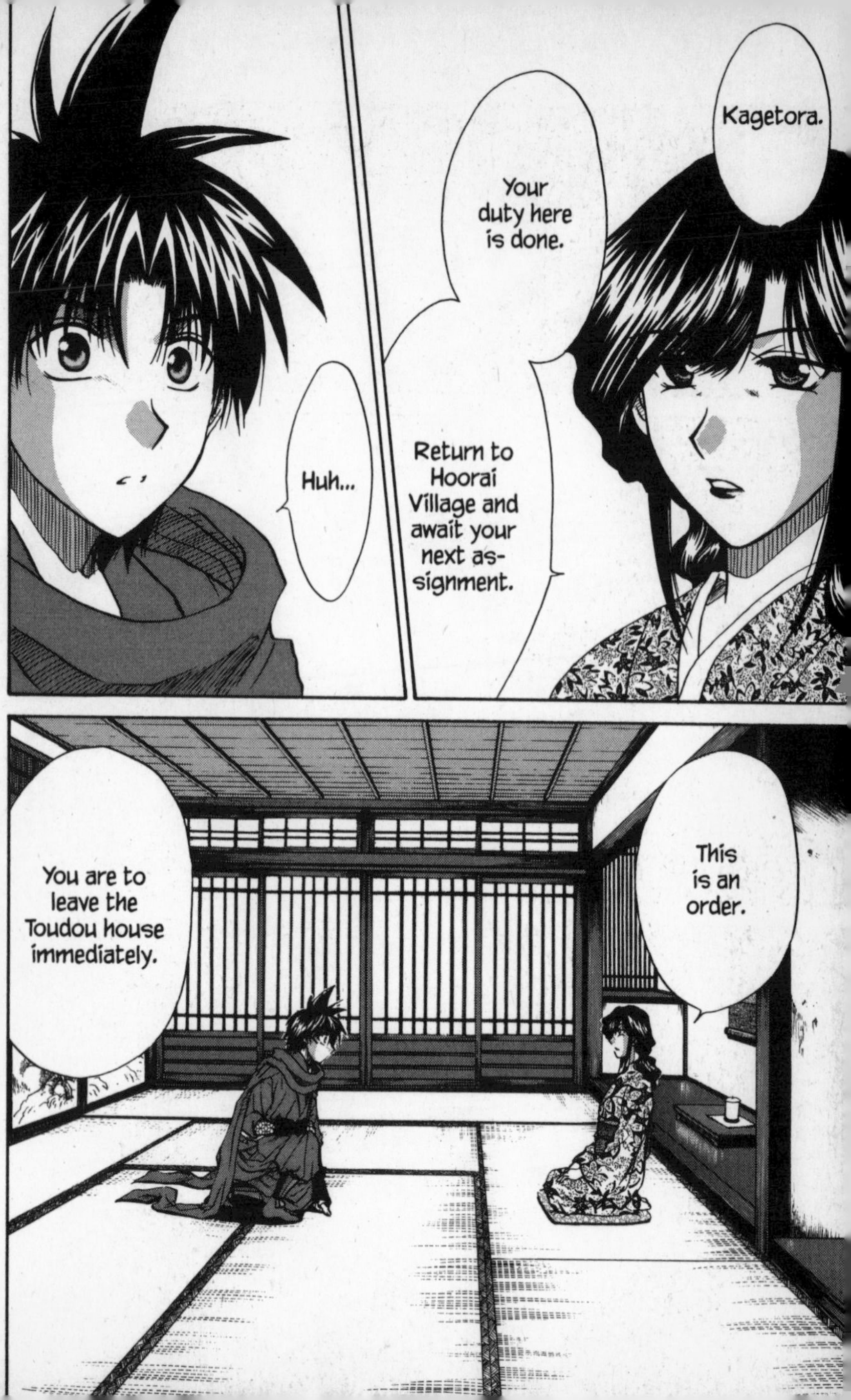
Kagetora.
Your duty here is done.
Return to Hoorai Village and await your next as-signment.
Huh...
This is an order.
You are to leave the Toudou house immediately.

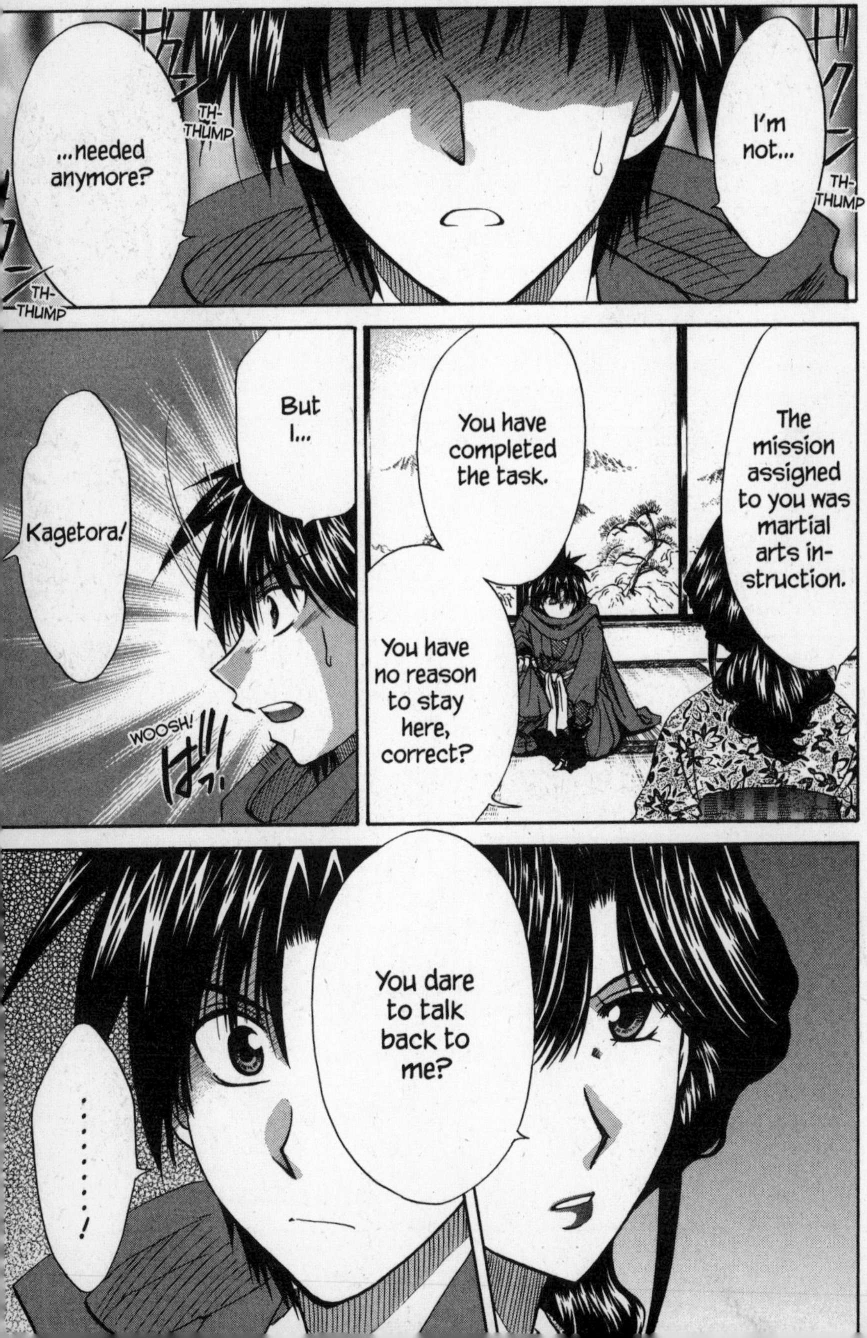
I'm not...
TH-THUMP
TH-THUMP
...needed anymore?
TH-THUMP
The mission assigned to you was martial arts instruction.
You have completed the task.
You have no reason to stay here, correct?
But I...
Kagetora!
WOOSH!
You dare to talk back to me?
.......!

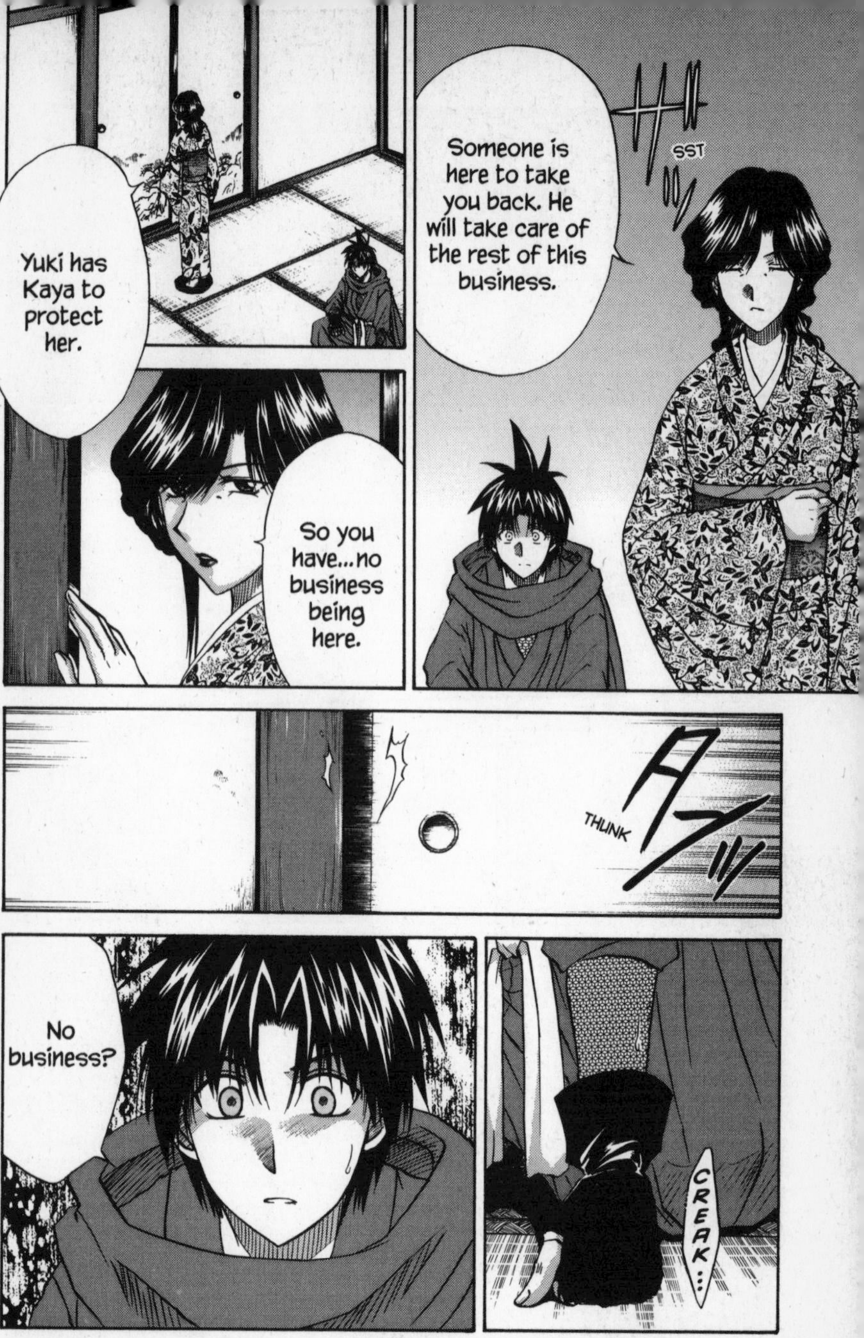
SST
Someone is here to take you back. He will take care of the rest of this business.
Yuki has Kaya to protect her.
So you have...no business being here.
THUNK
CREAK...
No business?

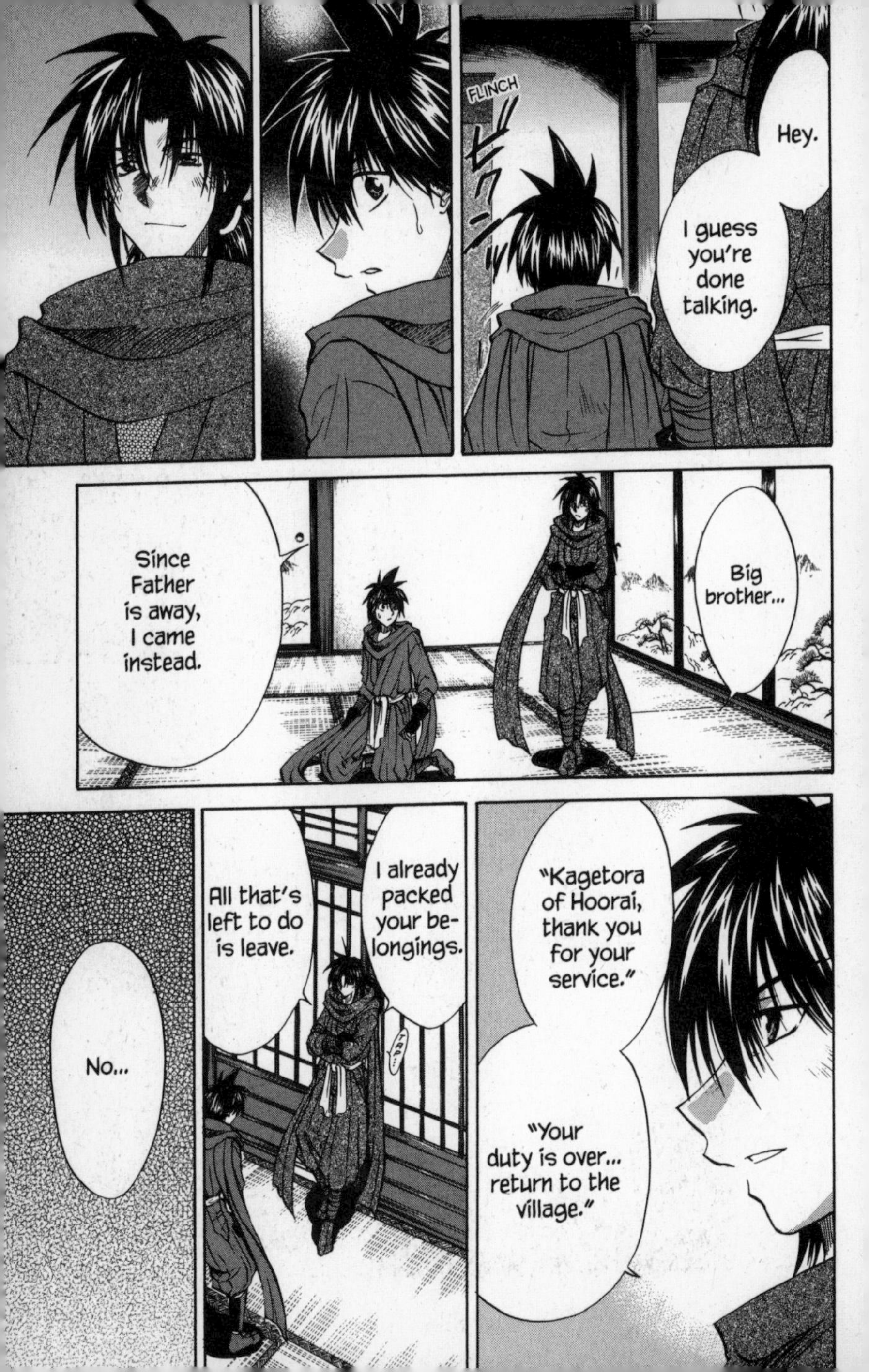

Hey.
I guess you're done talking.
FLINCH
Big brother...
Since Father is away, I came instead.
"Kagetora of Hoorai, thank you for your service."
"Your duty is over... return to the village."
I already packed your be-longings.
All that's left to do is leave.
No...

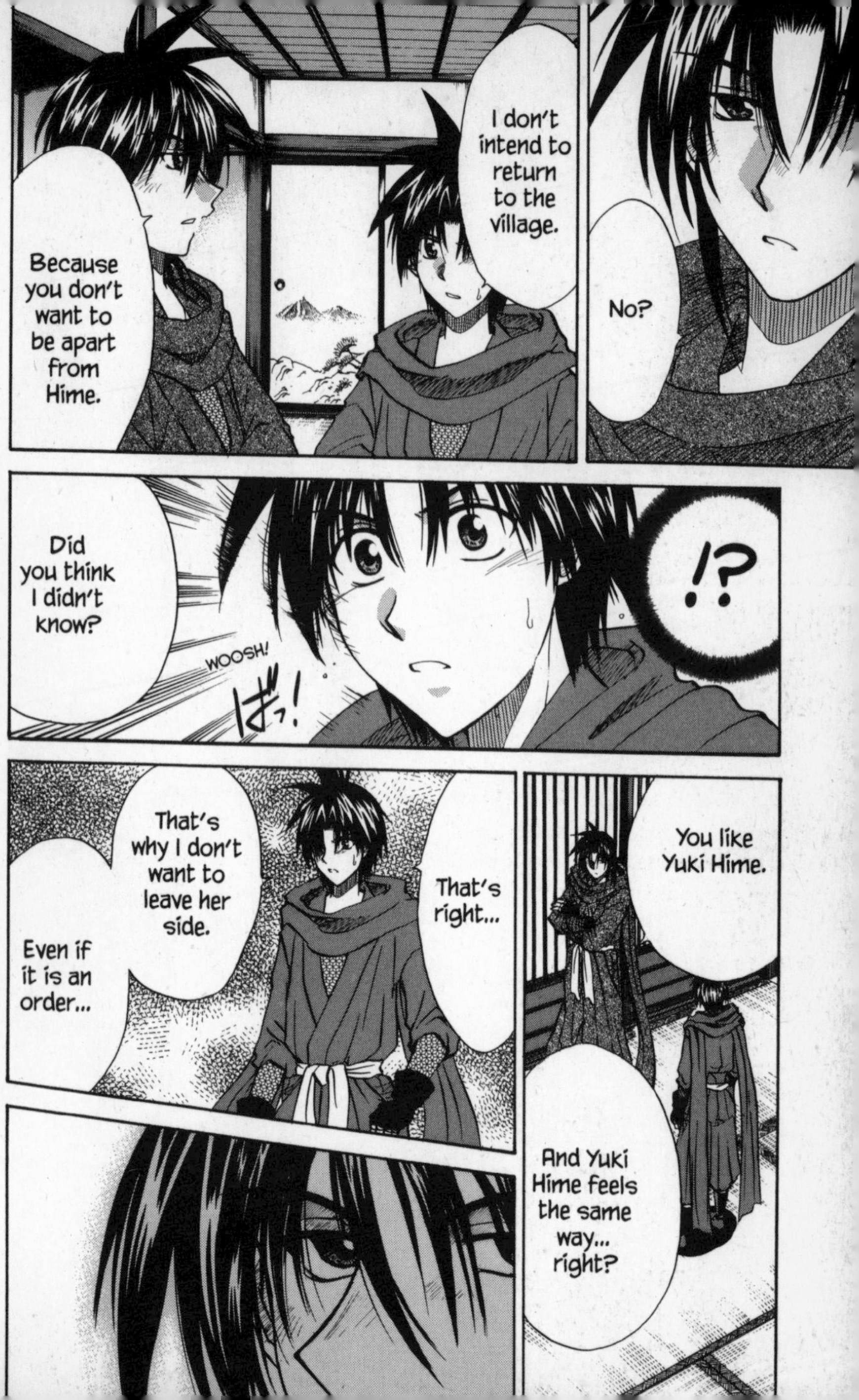
No?
I don't intend to return to the village.
Because you don't want to be apart from Hime.
!?
Did you think I didn't know?
WOOSH!
ばっ!
You like Yuki Hime.
And Yuki Hime feels the same way... right?
That's right...
That's why I don't want to leave her side.
Even if it is an order...

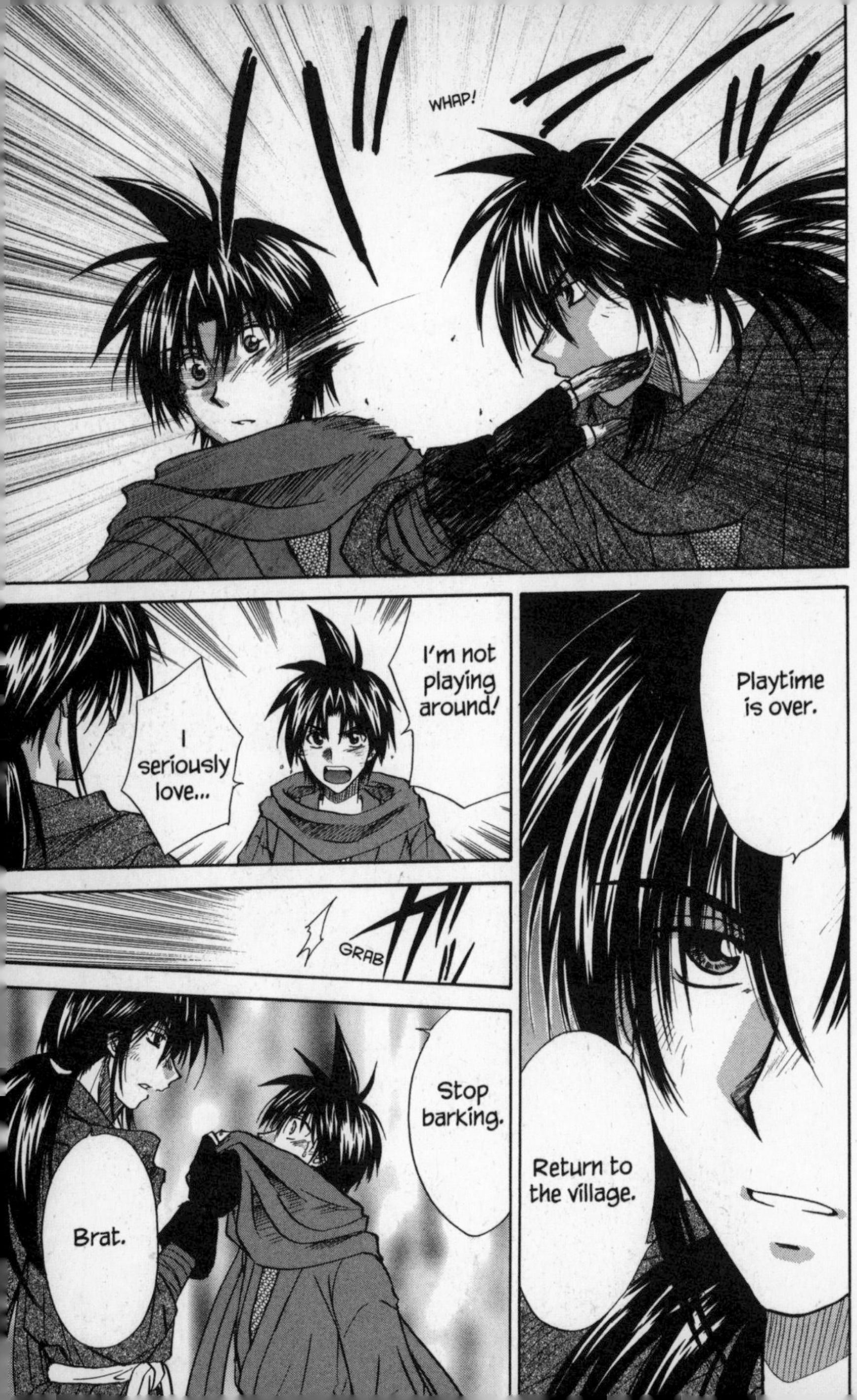
WHAP!
Playtime is over.
Return to the village.
I'm not playing around!
I seriously love...
GRAB
Stop barking.
Brat.

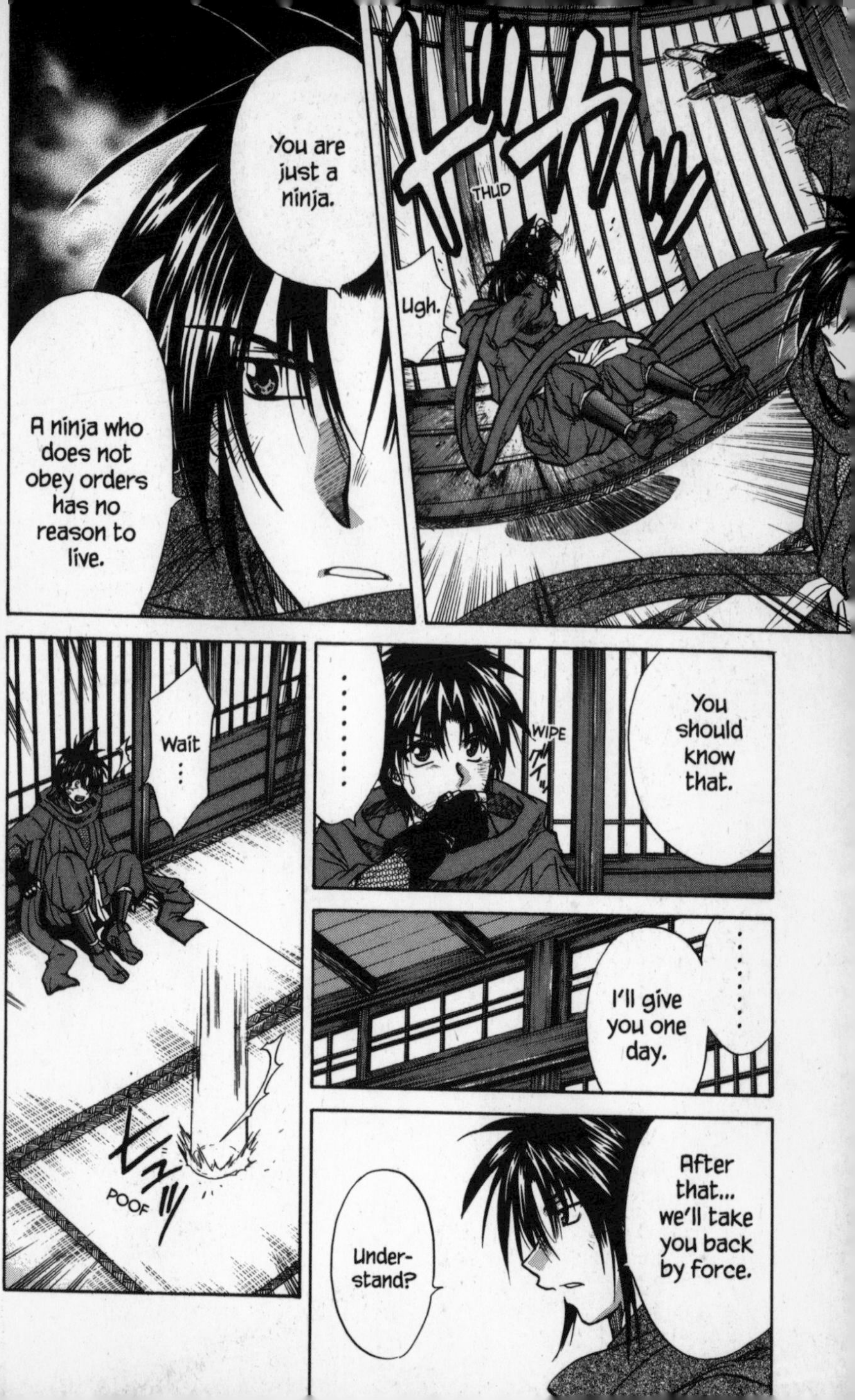
THUD
Ugh.
You are just a ninja.
A ninja who does not obey orders has no reason to live.
You should know that.
WIPE
......
......
I'll give you one day.
After that... we'll take you back by force.
Under-stand?
Wait ...
POOF

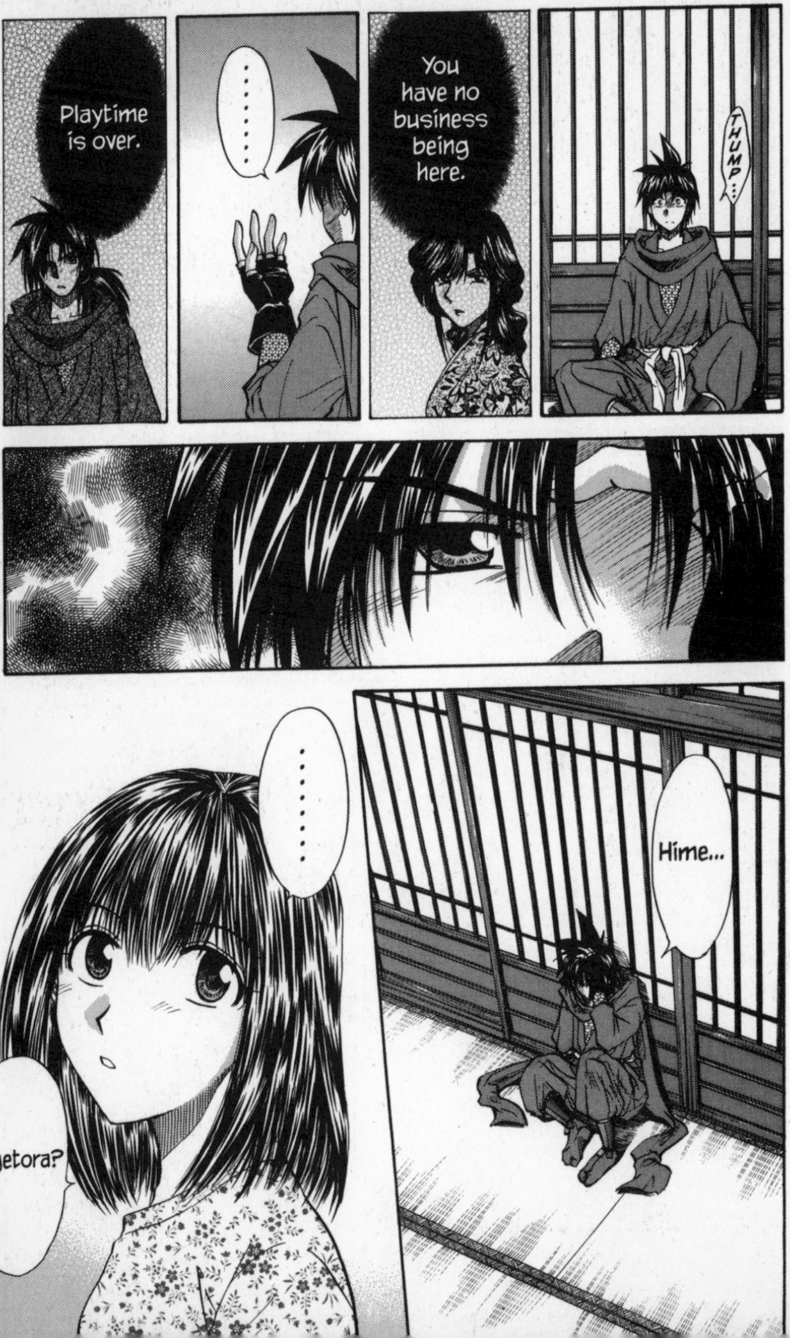
THUMP...
You have no business being here.
......
Playtime is over.
Hime...
......
Kagetora?

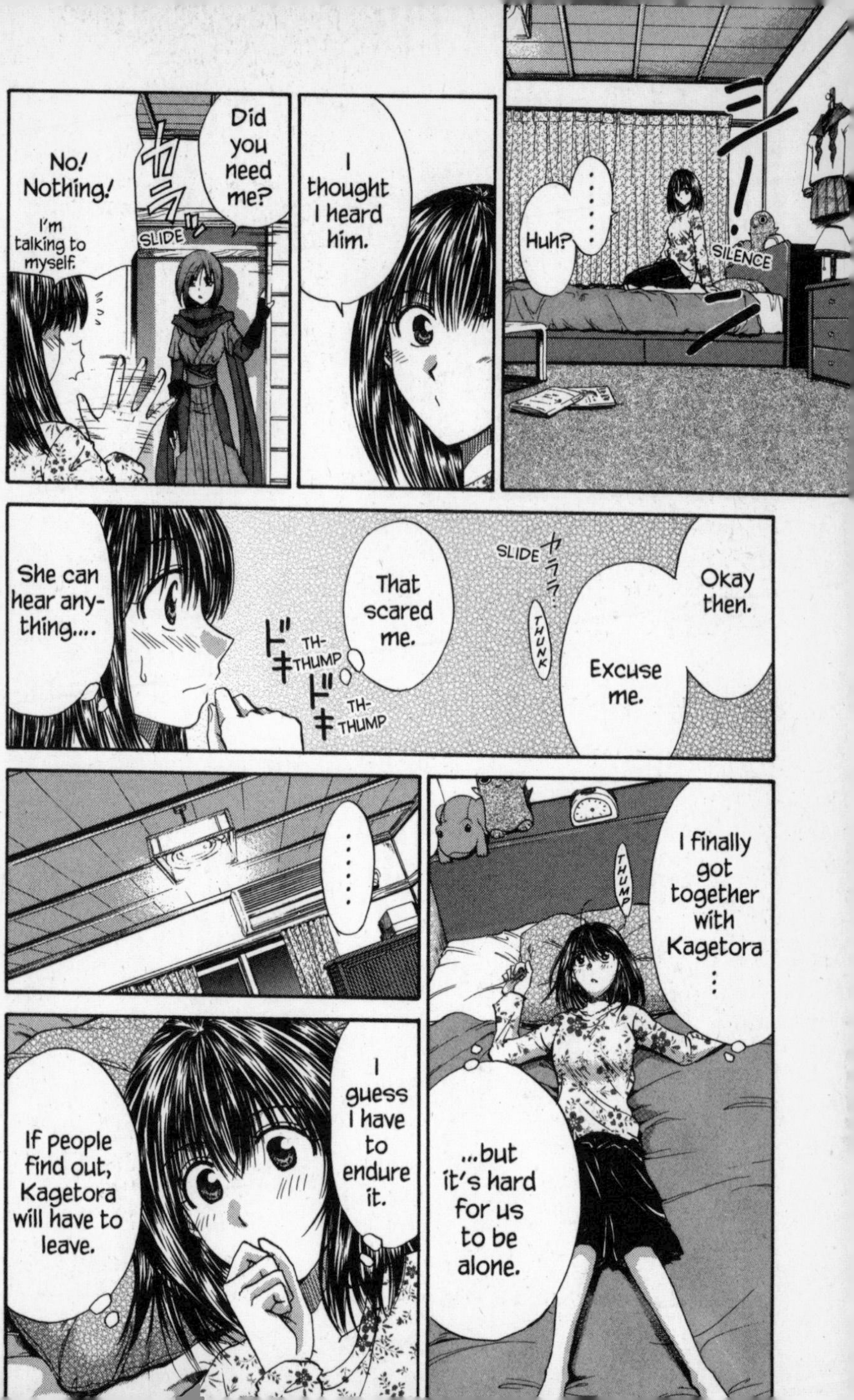
Huh?
......
SILENCE
I thought I heard him.
Did you need me?
SLIDE
No! Nothing!
I'm talking to myself.
Okay then.
Excuse me.
SLIDE
THUNK
That scared me.
TH-THUMP
TH-THUMP
She can hear anything....
I finally got together with Kagetora
...
THUMP
...but it's hard for us to be alone.
......
I guess I have to endure it.
If people find out, Kagetora will have to leave.

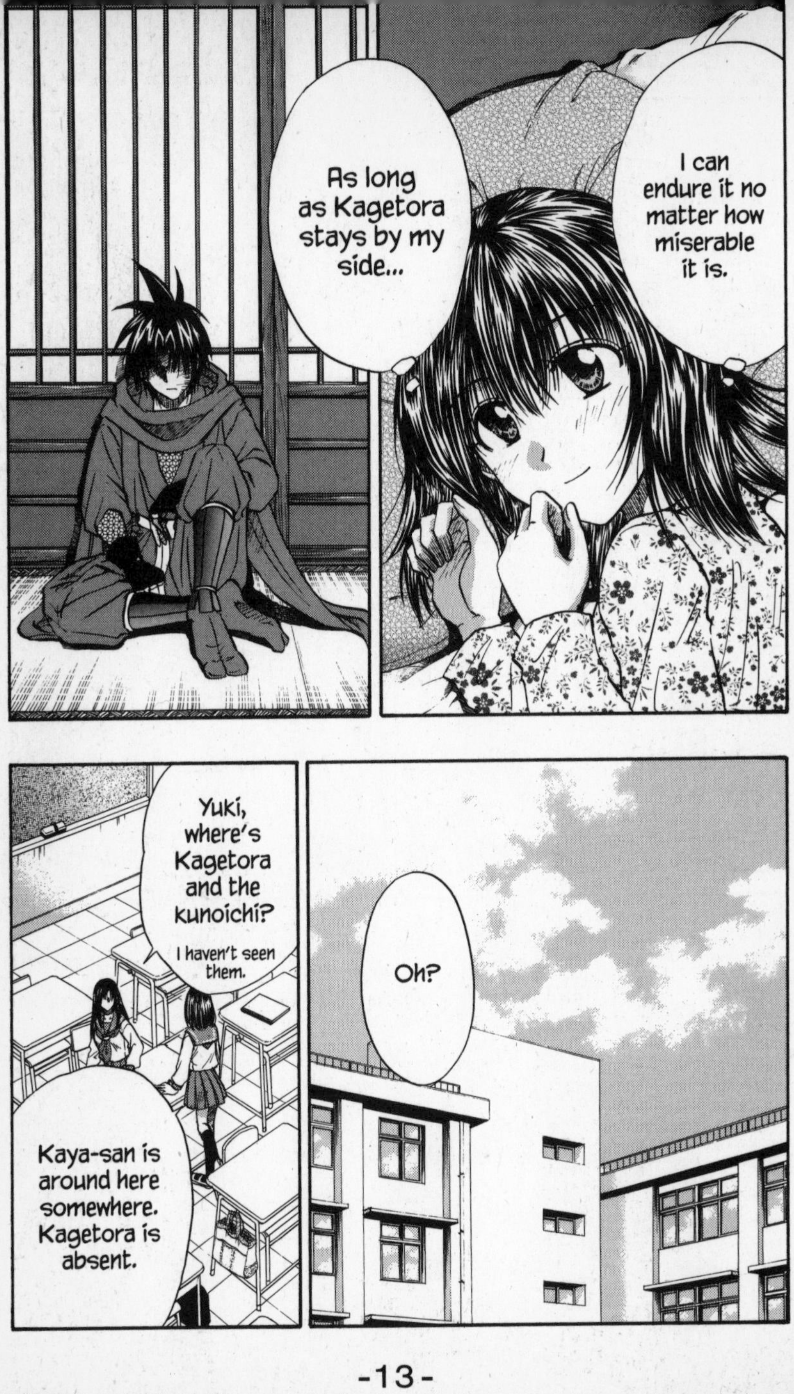
As long as Kagetora stays by my side...
I can endure it no matter how miserable it is.
Oh?
Yuki, where's Kagetora and the kunoichi?
I haven't seen them.
Kaya-san is around here somewhere. Kagetora is absent.

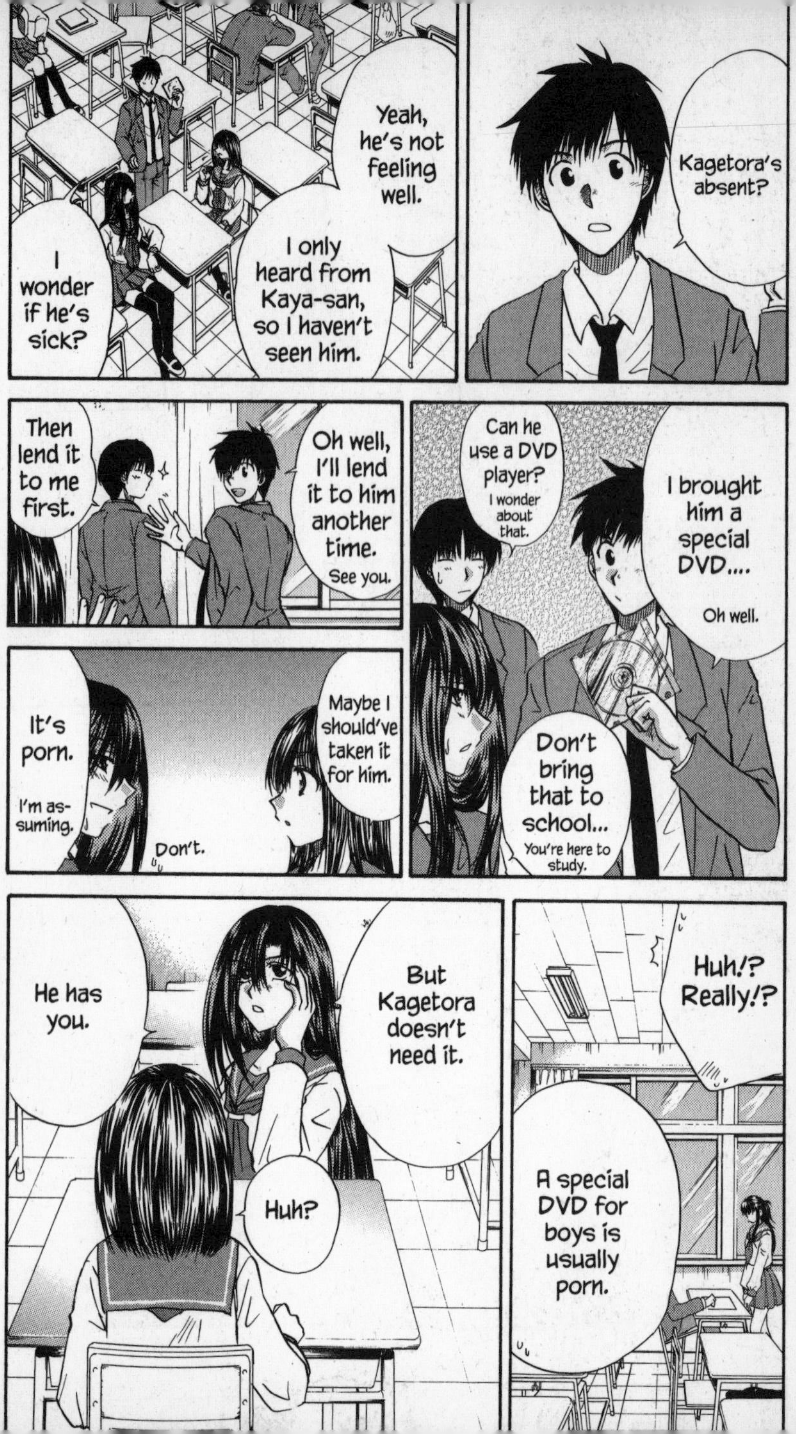
Kagetora's absent?
Yeah, he's not feeling well.
I only heard from Kaya-san, so I haven't seen him.
I wonder if he's sick?
I brought him a special DVD....
Oh well.
Can he use a DVD player?
I wonder about that.
Don't bring that to school...
You're here to study.
Oh well, I'll lend it to him another time.
See you.
Then lend it to me first.
Maybe I should've taken it for him.
It's porn.
I'm assuming.
Don't.
Huh!? Really!?
A special DVD for boys is usually porn.
But Kagetora doesn't need it.
He has you.
Huh?

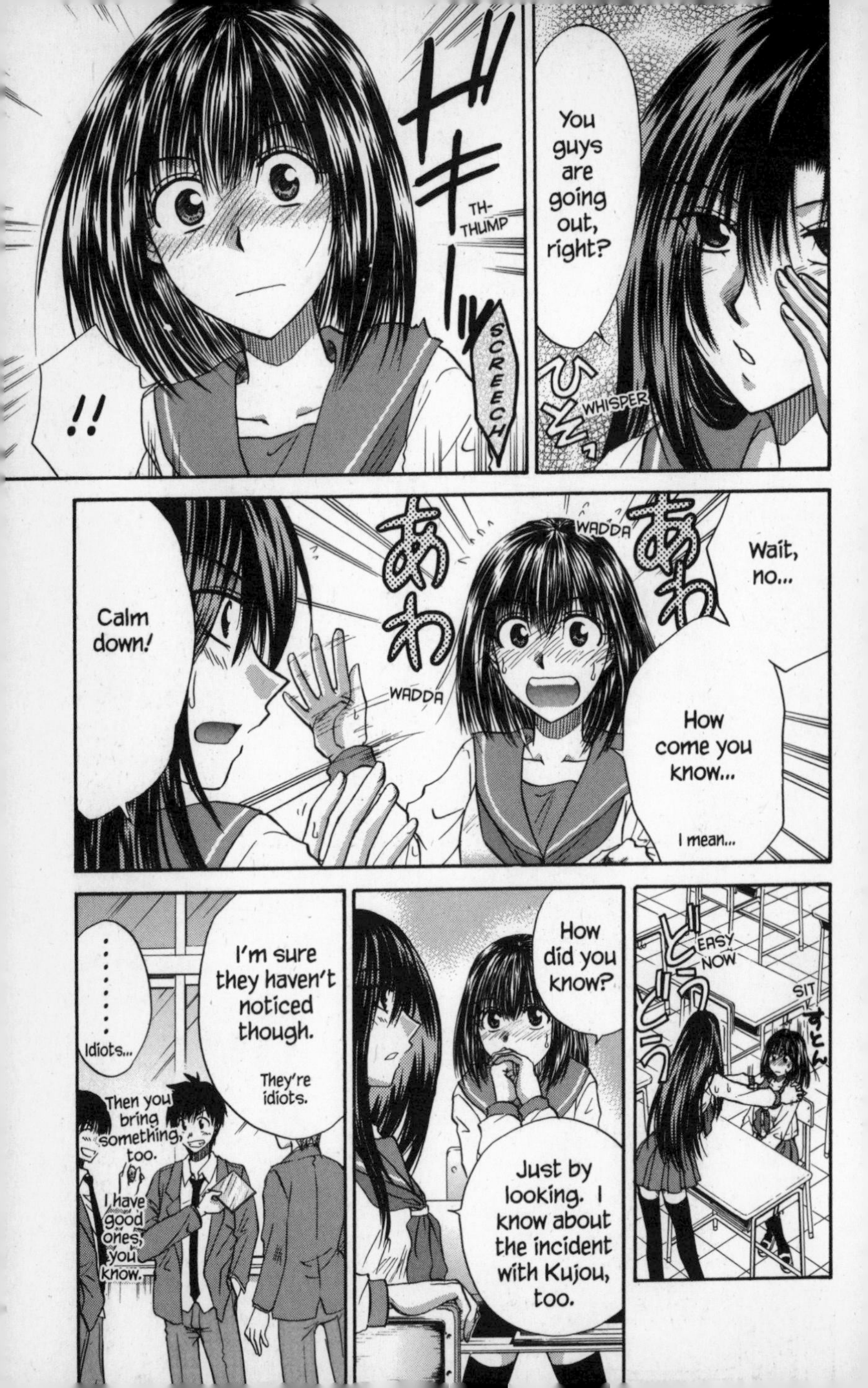

You guys are going out, right?
ひそ
WHISPER
TH-THUMP
SCREECH
!!
Wait, no...
あわ
WADDA
あわ
WADDA
How come you know...
I mean...
Calm down!
どうどう
EASY NOW
すとん
SIT
How did you know?
Just by looking. I know about the incident with Kujou, too.
I'm sure they haven't noticed though.
They're idiots.
......
Idiots...
Then you bring something, too.
I have good ones, you know.

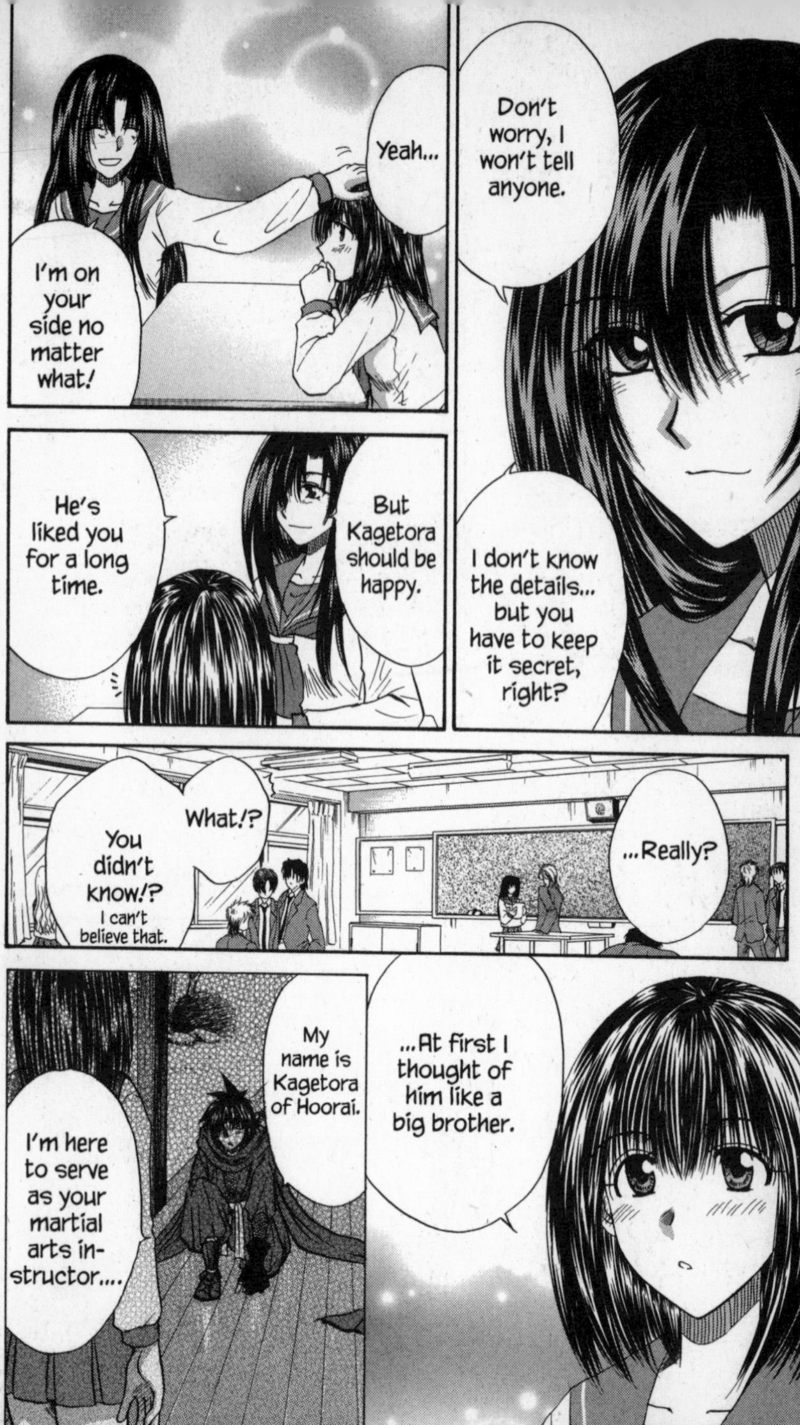
Don't worry, I won't tell anyone.
I don't know the details... but you have to keep it secret, right?
Yeah...
I'm on your side no matter what!
But Kagetora should be happy.
He's liked you for a long time.
...Really?
What!?
You didn't know!?
I can't believe that.
...At first I thought of him like a big brother.
My name is Kagetora of Hoorai.
I'm here to serve as your martial arts instructor....

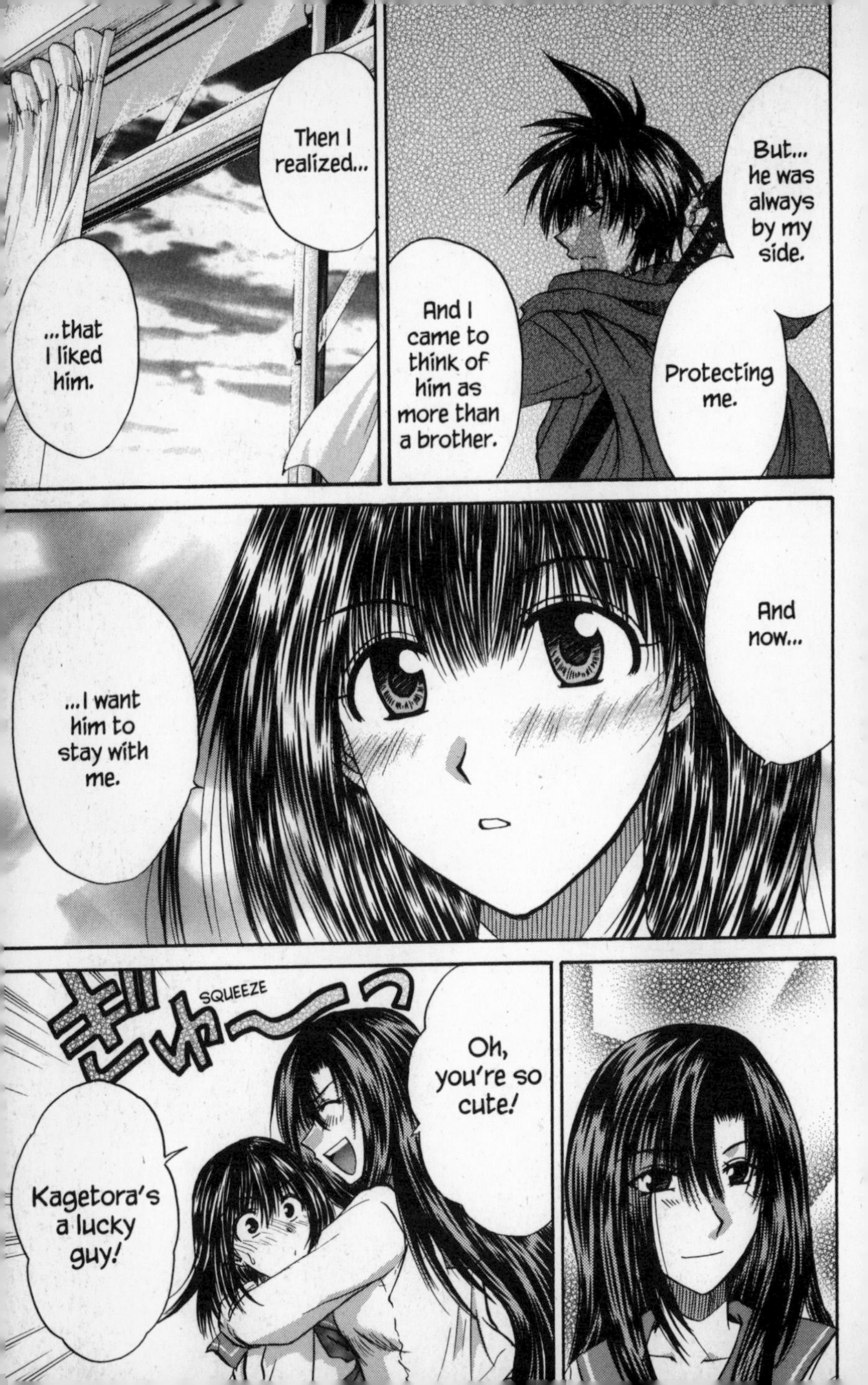
But... he was always by my side.
Protecting me.
And I came to think of him as more than a brother.
Then I realized...
...that I liked him.
And now...
...I want him to stay with me.
ぎゅ～っ
SQUEEZE
Oh, you're so cute!
Kagetora's a lucky guy!

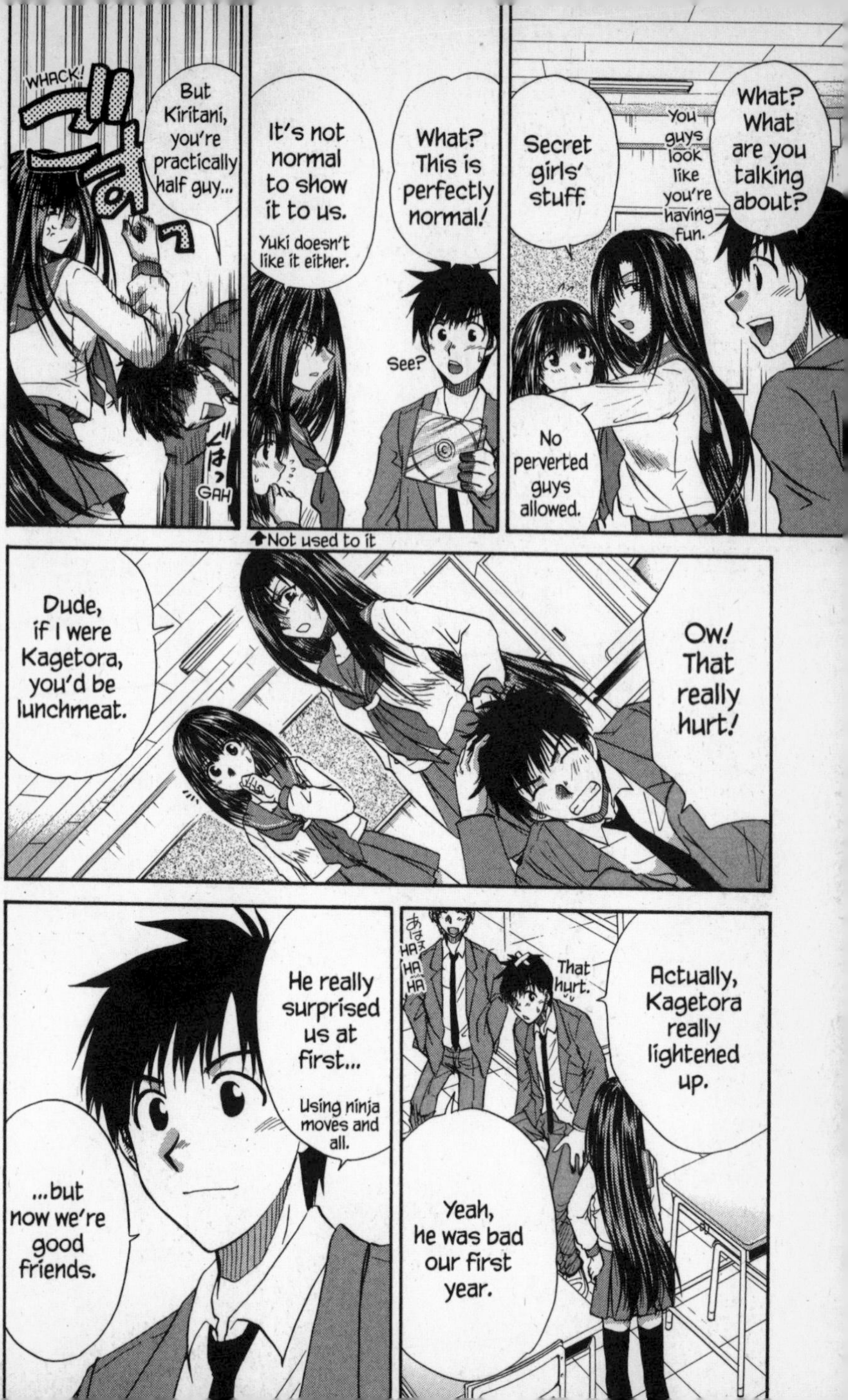
What? What are you talking about?
You guys look like you're having fun.
Secret girls' stuff.
No perverted guys allowed.
What? This is perfectly normal!
See?
It's not normal to show it to us.
Yuki doesn't like it either.
Not used to it
But Kiritani, you're practically half guy...
WHACK!
GAH
Ow! That really hurt!
Dude, if I were Kagetora, you'd be lunchmeat.
Actually, Kagetora really lightened up.
That hurt.
HA HA HA
Yeah, he was bad our first year.
He really surprised us at first...
Using ninja moves and all.
...but now we're good friends.

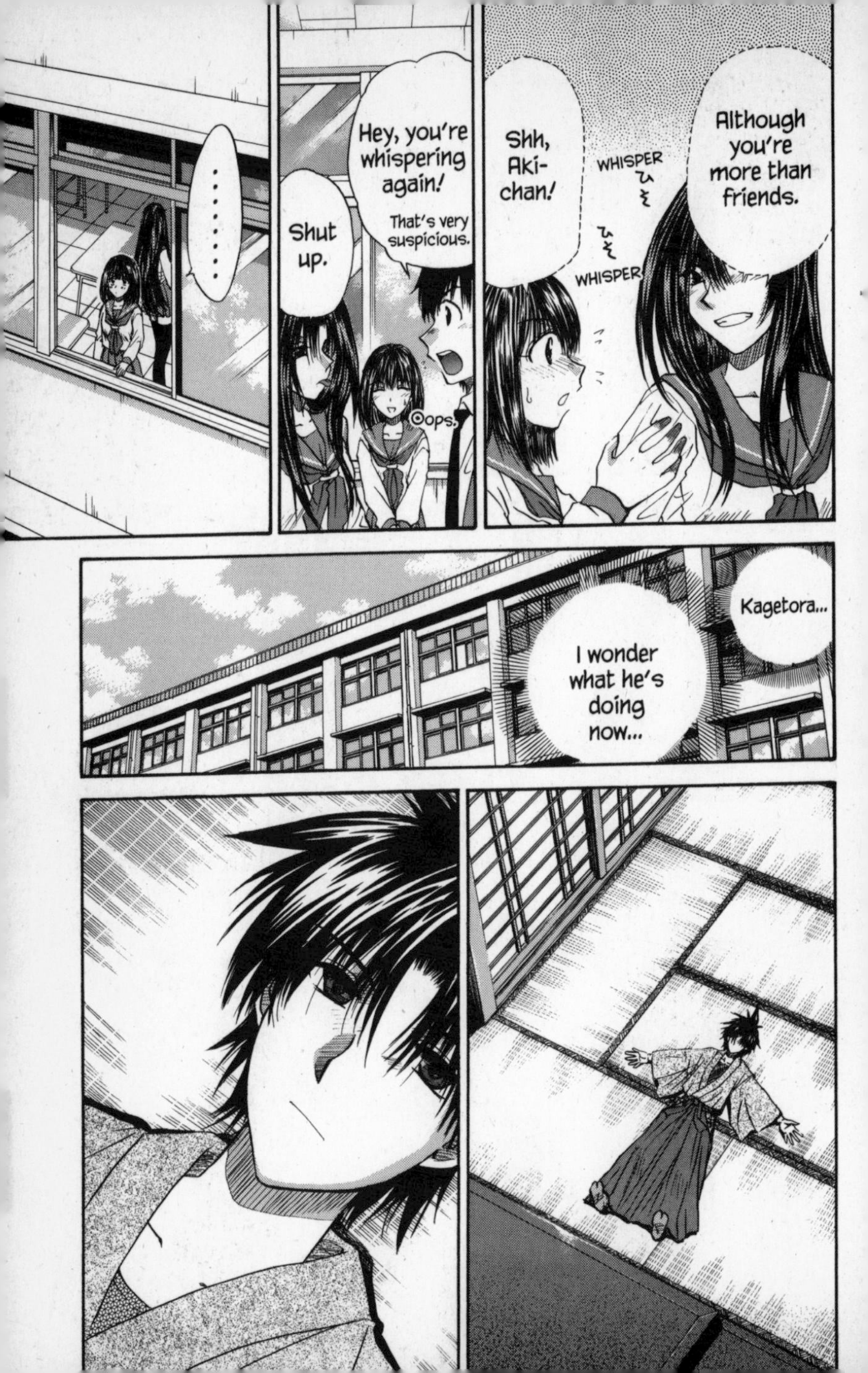
Although you're more than friends.
WHISPER ひそ
ひそ WHISPER
Shh, Aki-chan!
Hey, you're whispering again!
That's very suspicious.
Shut up.
Oops.
......
Kagetora...
I wonder what he's doing now...

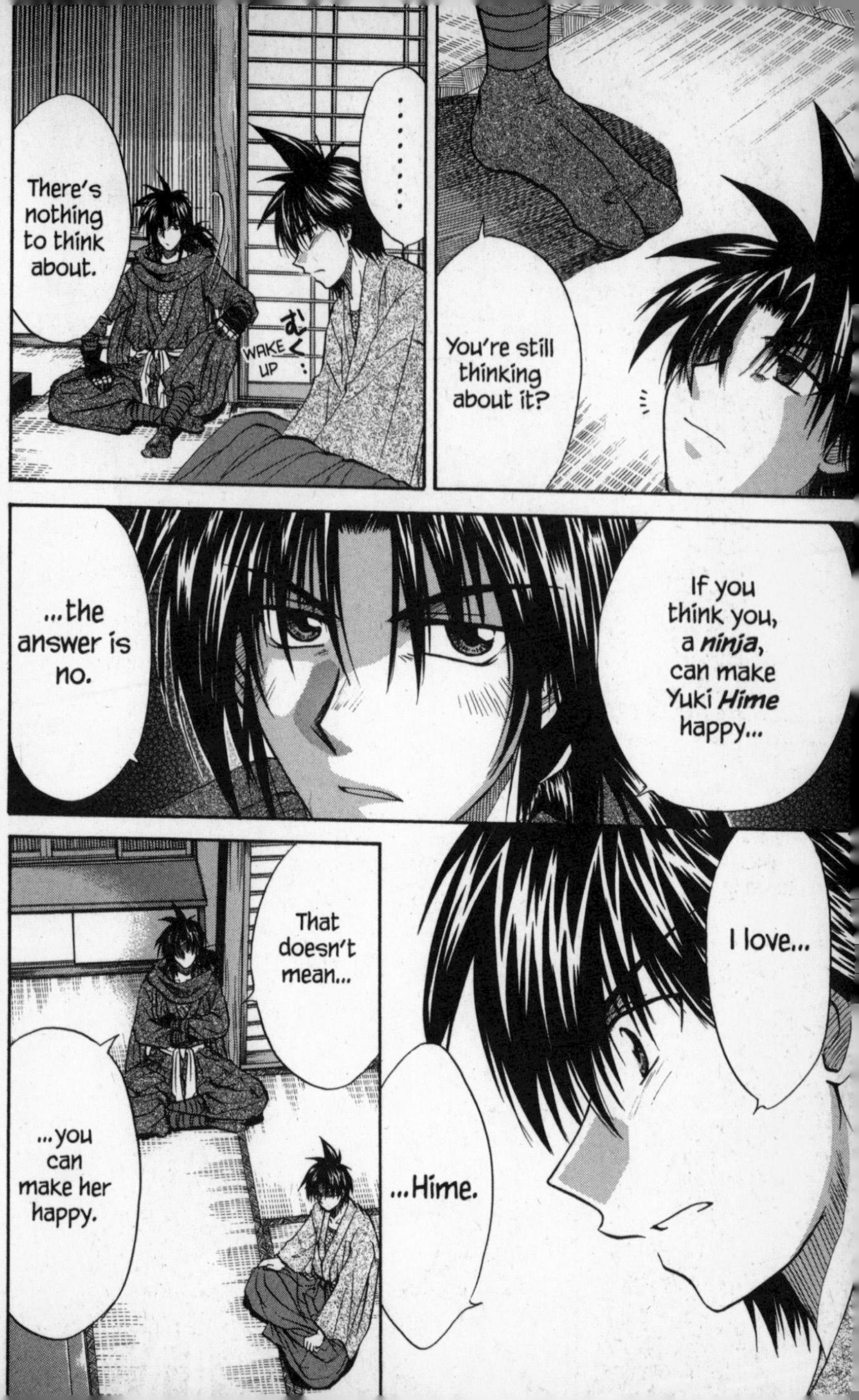
You're still thinking about it?
......
むく
WAKE UP
There's nothing to think about.
If you think you, a *ninja*, can make Yuki *Hime* happy...
...the answer is no.
I love...
...Hime.
That doesn't mean...
...you can make her happy.

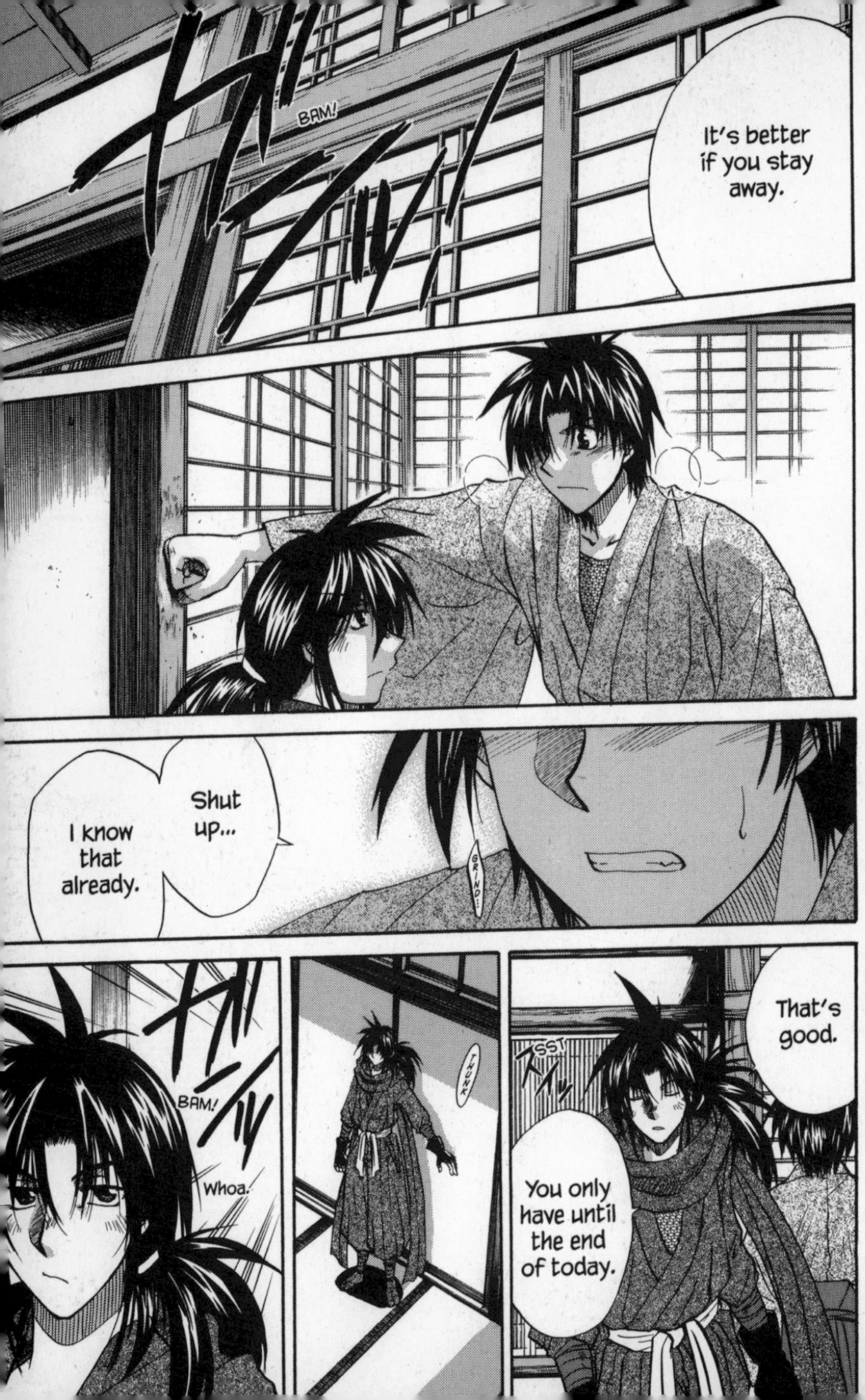
It's better if you stay away.
BAM!
Shut up...
I know that already.
GRIND...
That's good.
SSST
You only have until the end of today.
THUNK
BAM!
Whoa.

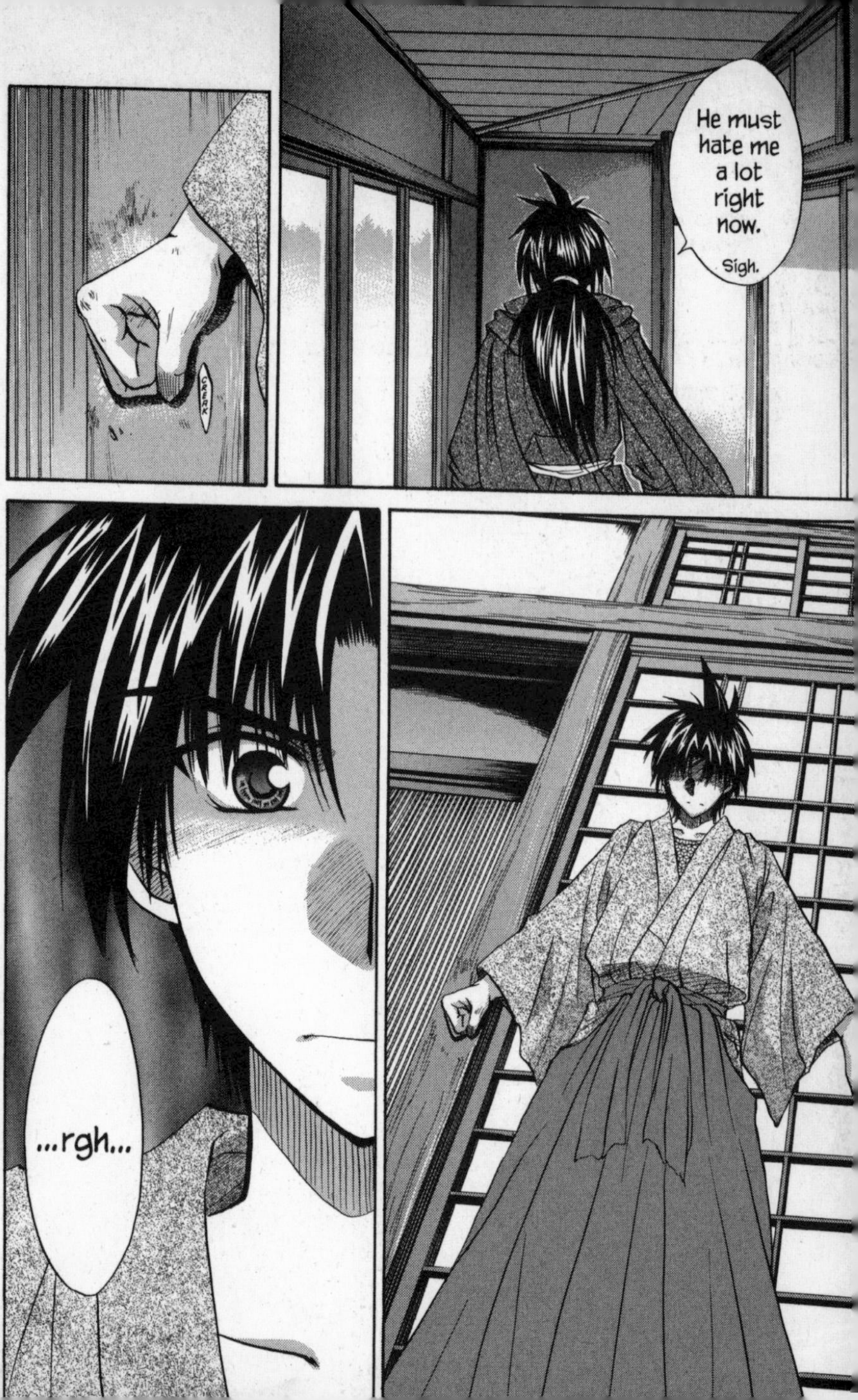
He must hate me a lot right now.
Sigh.
CRERK
...rgh...

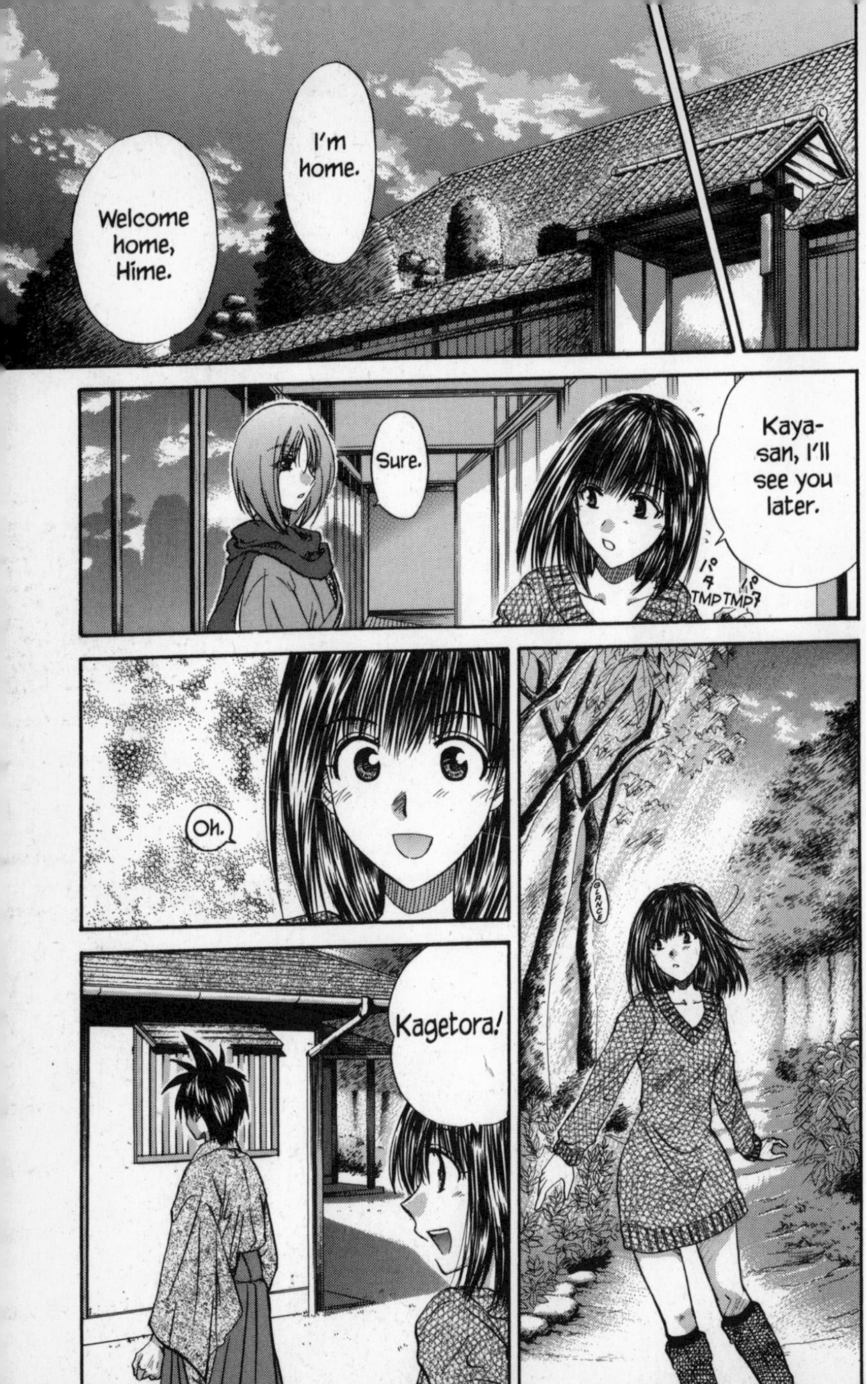
I'm home.
Welcome home, Hime.
Kaya-san, I'll see you later.
TMP TMP
Sure.
GLANCE
Oh.
Kagetora!

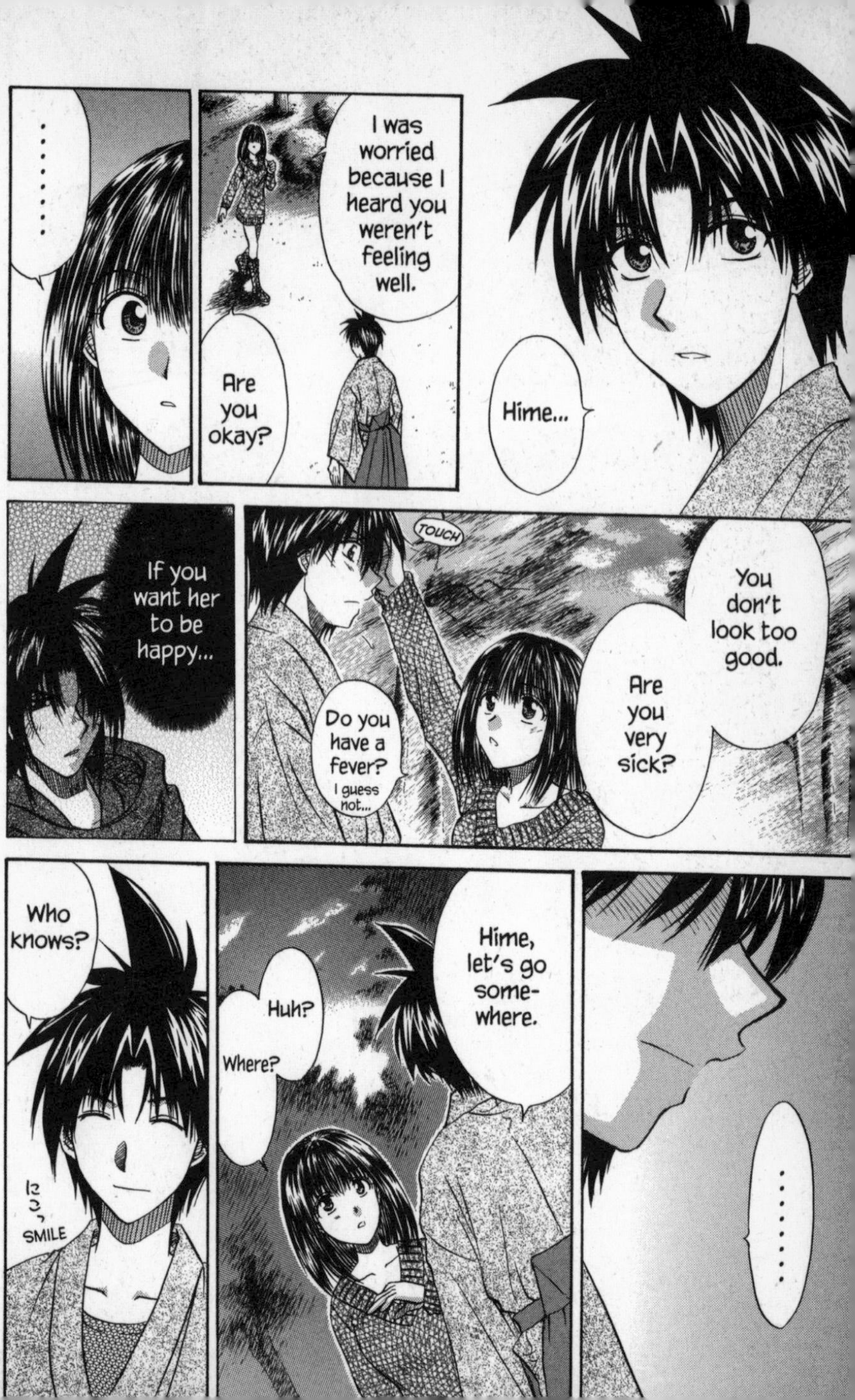
Hime...
I was worried because I heard you weren't feeling well.
Are you okay?
......
You don't look too good.
Are you very sick?
TOUCH
Do you have a fever?
I guess not...
If you want her to be happy...
......
Hime, let's go somewhere.
Huh?
Where?
Who knows?
にこっ
SMILE

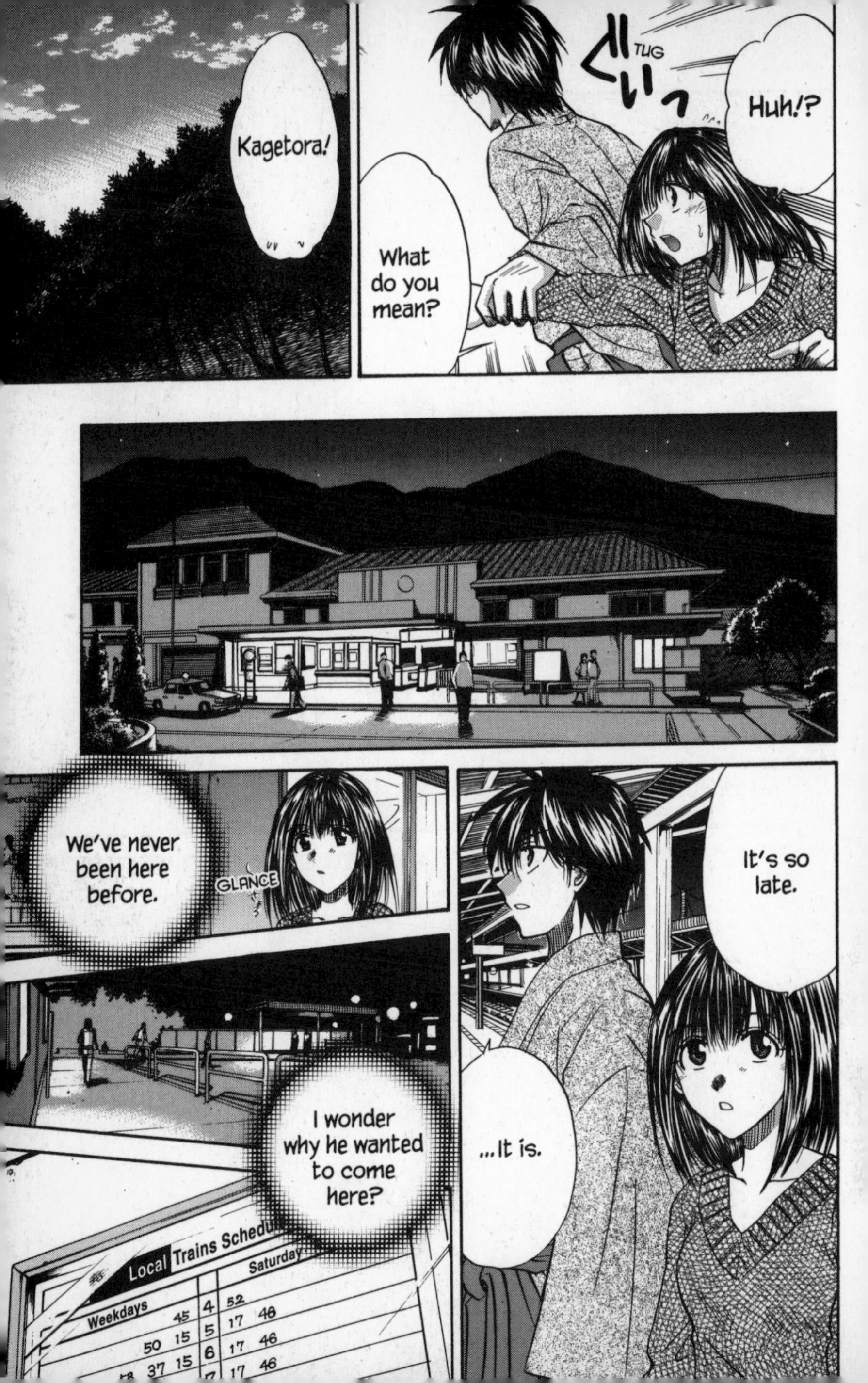
Huh!?
TUG
What do you mean?
Kagetora!
It's so late.
...It is.
We've never been here before.
GLANCE
I wonder why he wanted to come here?
Local Trains Schedu
Weekdays
Saturday

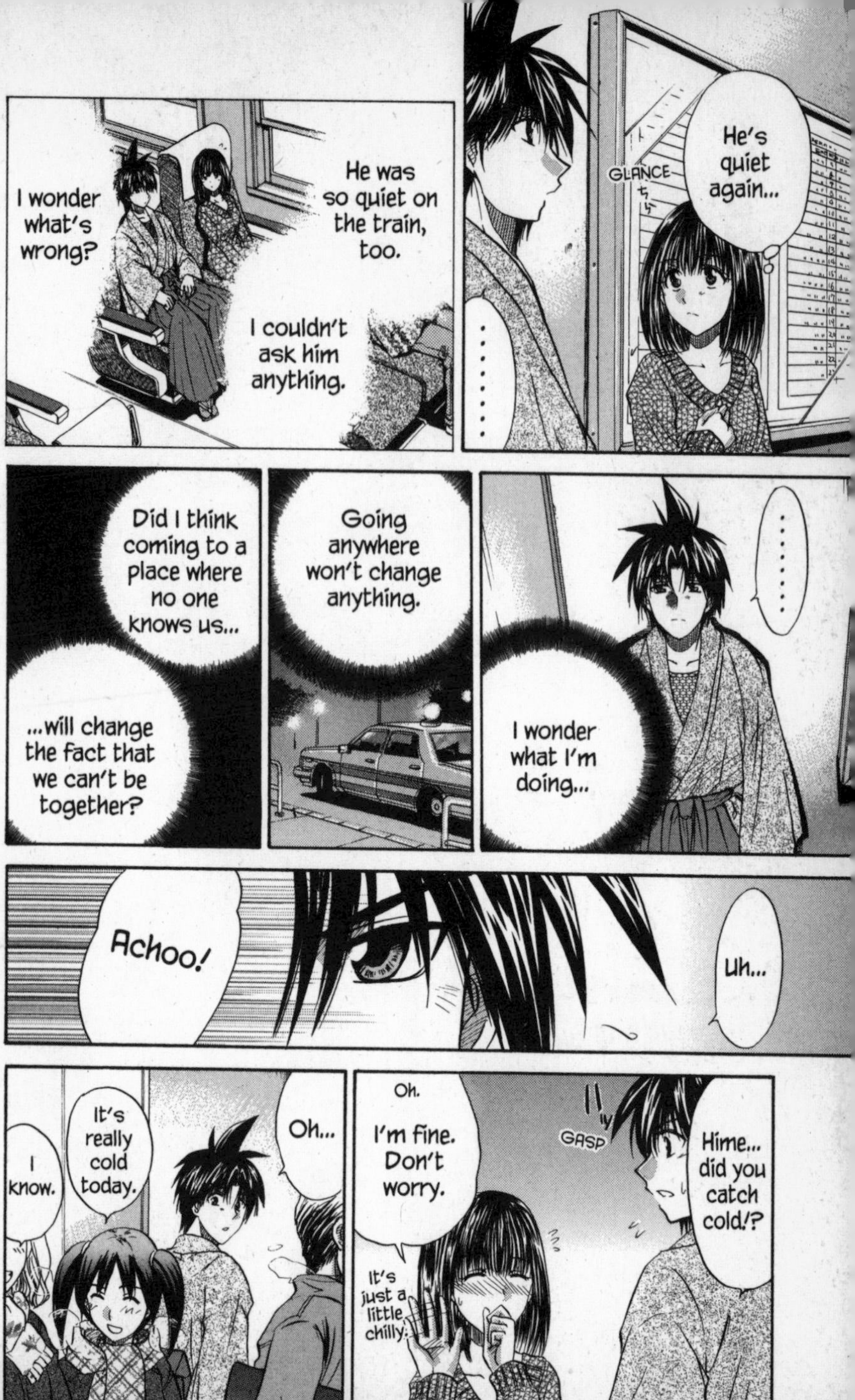
GLANCE
He's quiet again...
......
He was so quiet on the train, too.
I wonder what's wrong?
I couldn't ask him anything.
......
I wonder what I'm doing...
Going anywhere won't change anything.
Did I think coming to a place where no one knows us...
...will change the fact that we can't be together?
Uh...
Achoo!
GASP
Hime... did you catch cold!?
Oh.
I'm fine. Don't worry.
It's just a little chilly.
Oh...
It's really cold today.
I know.

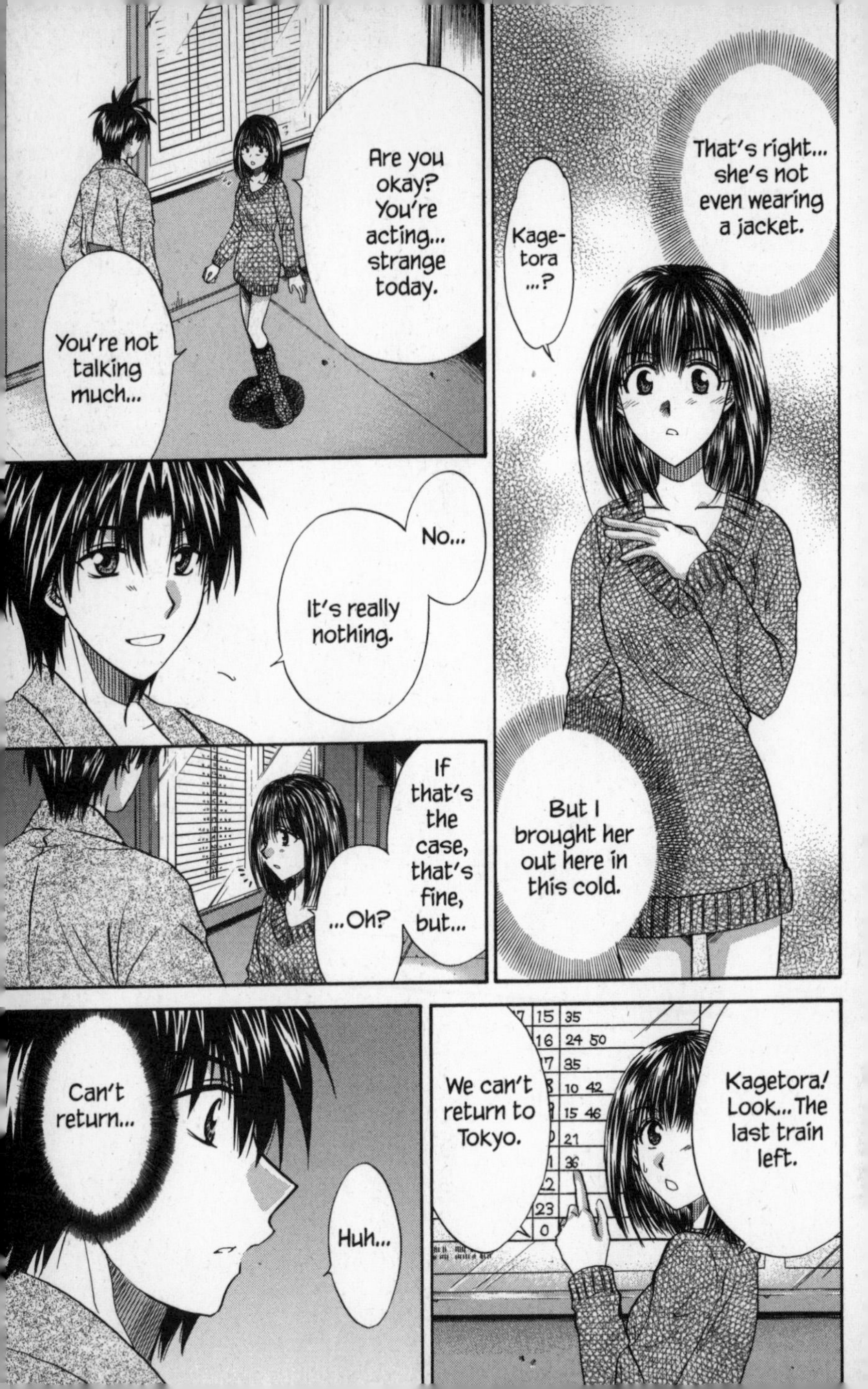
That's right... she's not even wearing a jacket.
Kagetora...?
But I brought her out here in this cold.
Are you okay? You're acting... strange today.
You're not talking much...
No...
It's really nothing.
If that's the case, that's fine, but...
...Oh?
Kagetora! Look... The last train left.
We can't return to Tokyo.
Huh...
Can't return...

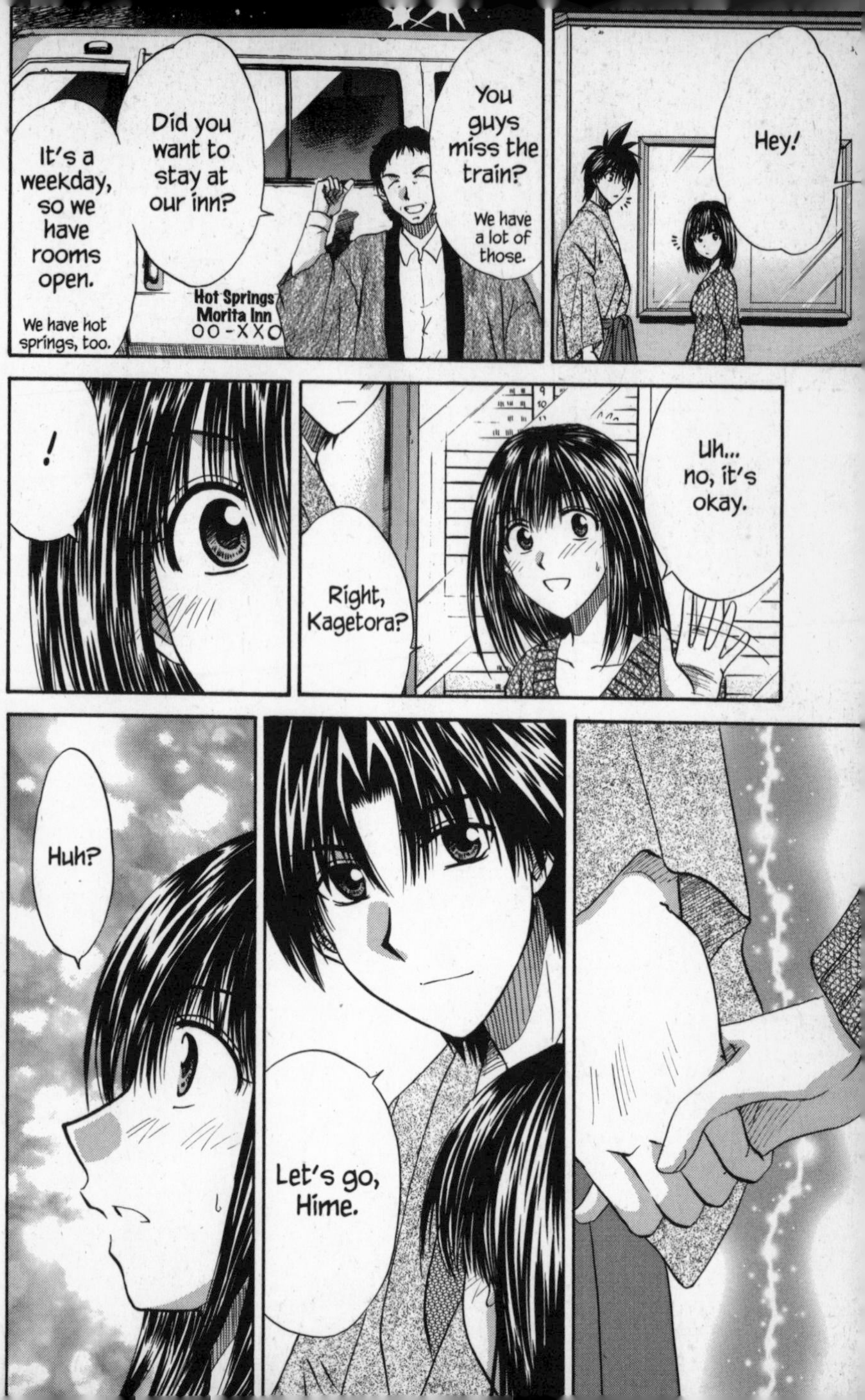
Hey!
You guys miss the train?
We have a lot of those.
Did you want to stay at our inn?
Hot Springs Morita Inn OO-XXO
It's a weekday, so we have rooms open.
We have hot springs, too.
Uh... no, it's okay.
Right, Kagetora?
!
Let's go, Hime.
Huh?

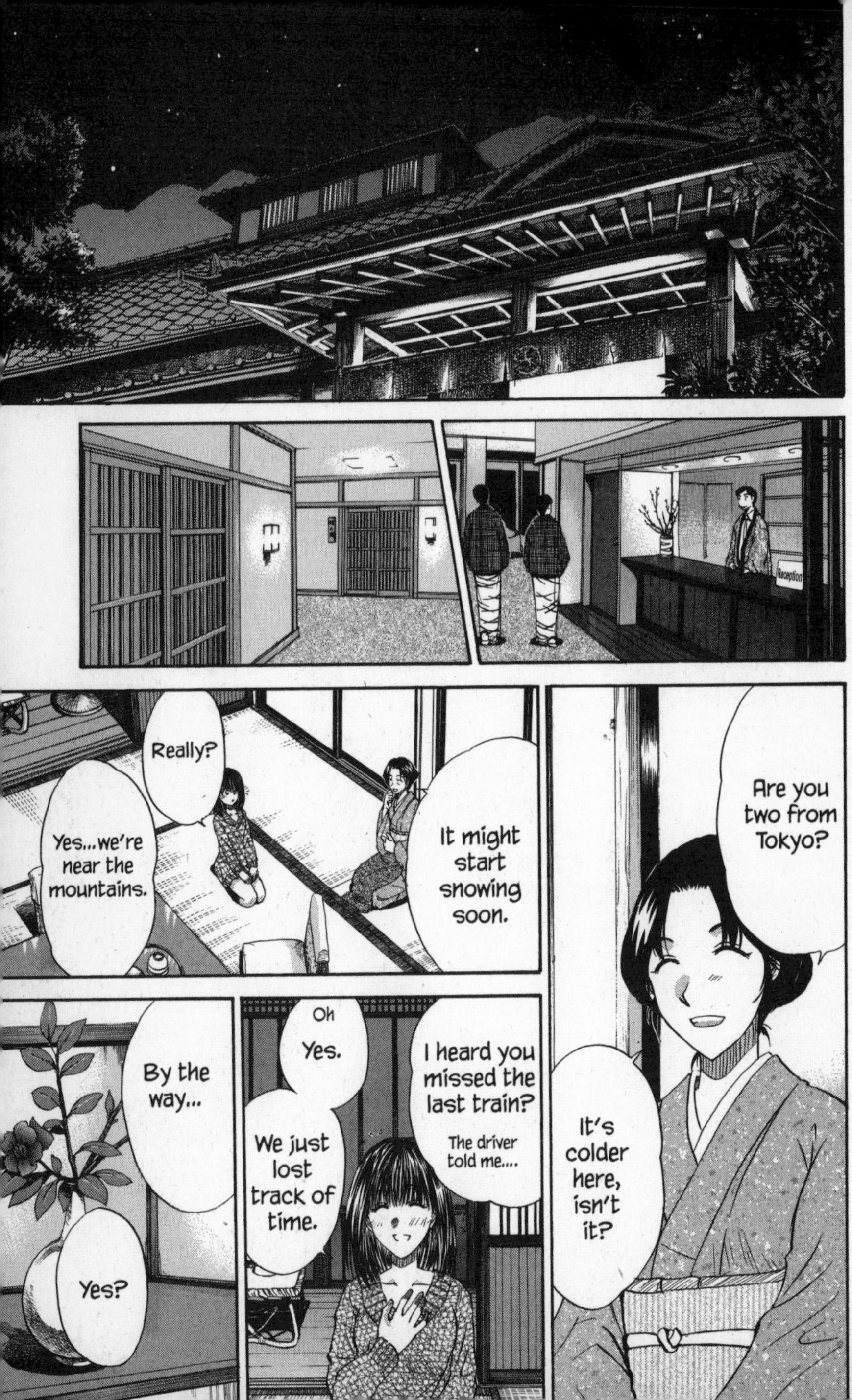
Reception
Are you two from Tokyo?
It's colder here, isn't it?
It might start snowing soon.
Really?
Yes...we're near the mountains.
I heard you missed the last train?
The driver told me....
Oh
Yes.
We just lost track of time.
By the way...
Yes?

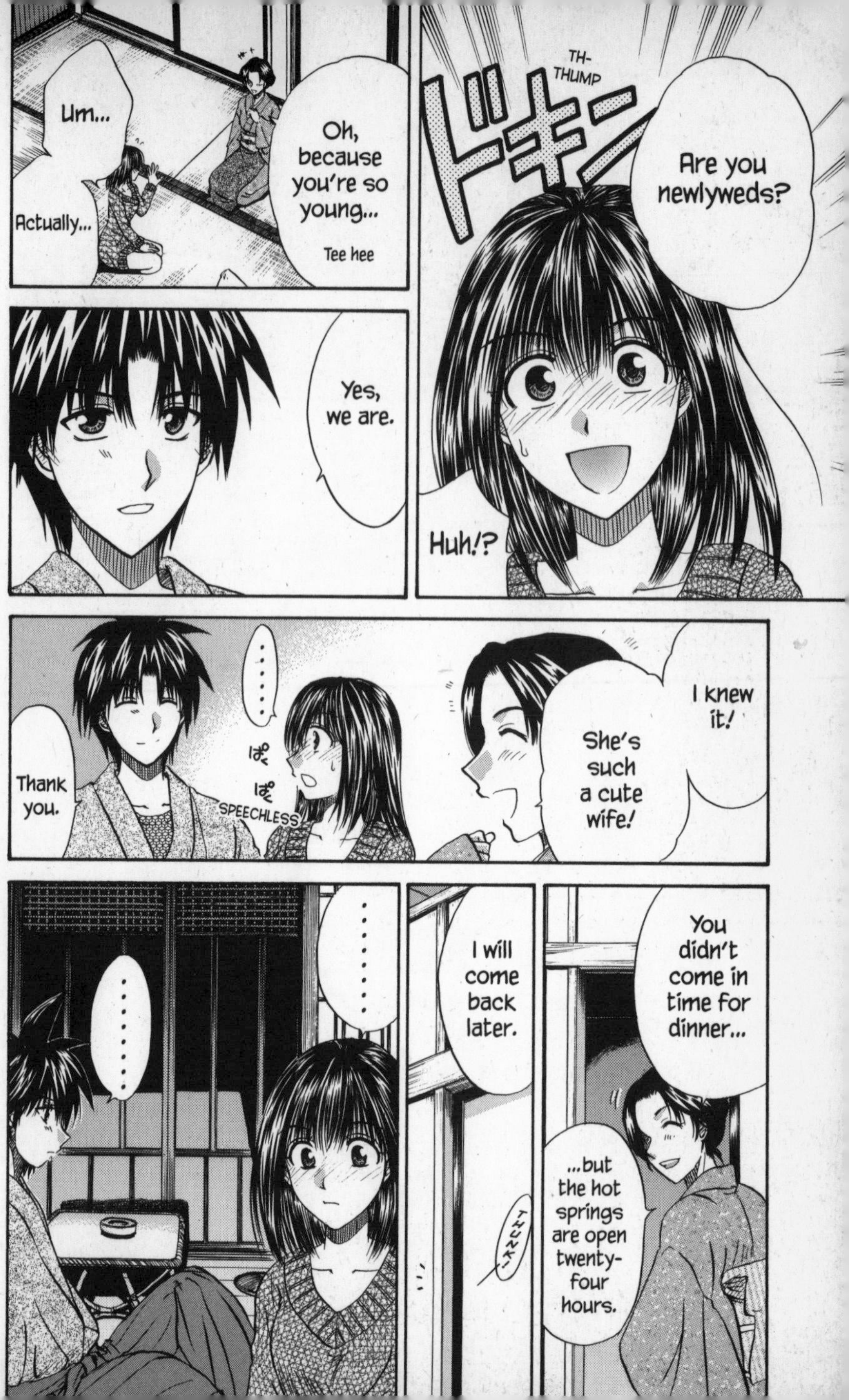
TH-THUMP
ドキーン
Are you newlyweds?
Huh!?
Um...
Actually...
Oh, because you're so young...
Tee hee
Yes, we are.
I knew it!
She's such a cute wife!
......
ぱく ぱく
SPEECHLESS
Thank you.
You didn't come in time for dinner...
...but the hot springs are open twenty-four hours.
THUNK
I will come back later.
......
......

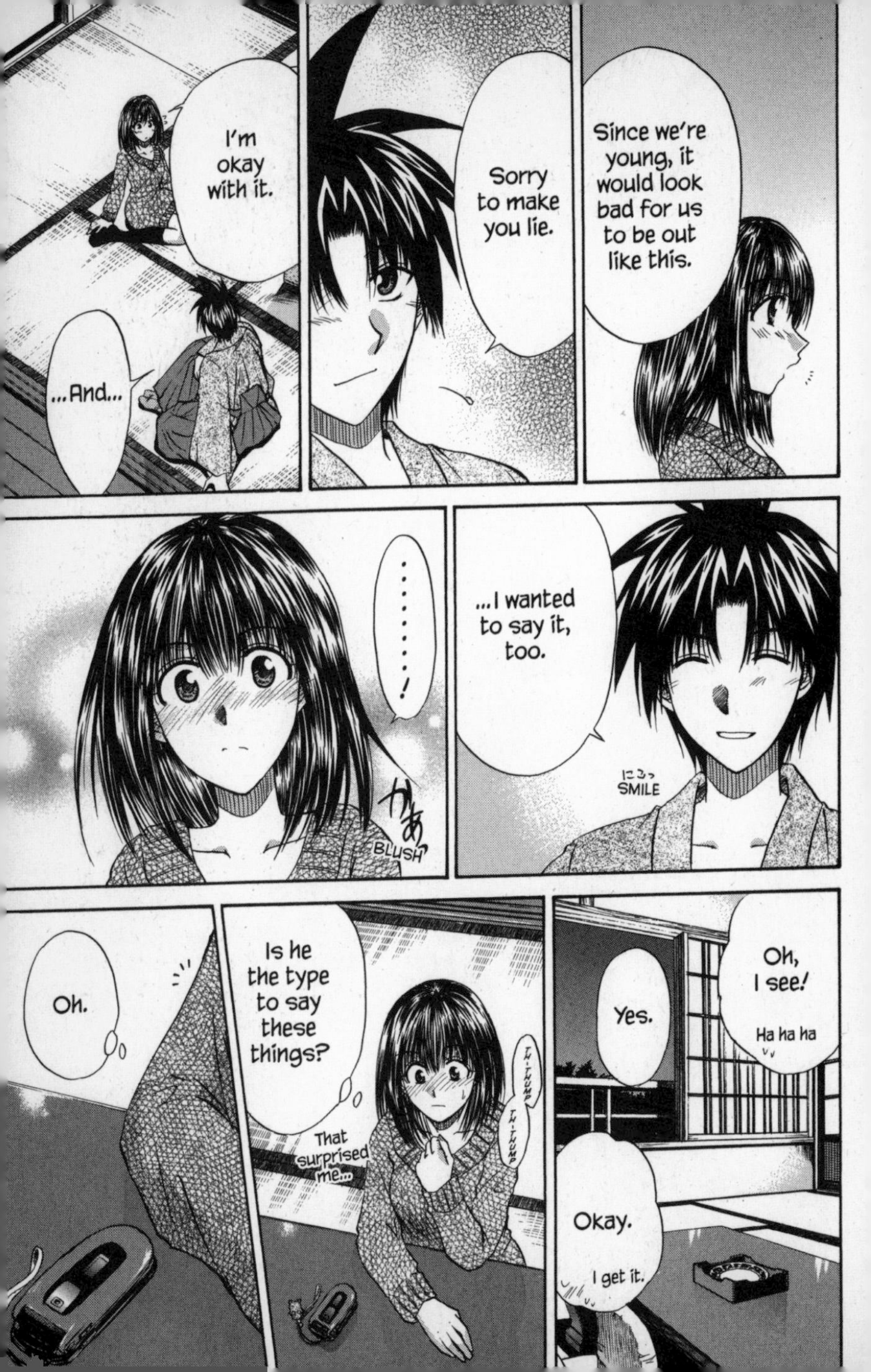
Since we're young, it would look bad for us to be out like this.
Sorry to make you lie.
I'm okay with it.
...And...
...I wanted to say it, too.
にこっ
SMILE
.......!
かあ
BLUSH
Oh, I see!
Ha ha ha
Yes.
Okay.
I get it.
Is he the type to say these things?
TH-THUMP
TH-THUMP
That surprised me...
Oh.

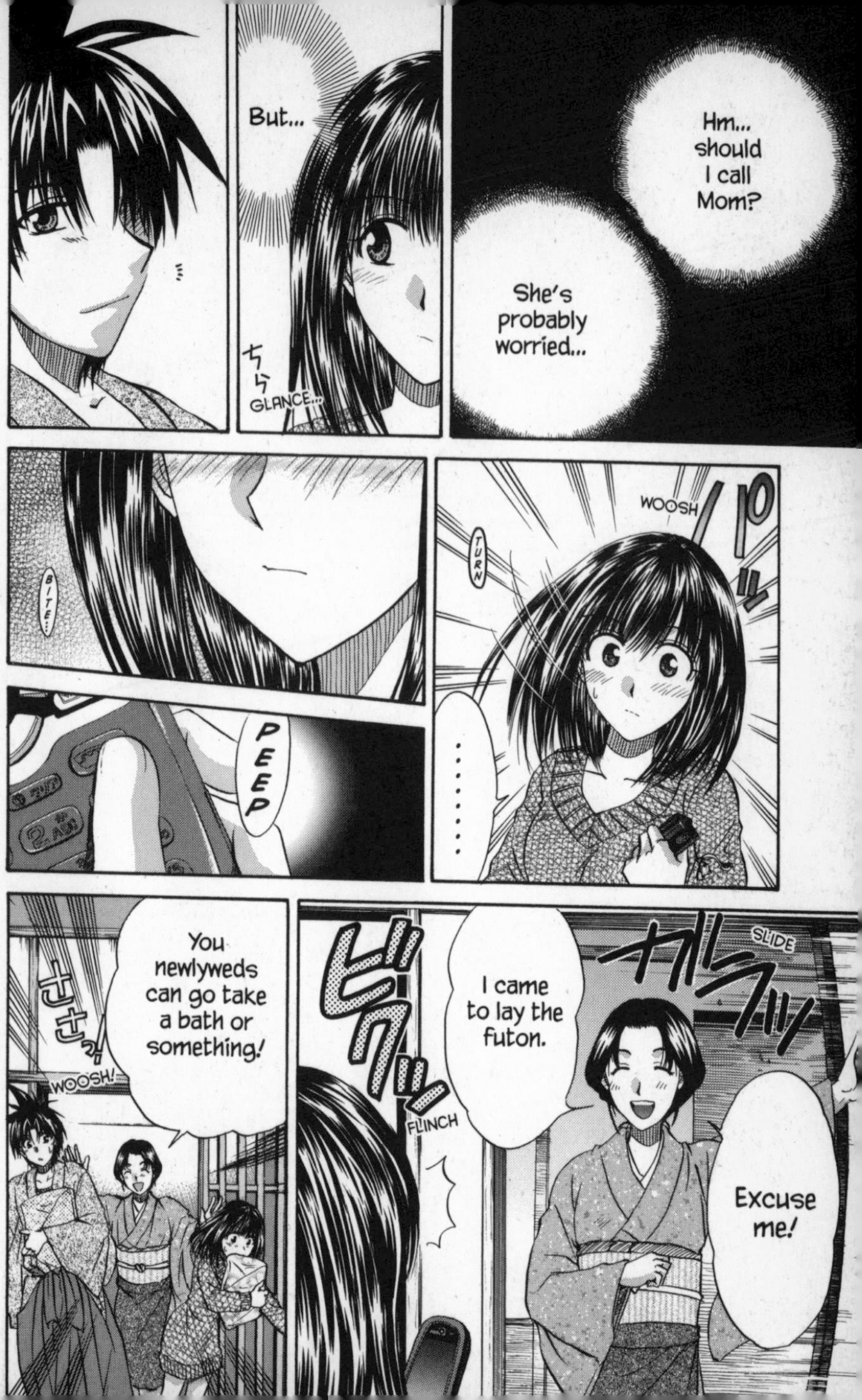
Hm... should I call Mom?
She's probably worried...
But...
GLANCE...
WOOSH
TURN
......
BITE...
PEEP
SLIDE
Excuse me!
I came to lay the futon.
FLINCH
You newlyweds can go take a bath or something!
WOOSH!

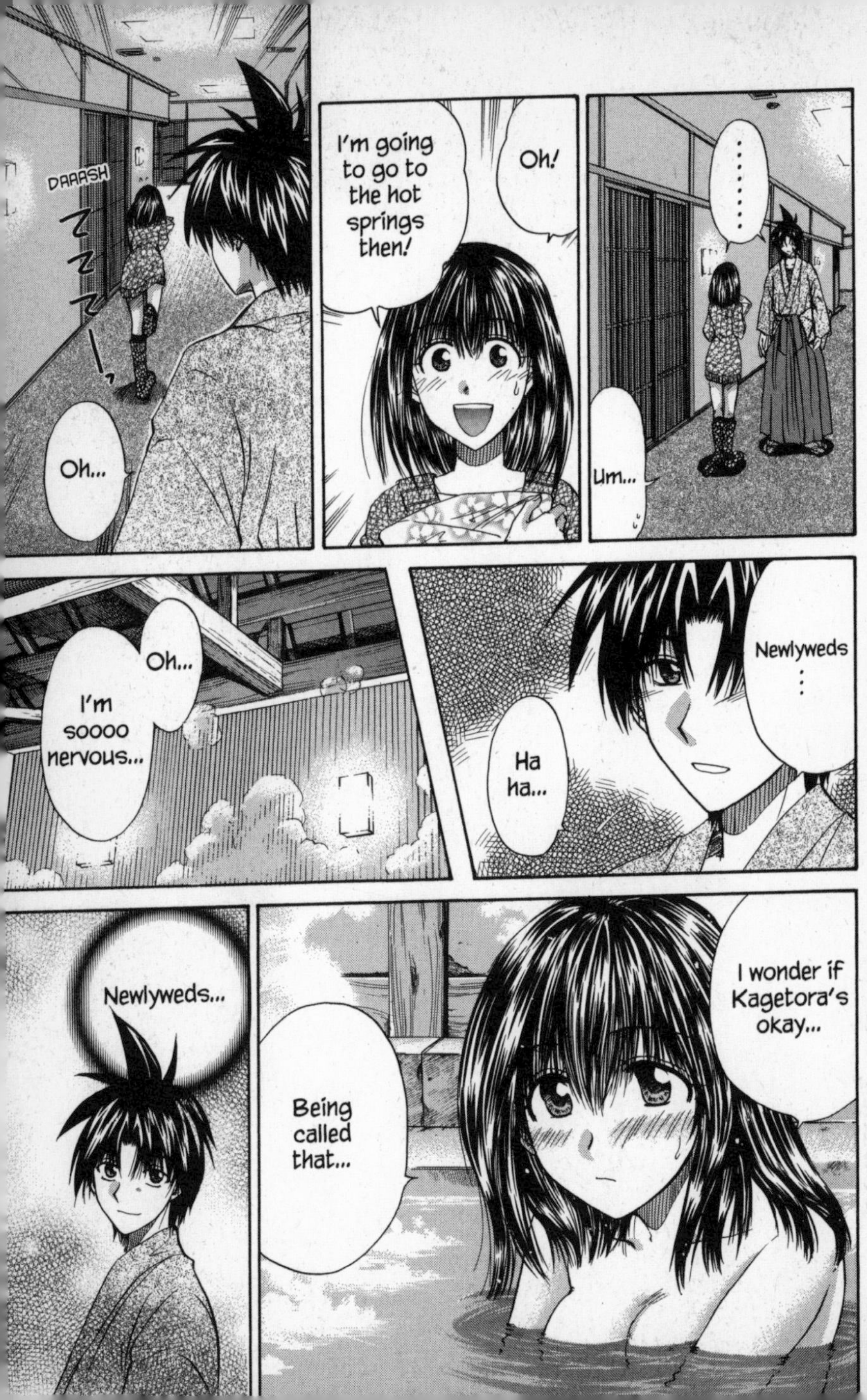

......
Um...
Oh!
I'm going to go to the hot springs then!
DAAASH
Oh...
Newlyweds...
Ha ha...
Oh...
I'm soooo nervous...
I wonder if Kagetora's okay...
Being called that...
Newlyweds...

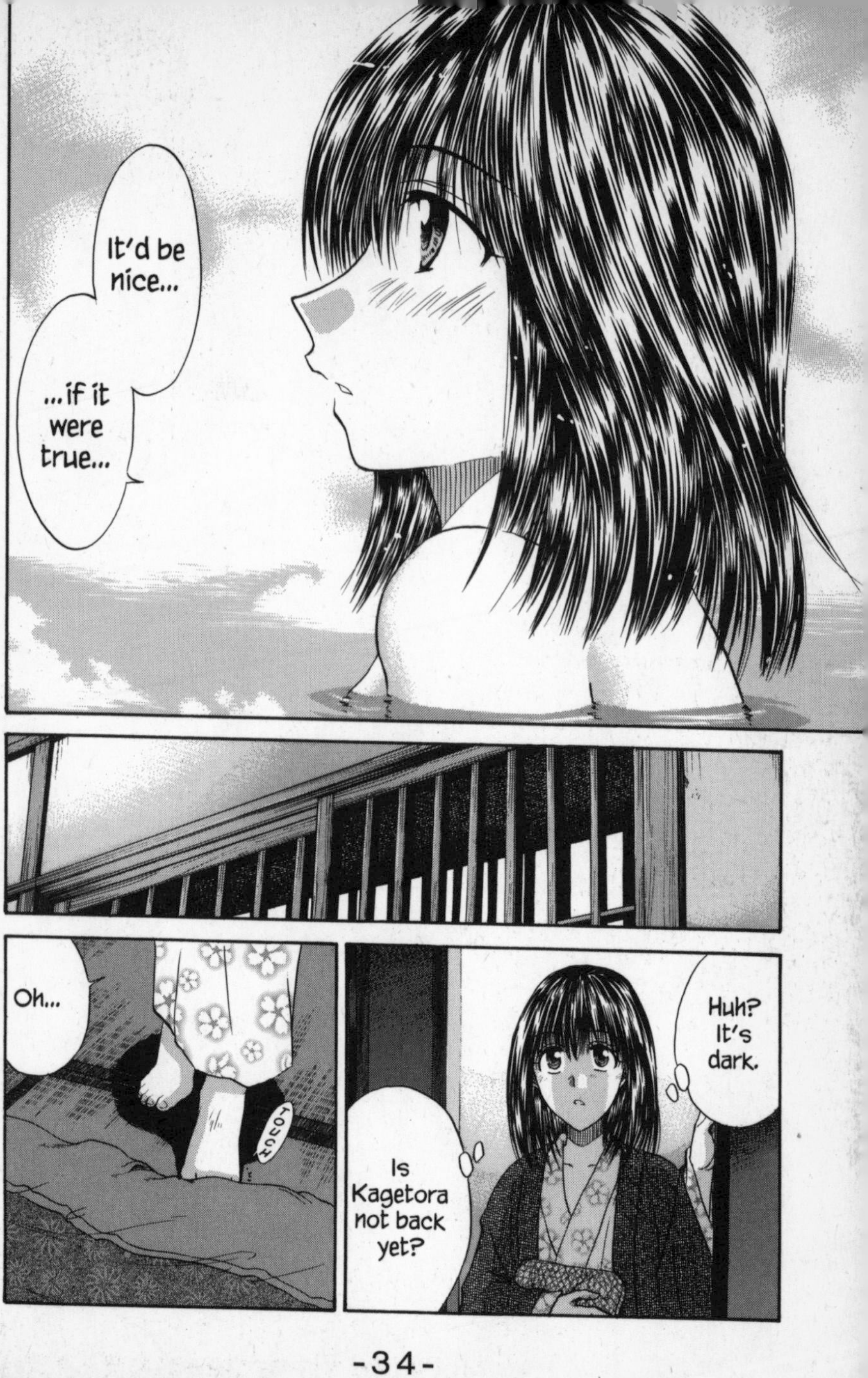
It'd be nice...
...if it were true...
Huh? It's dark.
Is Kagetora not back yet?
Oh...
TOUCH

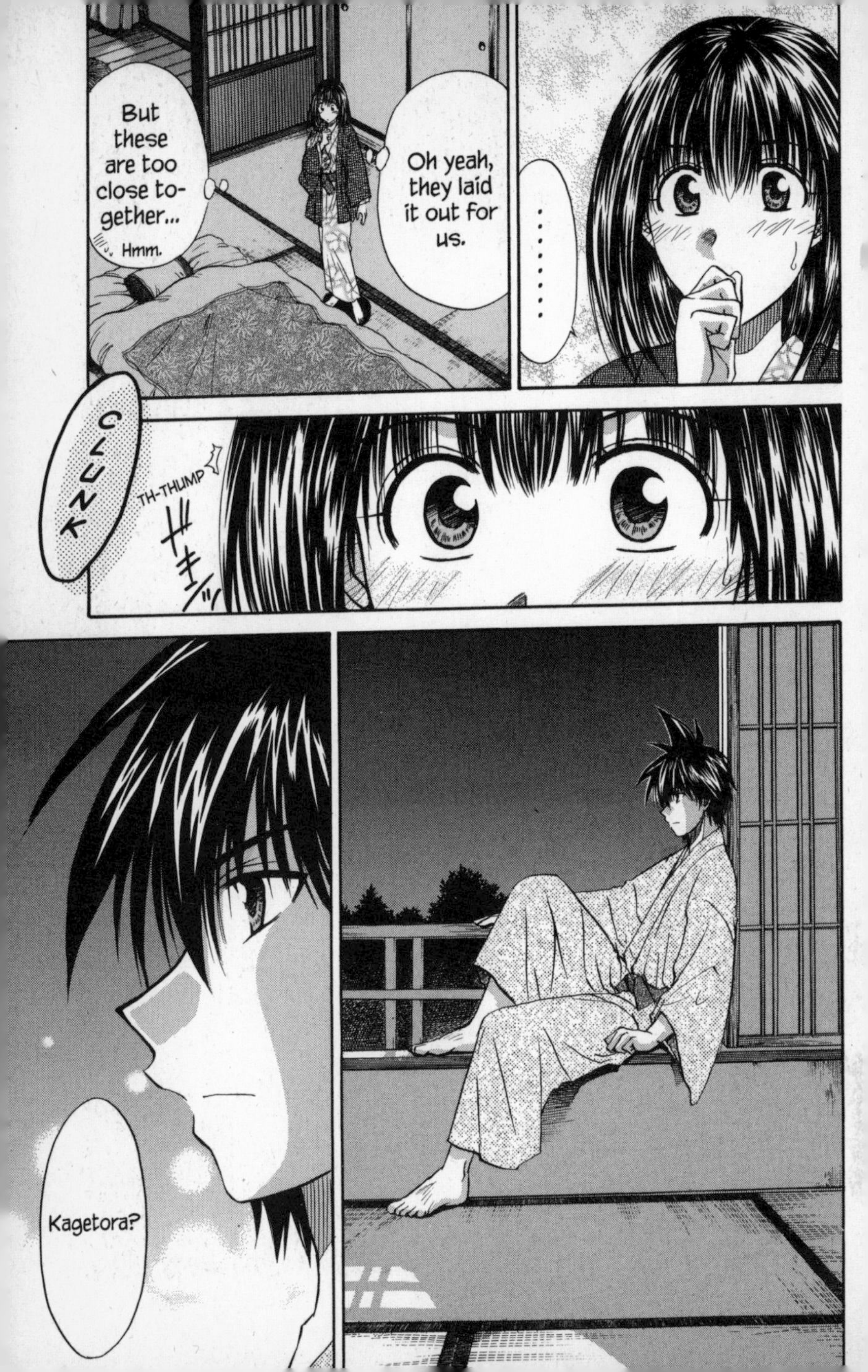
......
Oh yeah, they laid it out for us.
But these are too close to-gether...
Hmm.
CLUNK
TH-THUMP
Kagetora?

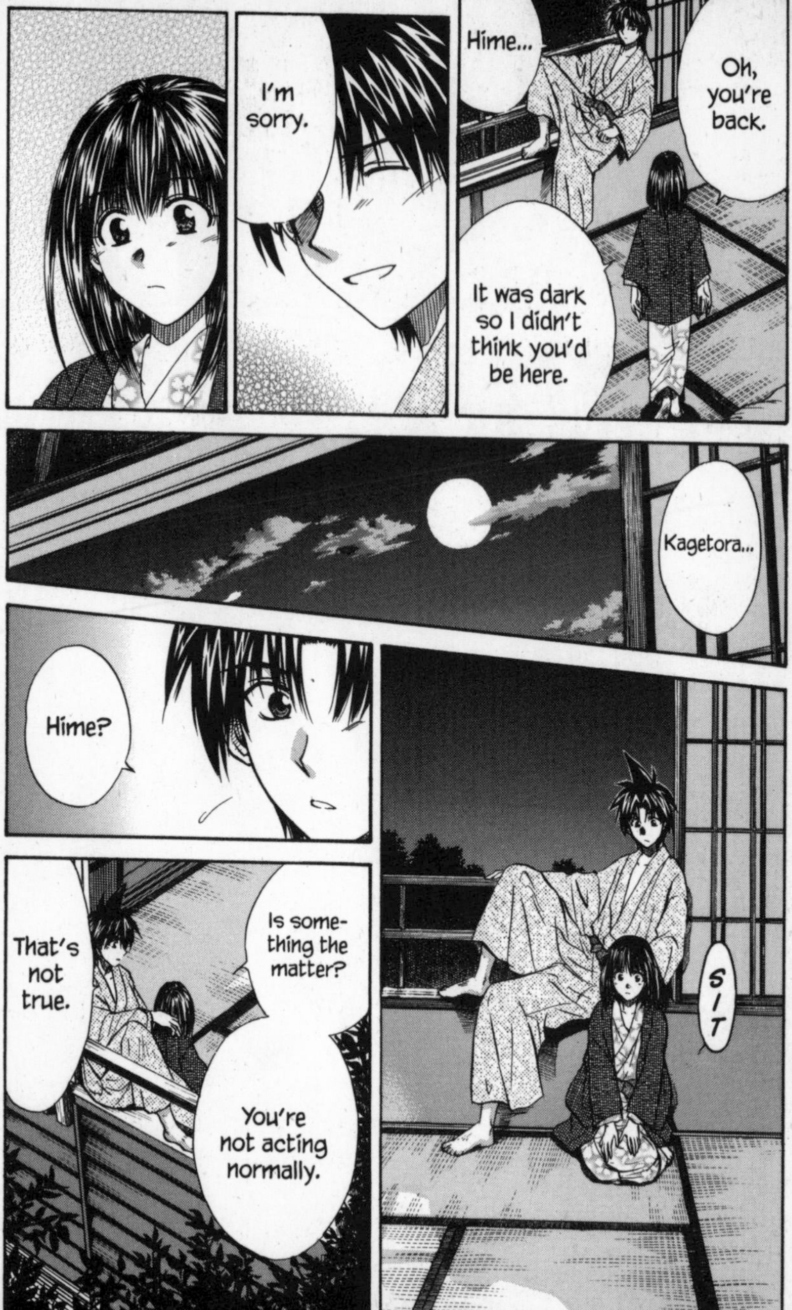
Oh, you're back.
Hime...
It was dark so I didn't think you'd be here.
I'm sorry.
Kagetora...
S I T
Hime?
Is some-thing the matter?
You're not acting normally.
That's not true.

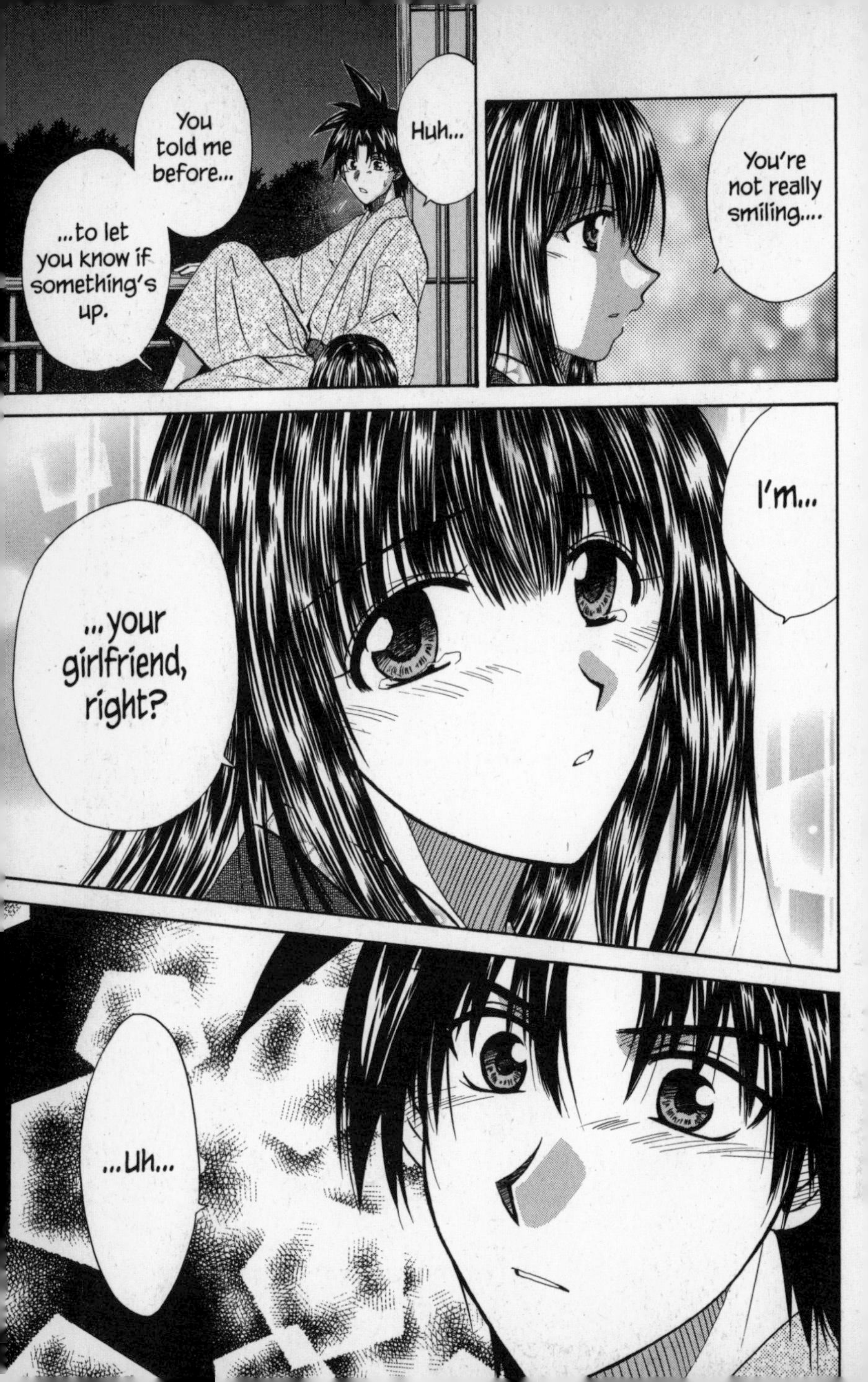
You're not really smiling....
Huh...
You told me before...
...to let you know if something's up.
I'm...
...your girlfriend, right?
...uh...

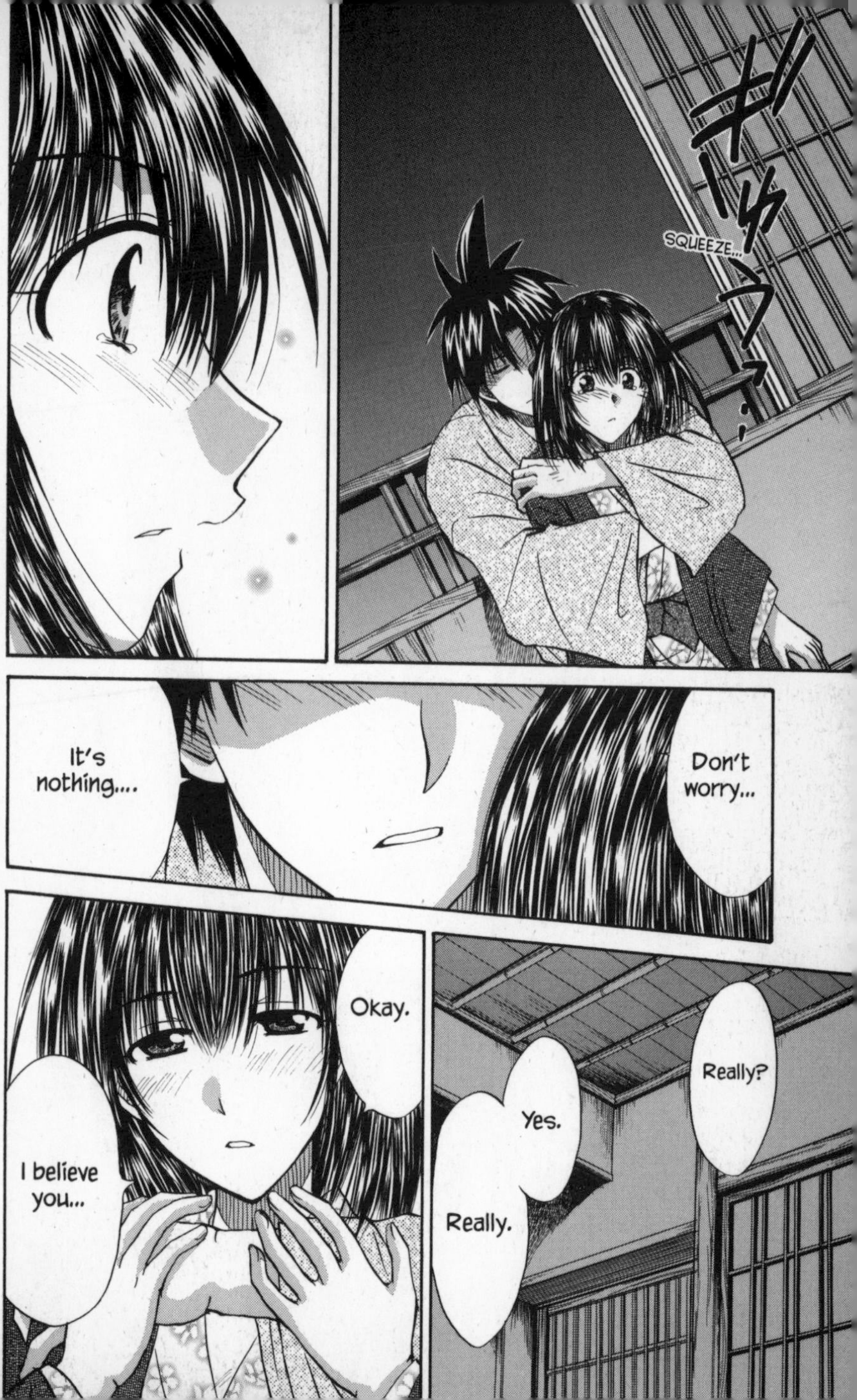
SQUEEZE...
Don't worry...
It's nothing....
Really?
Yes.
Really.
Okay.
I believe you...

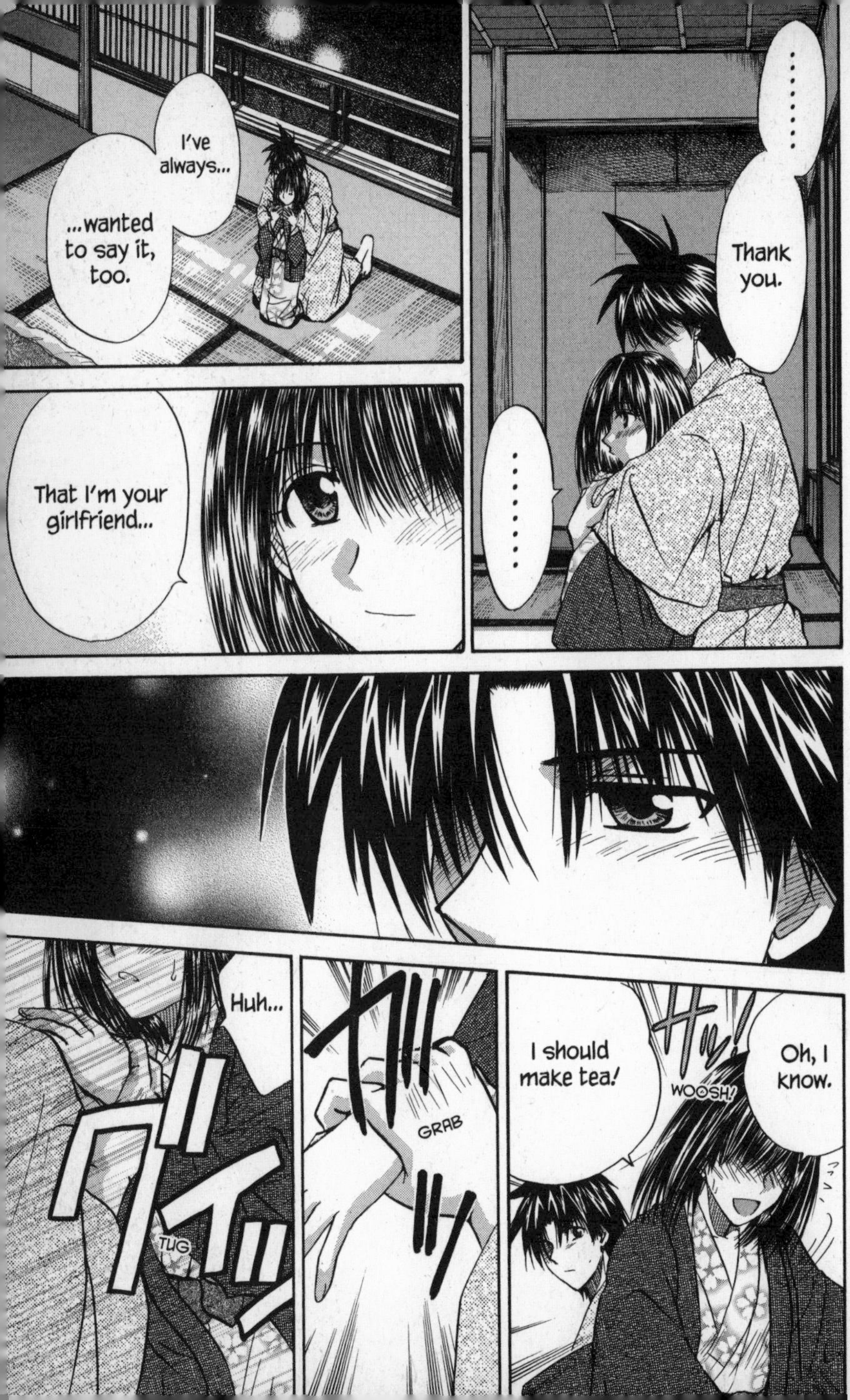
......
Thank you.
......
I've always...
...wanted to say it, too.
That I'm your girlfriend...
Oh, I know.
WOOSH!
I should make tea!
GRAB
Huh...
TUG

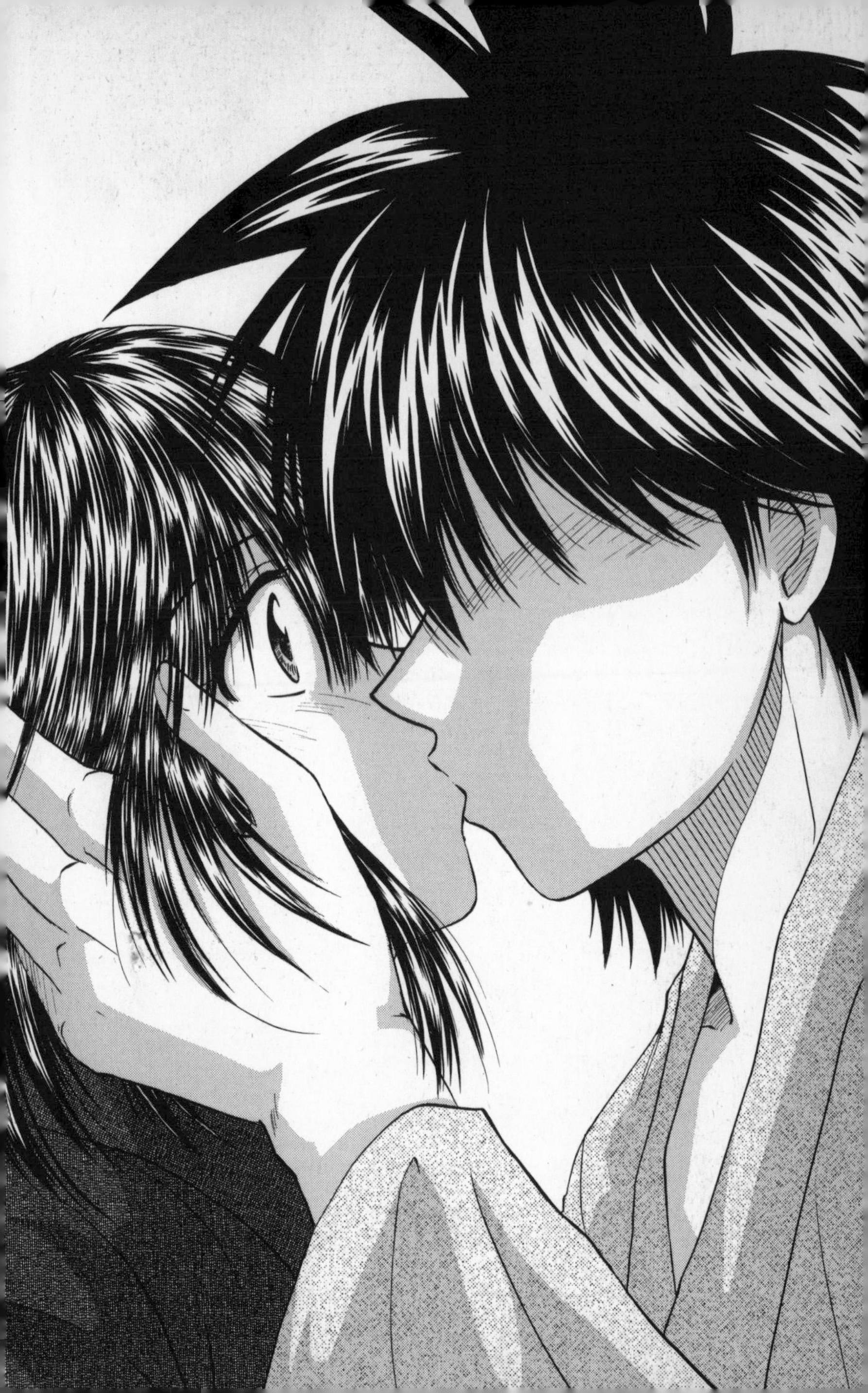

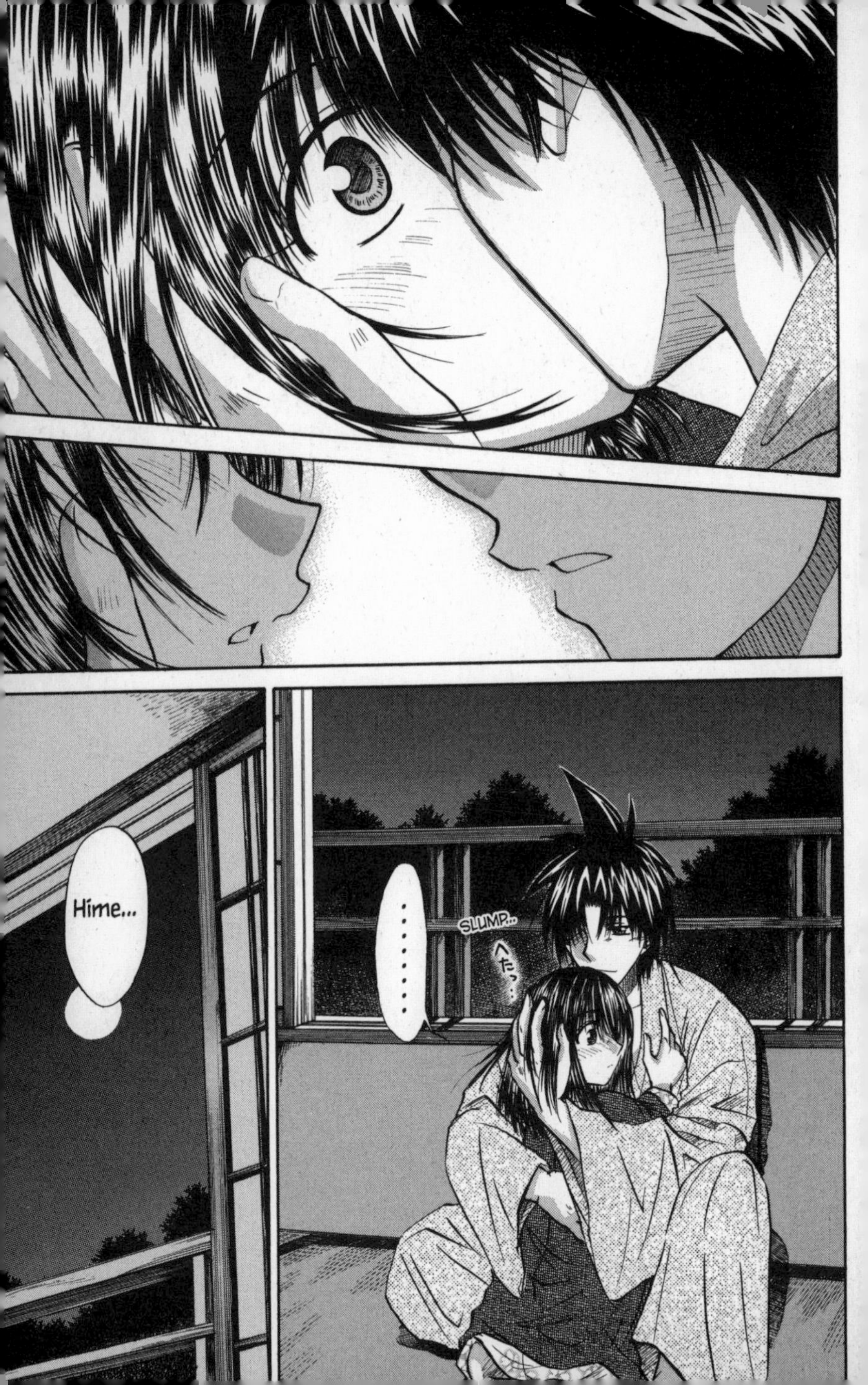
SLUMP...
へたっ…
....
Hime...

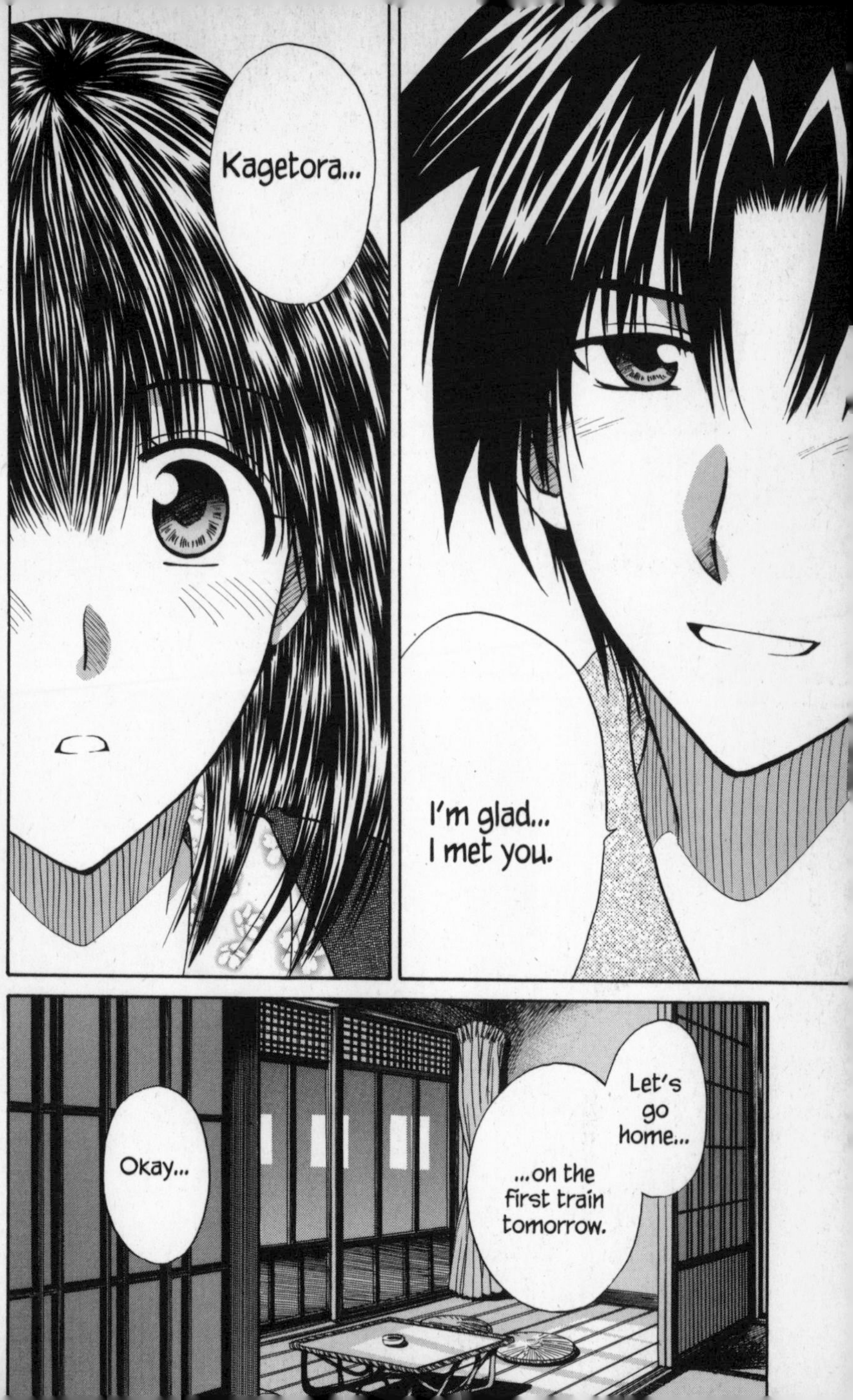
I'm glad... I met you.
Kagetora...
Let's go home...
...on the first train tomorrow.
Okay...

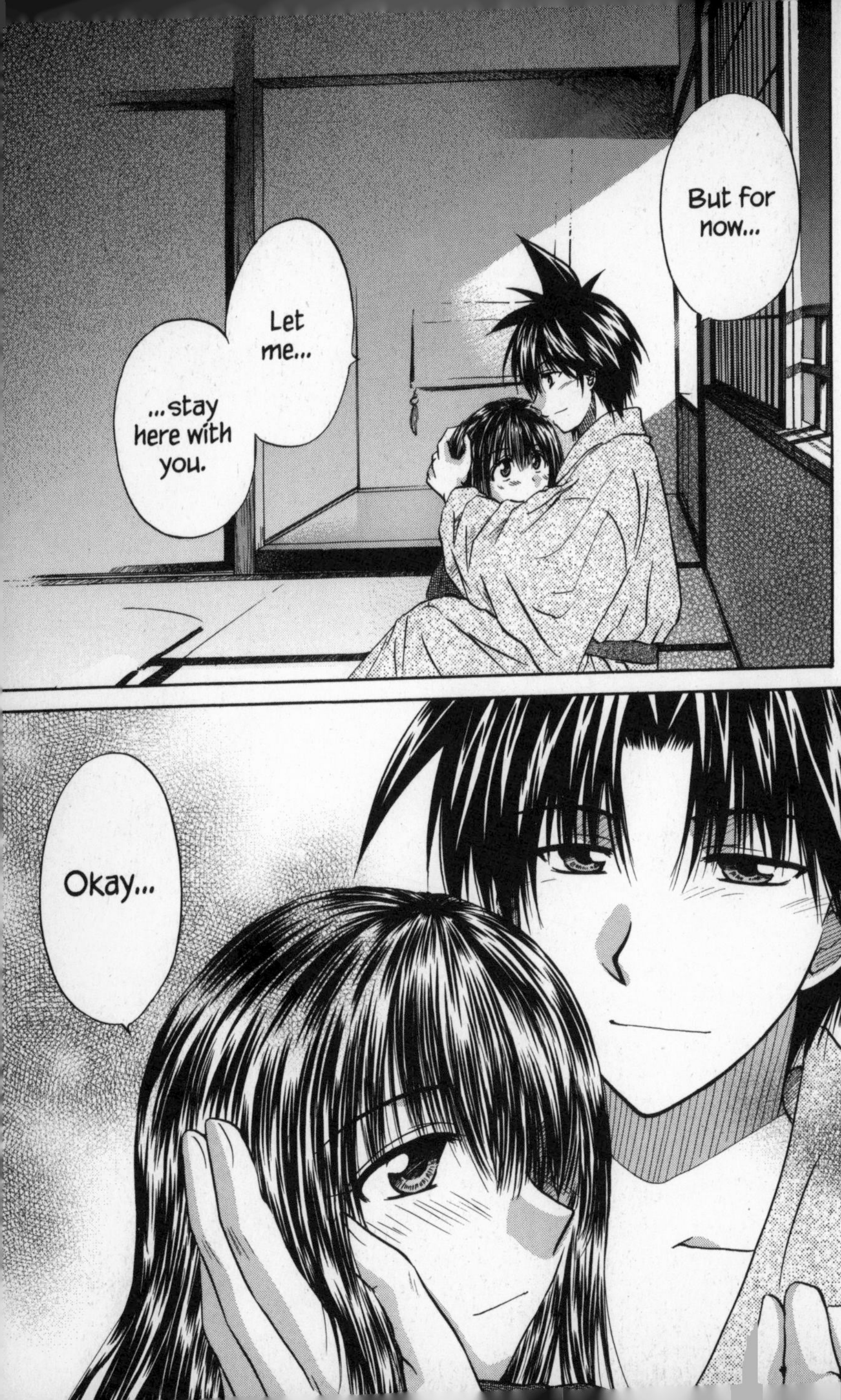
But for now...
Let me...
...stay here with you.
Okay...

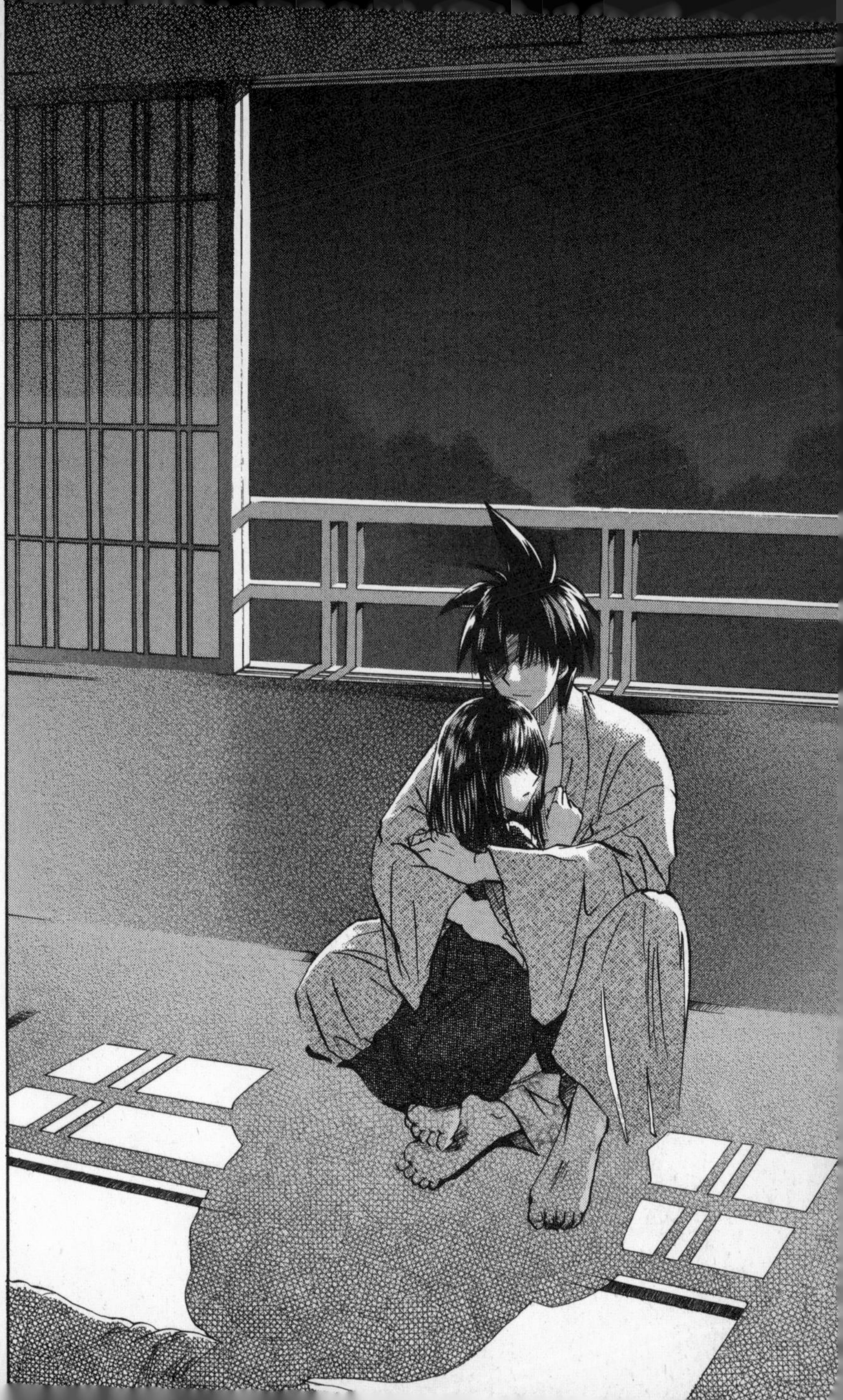

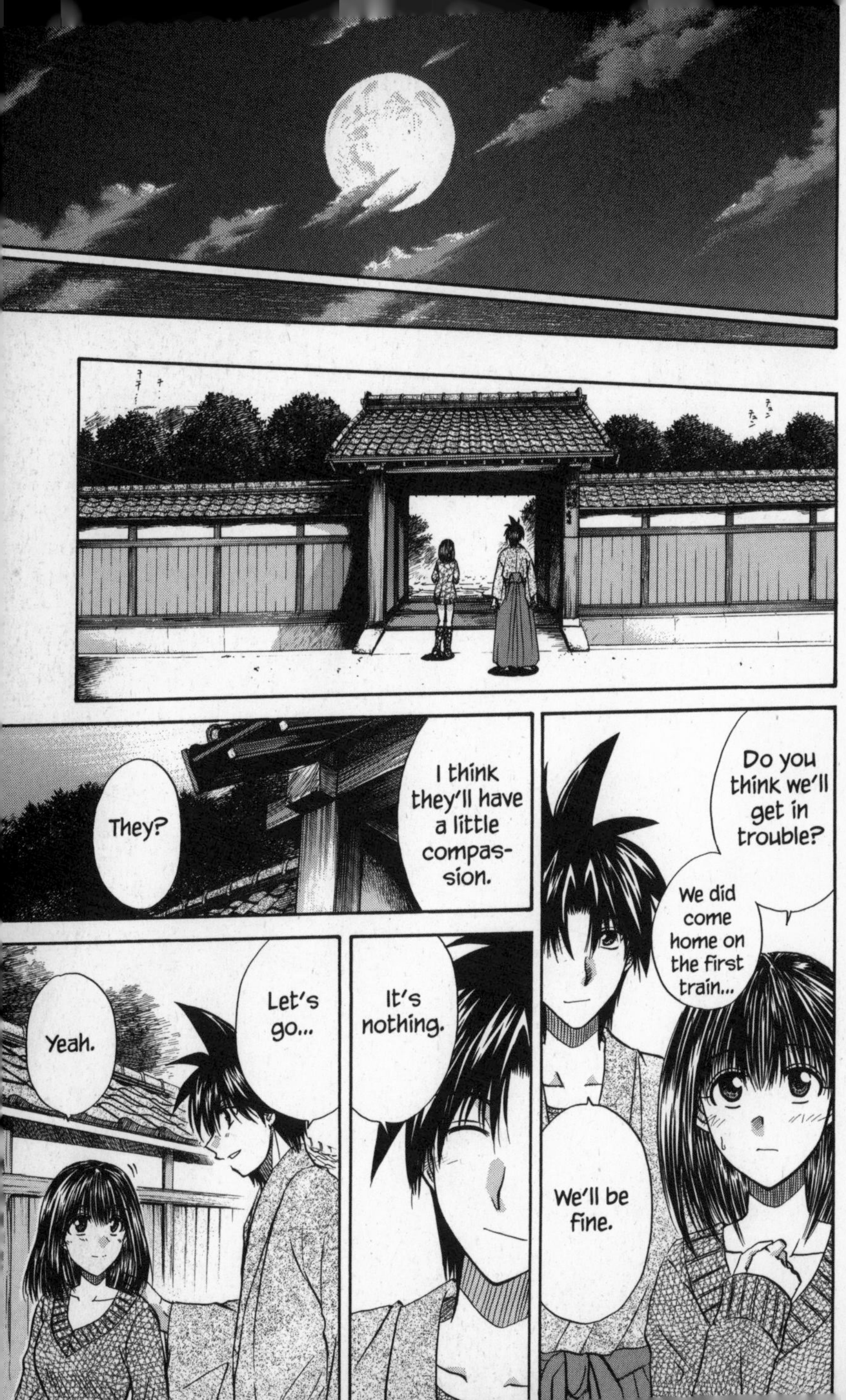
Do you think we'll get in trouble?
We did come home on the first train...
We'll be fine.
I think they'll have a little compas-sion.
They?
It's nothing.
Let's go...
Yeah.

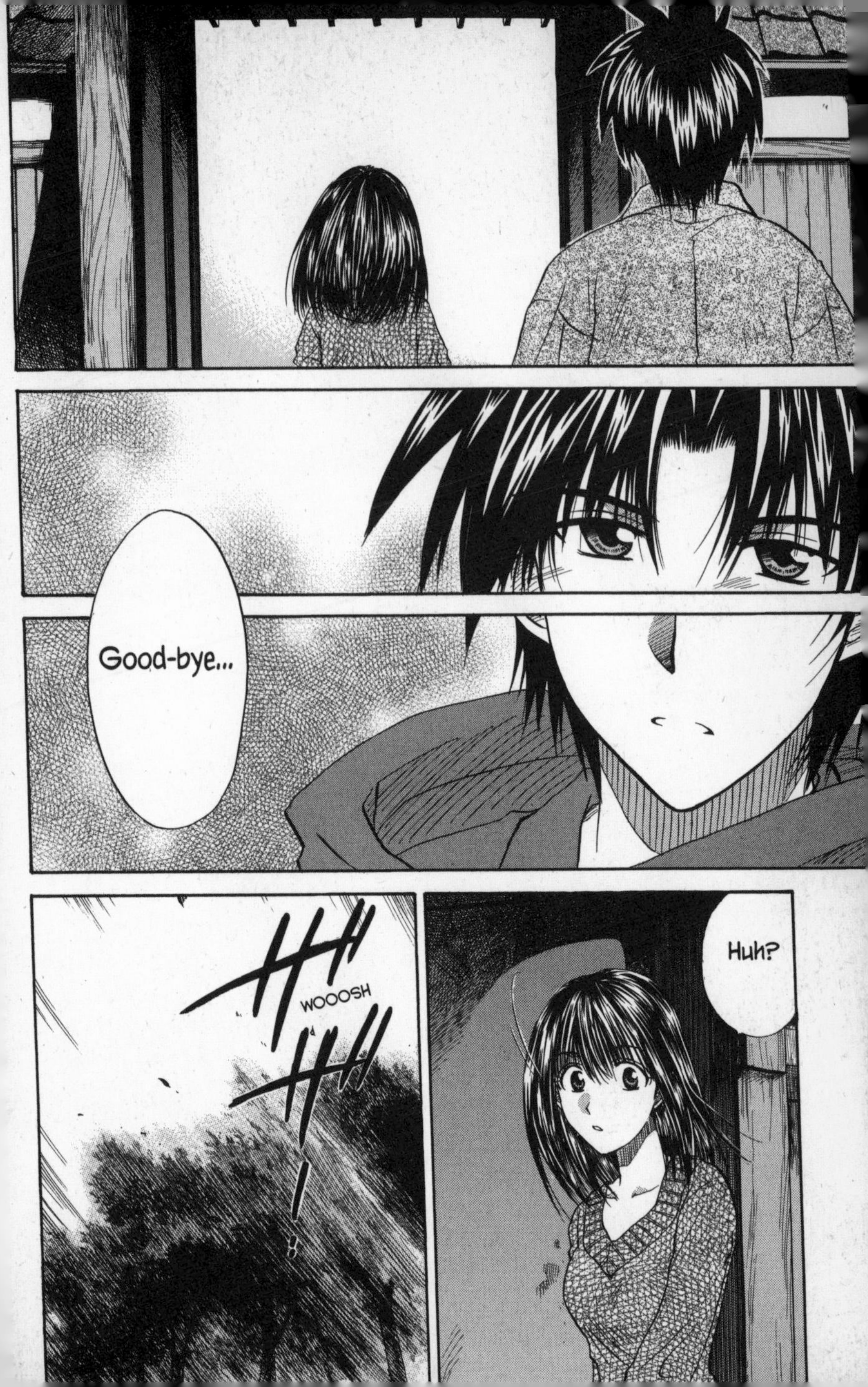
Good-bye...
Huh?
WOOOSH

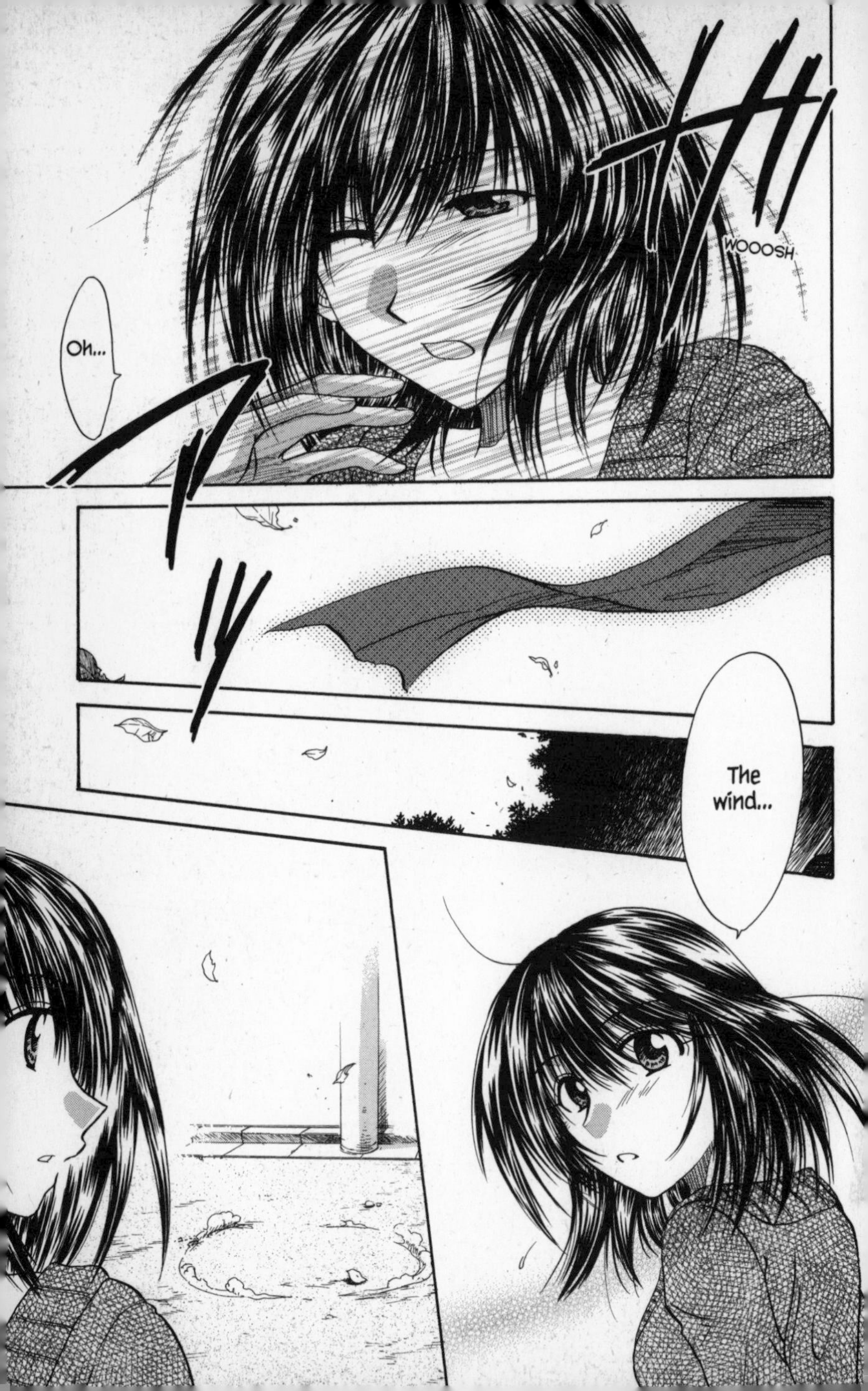
WOOOSH
Oh...
The wind...

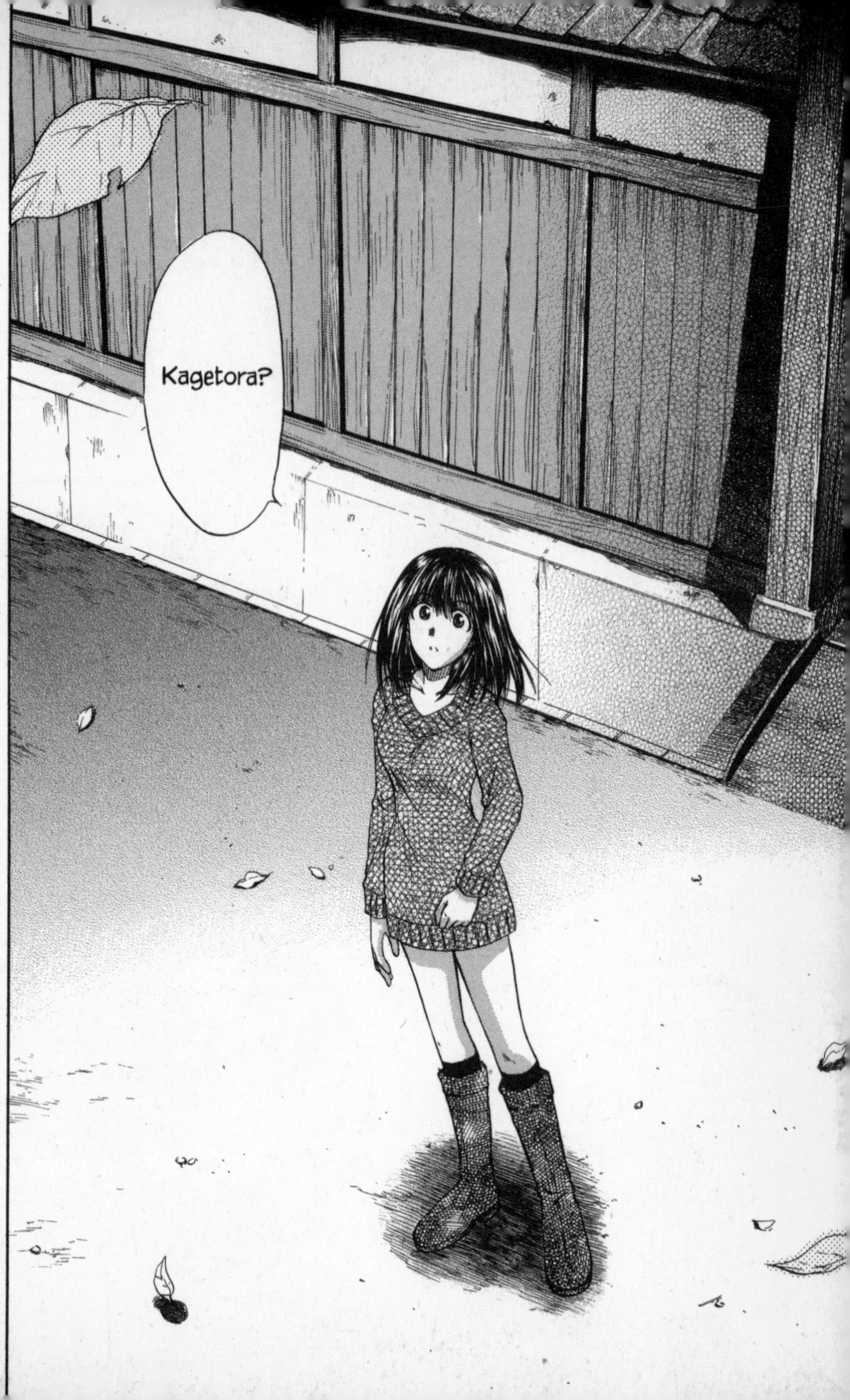
Kagetora?

KAGETORA
カゲトラ

#49 This Is an Order

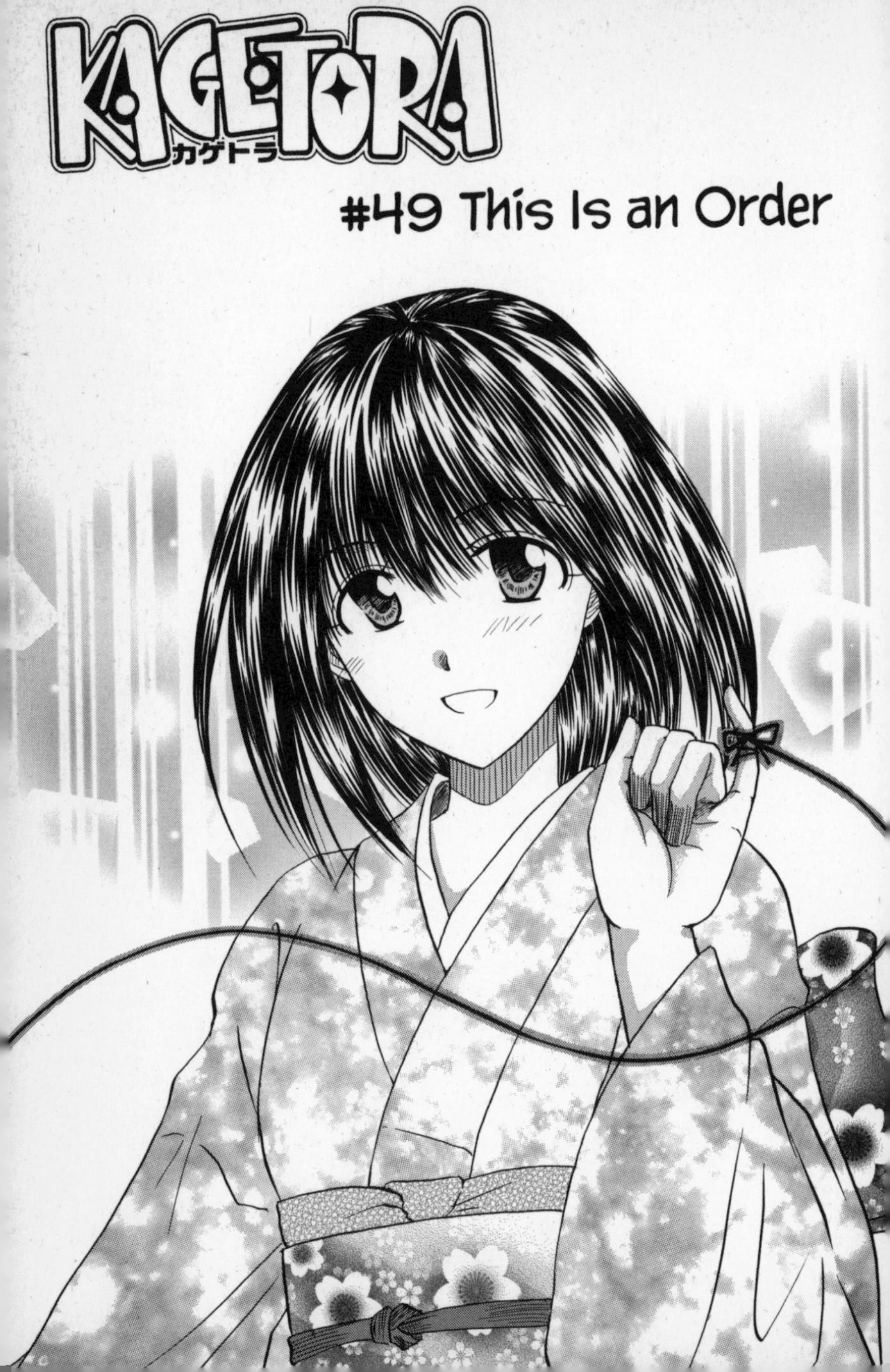

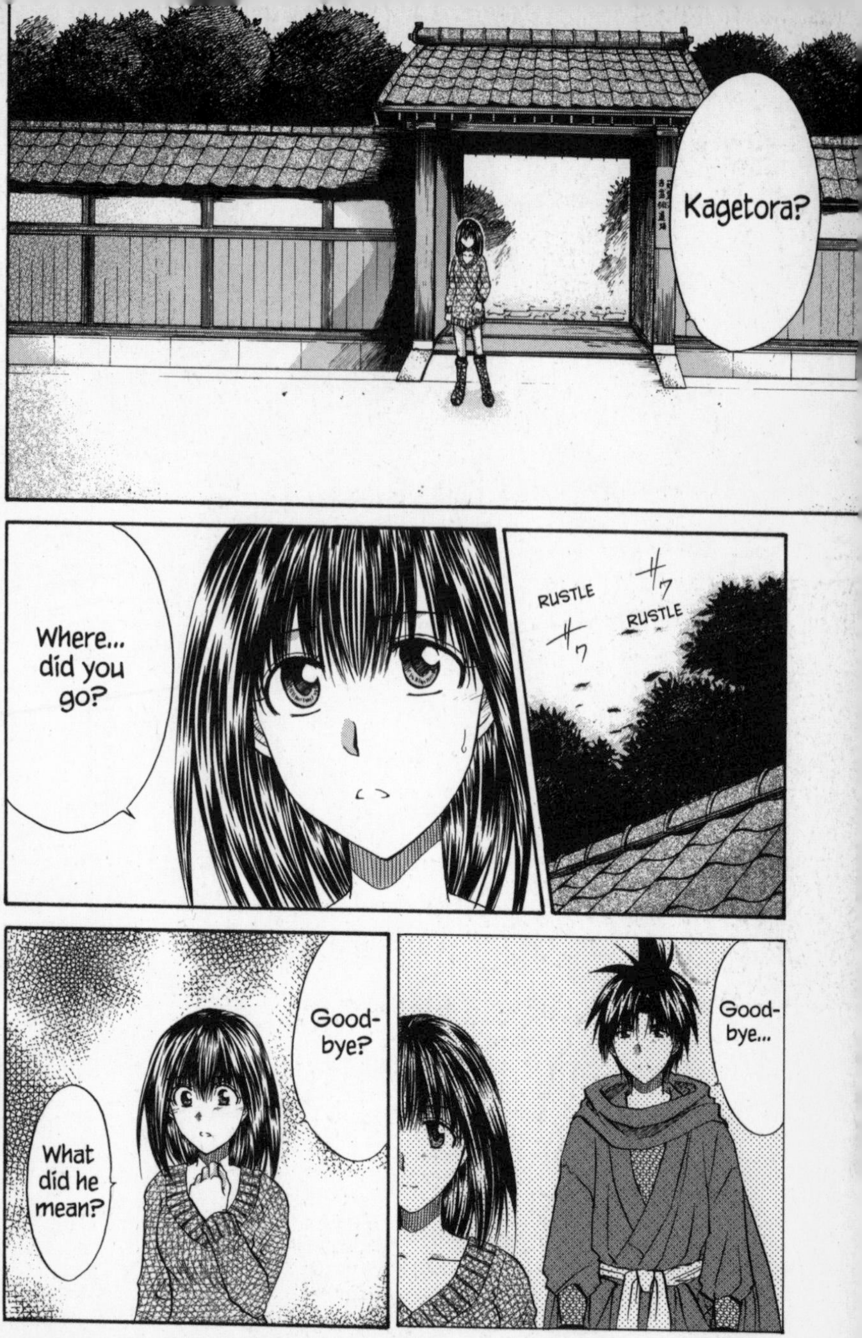
Kagetora?
ザワ
RUSTLE
ザワ
RUSTLE
Where... did you go?
Good-bye...
Good-bye?
What did he mean?

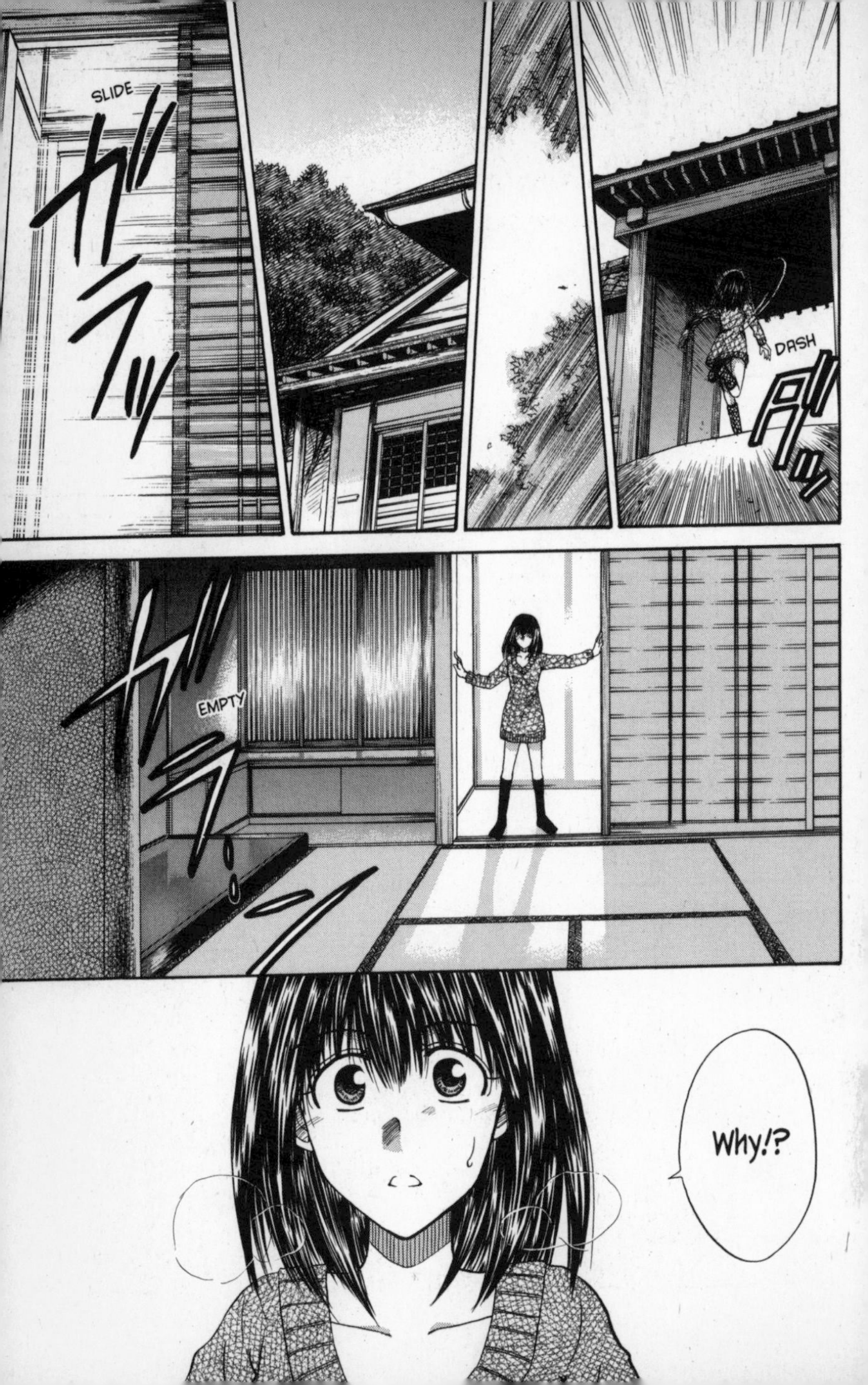
DASH
SLIDE
EMPTY
Why!?

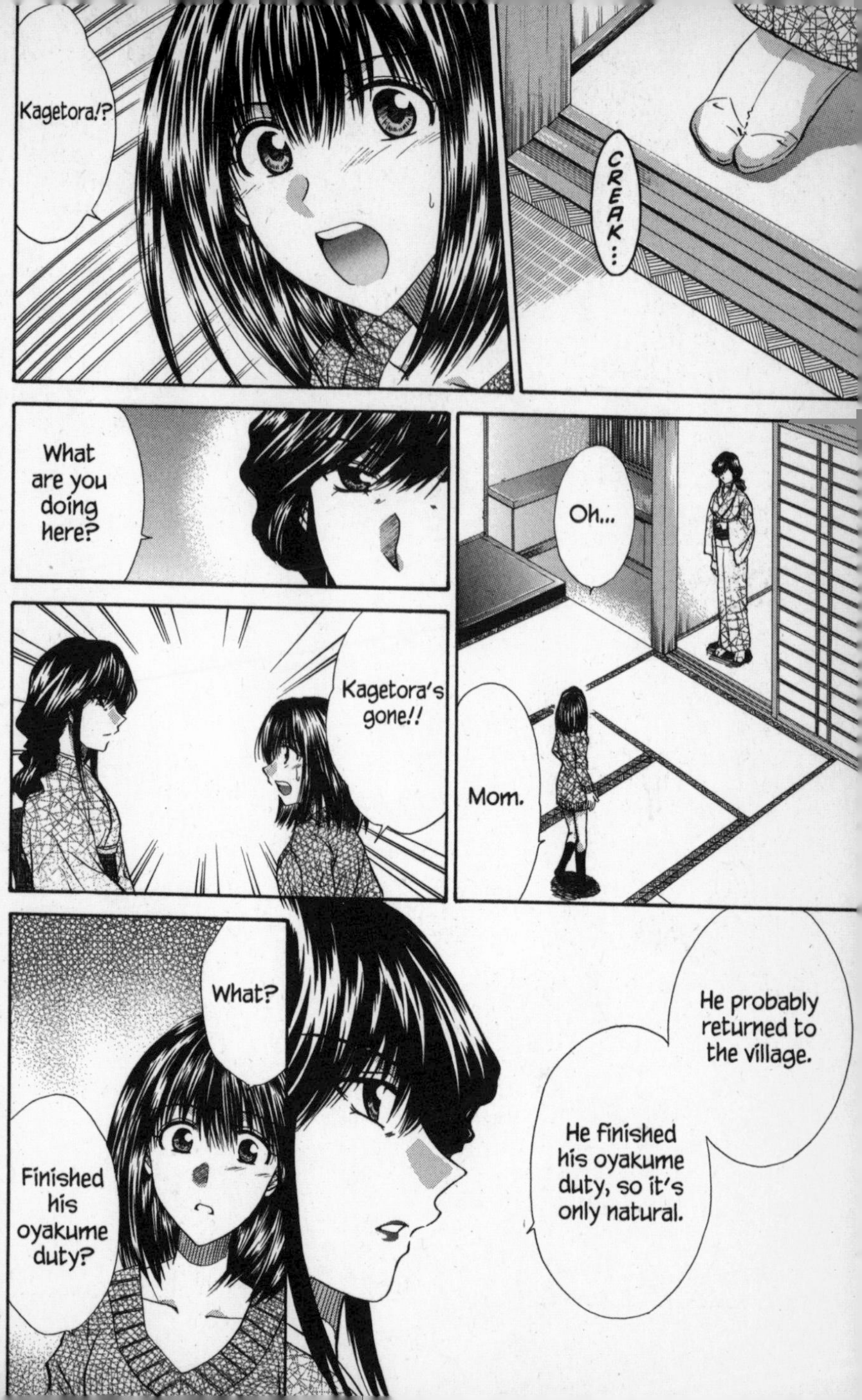
CREAK...
Kagetora!?
Oh...
Mom.
What are you doing here?
Kagetora's gone!!
He probably returned to the village.
He finished his oyakume duty, so it's only natural.
What?
Finished his oyakume duty?

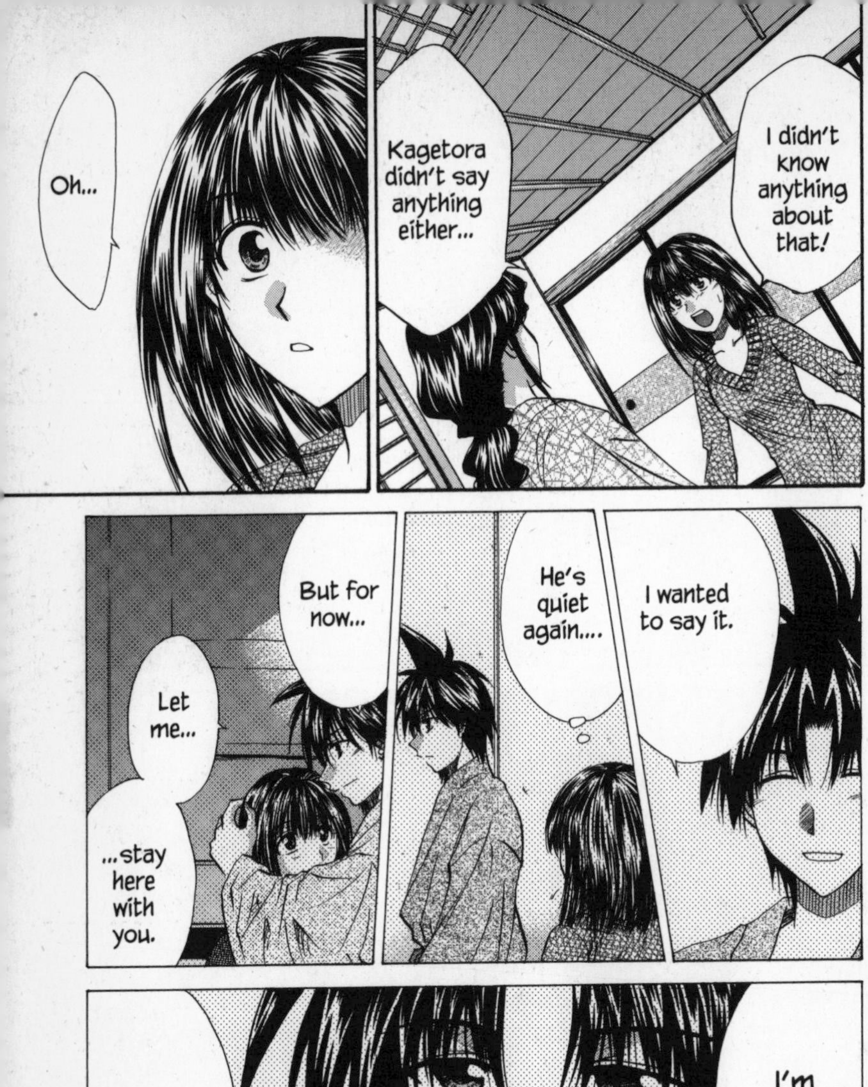
I didn't know anything about that!
Kagetora didn't say anything either...
Oh...
I wanted to say it.
He's quiet again....
But for now...
Let me...
...stay here with you.
I'm glad...
...I met you.

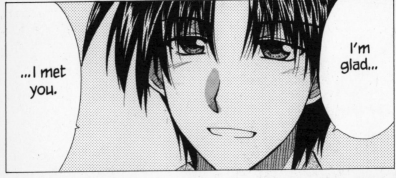

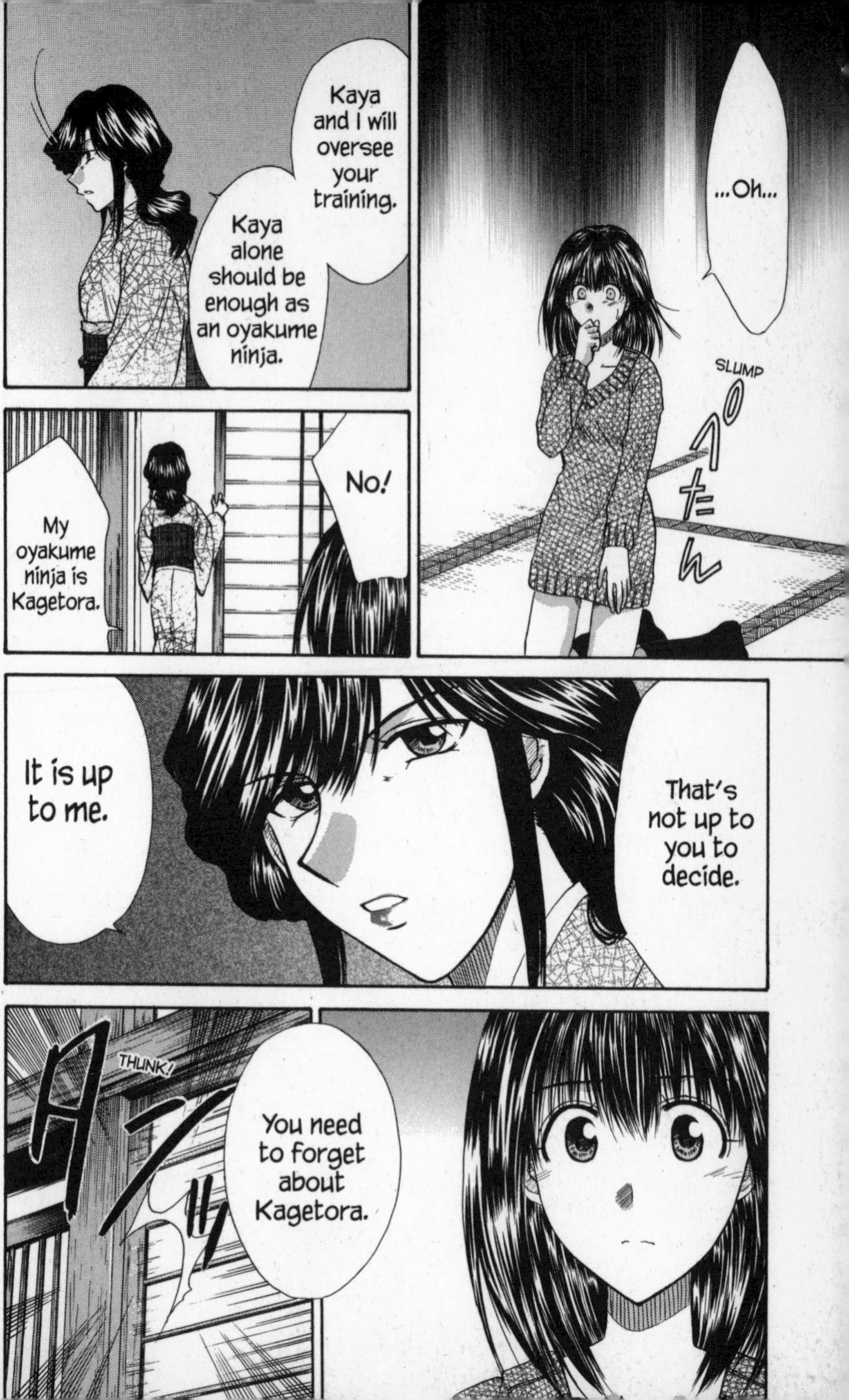

...Oh...
SLUMP
ぺたん
Kaya and I will oversee your training.
Kaya alone should be enough as an oyakume ninja.
No!
My oyakume ninja is Kagetora.
That's not up to you to decide.
It is up to me.
You need to forget about Kagetora.
THUNK!

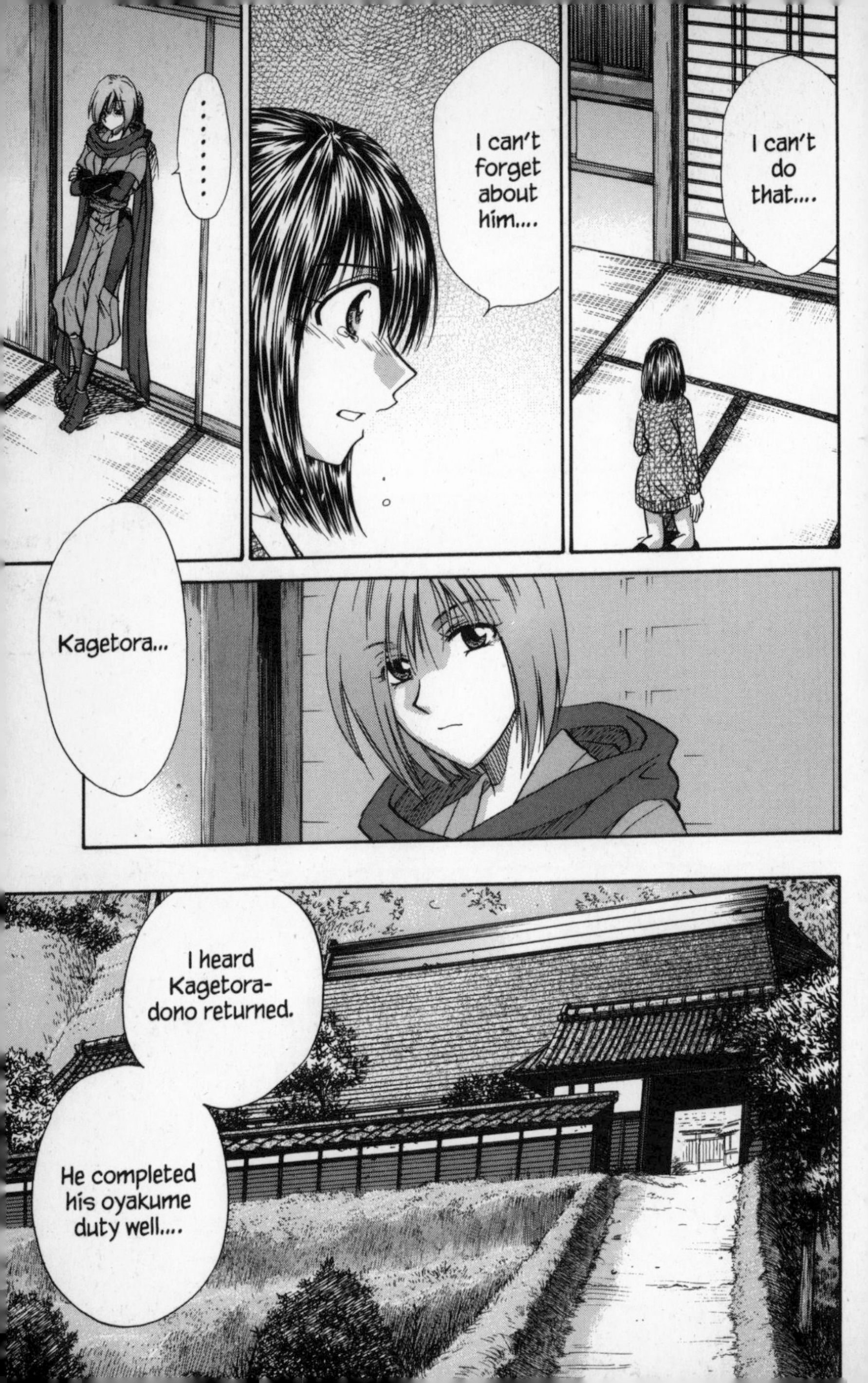
I can't do that....
I can't forget about him....
......
Kagetora...
I heard Kagetora-dono returned.
He completed his oyakume duty well....

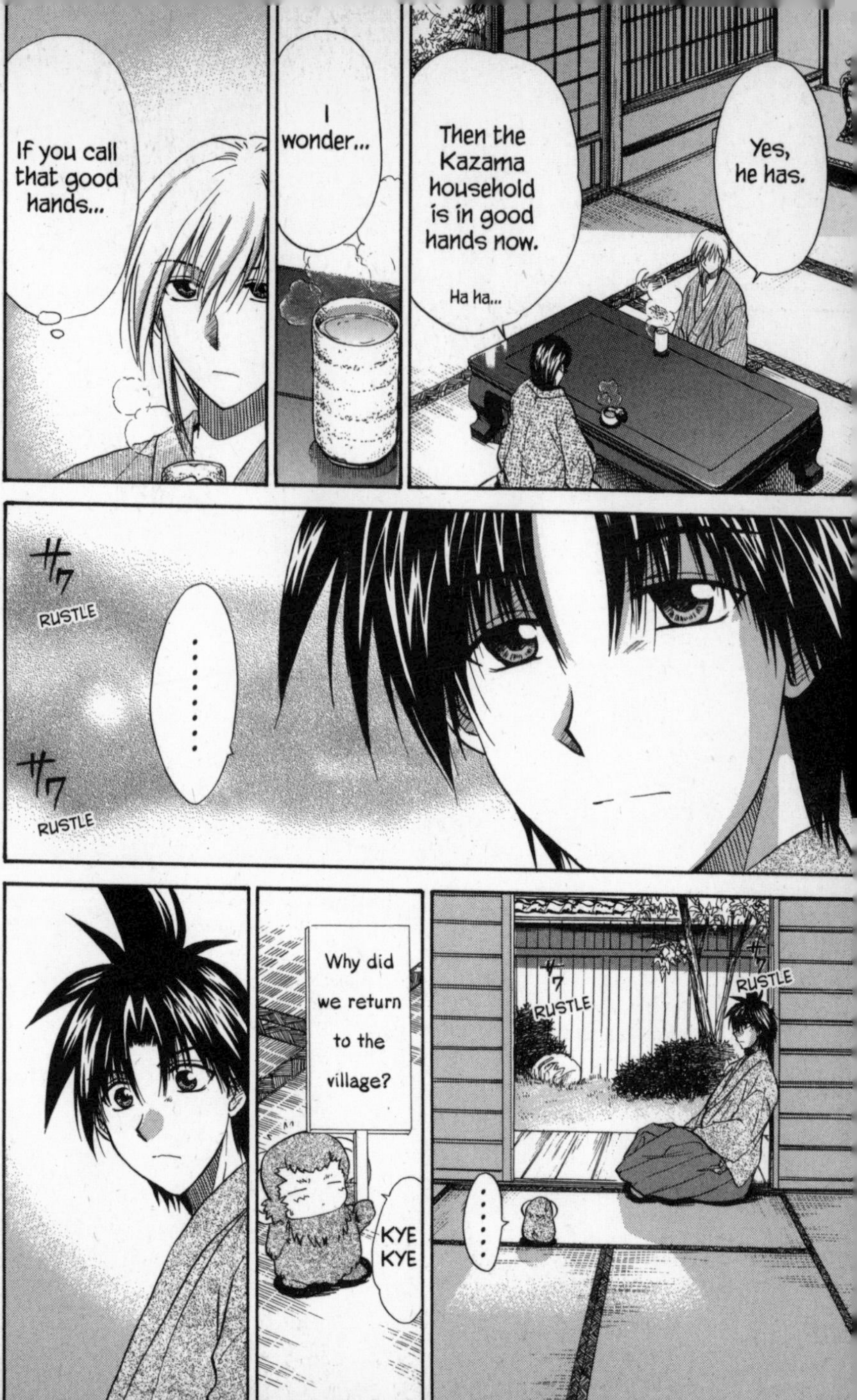

Yes, he has.
Then the Kazama household is in good hands now.
Ha ha...
I wonder...
If you call that good hands...
......
RUSTLE
RUSTLE
RUSTLE
RUSTLE
......
Why did we return to the village?
KYE KYE

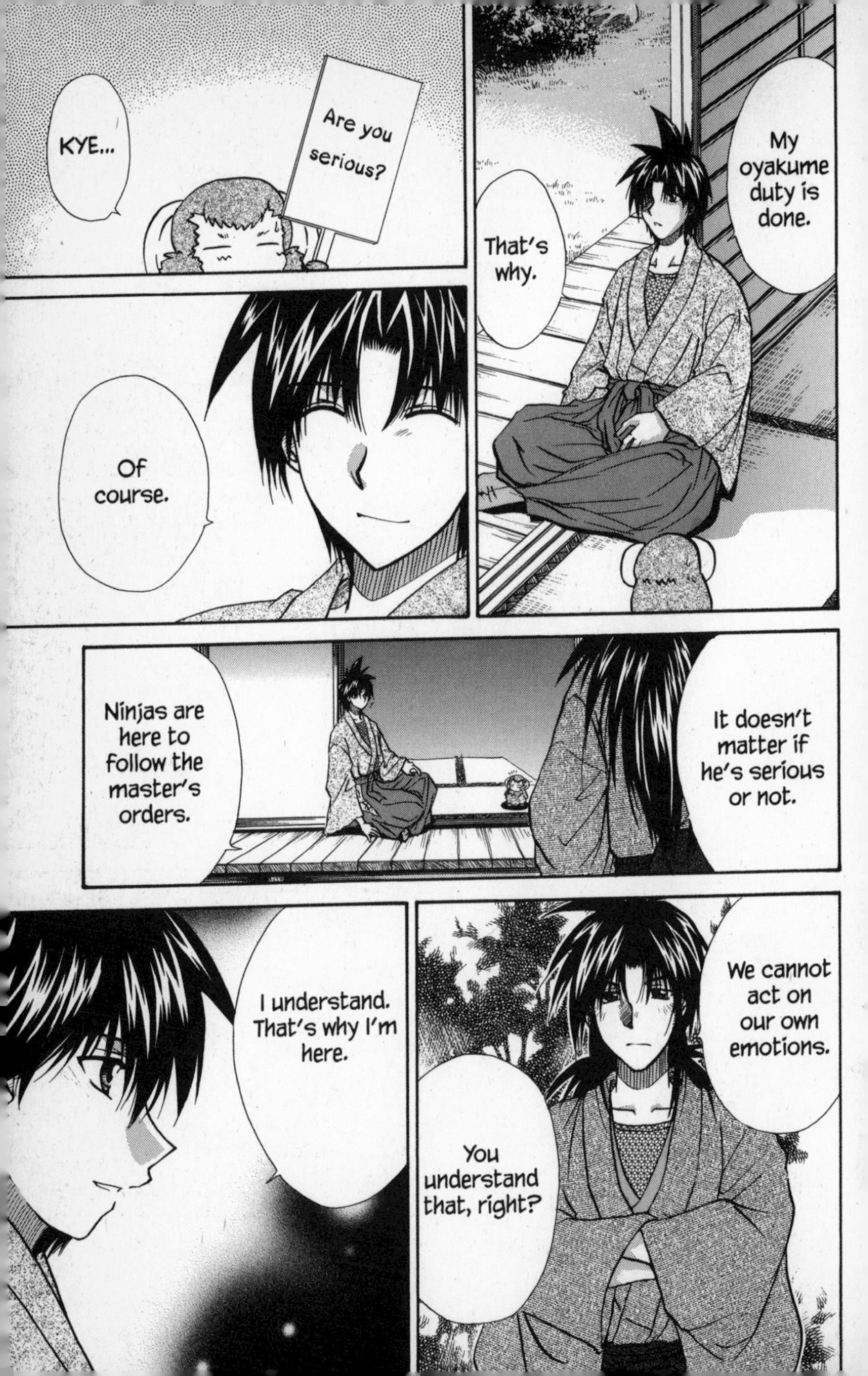
My oyakume duty is done.
That's why.
Are you serious?
KYE...
Of course.
It doesn't matter if he's serious or not.
Ninjas are here to follow the master's orders.
We cannot act on our own emotions.
You understand that, right?
I understand. That's why I'm here.

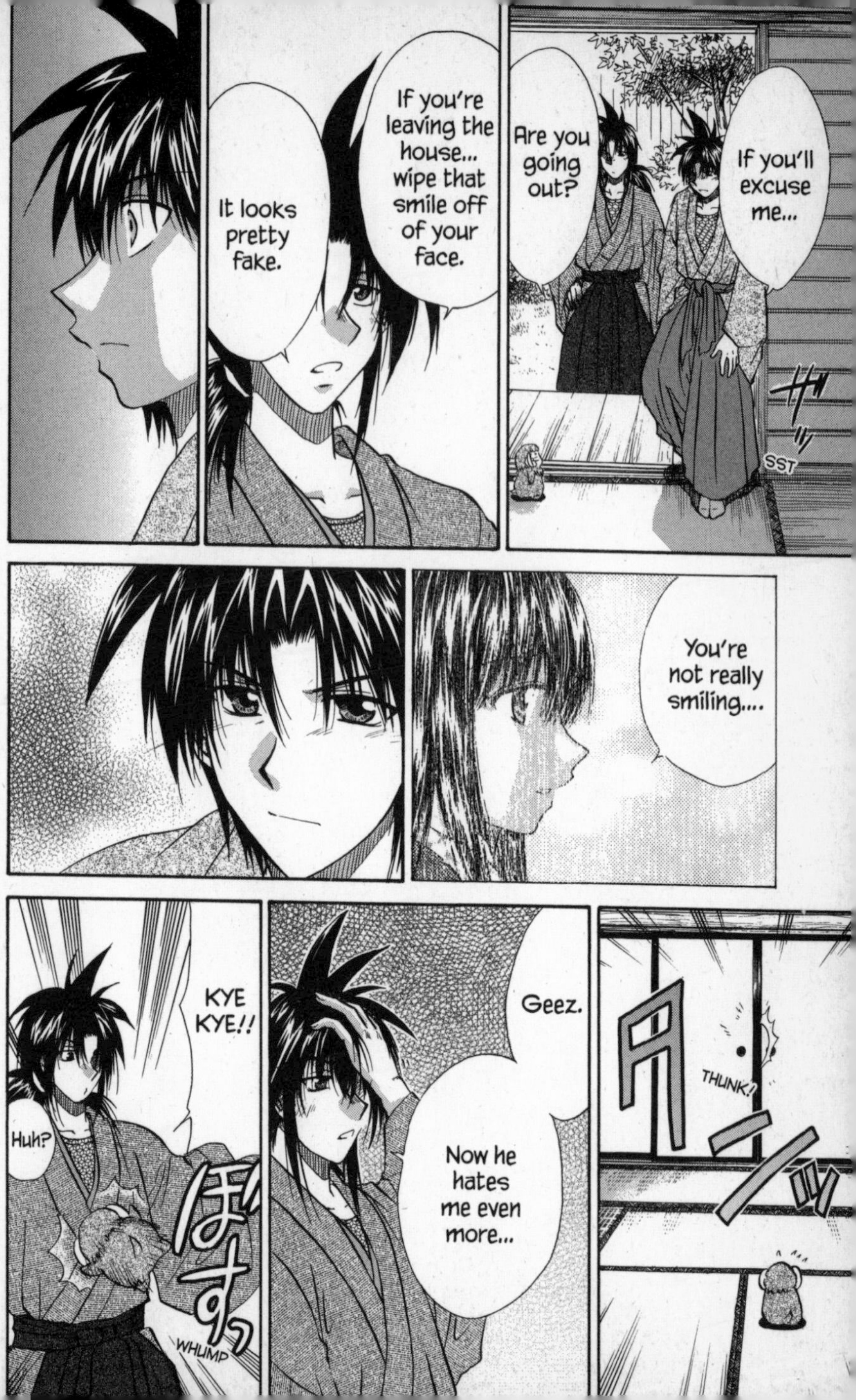
If you'll excuse me...
SST
Are you going out?
If you're leaving the house... wipe that smile off of your face.
It looks pretty fake.
You're not really smiling....
THUNK!
Geez.
Now he hates me even more...
KYE KYE!!
Huh?
WHUMP

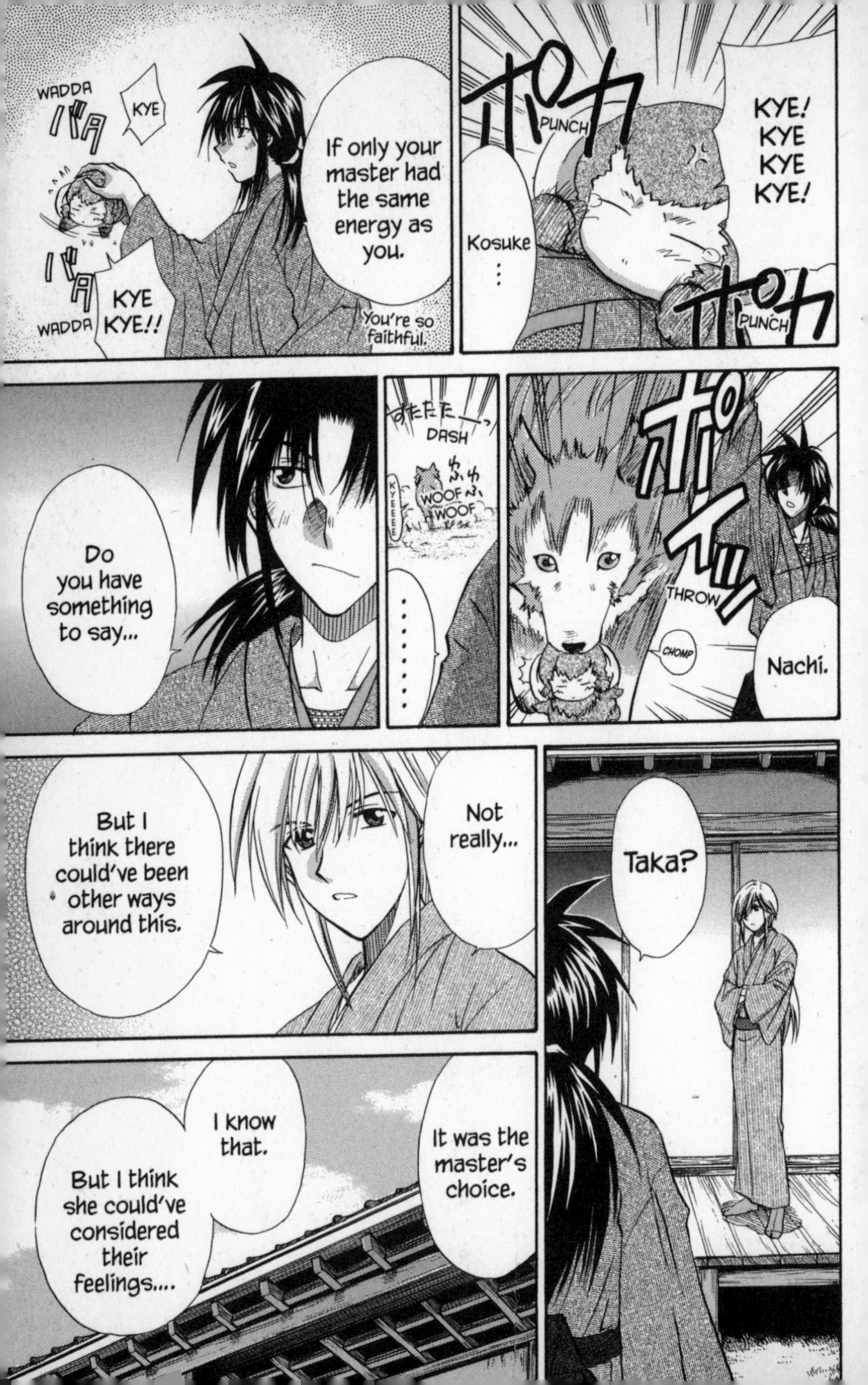

ポカ
PUNCH
KYE! KYE KYE KYE!
Kosuke...
ポカ
PUNCH
If only your master had the same energy as you.
KYE
WADDA
バタ
KYE KYE!!
WADDA
バタ
You're so faithful.
THROW
Nachi.
CHOMP
DASH
WOOF WOOF
KYEEEEE
....
Do you have something to say...
Taka?
Not really...
But I think there could've been other ways around this.
It was the master's choice.
I know that.
But I think she could've considered their feelings....

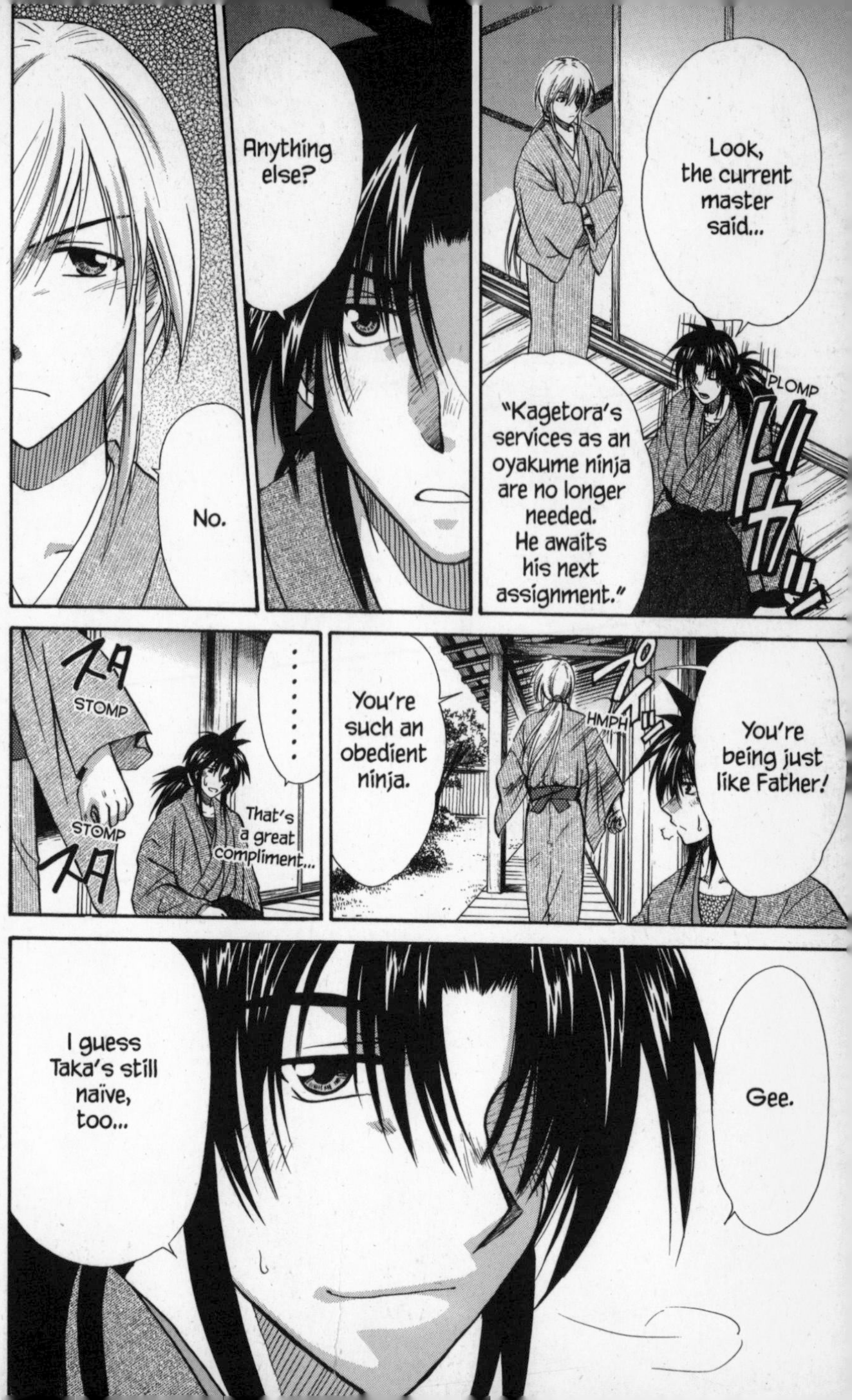
Look, the current master said...
PLOMP
"Kagetora's services as an oyakume ninja are no longer needed. He awaits his next assignment."
Anything else?
No.
You're being just like Father!
HMPH
You're such an obedient ninja.
......
STOMP
STOMP
That's a great compliment...
Gee.
I guess Taka's still naïve, too...

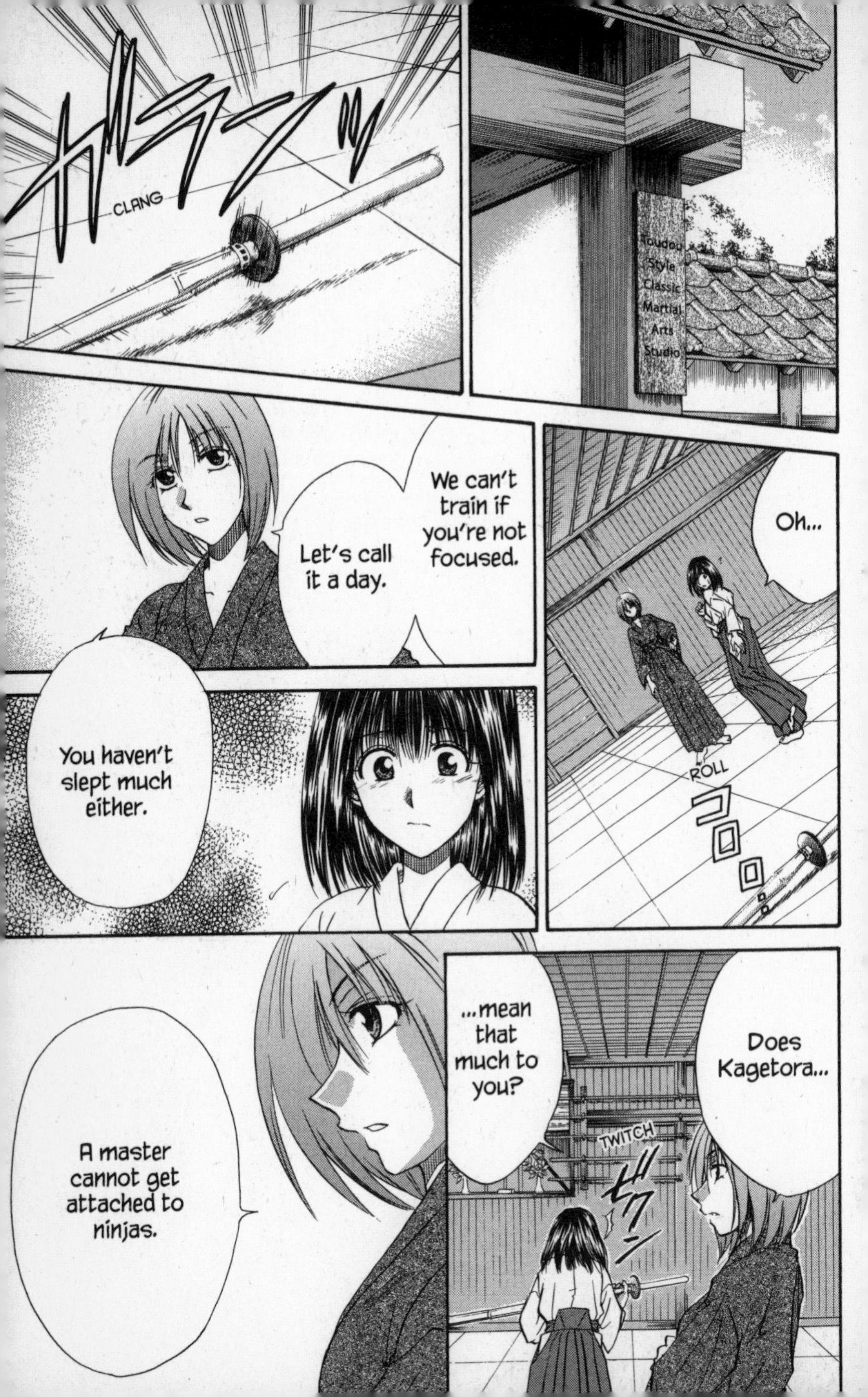
Toudou Style Classic Martial Arts Studio
CLANG
Oh...
ROLL
We can't train if you're not focused.
Let's call it a day.
You haven't slept much either.
Does Kagetora...
...mean that much to you?
TWITCH
A master cannot get attached to ninjas.

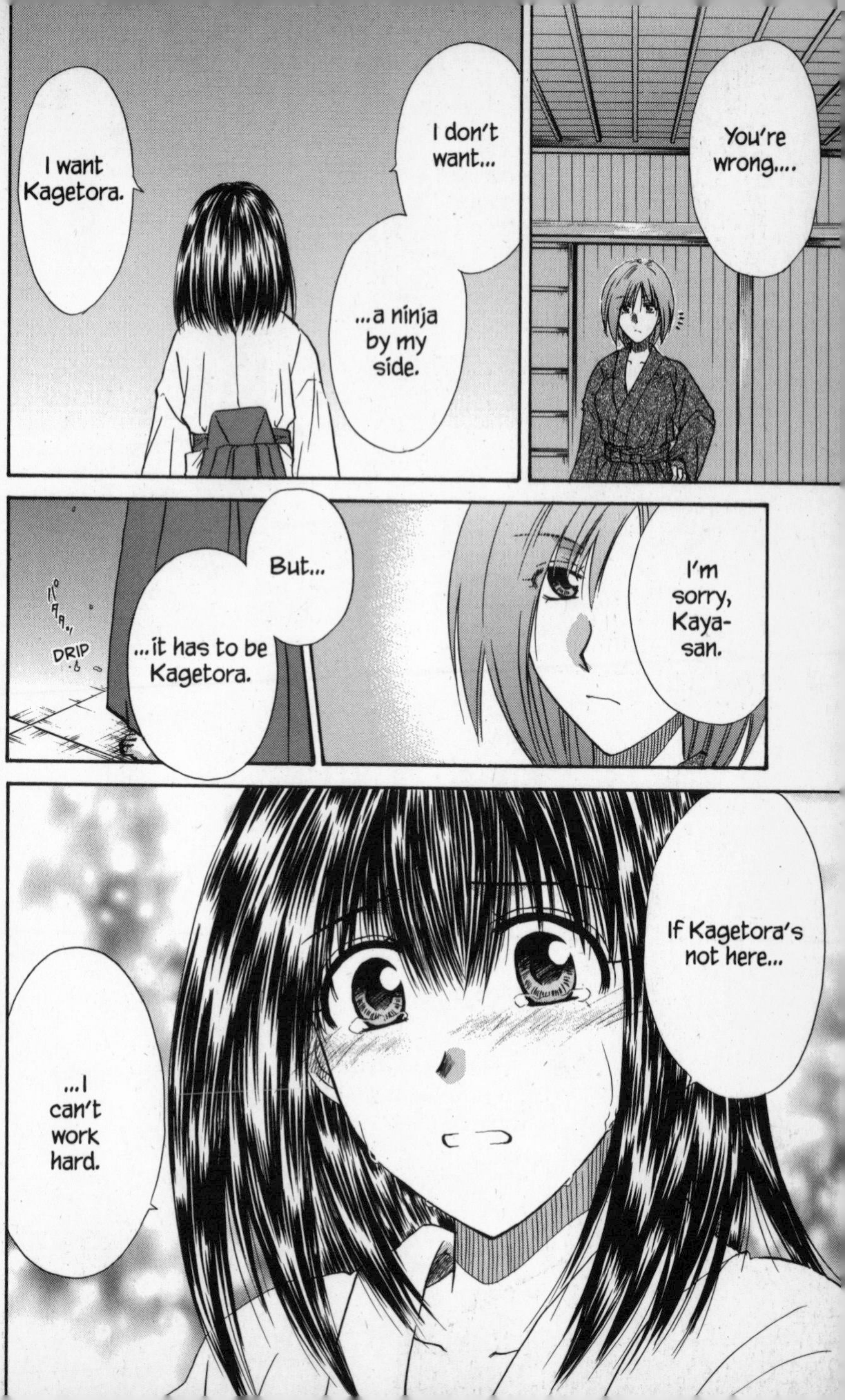
You're wrong....
I don't want...
...a ninja by my side.
I want Kagetora.
I'm sorry, Kaya-san.
But...
...it has to be Kagetora.
DRIP
If Kagetora's not here...
...I can't work hard.

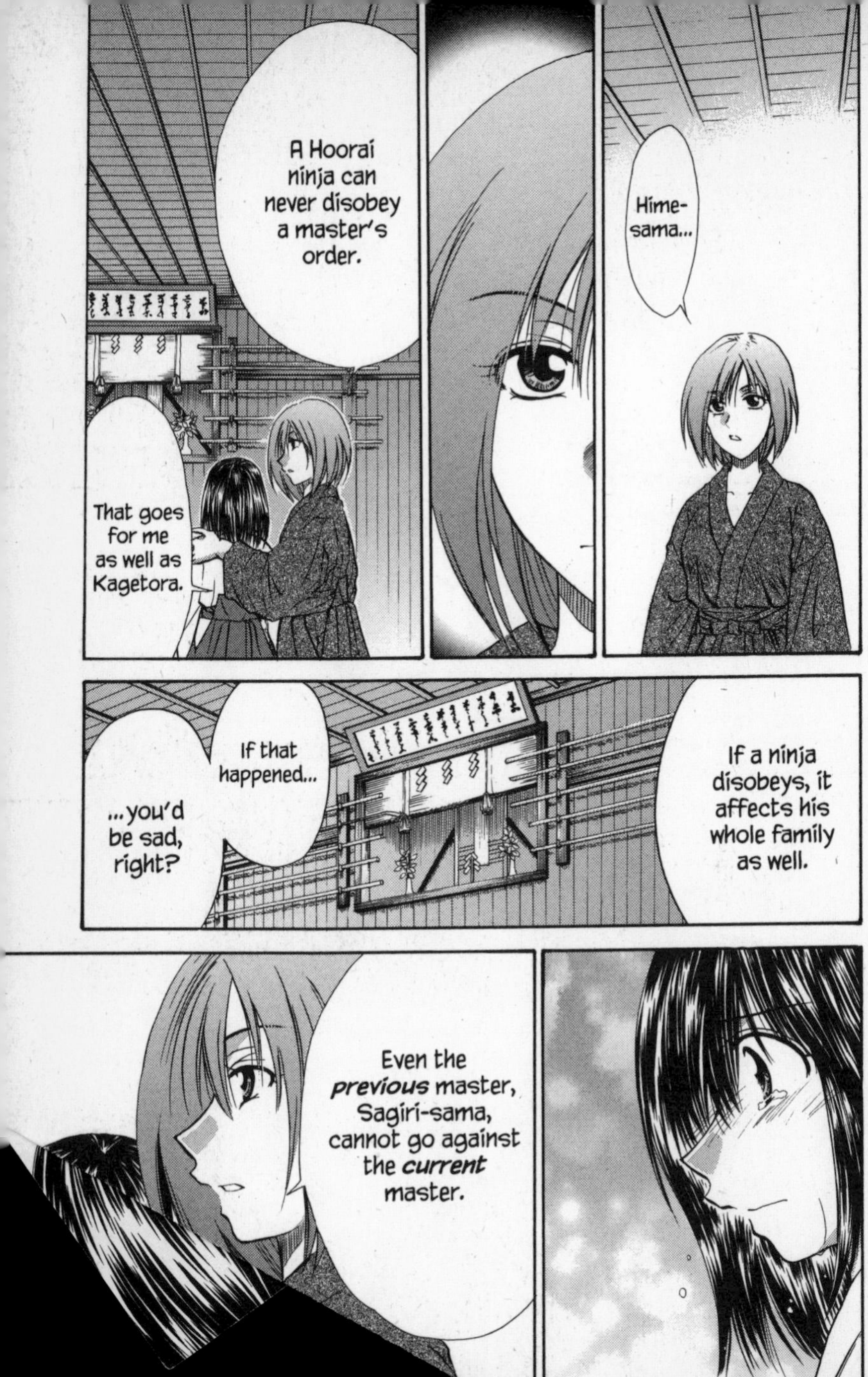
Hime-sama...
A Hoorai ninja can never disobey a master's order.
That goes for me as well as Kagetora.
If a ninja disobeys, it affects his whole family as well.
If that happened...
...you'd be sad, right?
Even the *previous* master, Sagiri-sama, cannot go against the *current* master.

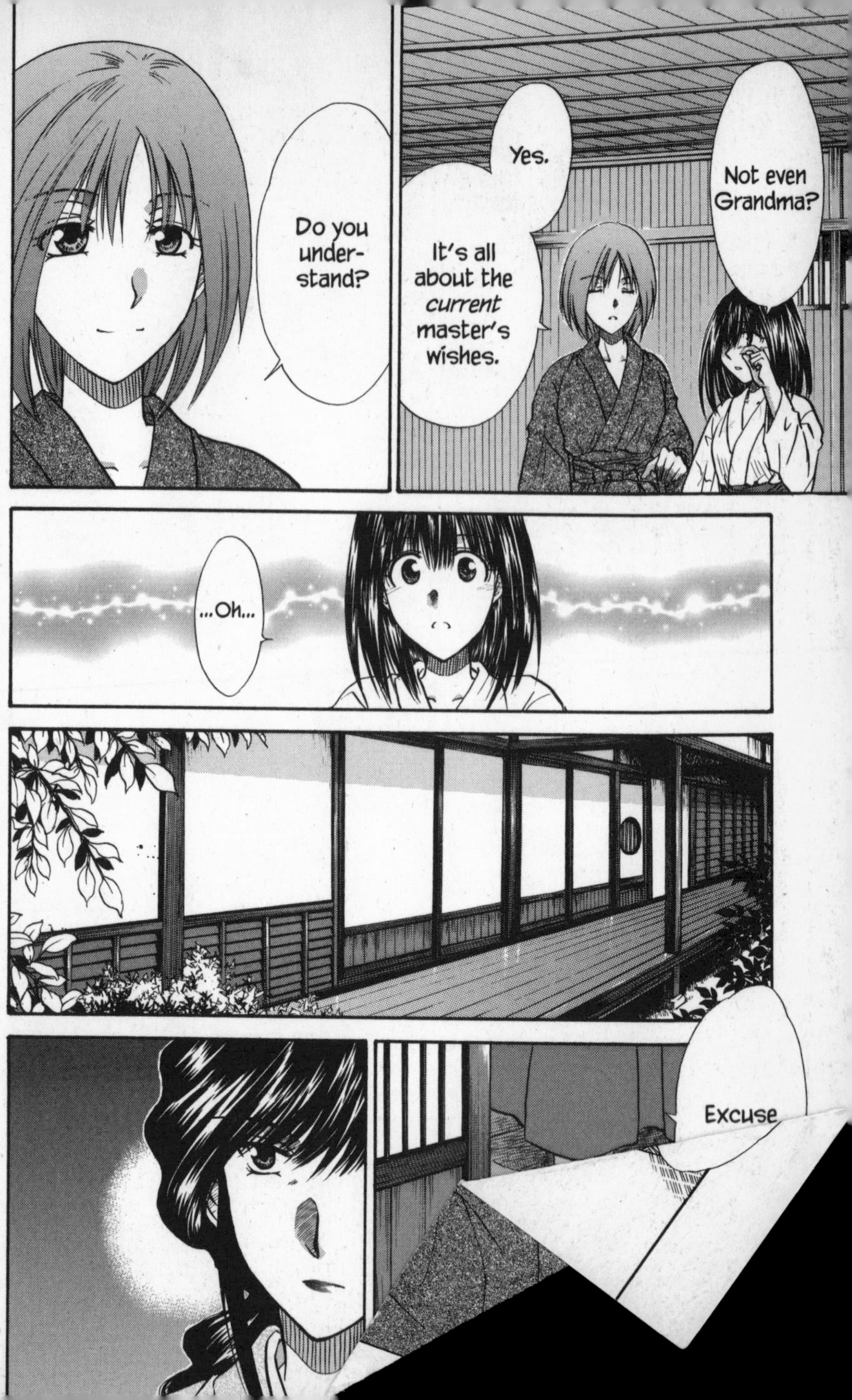
Not even Grandma?
Yes.
It's all about the *current* master's wishes.
Do you under-stand?
...Oh...
Excuse

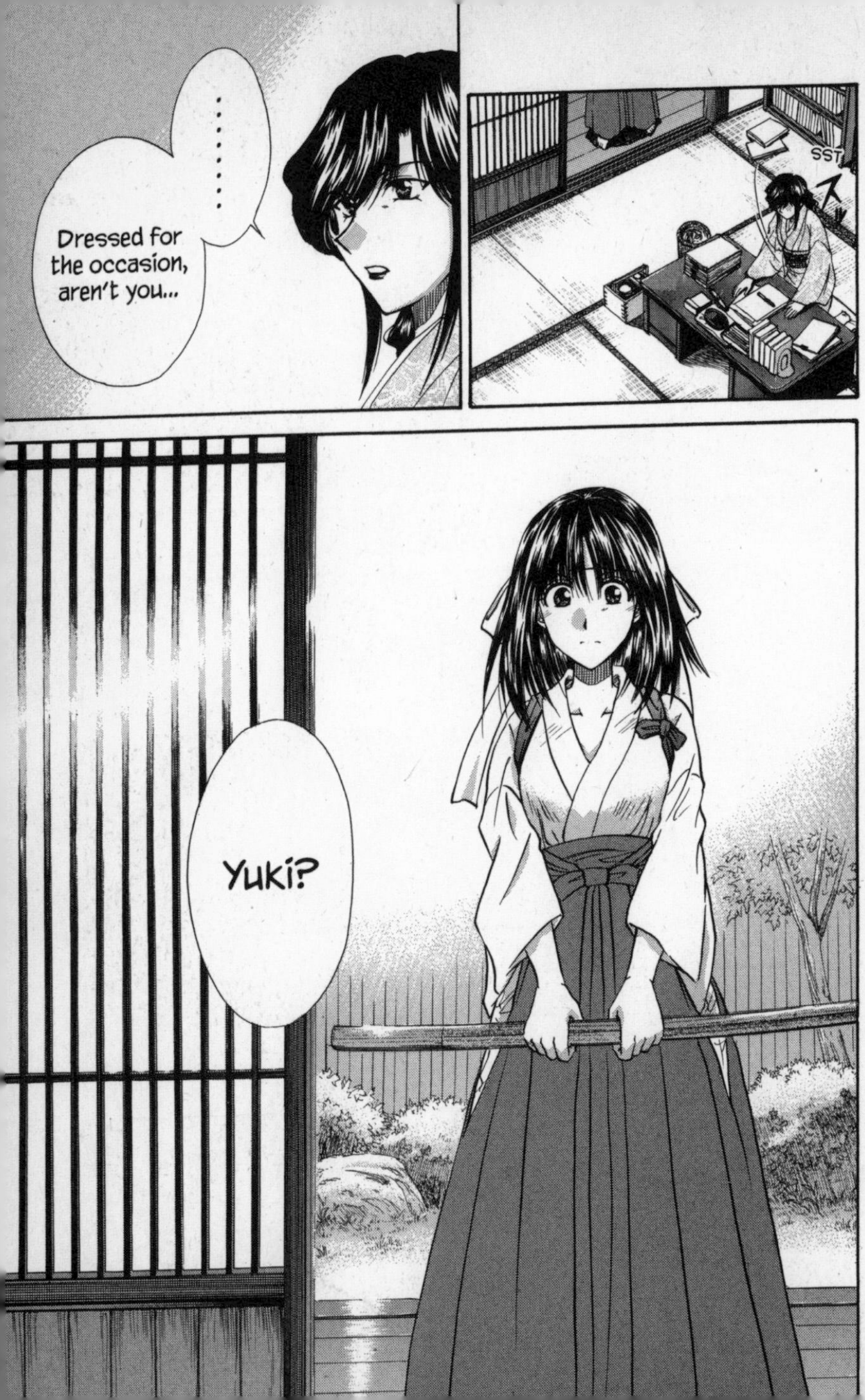
SST
......
Dressed for the occasion, aren't you...
Yuki?

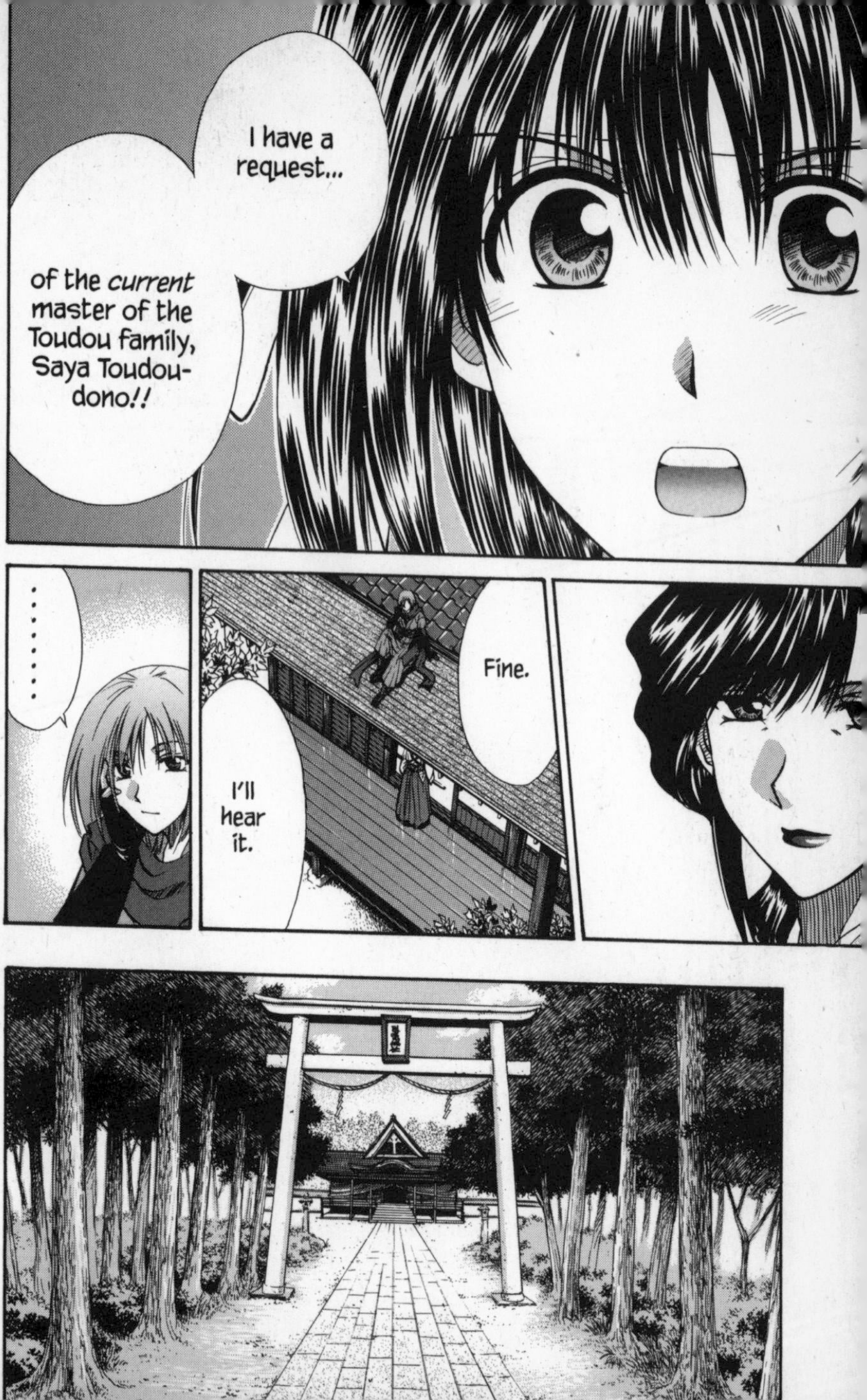
I have a request...
of the *current* master of the Toudou family, Saya Toudou-dono!!
Fine.
I'll hear it.
....

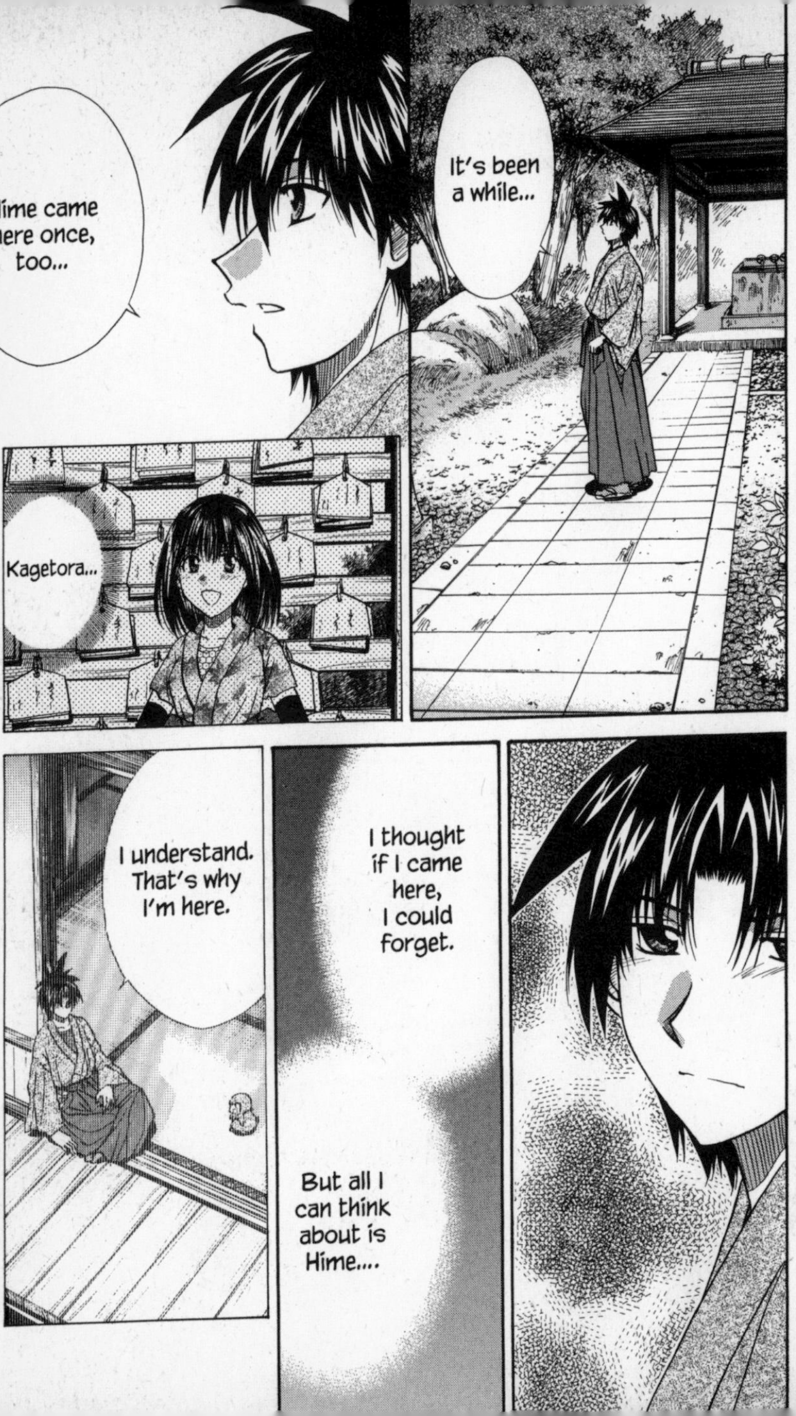
It's been a while...
Hime came here once, too...
Kagetora...
I thought if I came here, I could forget.
But all I can think about is Hime....
I understand. That's why I'm here.

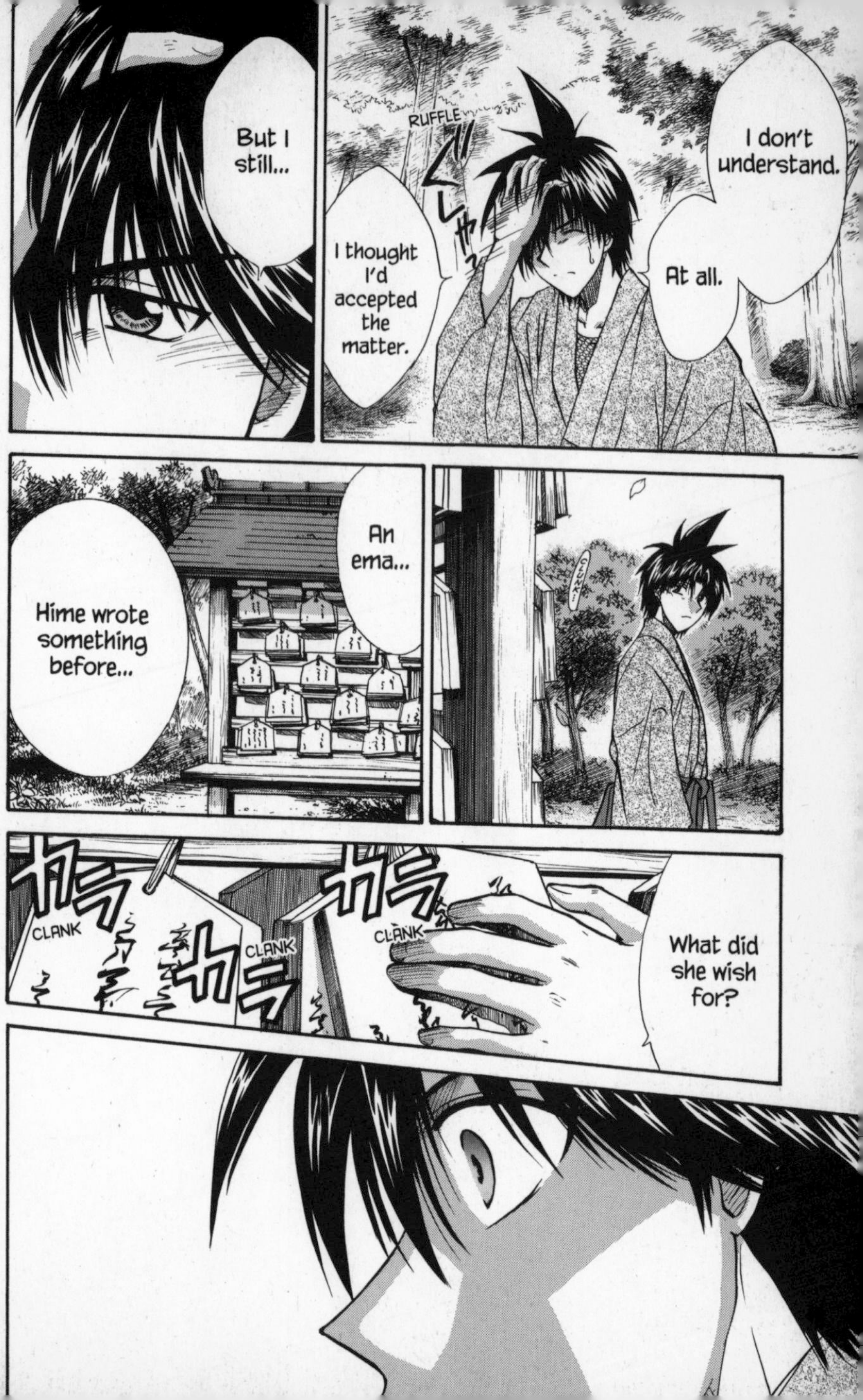
I don't understand.
At all.
RUFFLE
I thought I'd accepted the matter.
But I still...
CLINK
An ema...
Hime wrote something before...
What did she wish for?
CLANK
CLANK
CLANK

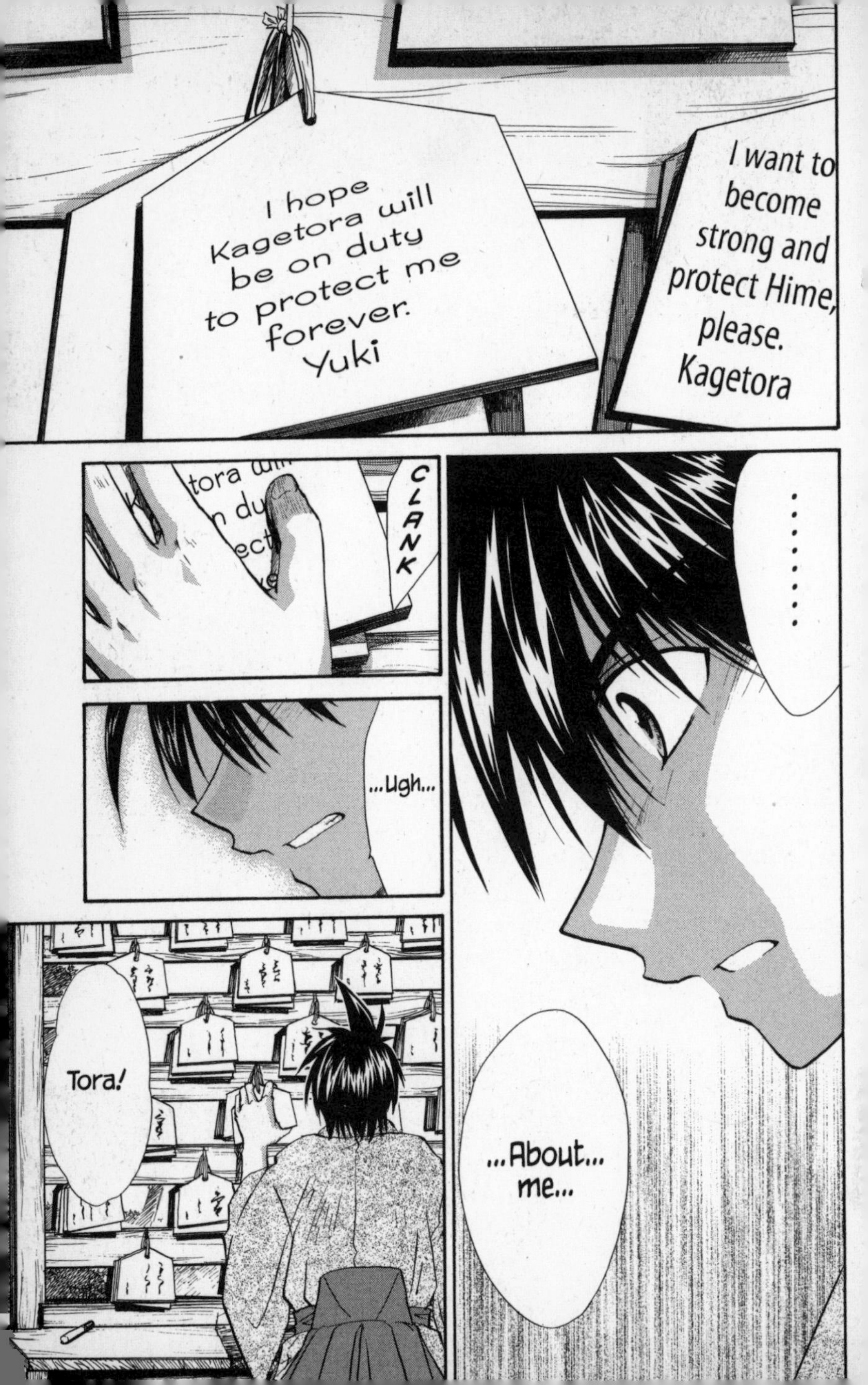
I want to become strong and protect Hime, please. Kagetora
I hope Kagetora will be on duty to protect me forever. Yuki
......
...About... me...
CLANK
...Ugh...
Tora!

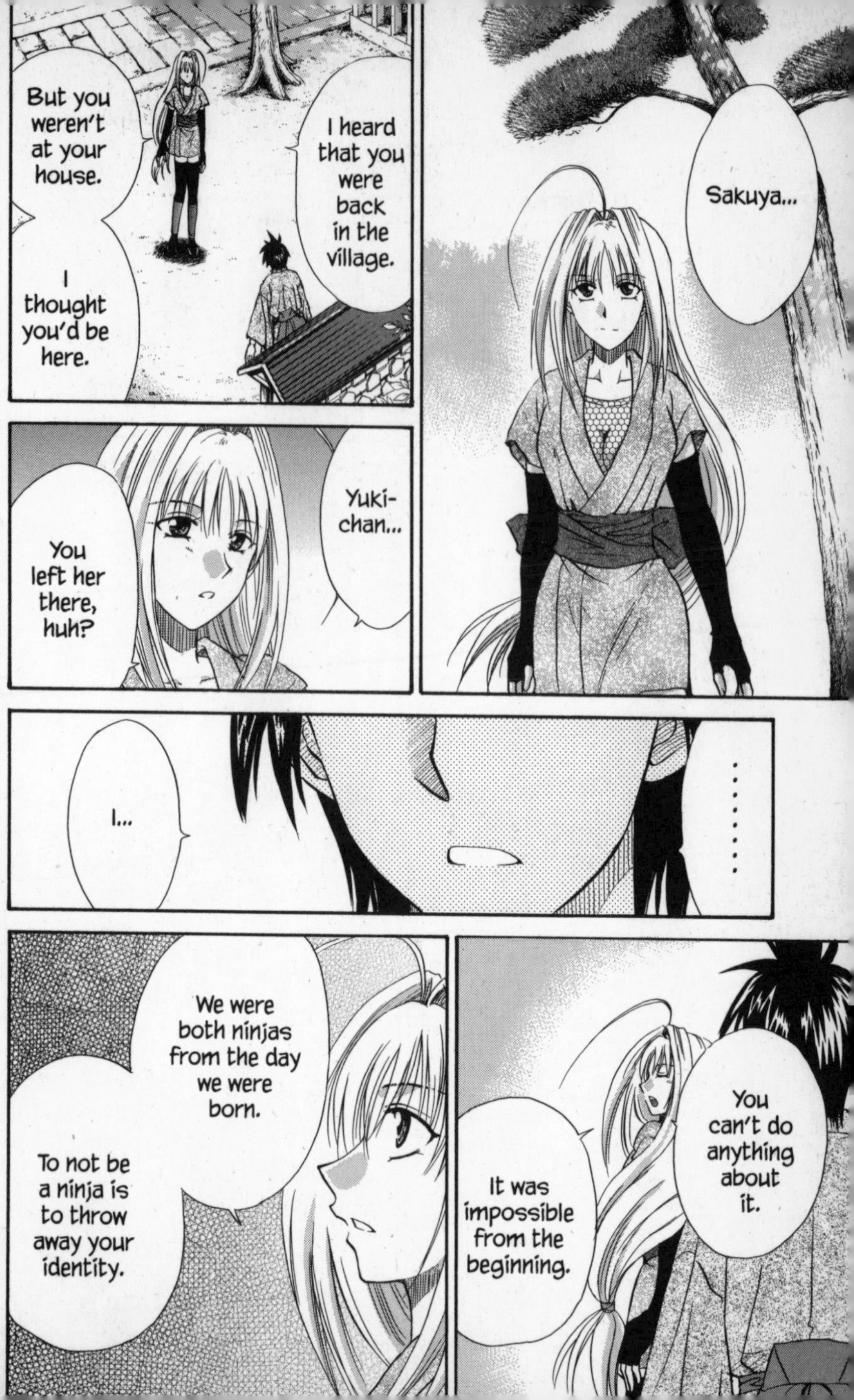
Sakuya...
I heard that you were back in the village.
But you weren't at your house.
I thought you'd be here.
Yuki-chan...
You left her there, huh?
....
I...
You can't do anything about it.
It was impossible from the beginning.
We were both ninjas from the day we were born.
To not be a ninja is to throw away your identity.

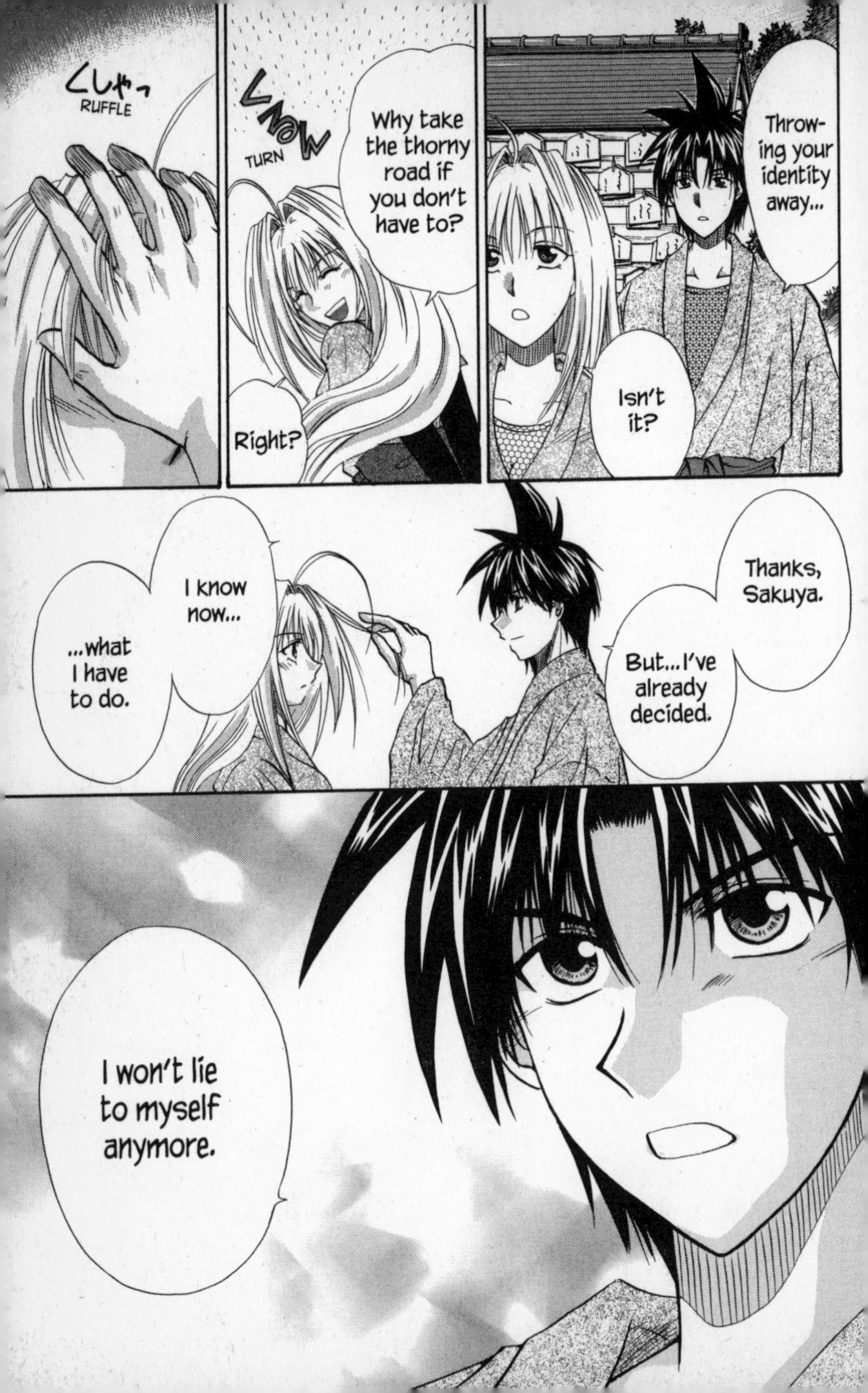
Throwing your identity away...
Isn't it?
TURN
Why take the thorny road if you don't have to?
Right?
くしゃっ
RUFFLE
Thanks, Sakuya.
But...I've already decided.
I know now...
...what I have to do.
I won't lie to myself anymore.

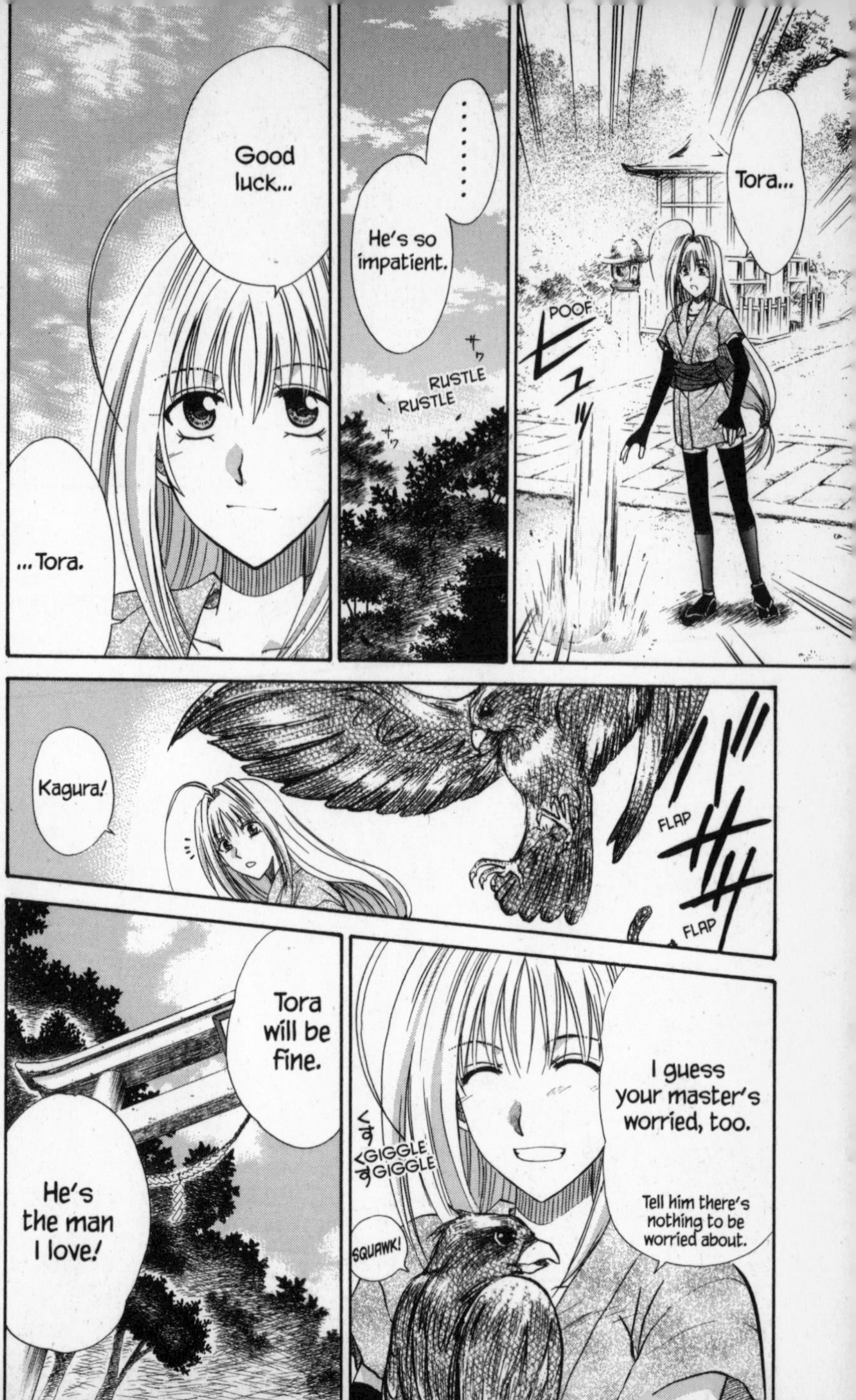
Tora...
POOF
......
He's so impatient.
RUSTLE
RUSTLE
Good luck...
...Tora.
Kagura!
FLAP
FLAP
I guess your master's worried, too.
GIGGLE
GIGGLE
Tell him there's nothing to be worried about.
SQUAWK!
Tora will be fine.
He's the man I love!

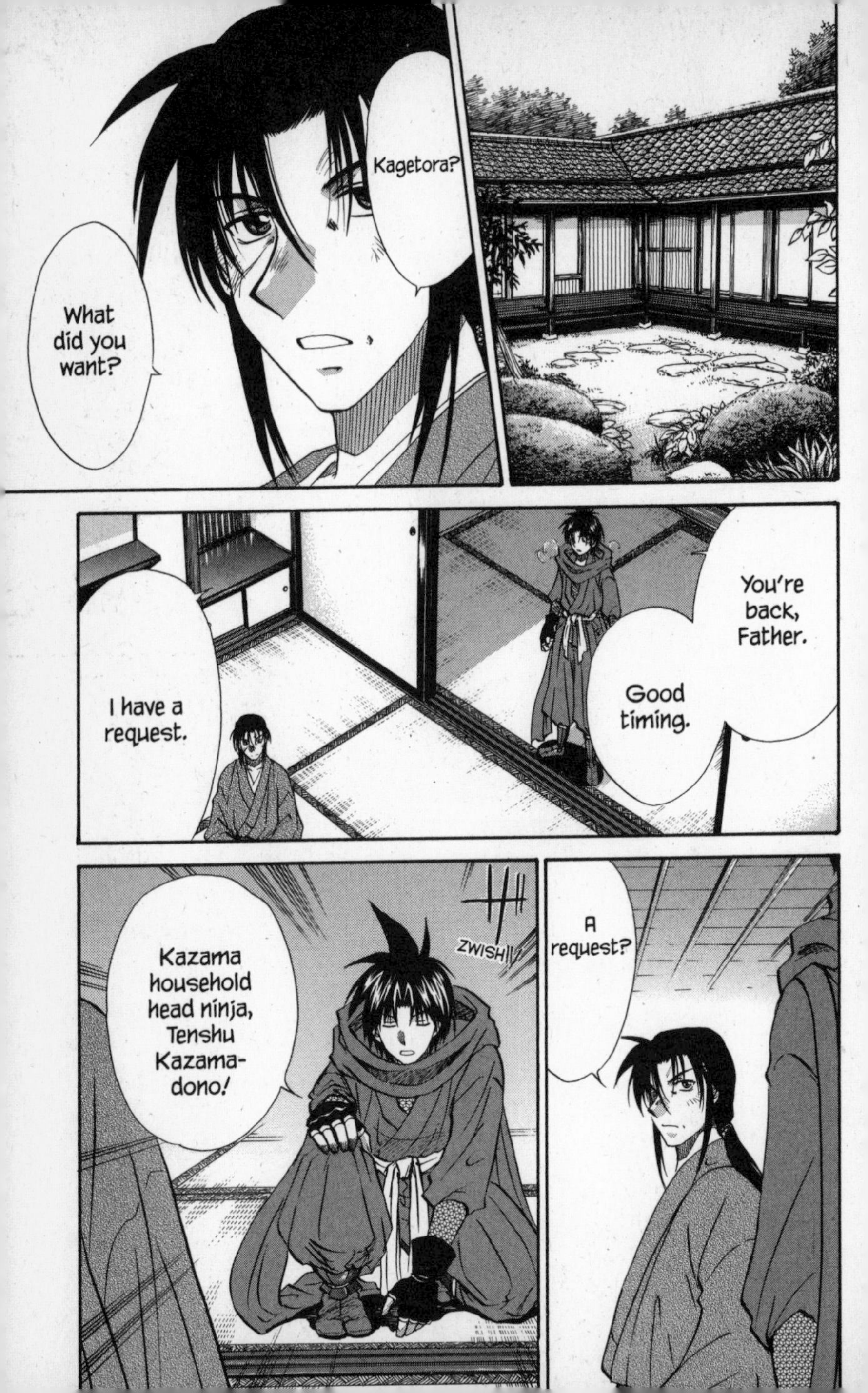
Kagetora?
What did you want?
You're back, Father.
Good timing.
I have a request.
A request?
ZWISH!!
Kazama household head ninja, Tenshu Kazama-dono!

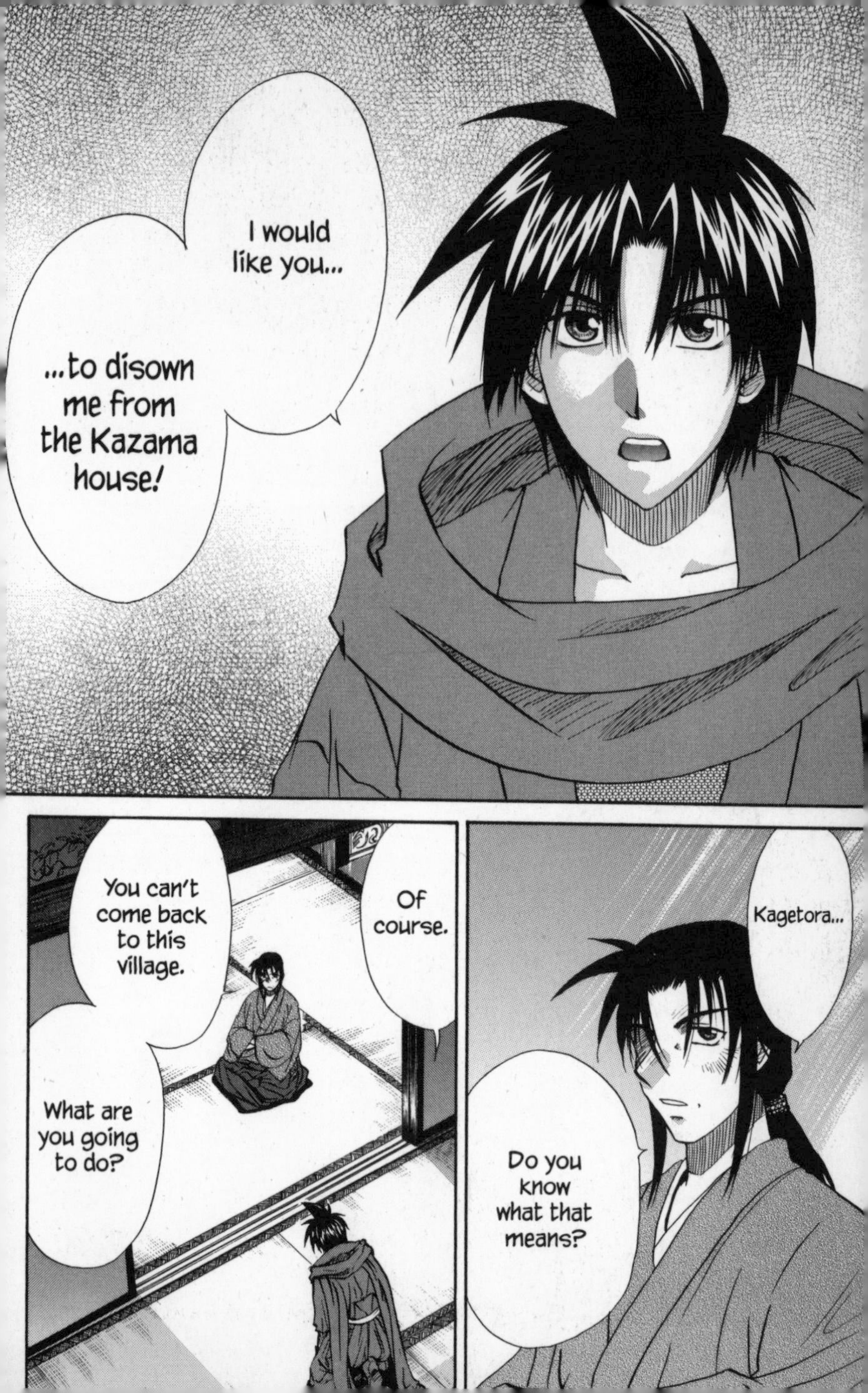
I would like you...
...to disown me from the Kazama house!
Kagetora...
Do you know what that means?
Of course.
You can't come back to this village.
What are you going to do?

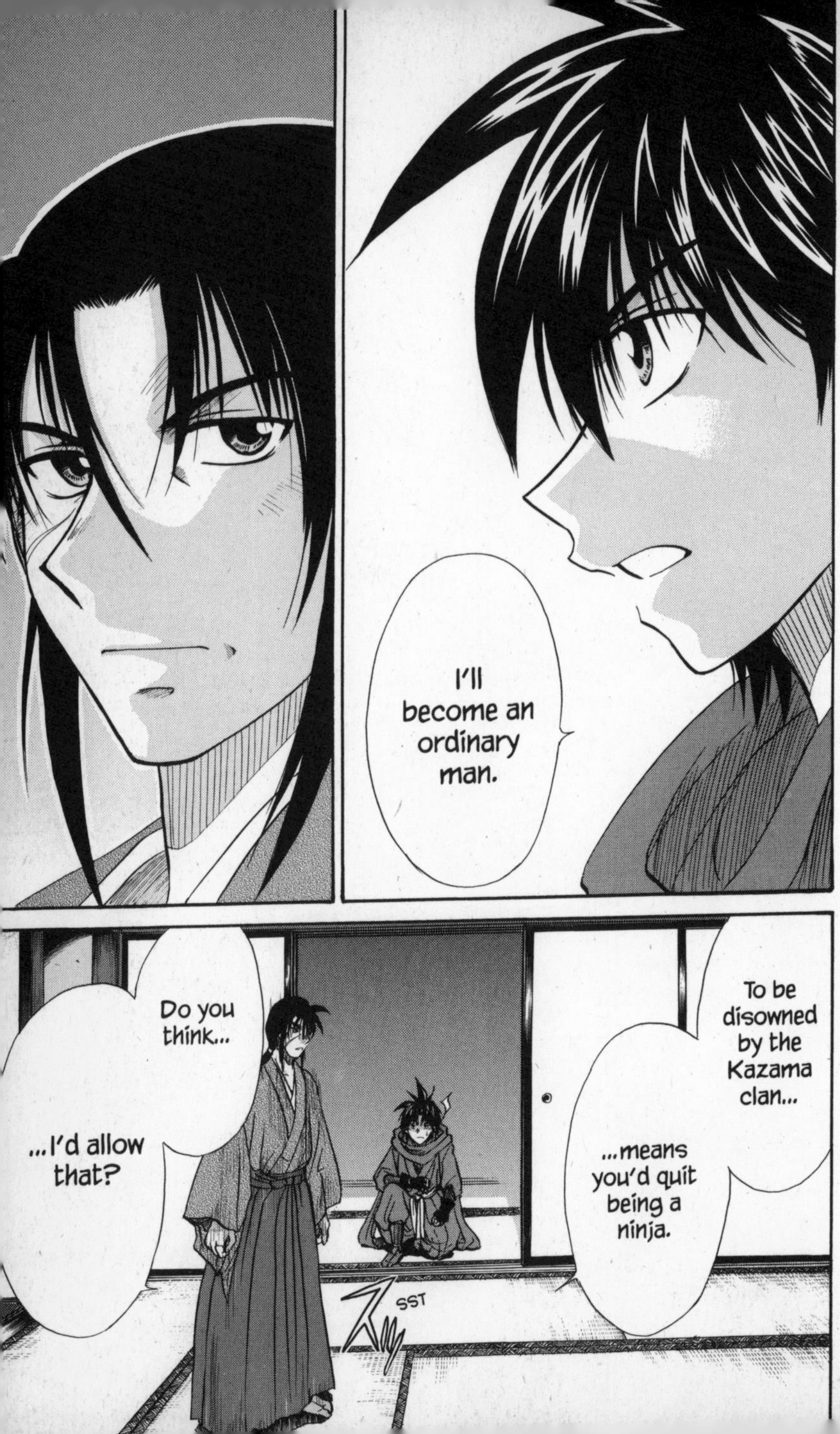
I'll become an ordinary man.
To be disowned by the Kazama clan...
...means you'd quit being a ninja.
Do you think...
...I'd allow that?
SST

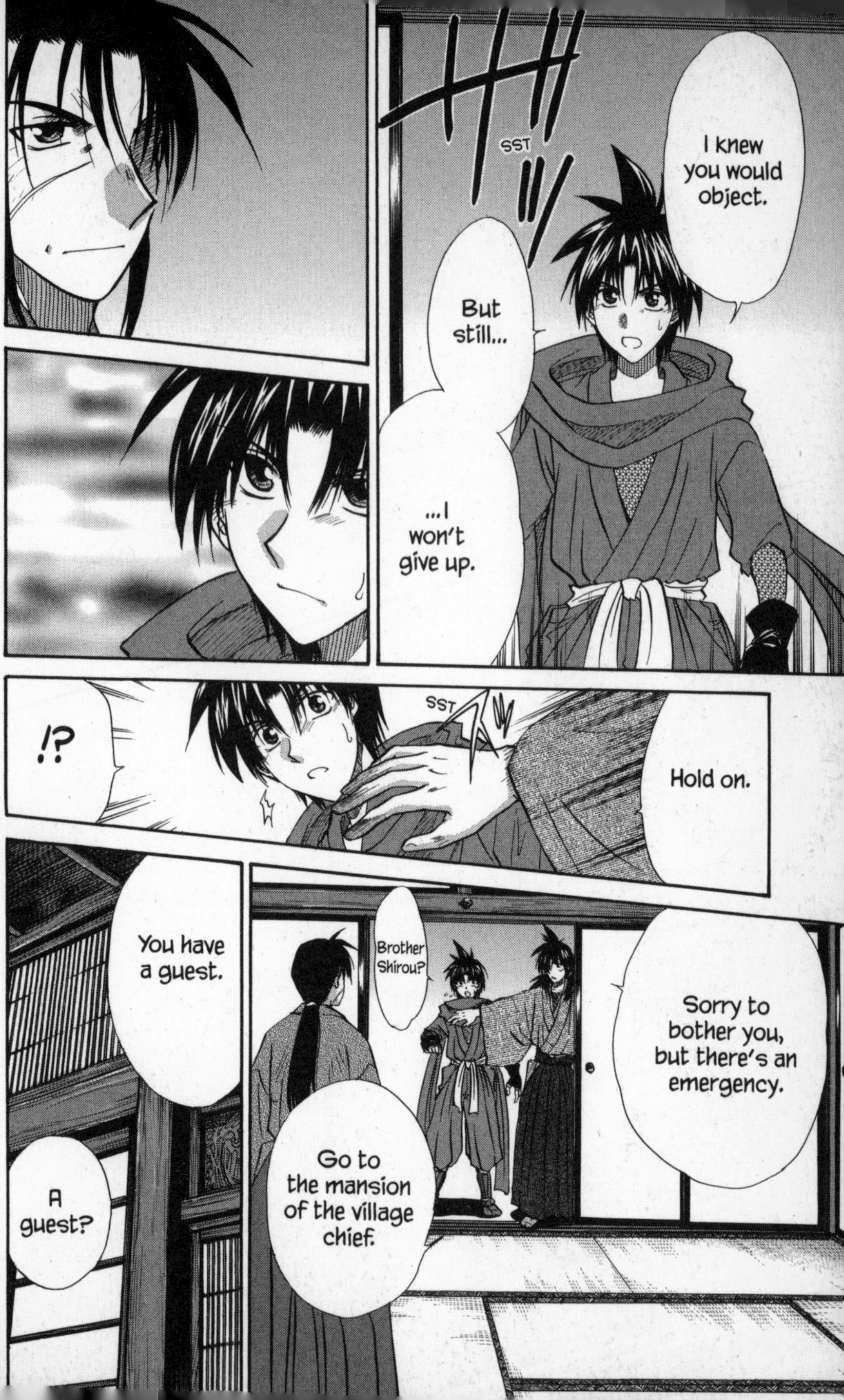
SST
I knew you would object.
But still...
...I won't give up.
SST
Hold on.
!?
Sorry to bother you, but there's an emergency.
Brother Shirou?
You have a guest.
Go to the mansion of the village chief.
A guest?

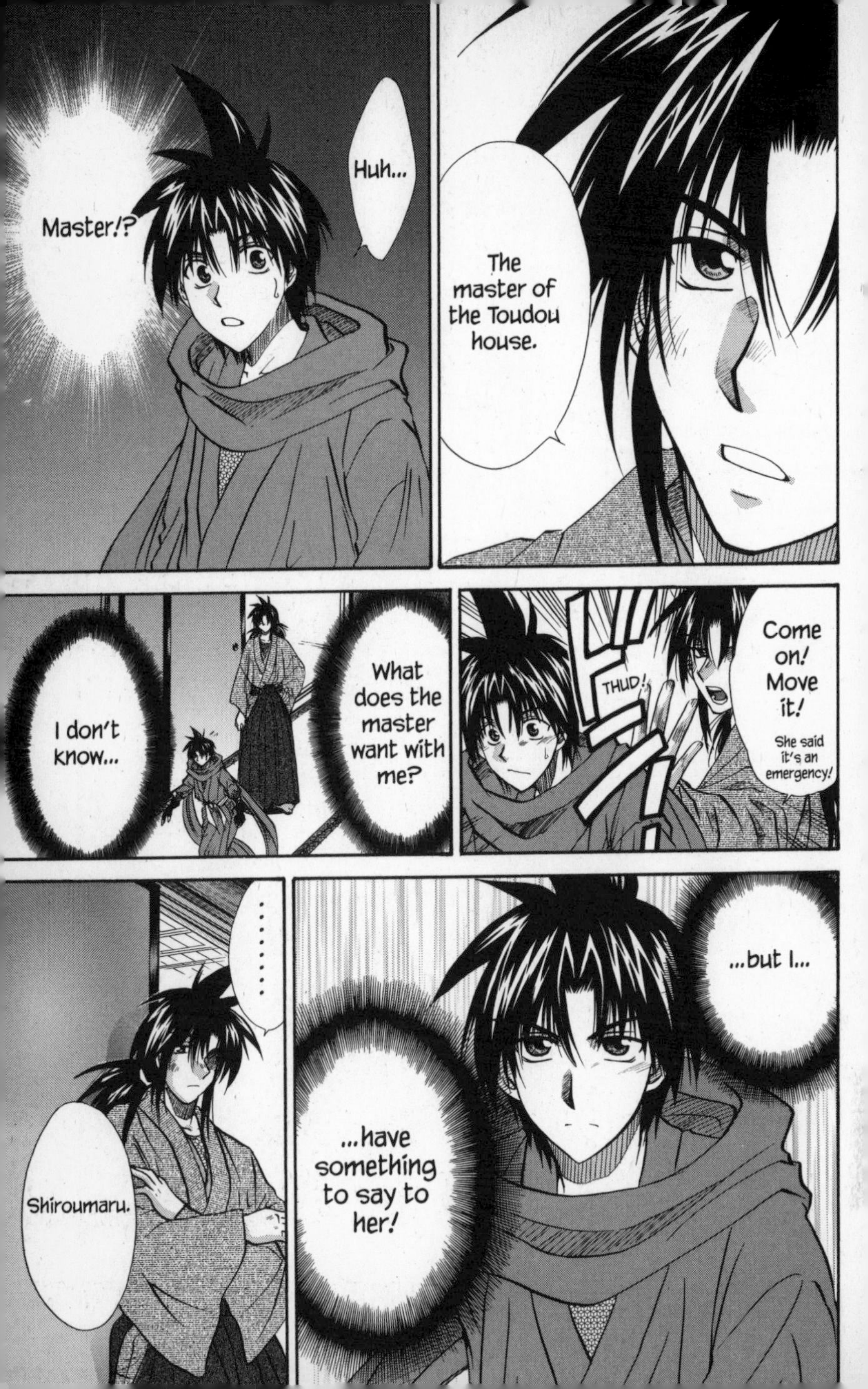

The master of the Toudou house.
Huh...
Master!?
Come on! Move it!
She said it's an emergency!
THUD!
What does the master want with me?
I don't know...
...but I...
...have something to say to her!
......
Shiroumaru.

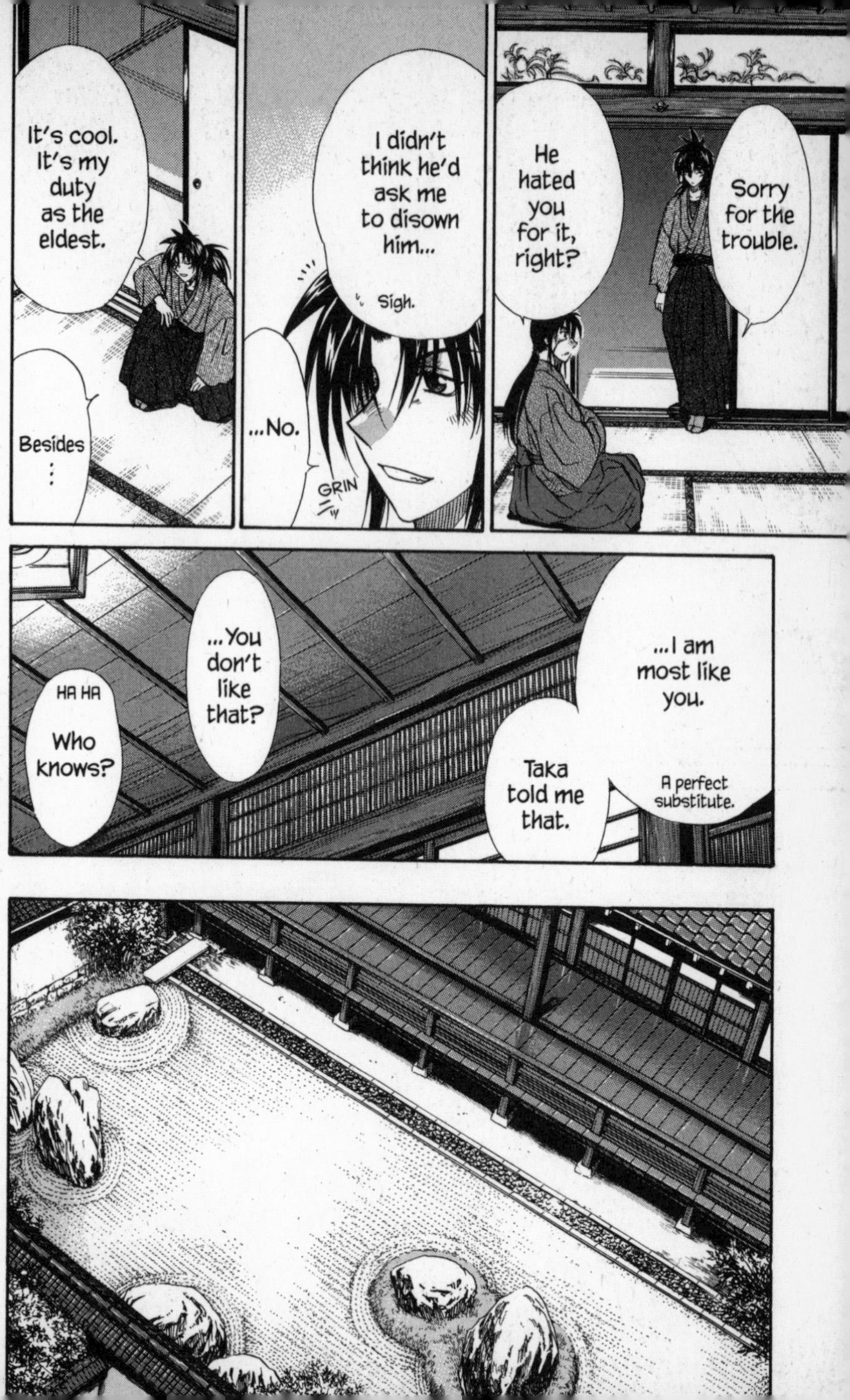
Sorry for the trouble.
He hated you for it, right?
I didn't think he'd ask me to disown him...
Sigh.
...No.
GRIN
It's cool. It's my duty as the eldest.
Besides...
...I am most like you.
A perfect substitute.
Taka told me that.
...You don't like that?
HA HA
Who knows?

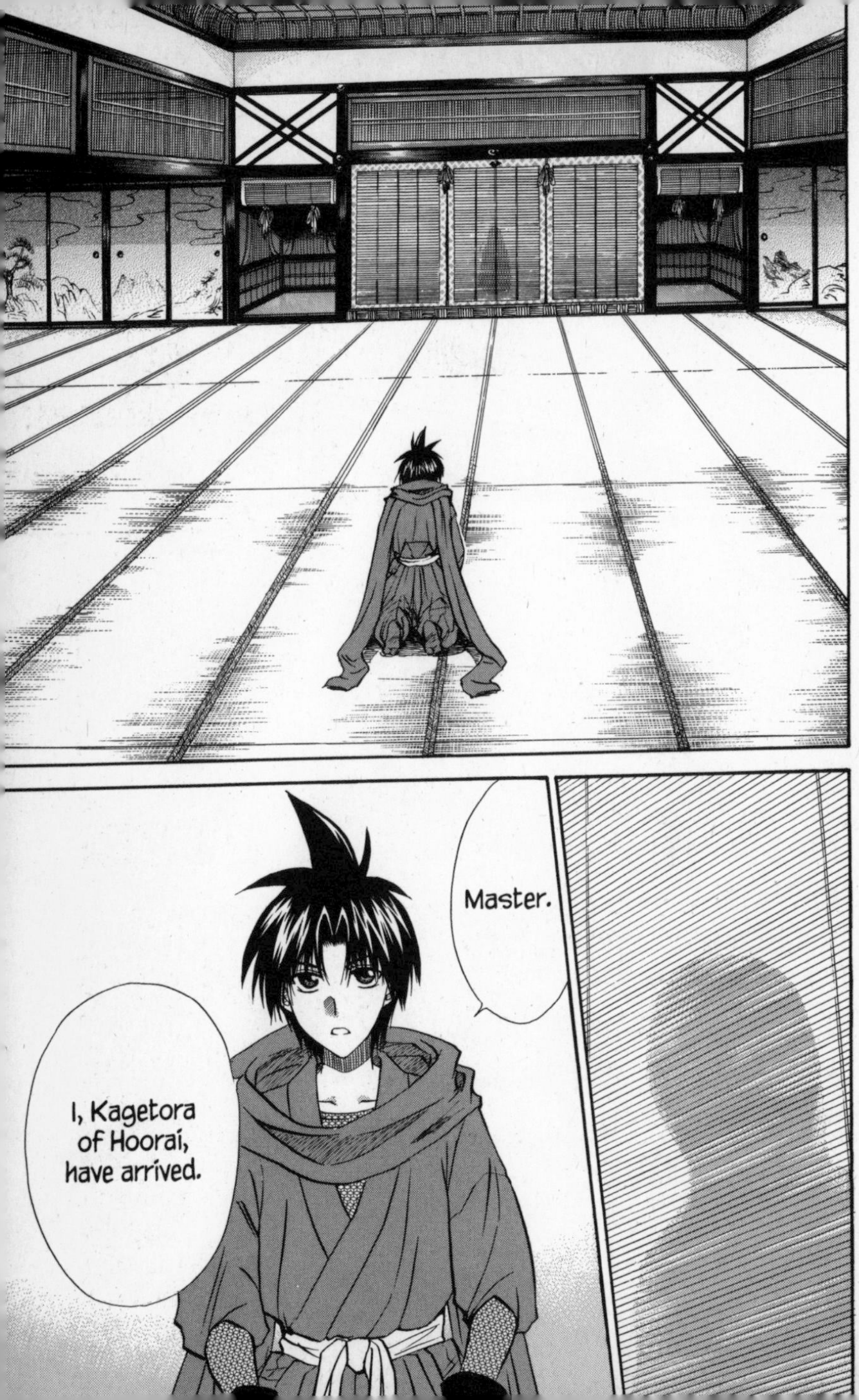
Master.
I, Kagetora of Hoorai, have arrived.

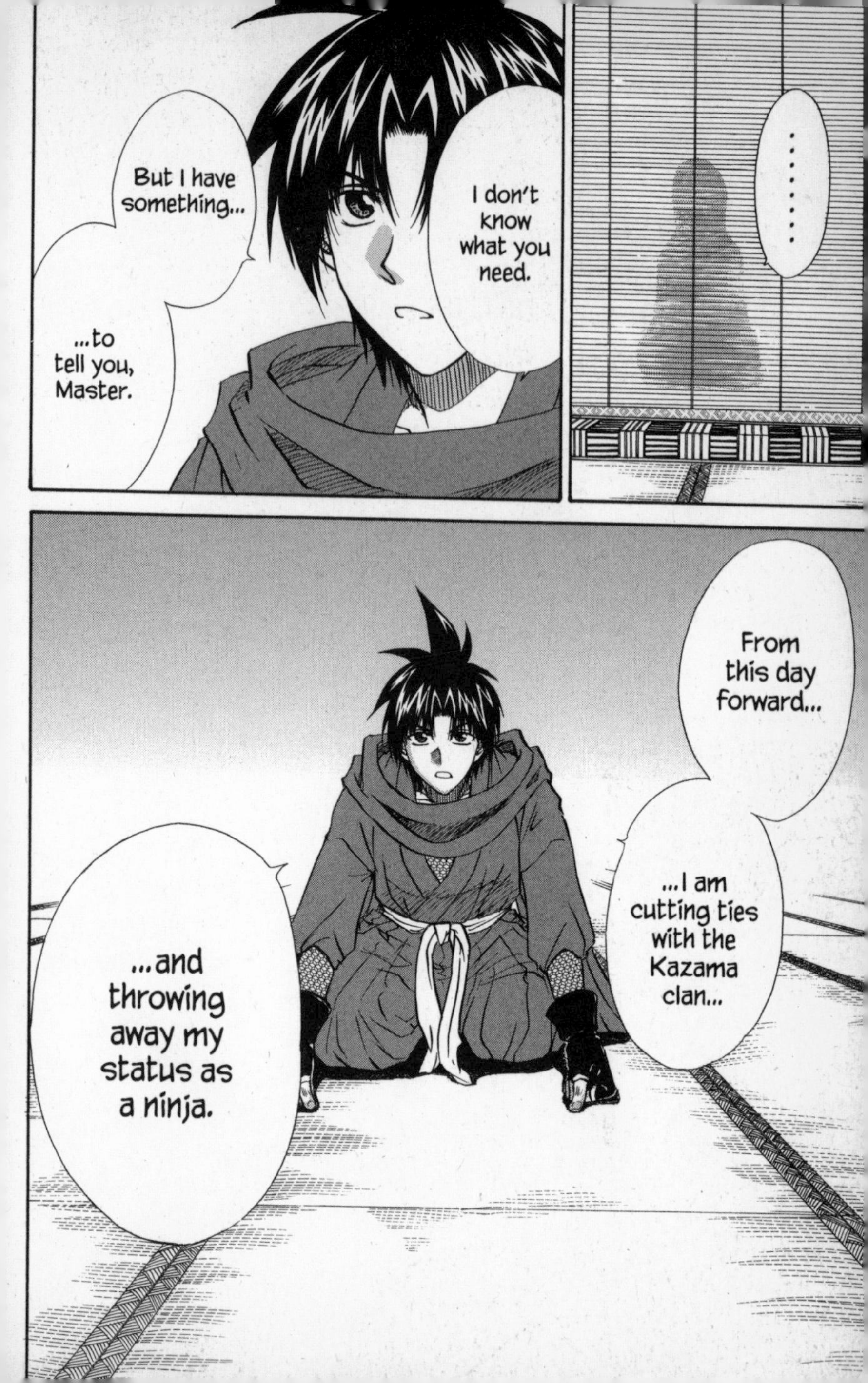
......
I don't know what you need.
But I have something...
...to tell you, Master.
From this day forward...
...I am cutting ties with the Kazama clan...
...and throwing away my status as a ninja.

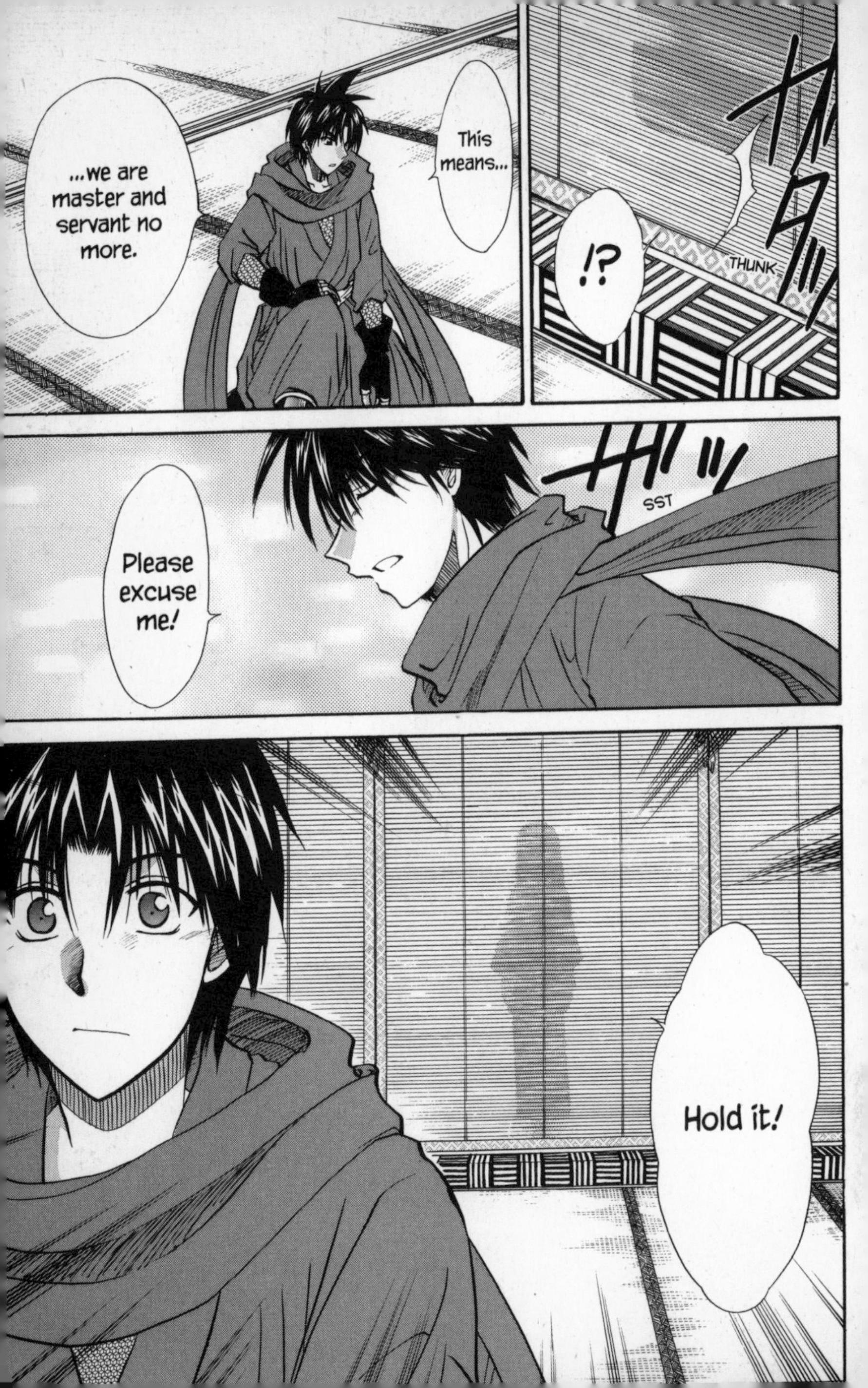
THUNK
!?
This means...
...we are master and servant no more.
SST
Please excuse me!
Hold it!

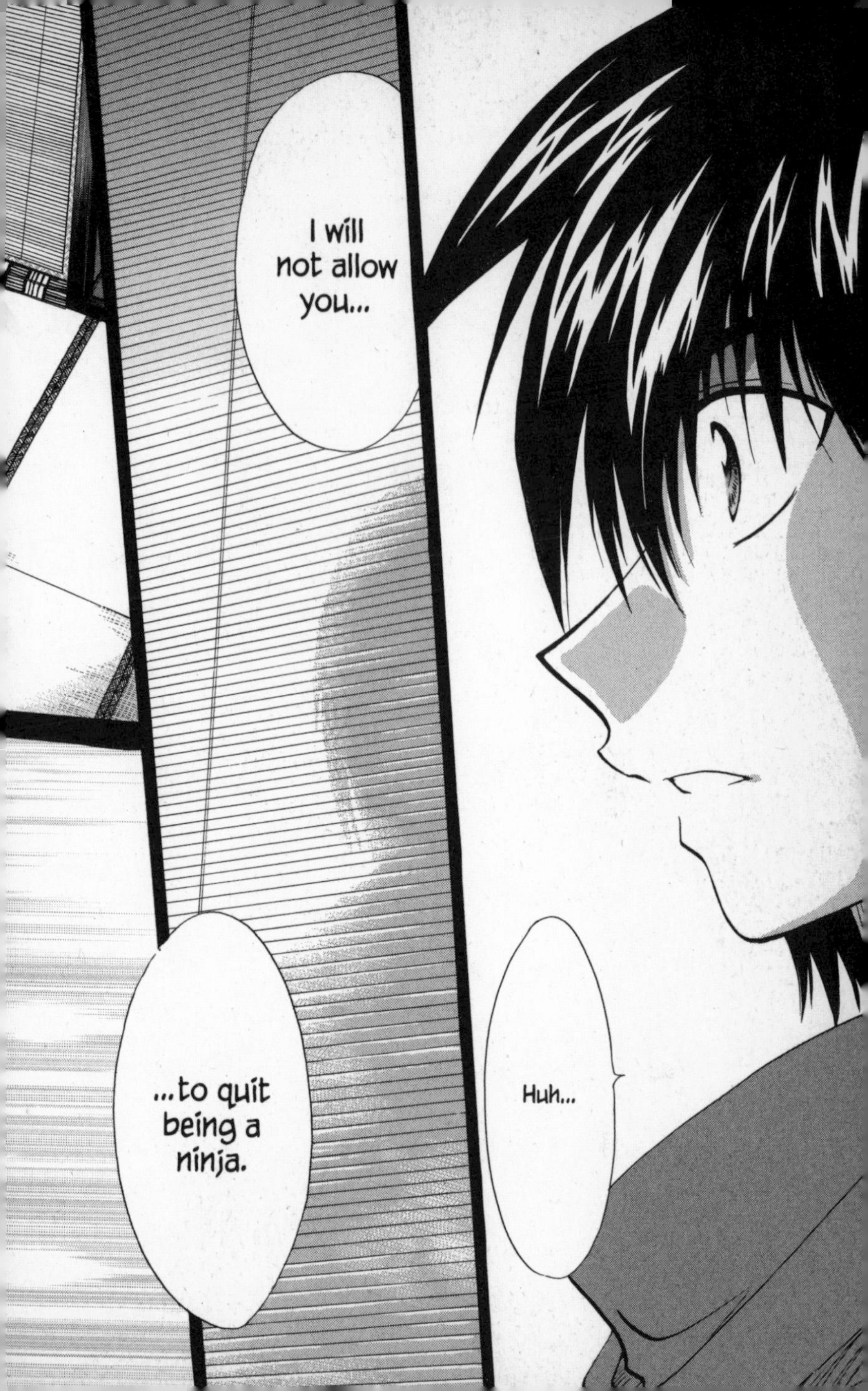
Huh...
I will not allow you...
...to quit being a ninja.

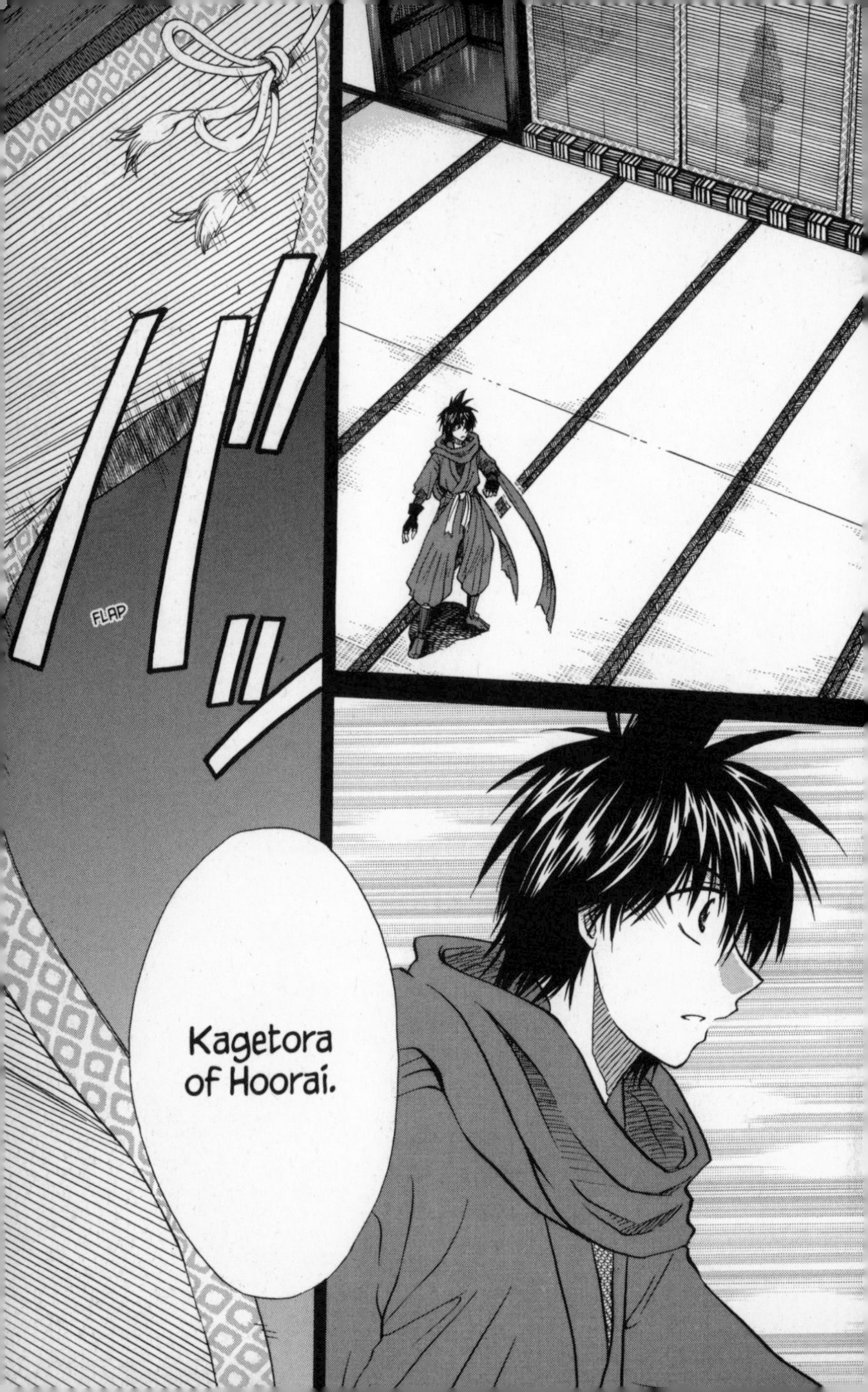
FLAP
Kagetora of Hoorai.

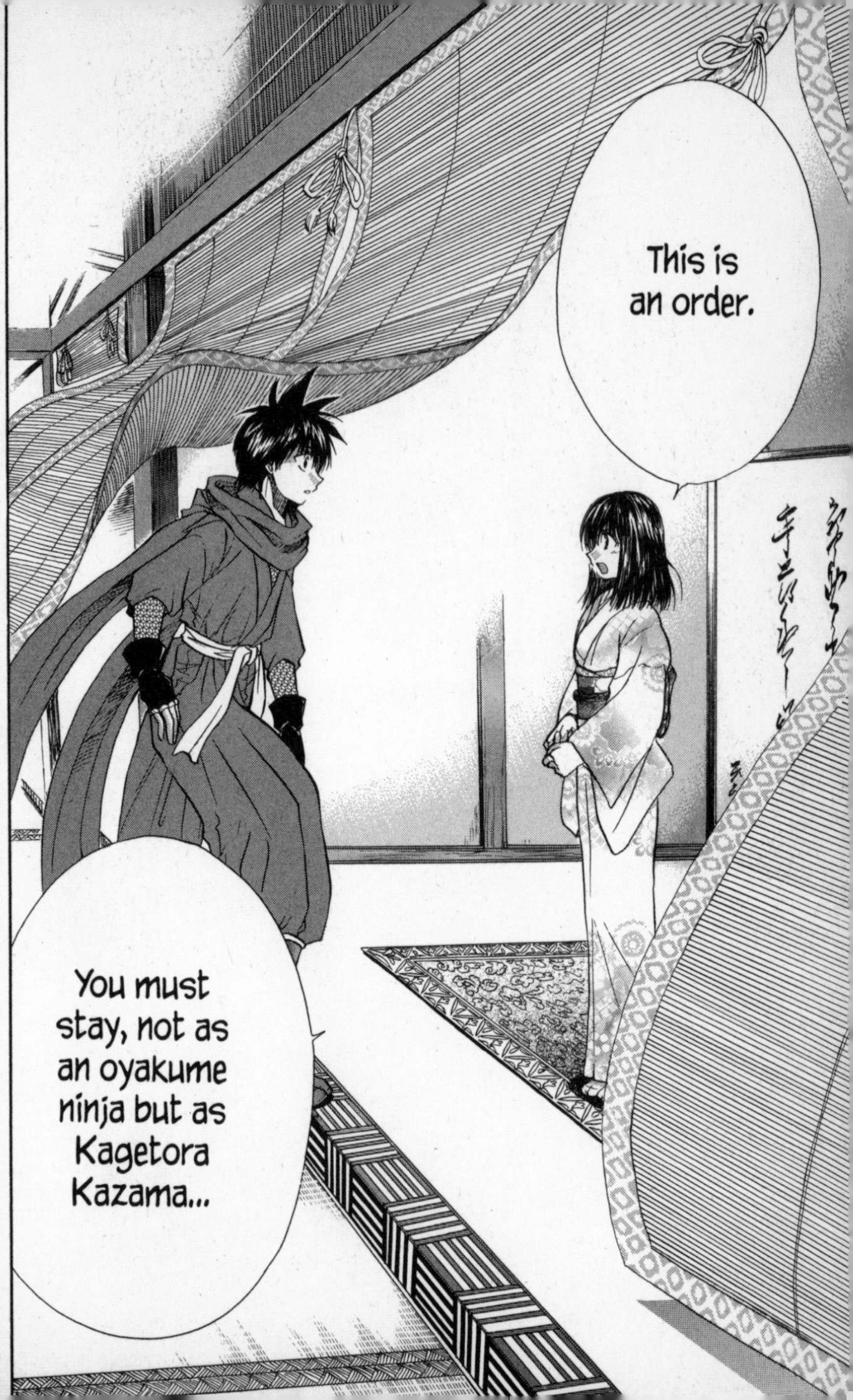
This is an order.
You must stay, not as an oyakume ninja but as Kagetora Kazama...

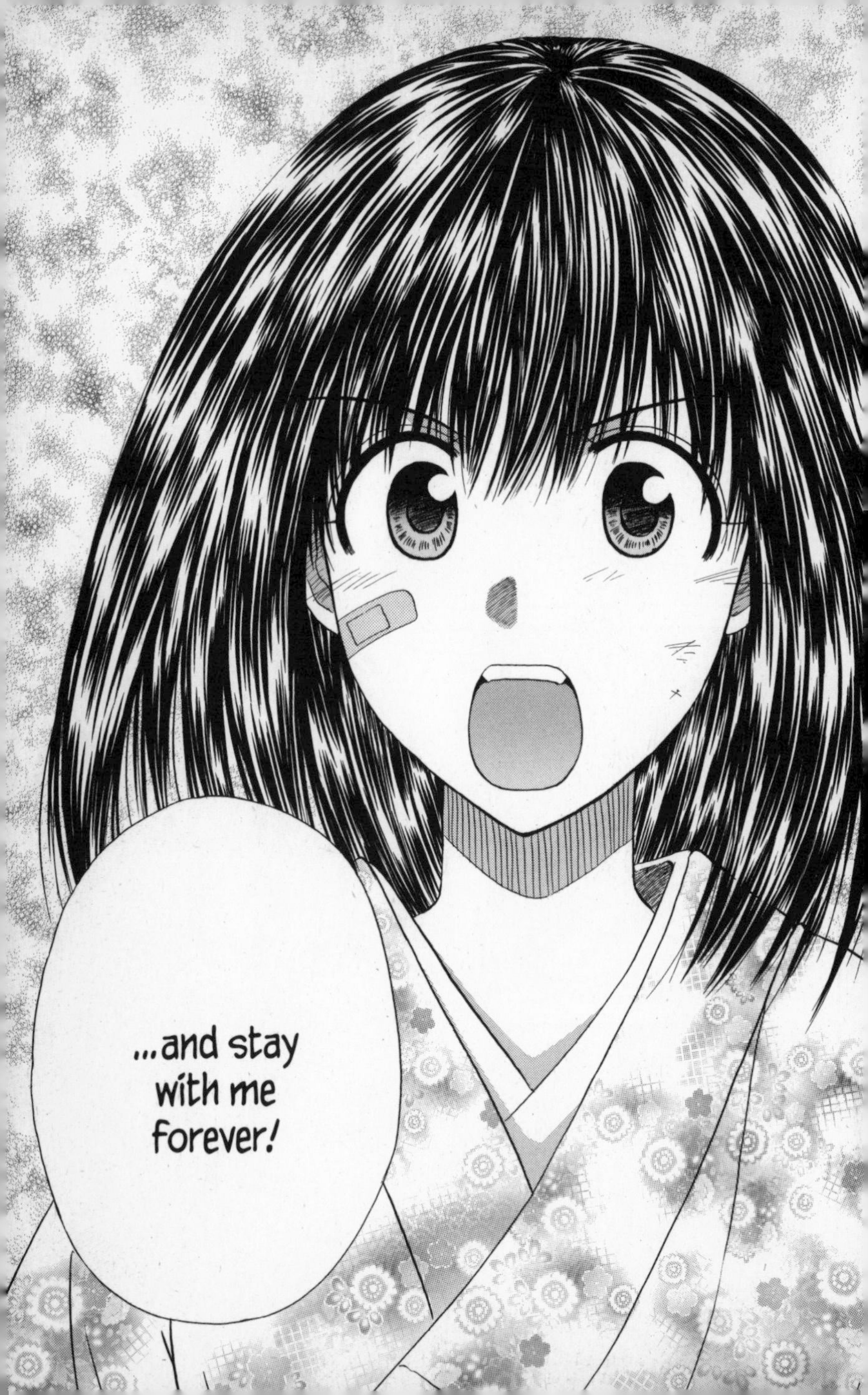
...and stay with me forever!

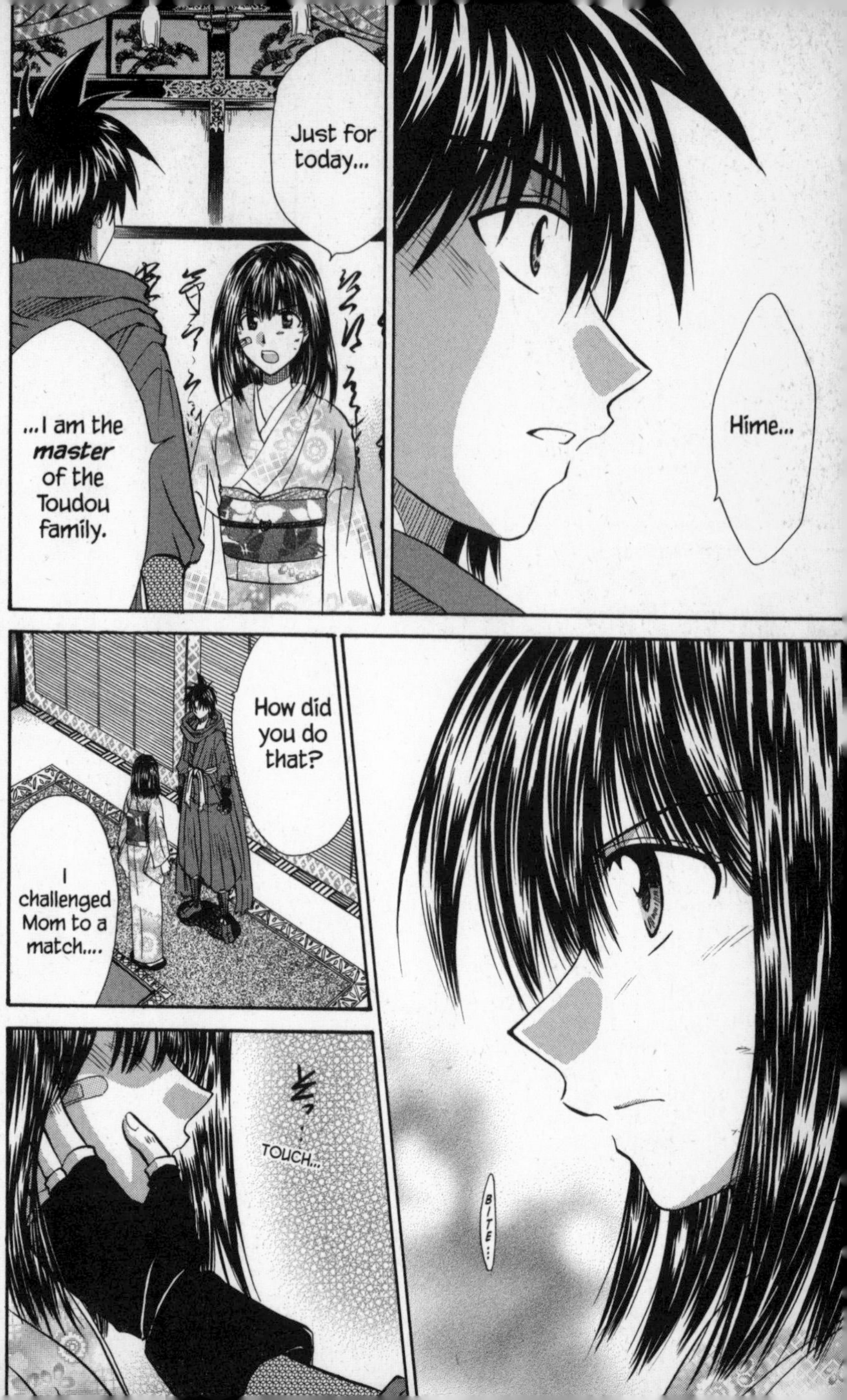

Hime...
Just for today...
...I am the *master* of the Toudou family.
How did you do that?
I challenged Mom to a match....
BITE...
TOUCH...

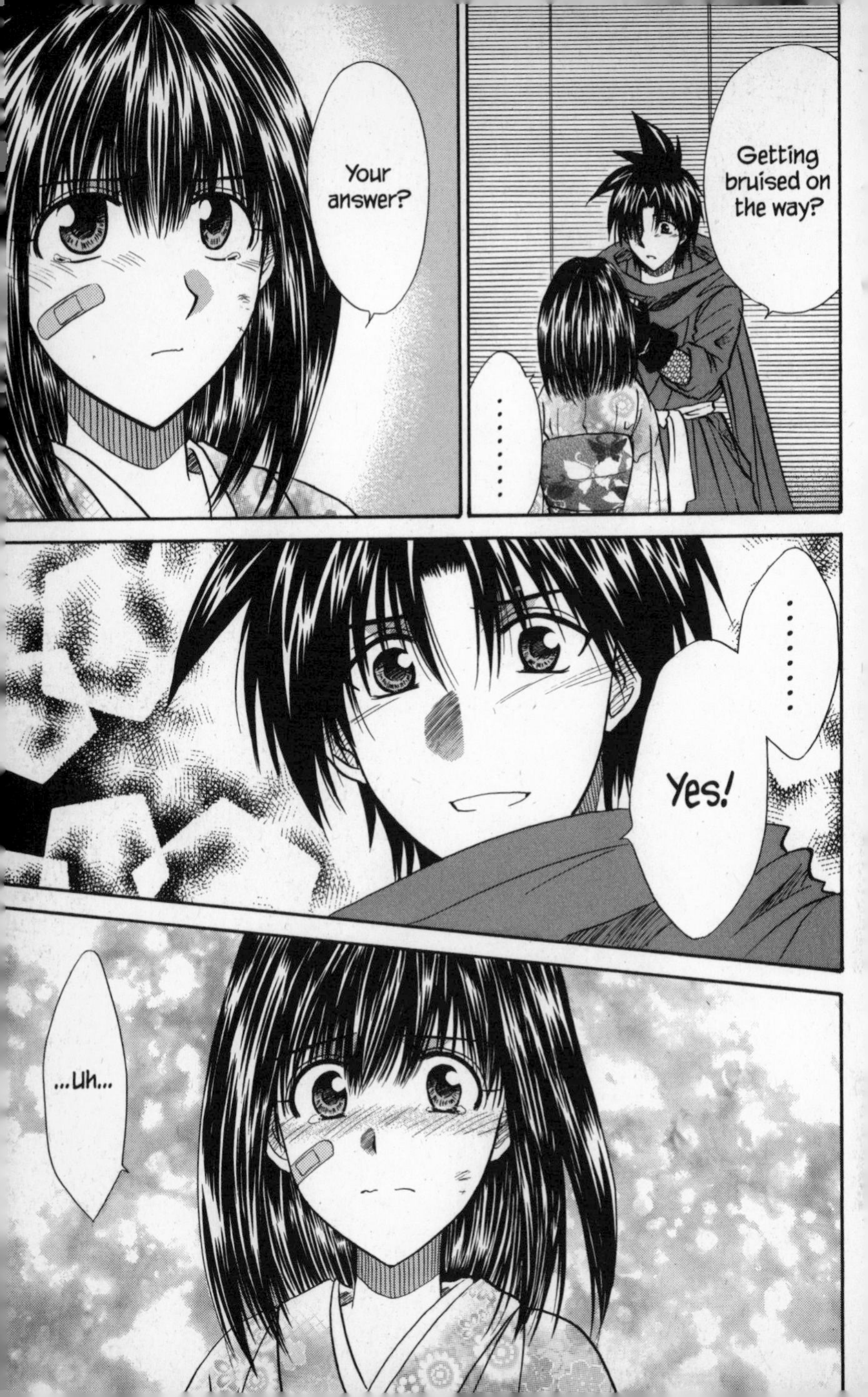
Getting bruised on the way?
......
Your answer?
......
Yes!
...uh...

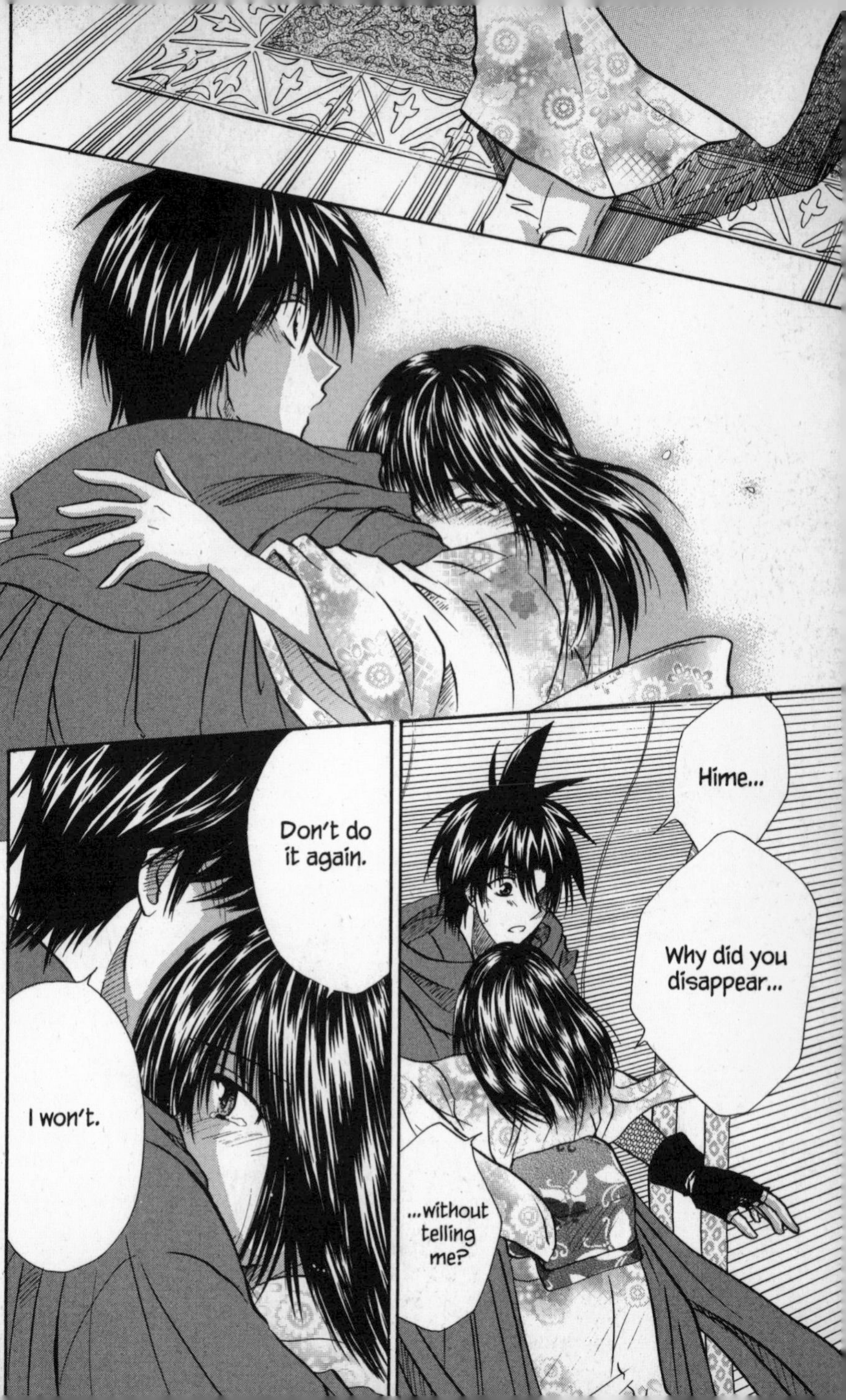
Hime...
Why did you disappear...
...without telling me?
Don't do it again.
I won't.

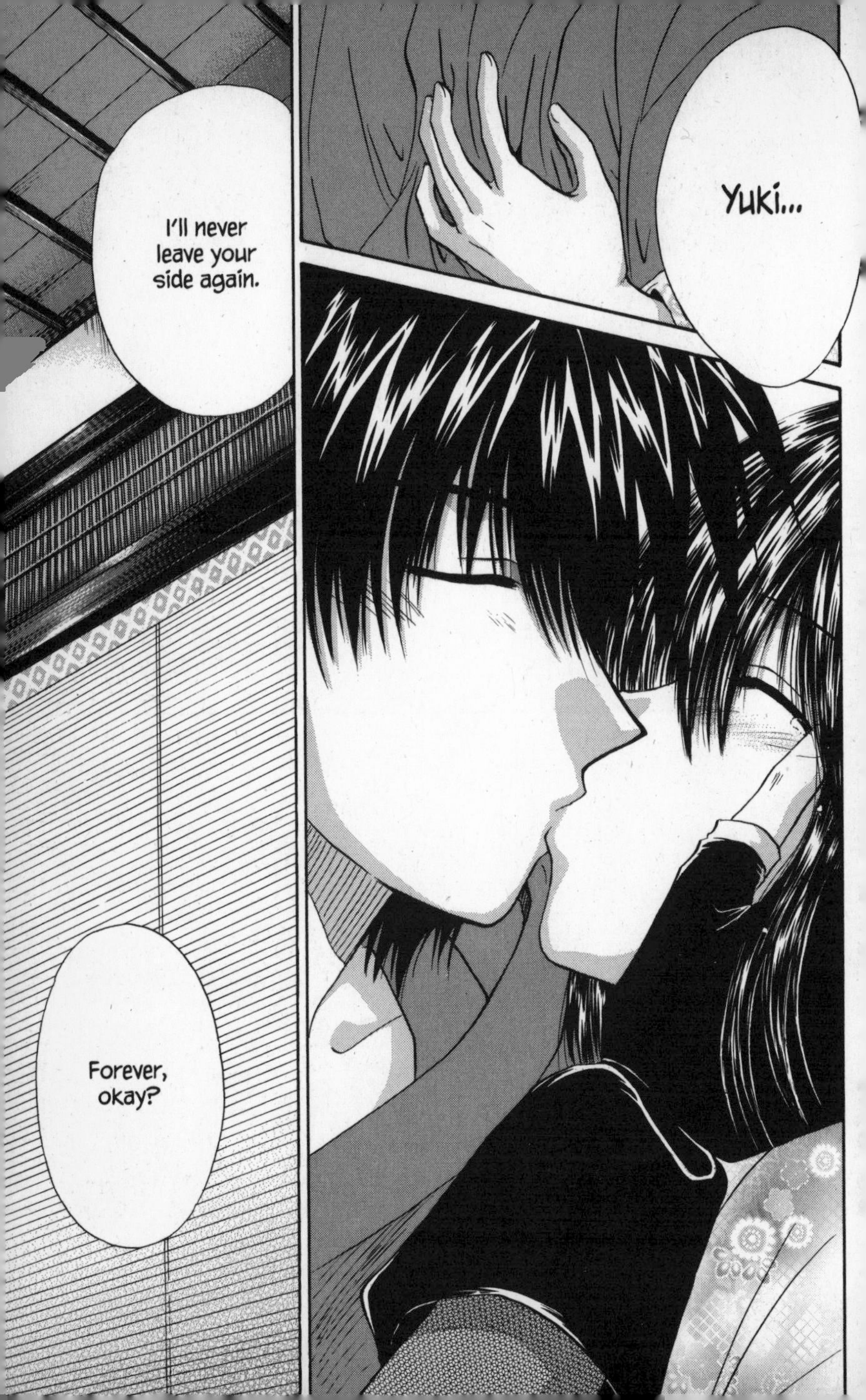
Yuki...
I'll never leave your side again.
Forever, okay?

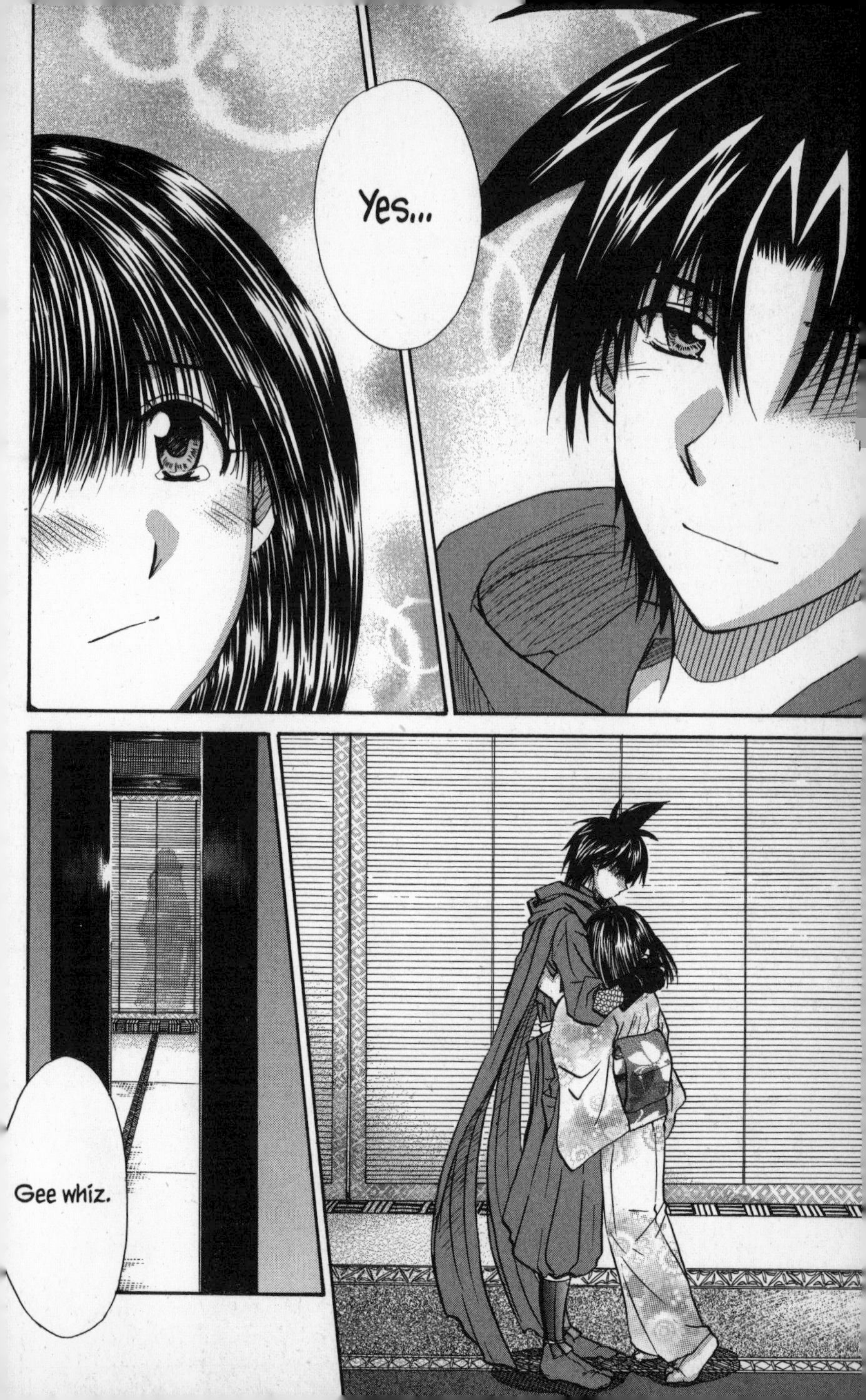
Yes...
Gee whiz.

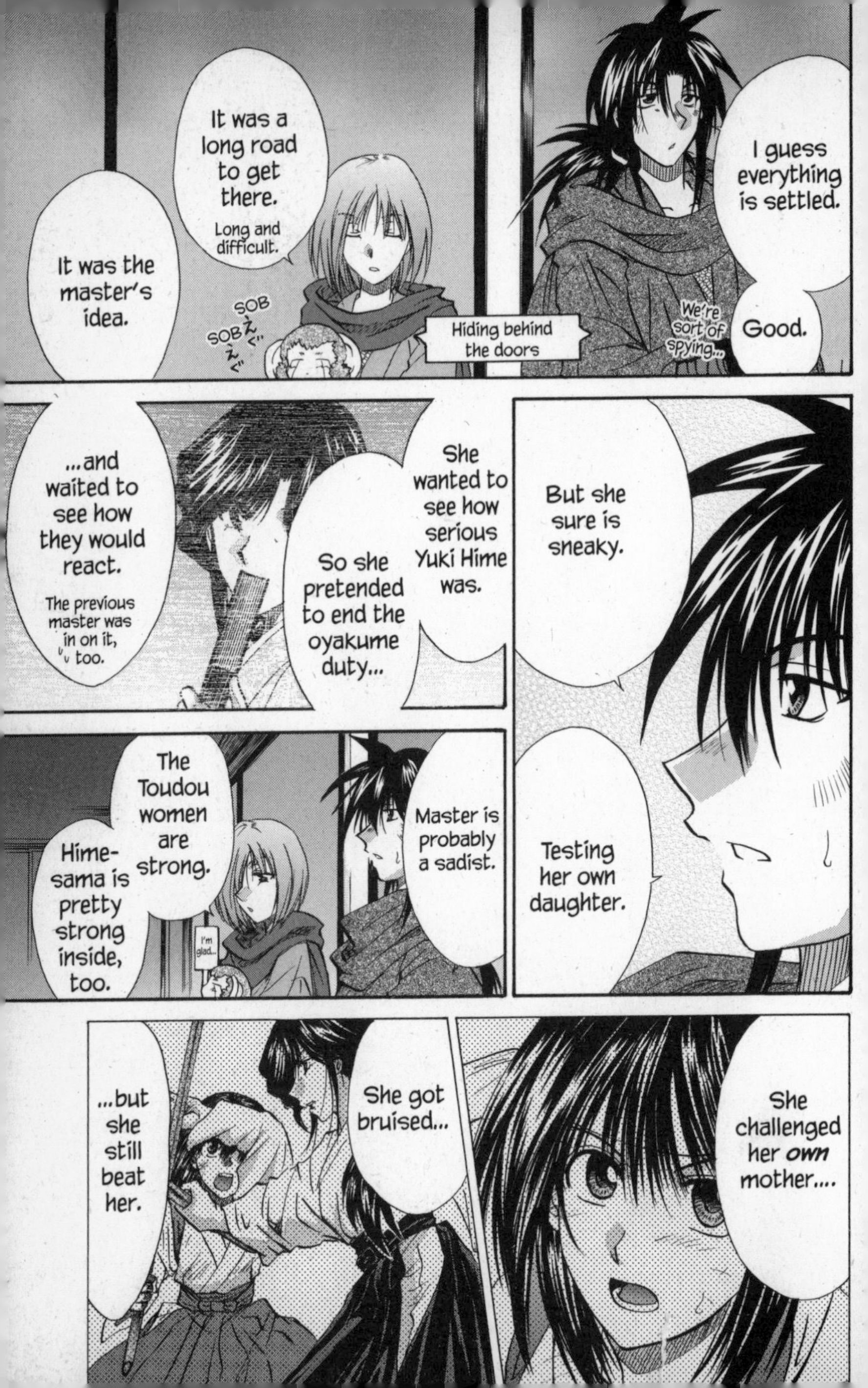
I guess everything is settled.
Good.
We're sort of spying...
Hiding behind the doors
It was a long road to get there.
Long and difficult.
It was the master's idea.
SOB えぐ
SOB えぐ
But she sure is sneaky.
Testing her own daughter.
She wanted to see how serious Yuki Hime was.
So she pretended to end the oyakume duty...
...and waited to see how they would react.
The previous master was in on it, too.
Master is probably a sadist.
The Toudou women are strong.
Hime-sama is pretty strong inside, too.
I'm glad...
She challenged her *own* mother....
She got bruised...
...but she still beat her.

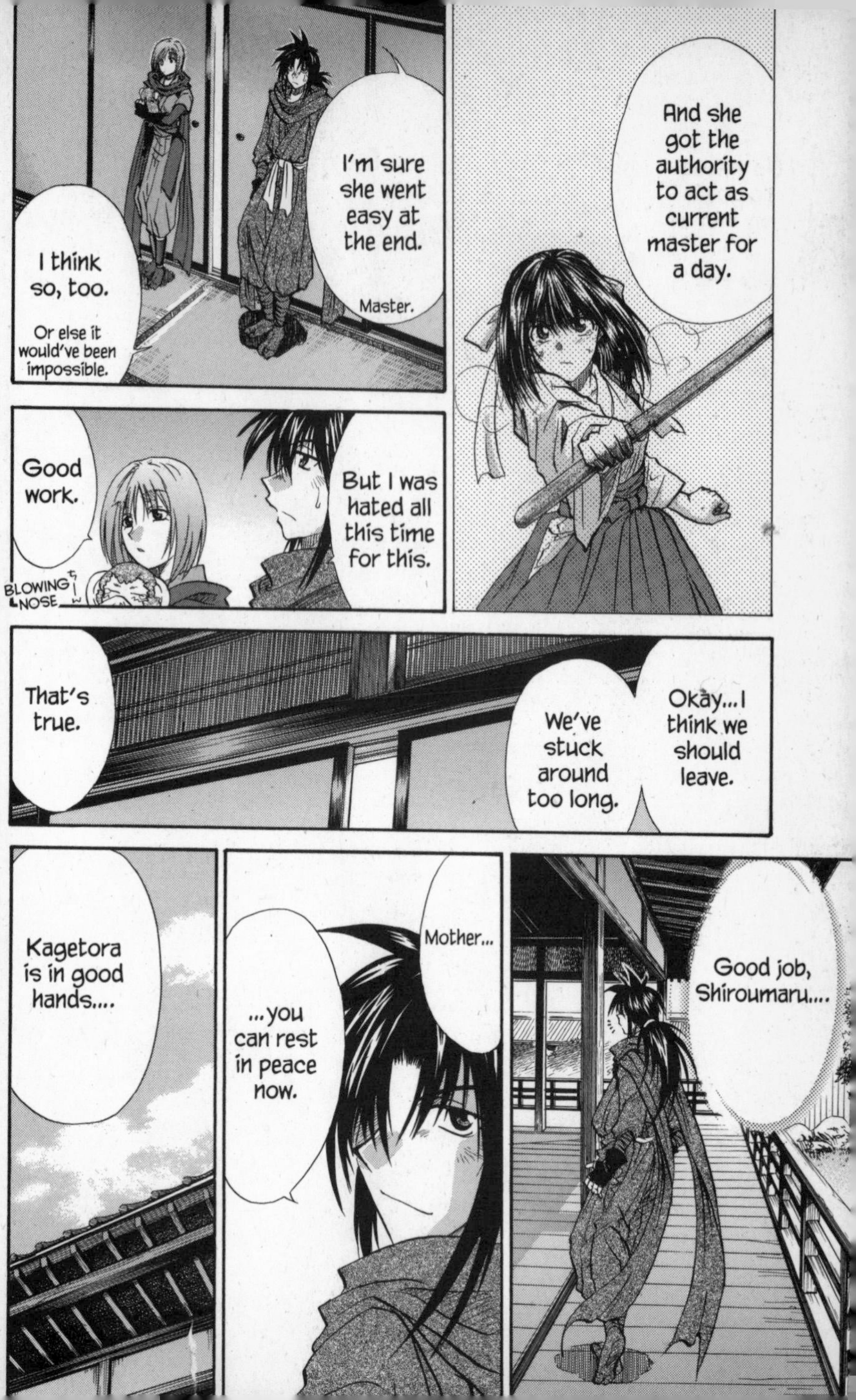
And she got the authority to act as current master for a day.
I'm sure she went easy at the end.
Master.
I think so, too.
Or else it would've been impossible.
But I was hated all this time for this.
Good work.
BLOWING NOSE
Okay...I think we should leave.
We've stuck around too long.
That's true.
Good job, Shiroumaru....
Mother...
...you can rest in peace now.
Kagetora is in good hands....

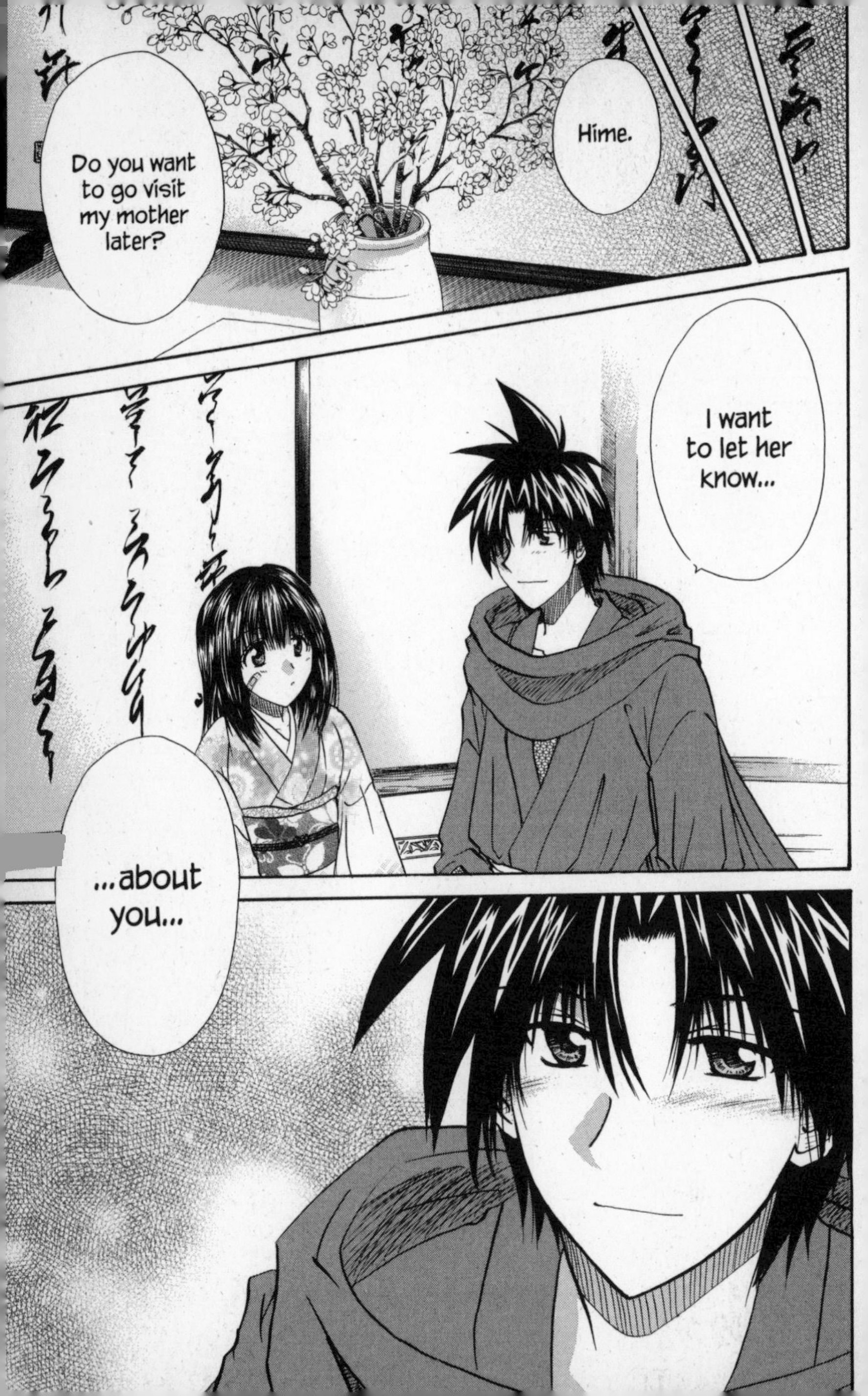
Hime.
Do you want to go visit my mother later?
I want to let her know...
...about you...

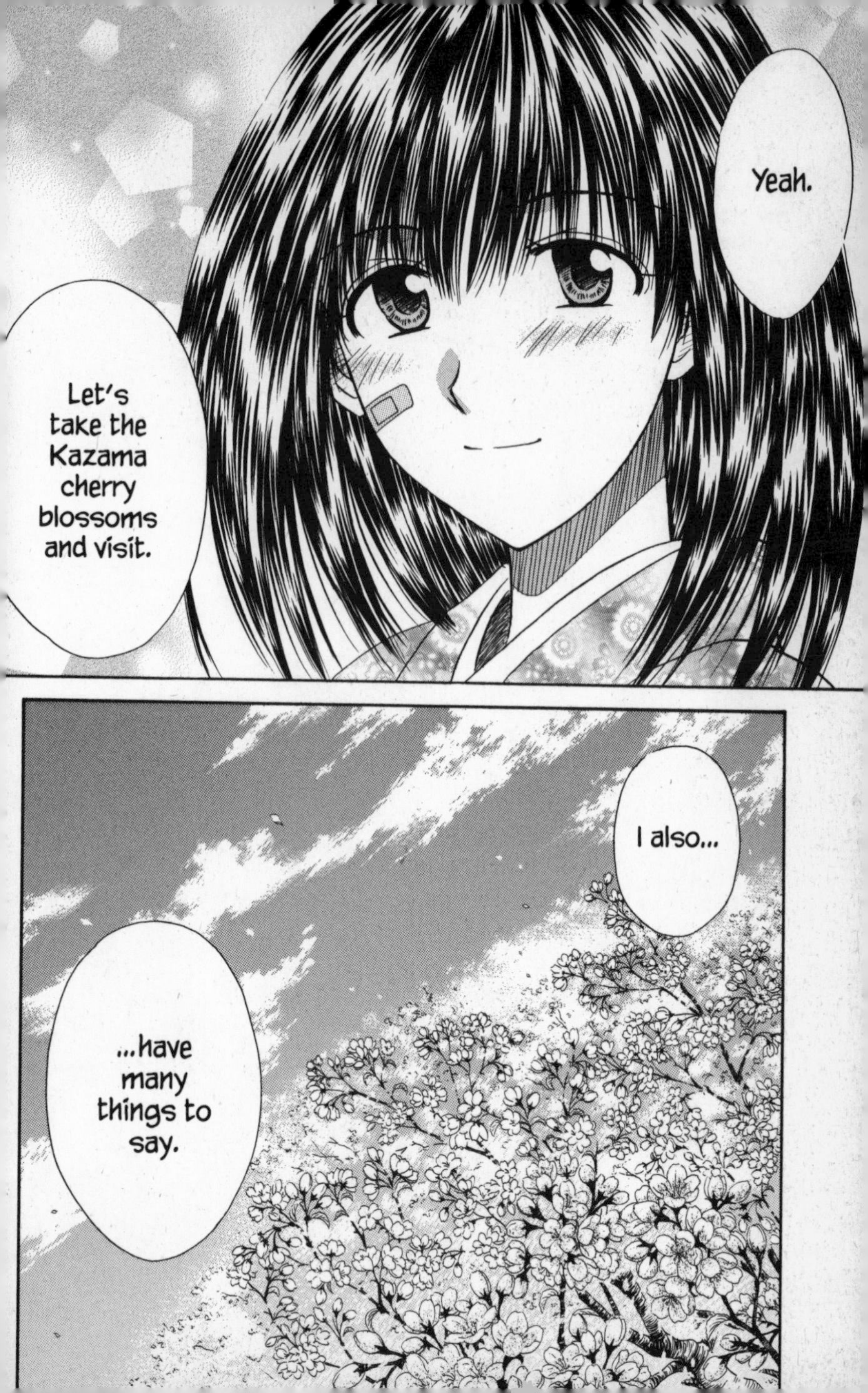
Yeah.
Let's take the Kazama cherry blossoms and visit.
I also...
...have many things to say.

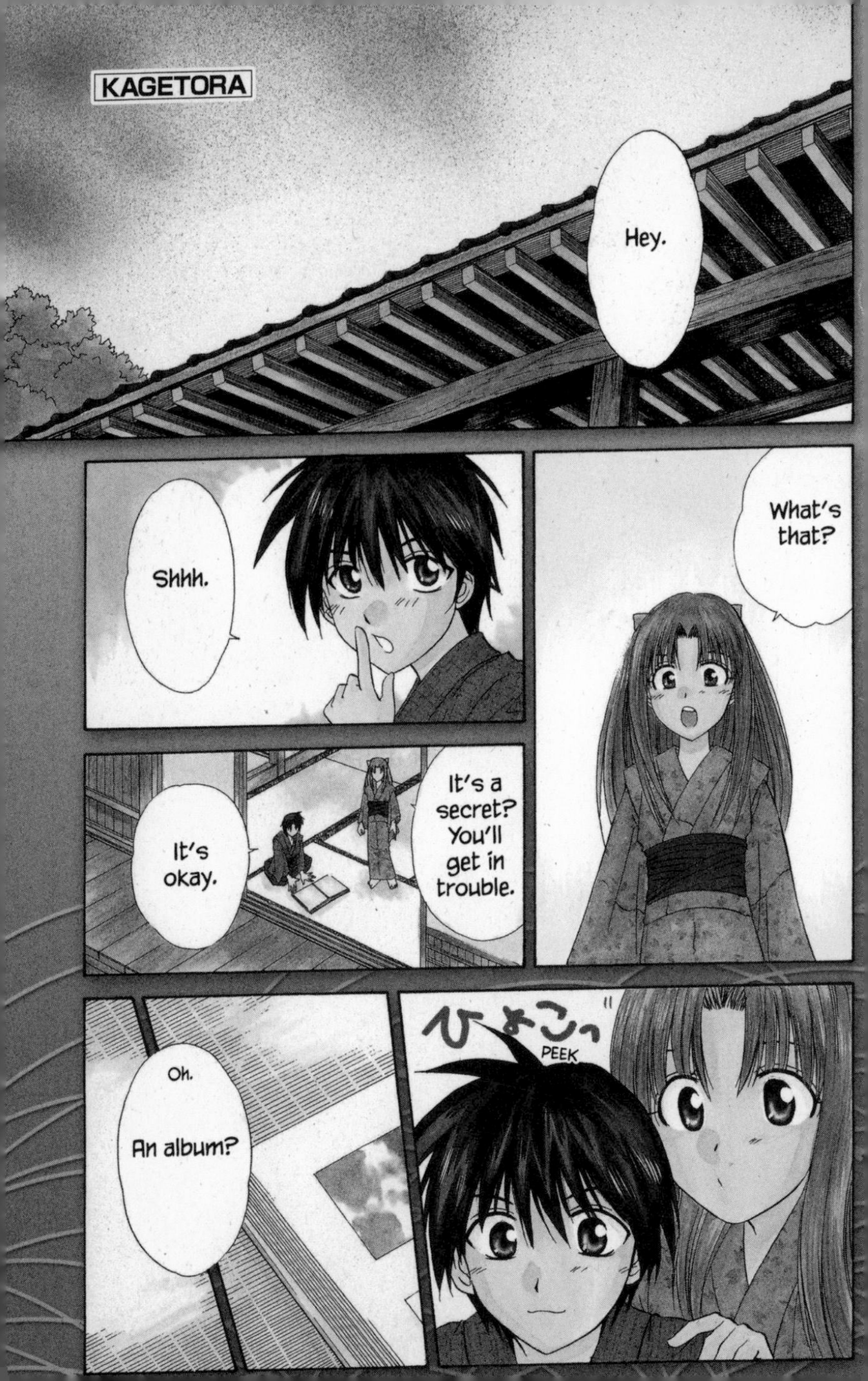
KAGETORA
Hey.
What's that?
Shhh.
It's a secret? You'll get in trouble.
It's okay.
ひょこっ
PEEK
Oh.
An album?

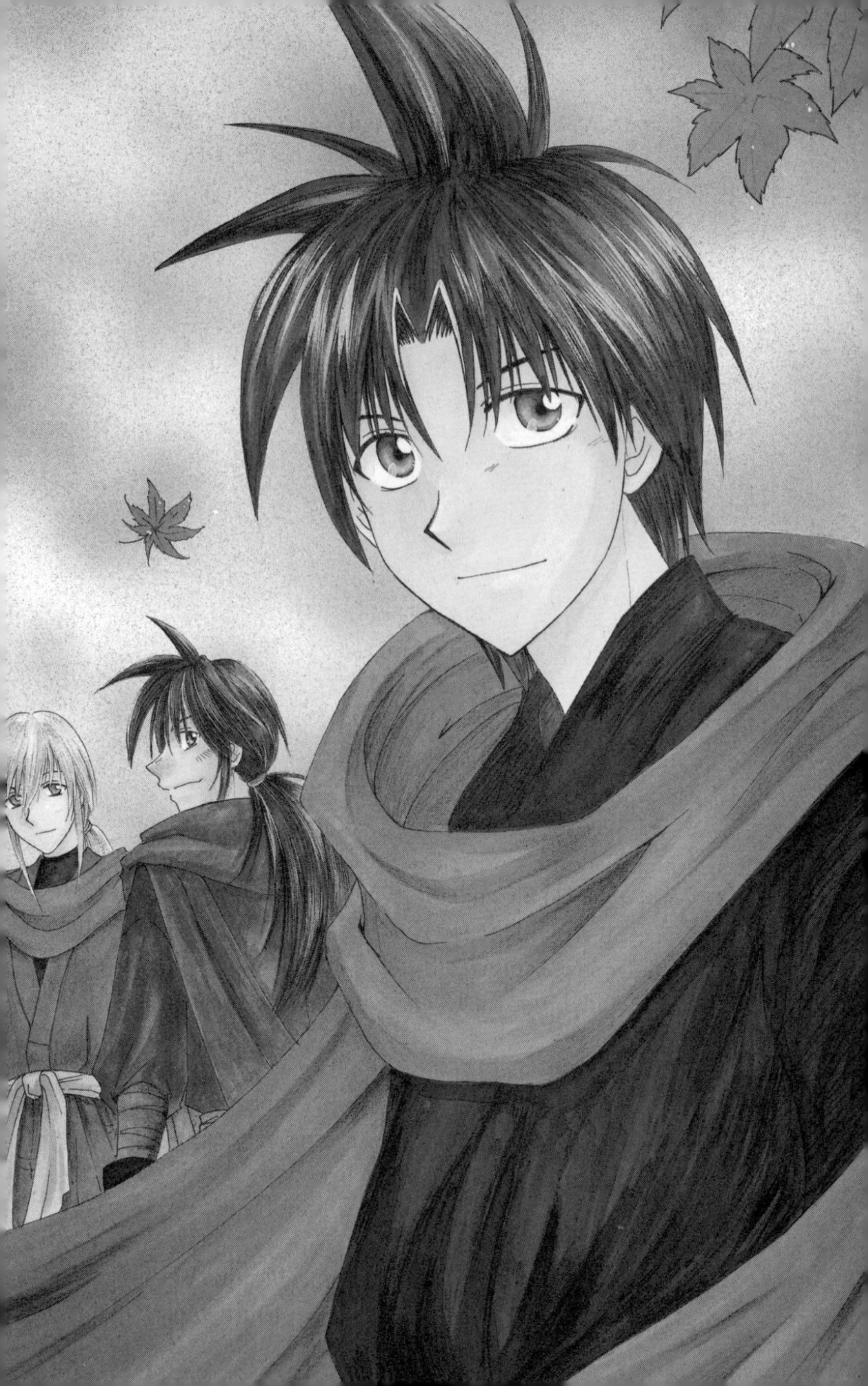

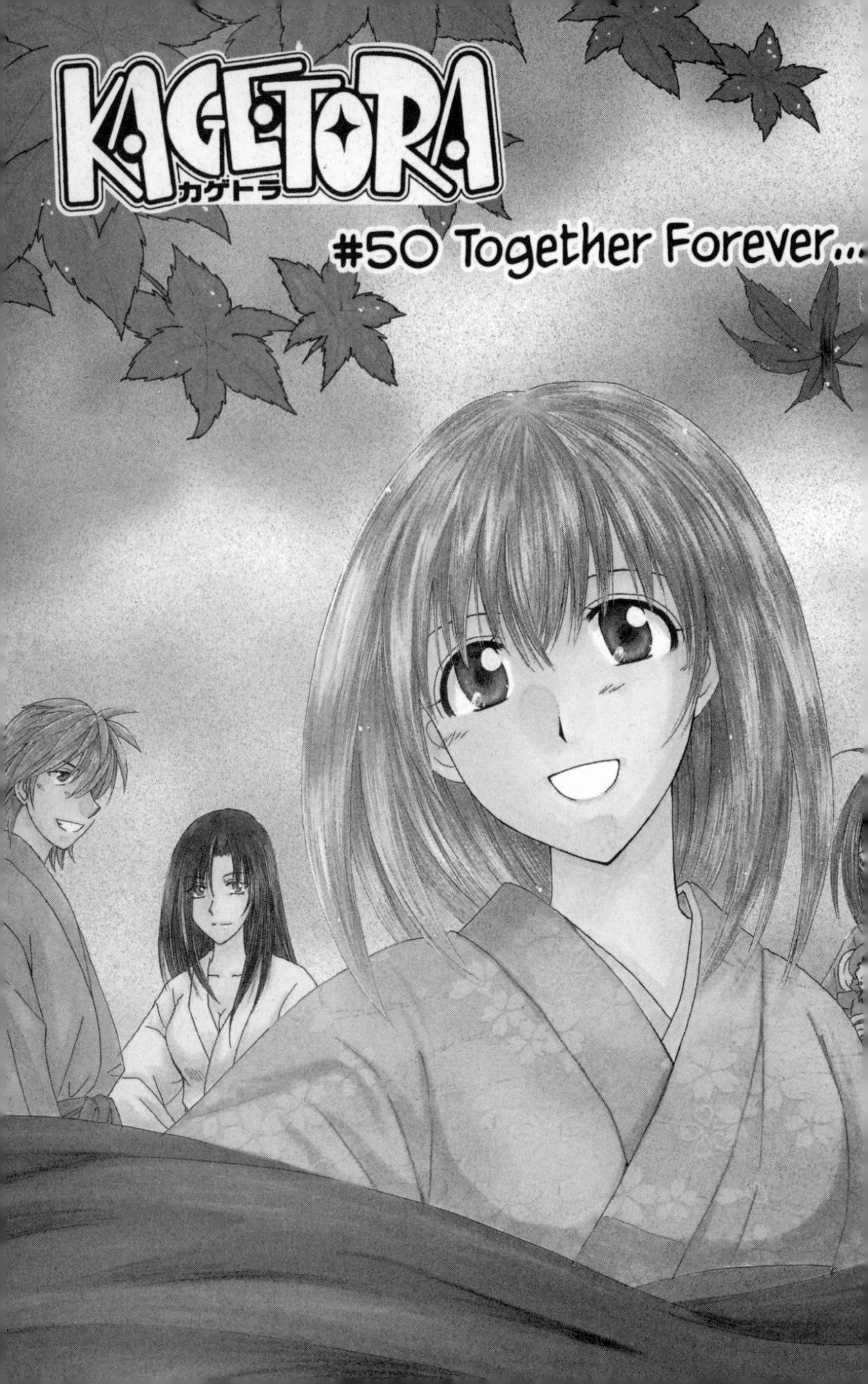
KAGETORA
カゲトラ
#50 Together Forever...

Side Note

These are the songs I was listening to while
I was working on the final chapter.
Kobukuro, "Together Forever"
Angela Aki, "This Love"
Lyrico, "Flower of Miracles"
Emiko Shiratori, "Amazing Grace"
And others...
The Kobukuro song is where I got the title.
(laugh)
I listened to Angela Aki throughout all
three chapters in this volume, and I was
listening to Lyrico throughout all of KAGETORA.
Maybe if you listen, while reading the book,
it'll be more dramatic...(laugh)

| Segami |

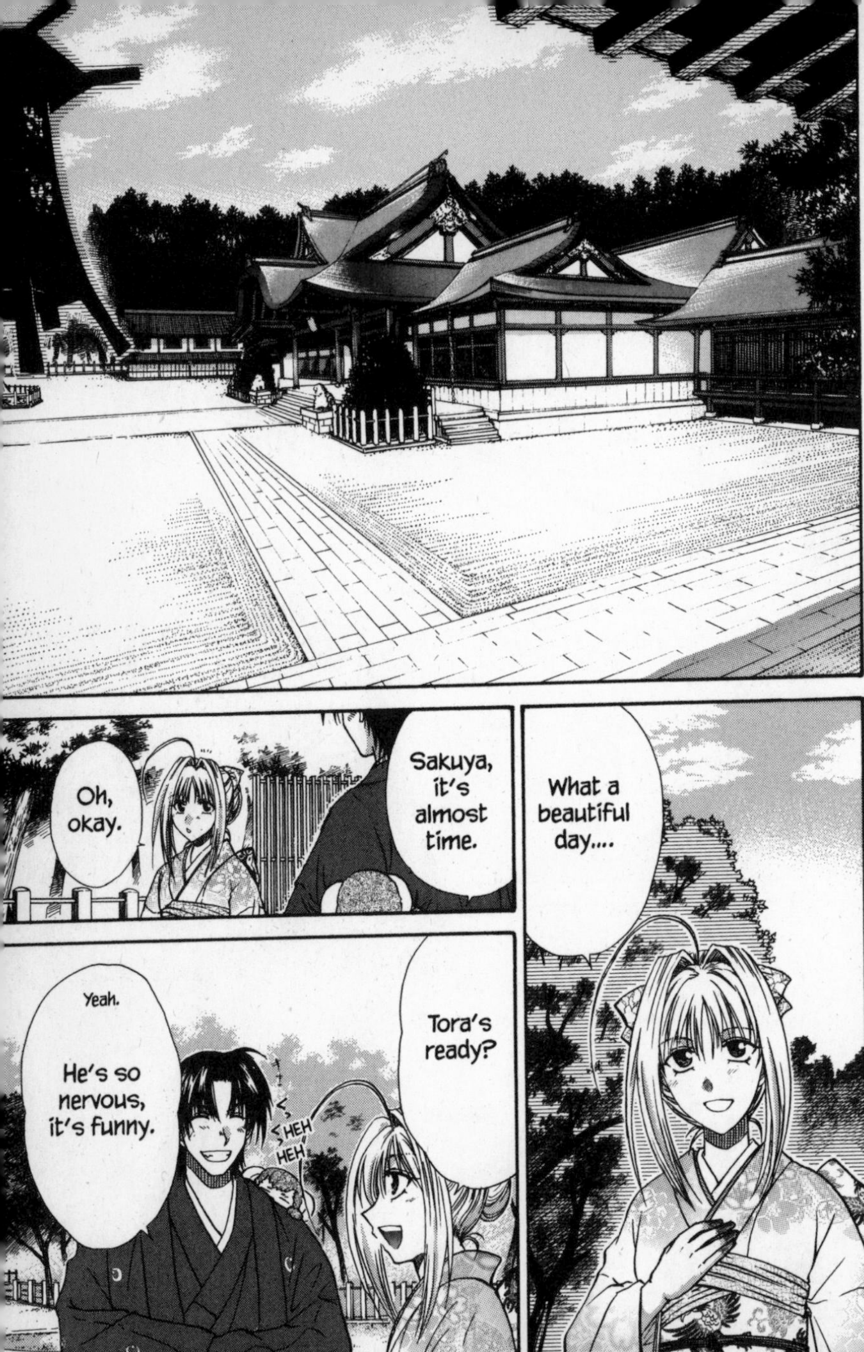
What a beautiful day....
Sakuya, it's almost time.
Oh, okay.
Tora's ready?
Yeah.
He's so nervous, it's funny.
HEH HEH

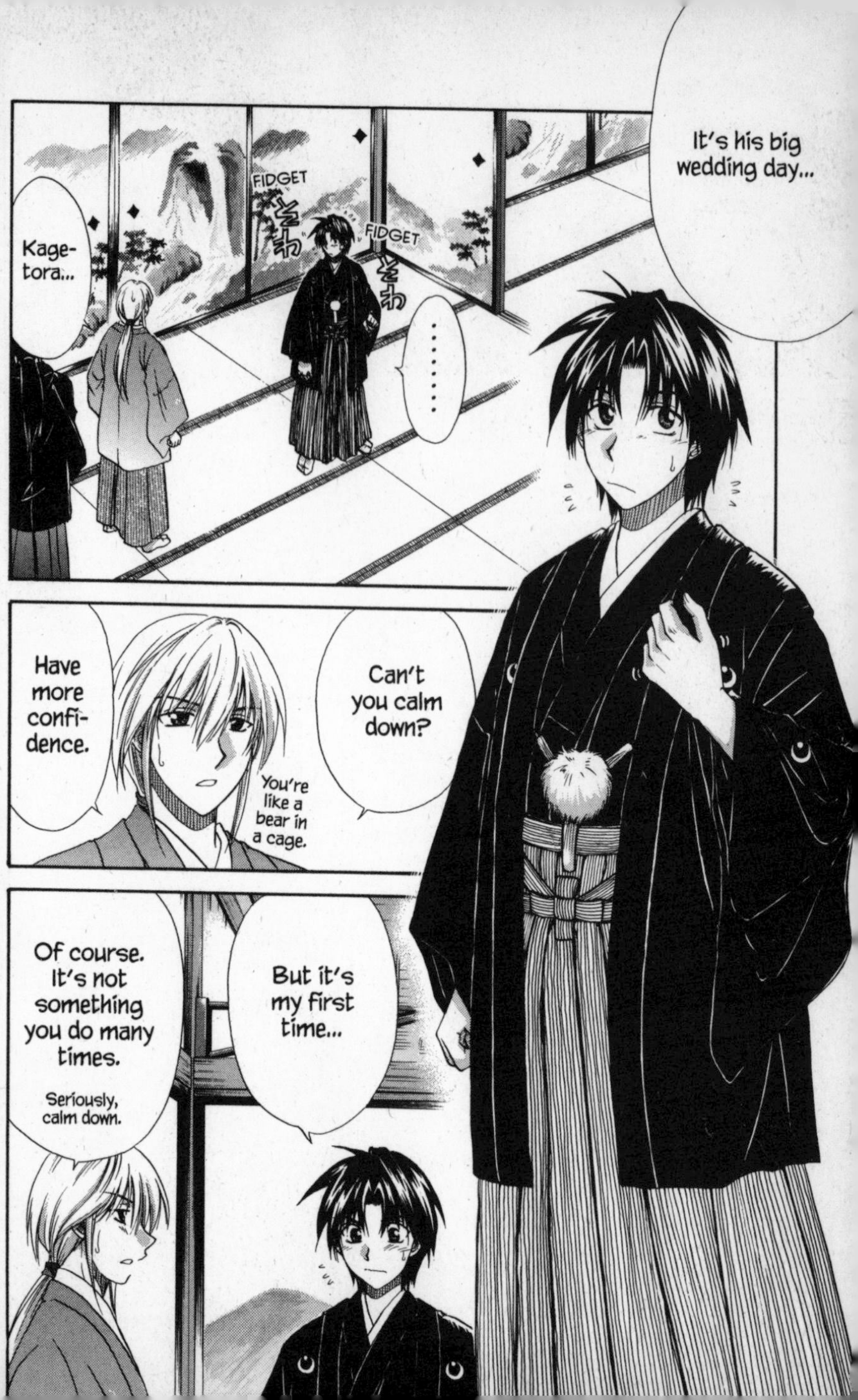
It's his big wedding day...
......
FIDGET
FIDGET
Kage-tora...
Can't you calm down?
You're like a bear in a cage.
Have more confi-dence.
But it's my first time...
Of course. It's not something you do many times.
Seriously, calm down.

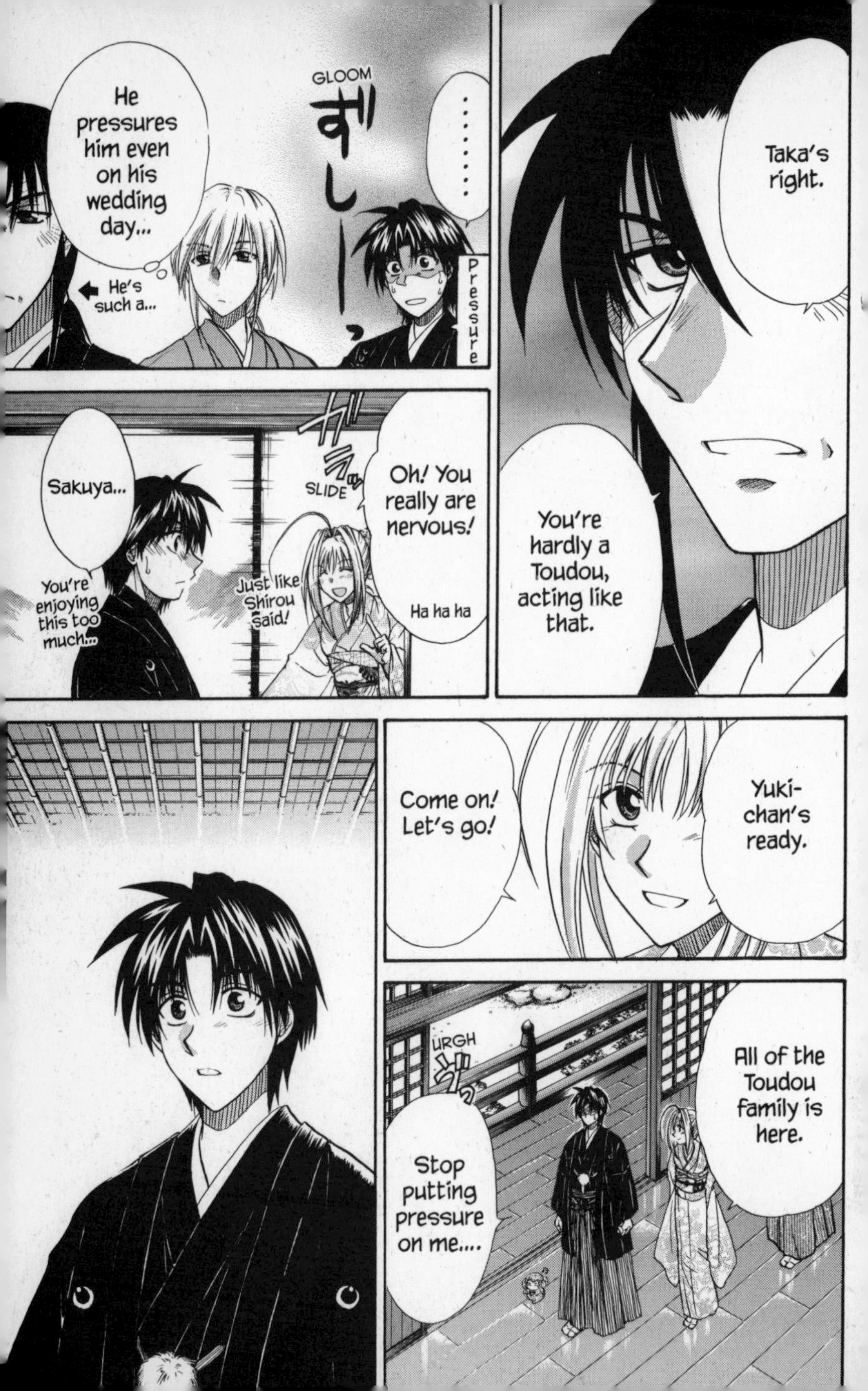
Taka's right.
You're hardly a Toudou, acting like that.
GLOOM
....
Pressure
He pressures him even on his wedding day...
He's such a...
SLIDE
Oh! You really are nervous!
Ha ha ha
Just like Shirou said!
Sakuya...
You're enjoying this too much...
Yuki-chan's ready.
Come on! Let's go!
All of the Toudou family is here.
URGH
Stop putting pressure on me....

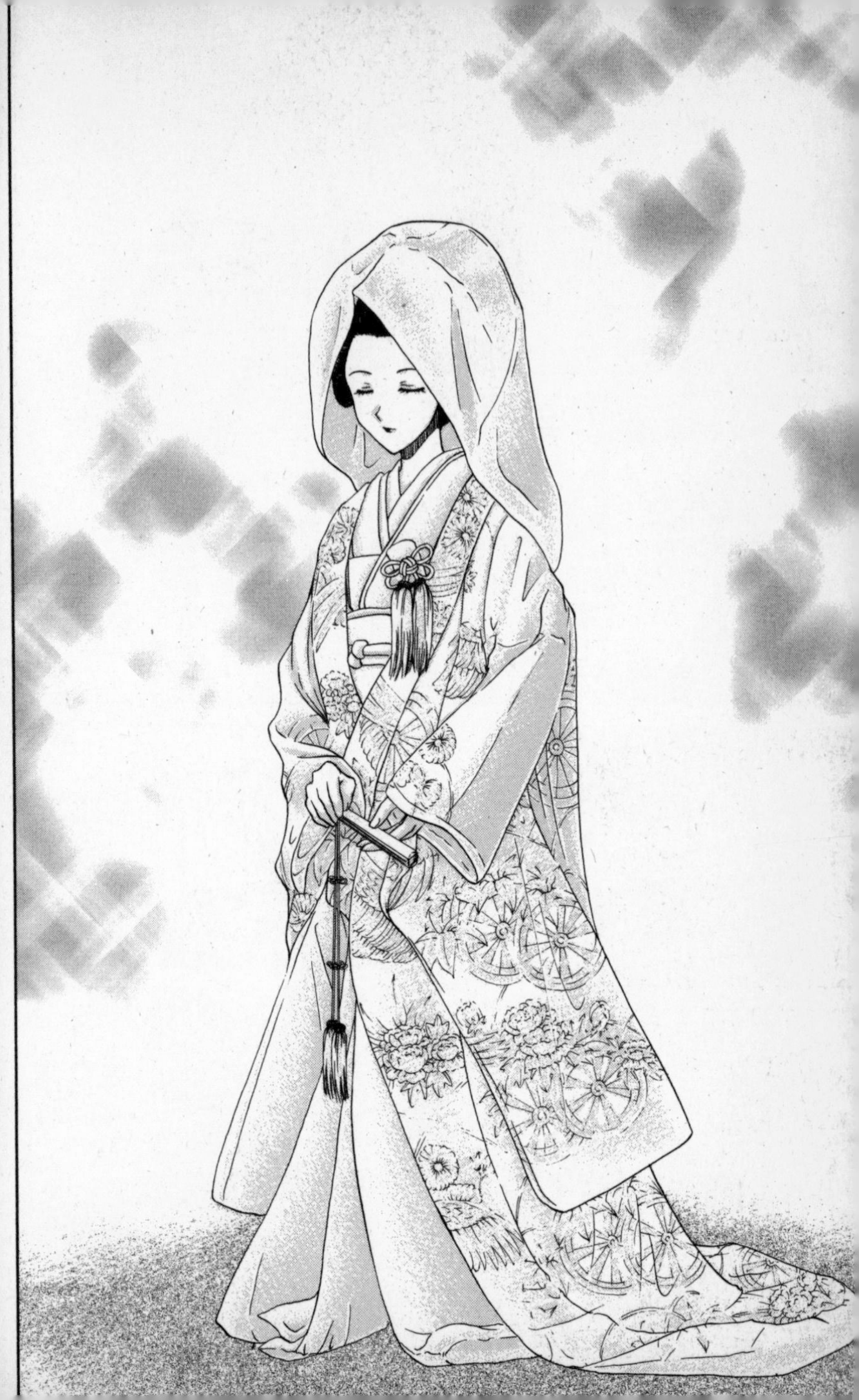

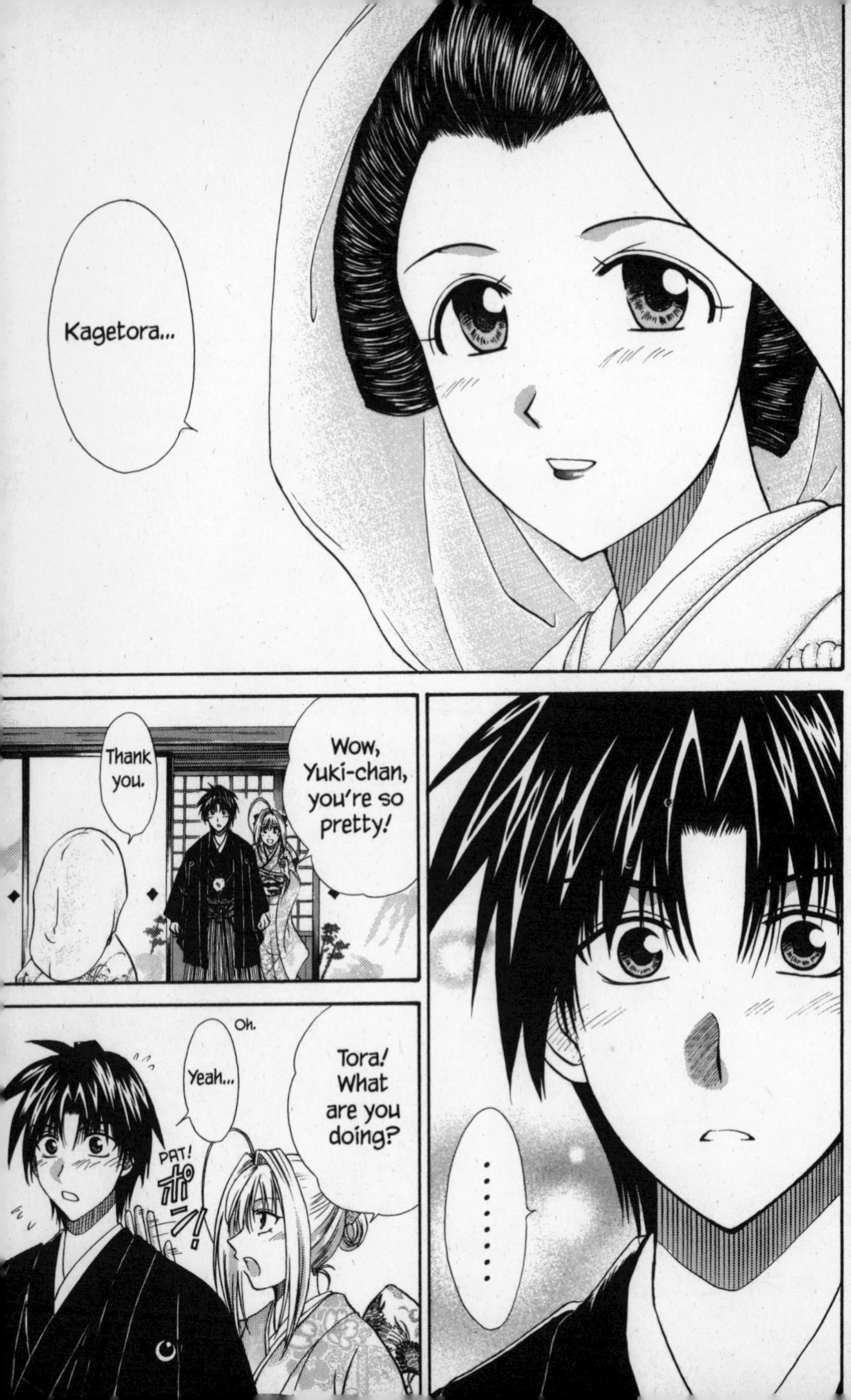
Kagetora...
......
Wow, Yuki-chan, you're so pretty!
Thank you.
Tora! What are you doing?
Oh.
Yeah...
PAT!

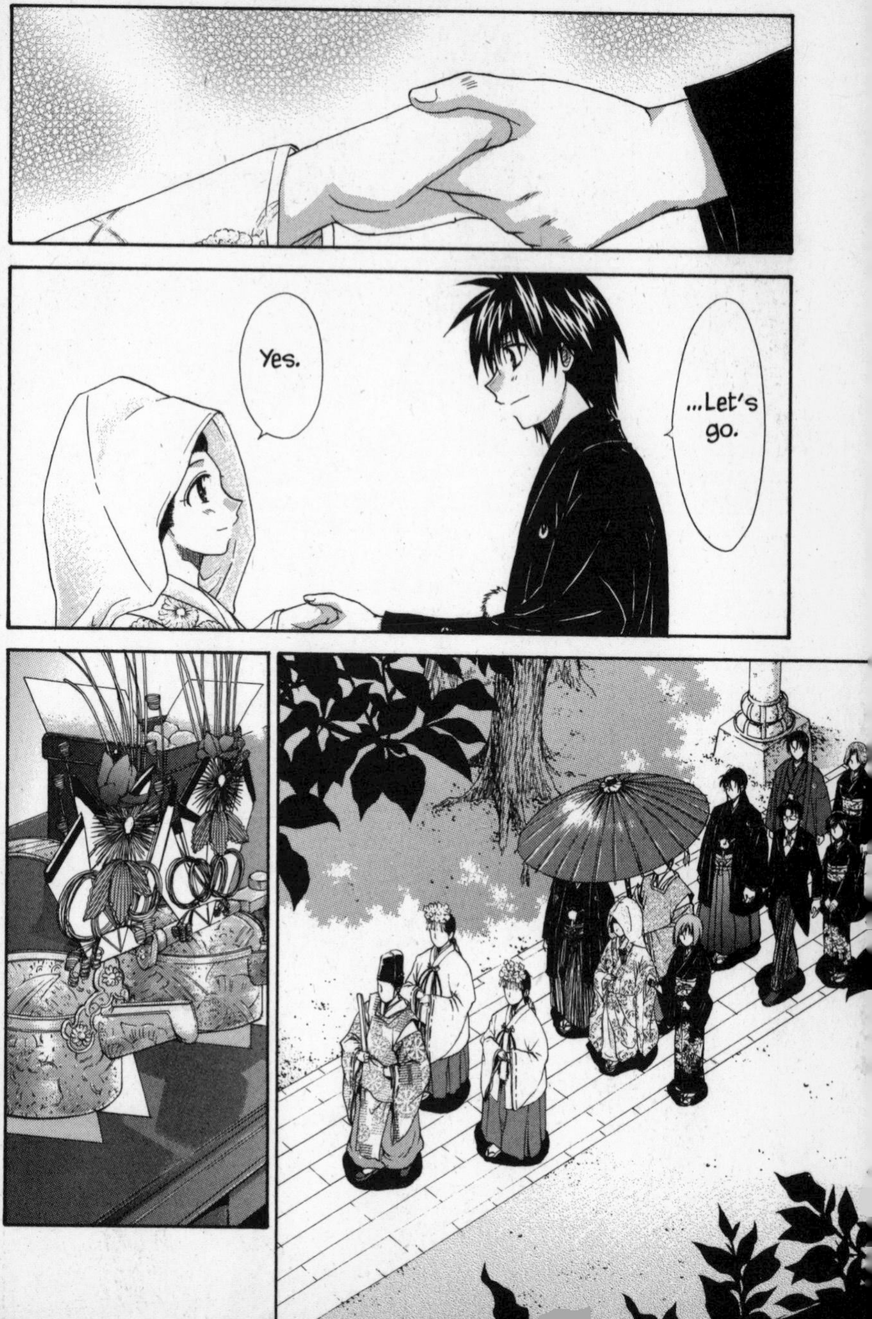
...Let's go.
Yes.

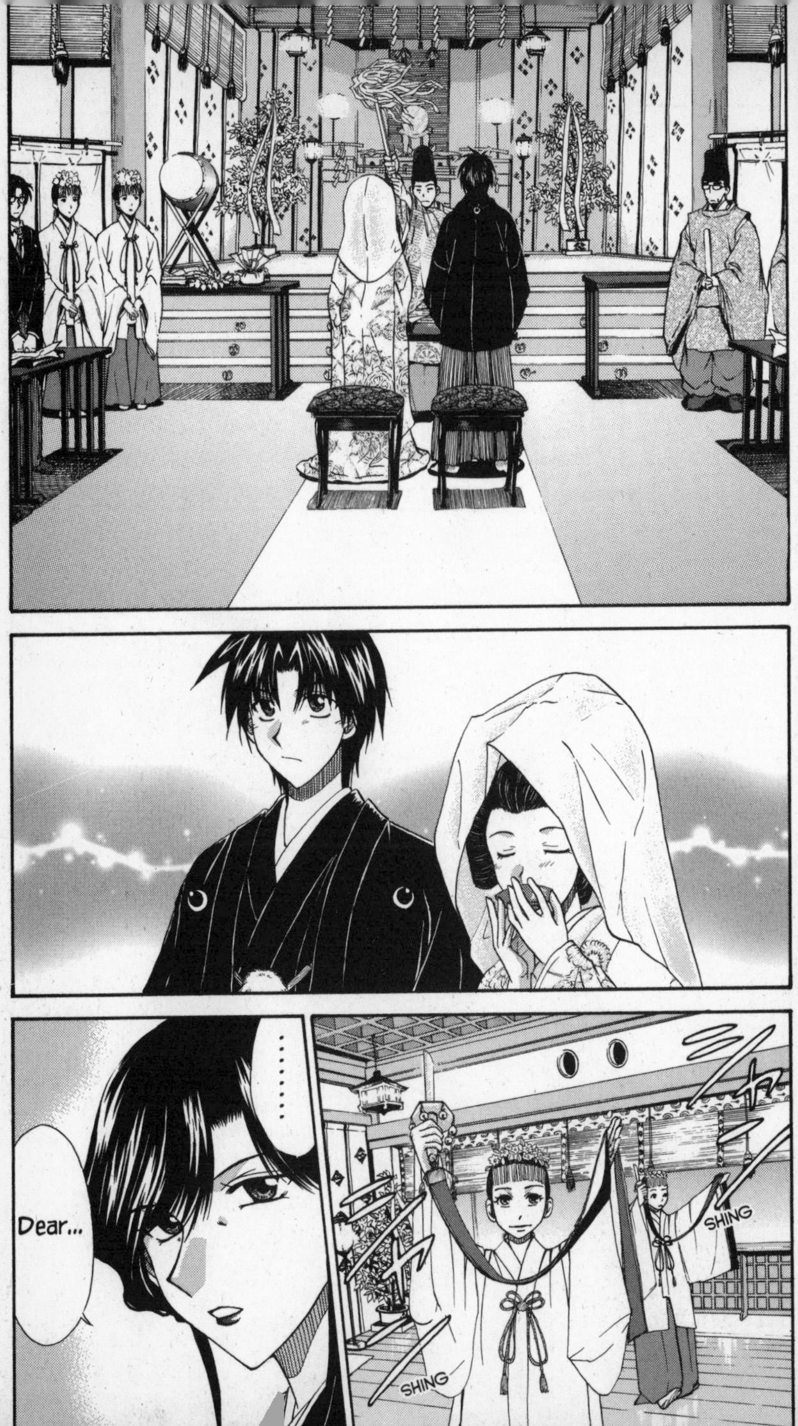
SHING
SHING
......
Dear...

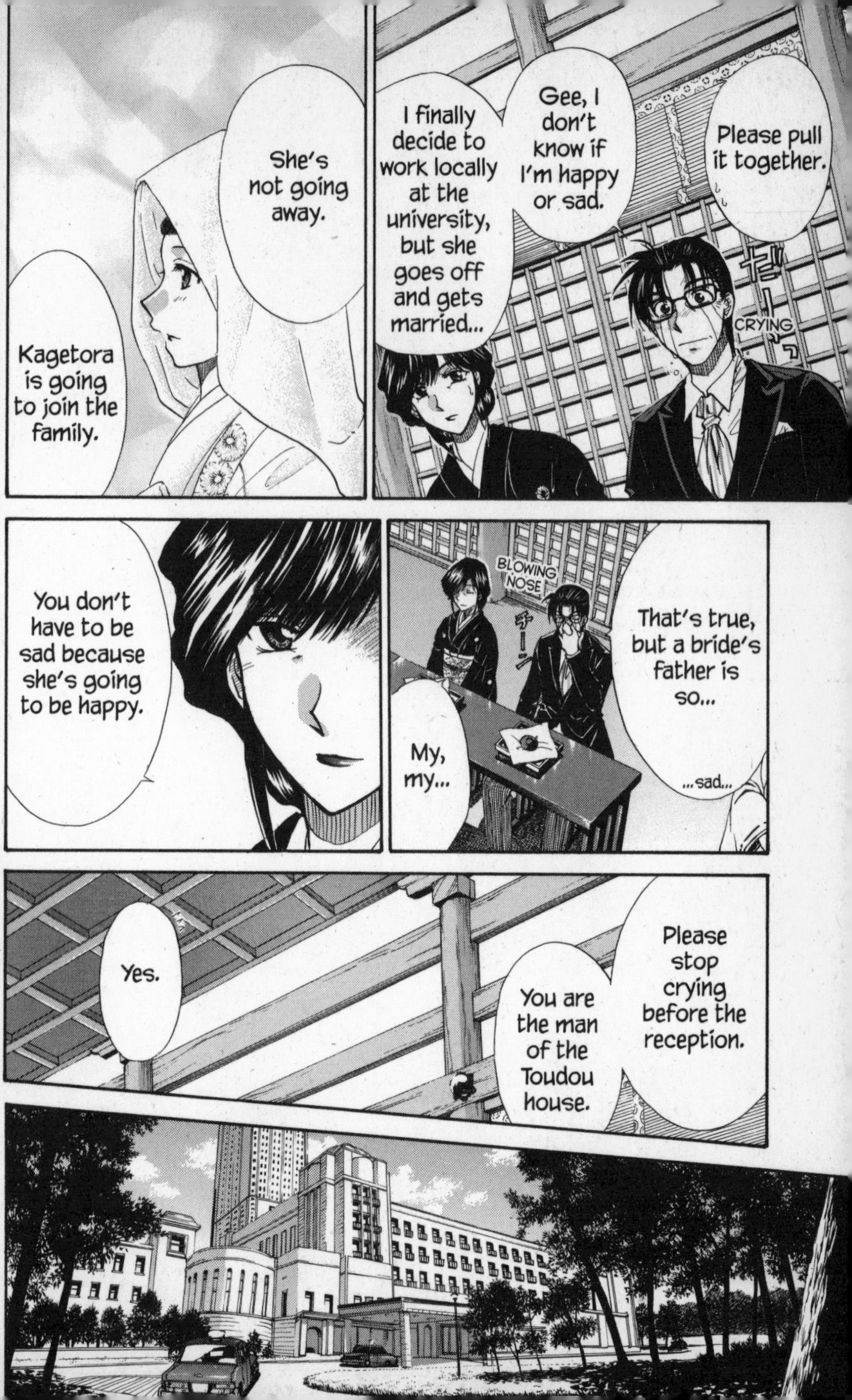
Please pull it together.
CRYING
Gee, I don't know if I'm happy or sad.
I finally decide to work locally at the university, but she goes off and gets married...
She's not going away.
Kagetora is going to join the family.
That's true, but a bride's father is so...
...sad...
BLOWING NOSE
My, my...
You don't have to be sad because she's going to be happy.
Please stop crying before the reception.
You are the man of the Toudou house.
Yes.

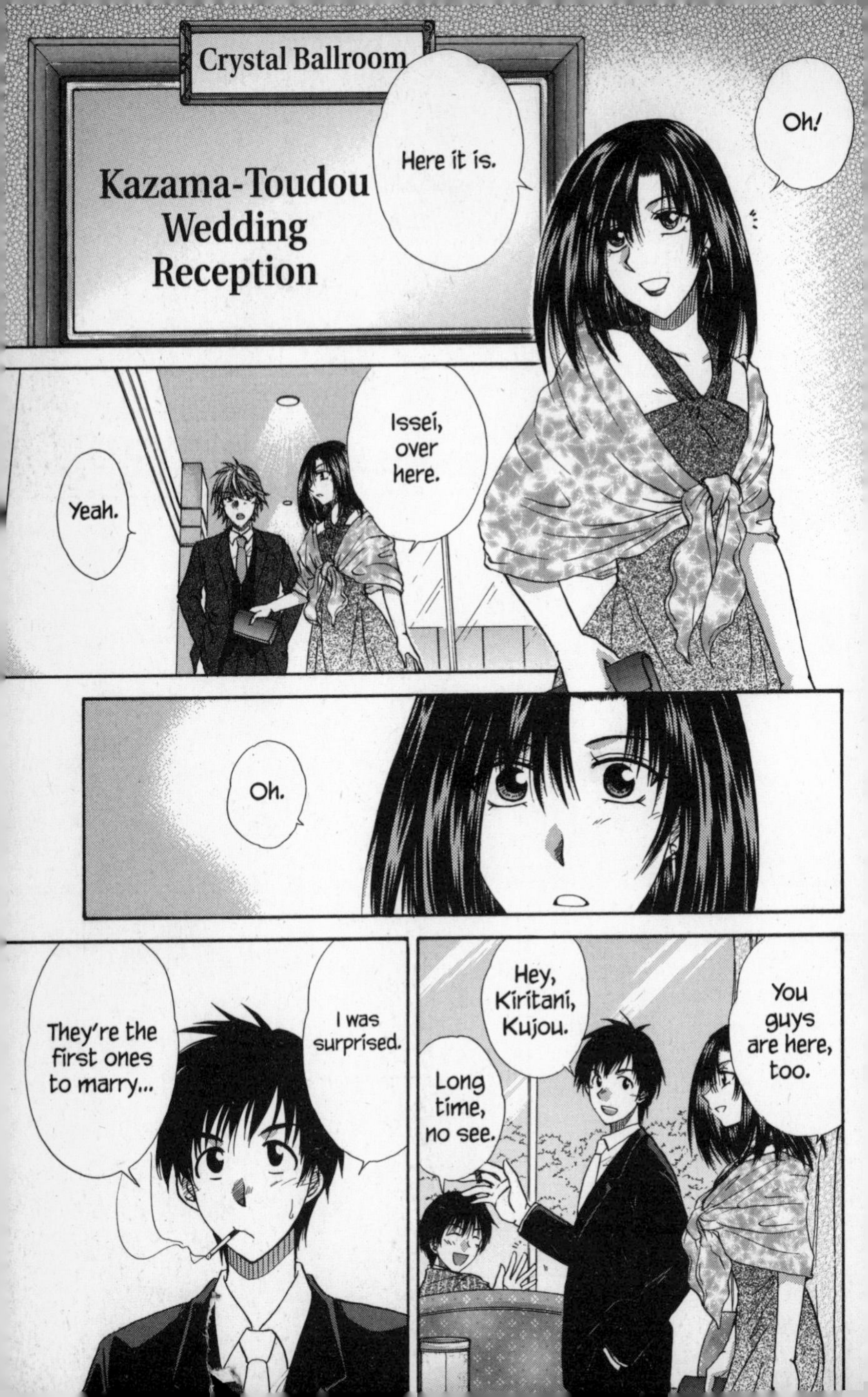

Oh!
Crystal Ballroom
Kazama-Toudou Wedding Reception
Here it is.
Issei, over here.
Yeah.
Oh.
You guys are here, too.
Hey, Kiritani, Kujou.
Long time, no see.
I was surprised.
They're the first ones to marry...

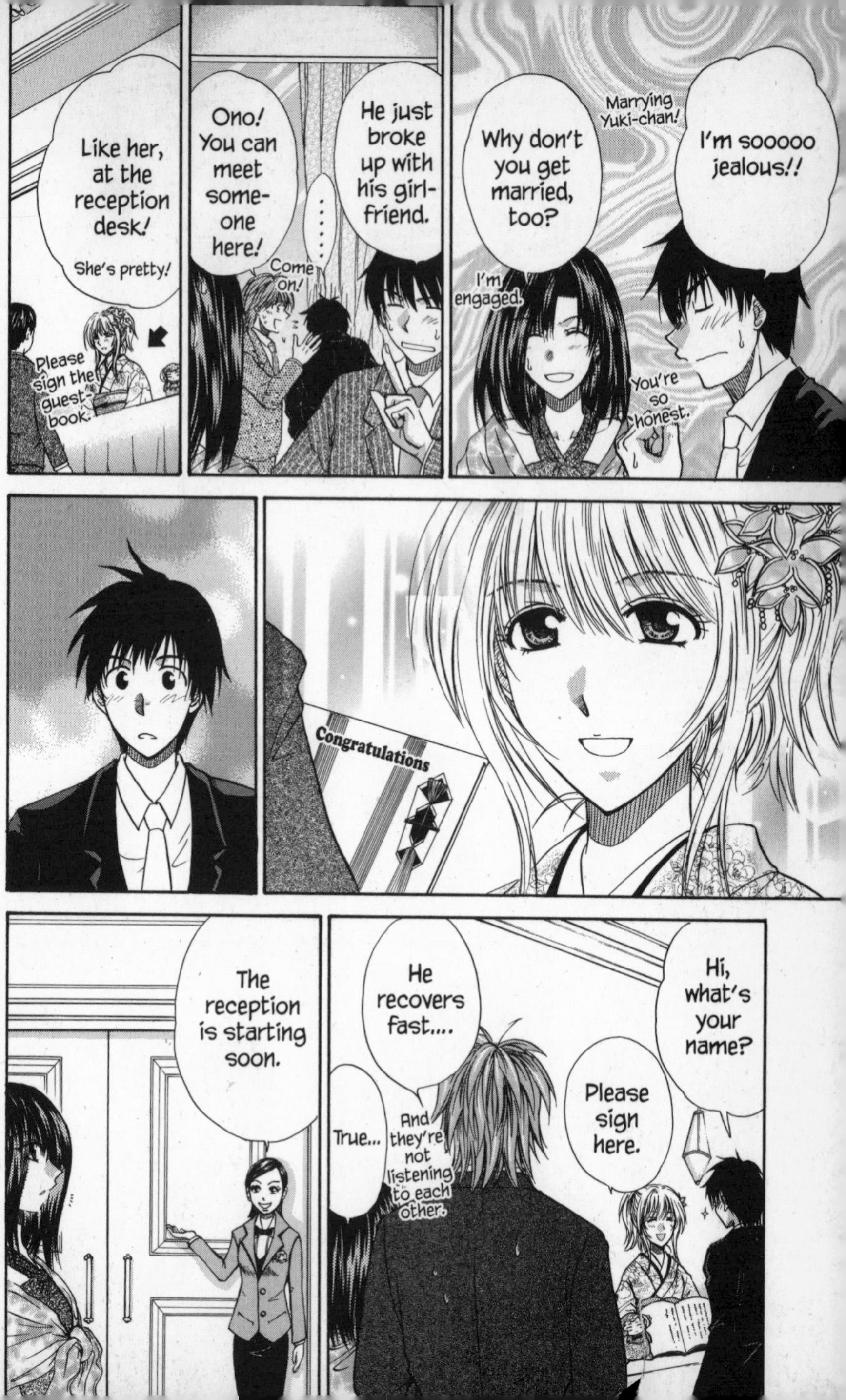
I'm sooooo jealous!!
Marrying Yuki-chan!
Why don't you get married, too?
I'm engaged.
You're so honest.
He just broke up with his girl-friend.
......
Ono! You can meet some-one here!
Come on!
Like her, at the reception desk!
She's pretty!
Please sign the guest-book.
Congratulations
Hi, what's your name?
Please sign here.
He recovers fast....
And they're not listening to each other.
True...
The reception is starting soon.

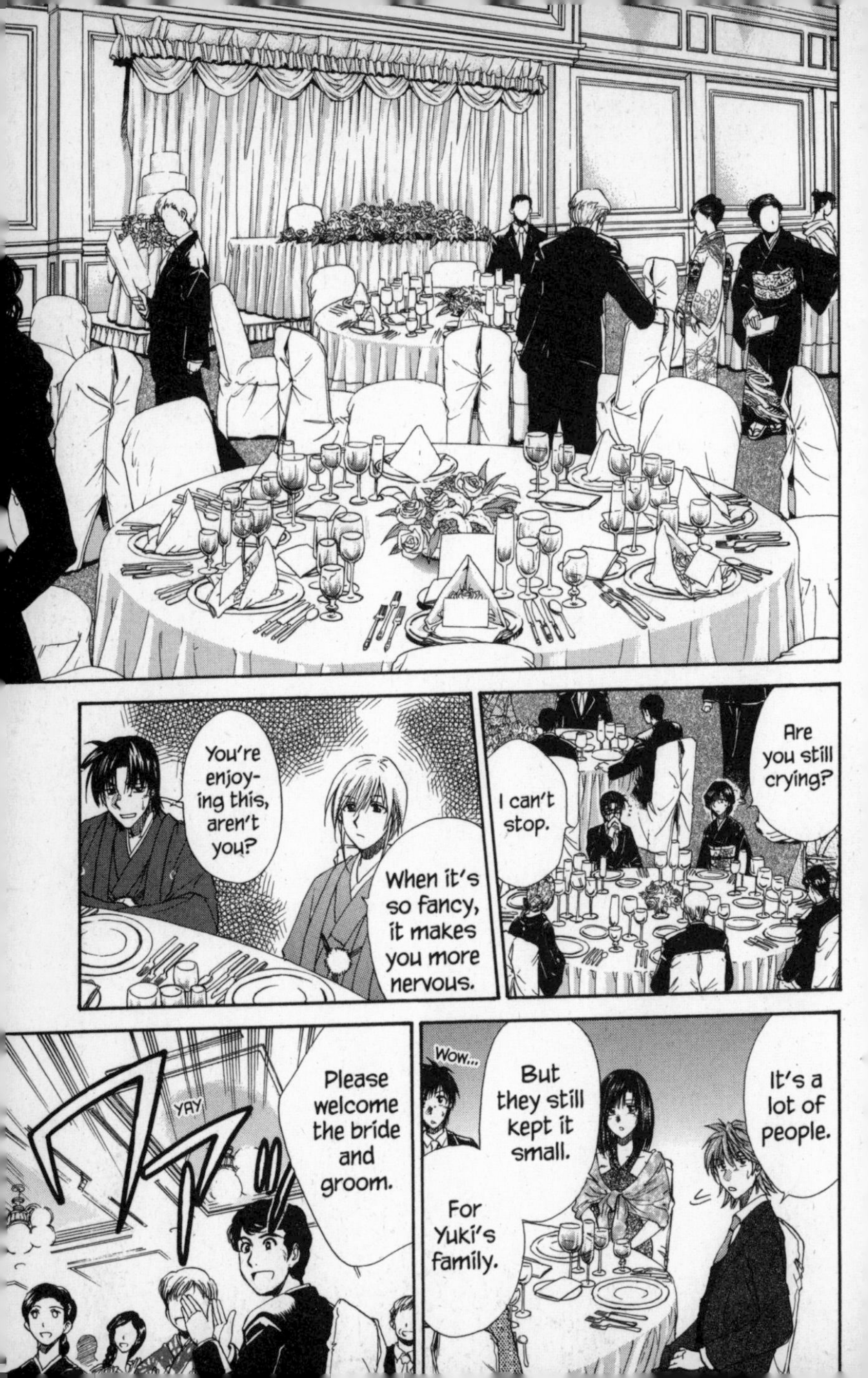
Are you still crying?
I can't stop.
You're enjoying this, aren't you?
When it's so fancy, it makes you more nervous.
It's a lot of people.
But they still kept it small.
Wow...
For Yuki's family.
Please welcome the bride and groom.
YAY

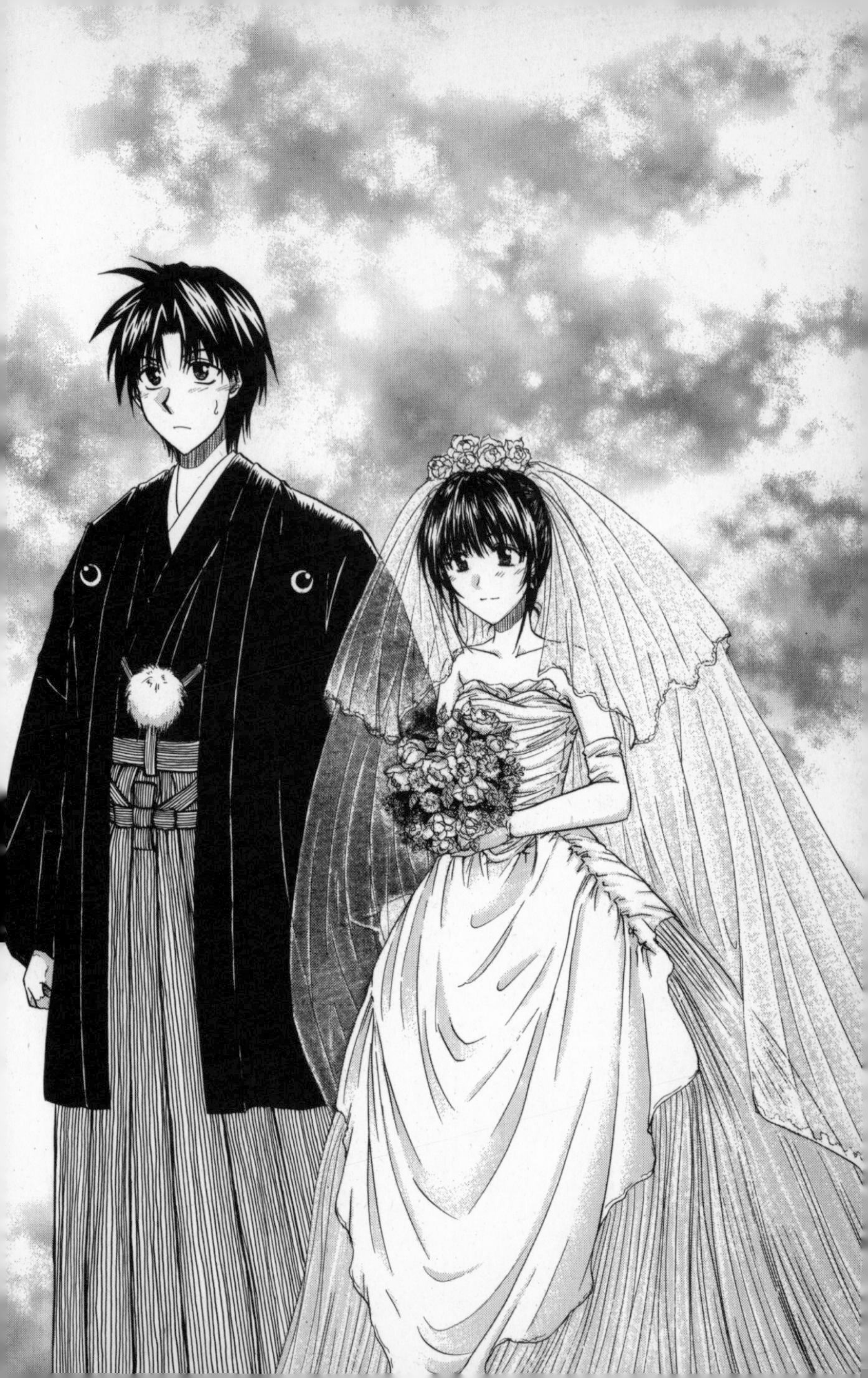

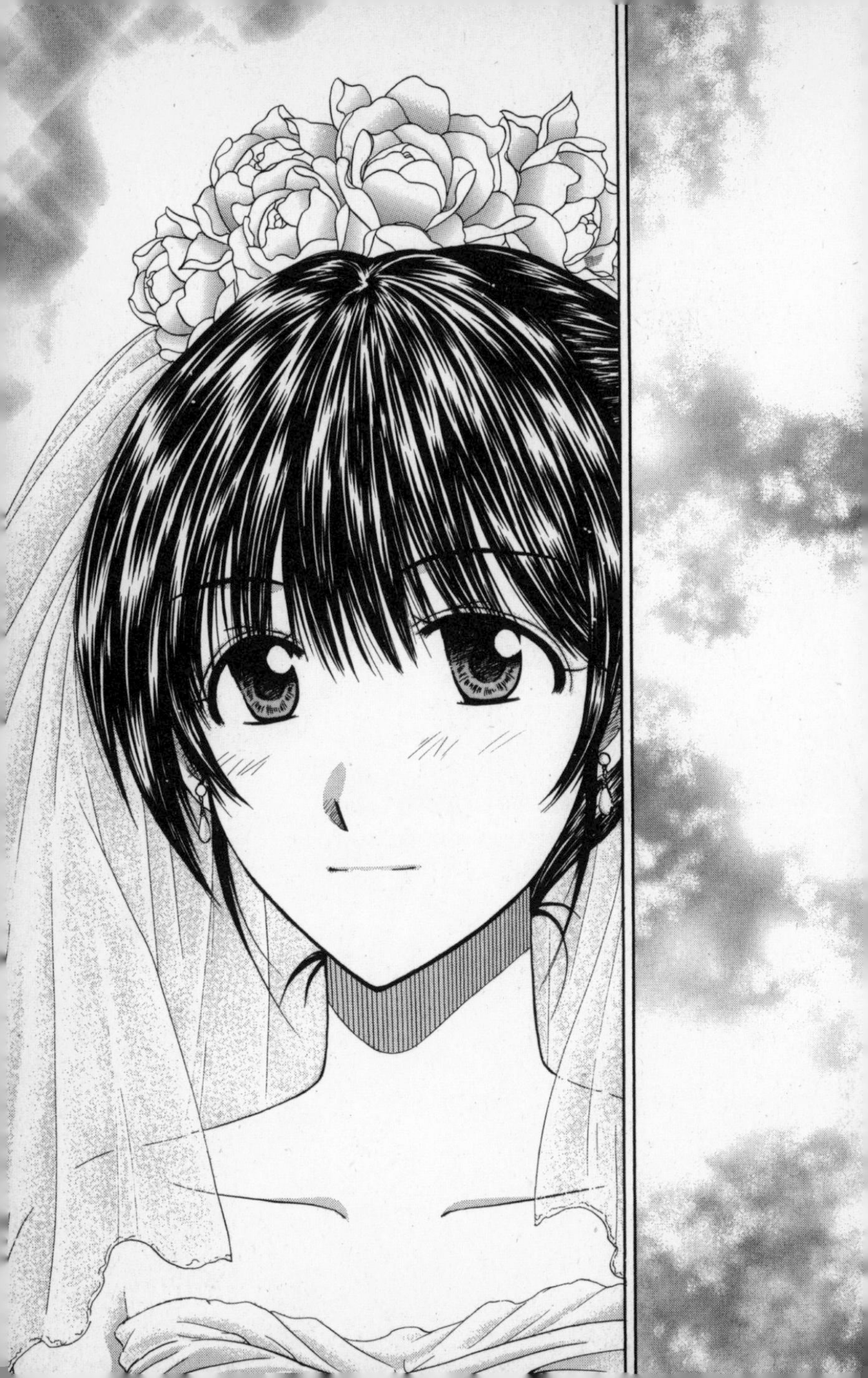

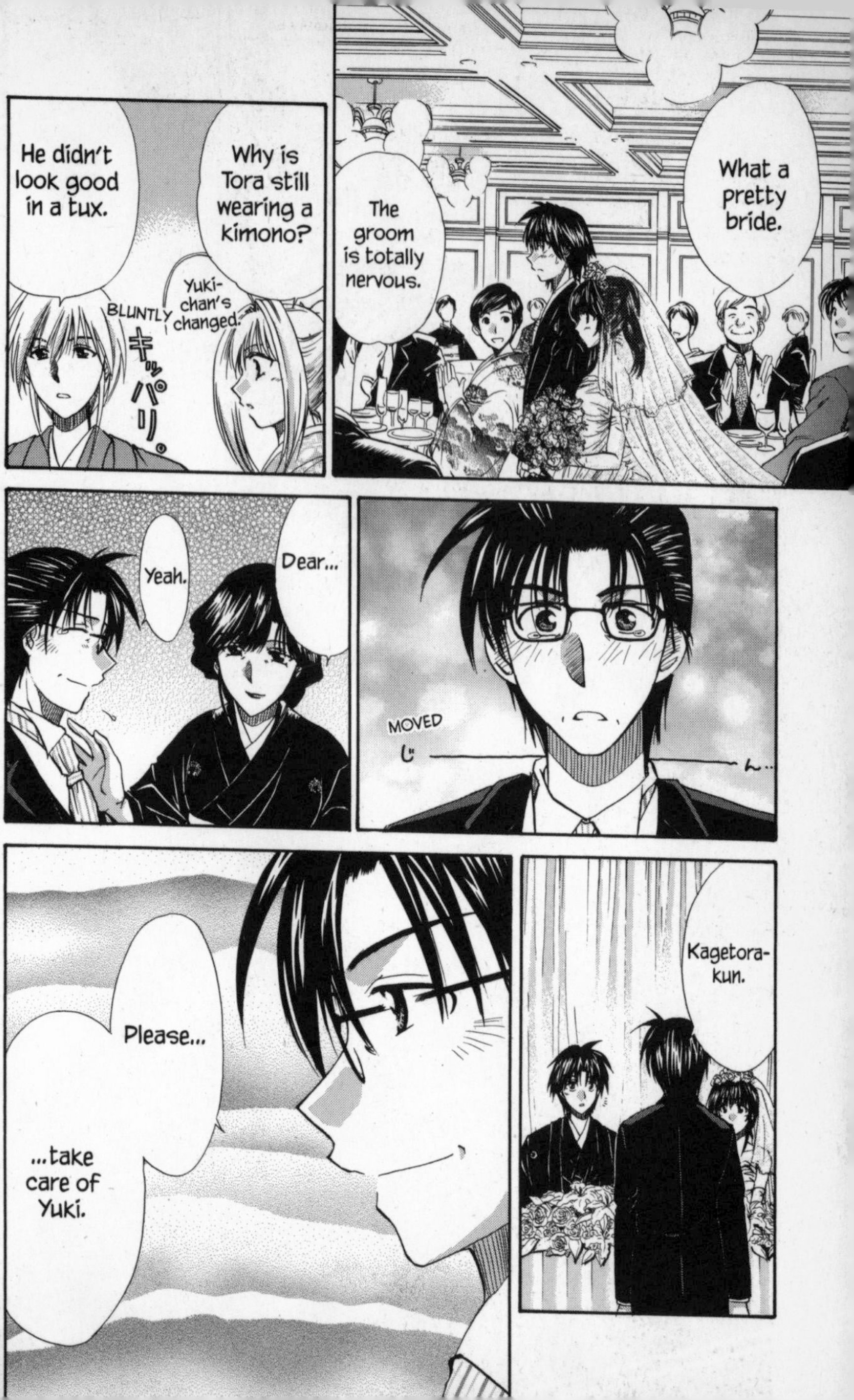
What a pretty bride.
The groom is totally nervous.
Why is Tora still wearing a kimono?
He didn't look good in a tux.
Yuki-chan's changed.
BLUNTLY
キッパリ。
MOVED
じ——ん…
Dear...
Yeah.
Kagetora-kun.
Please...
...take care of Yuki.

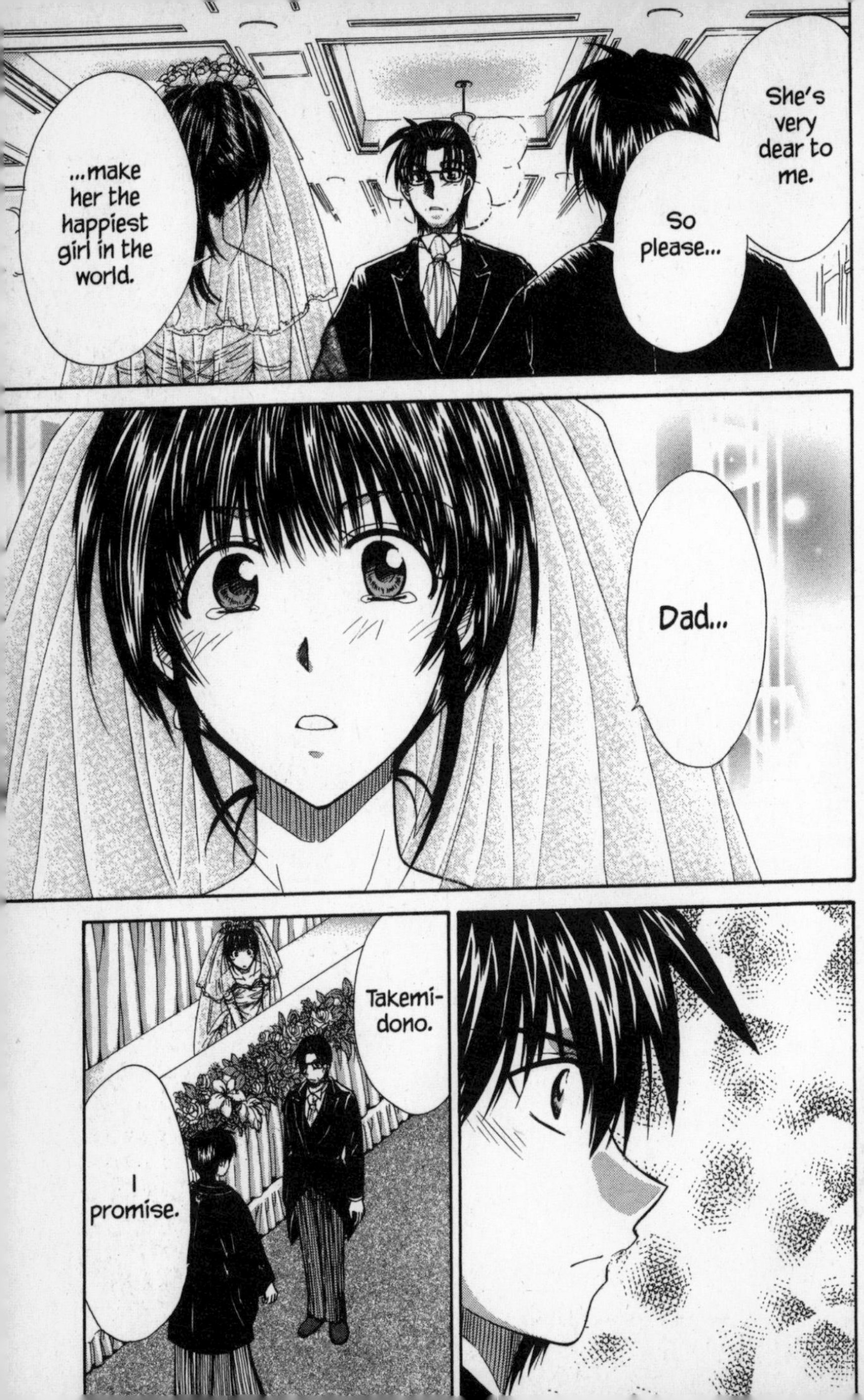
She's very dear to me.
So please...
...make her the happiest girl in the world.
Dad...
Takemi-dono.
I promise.

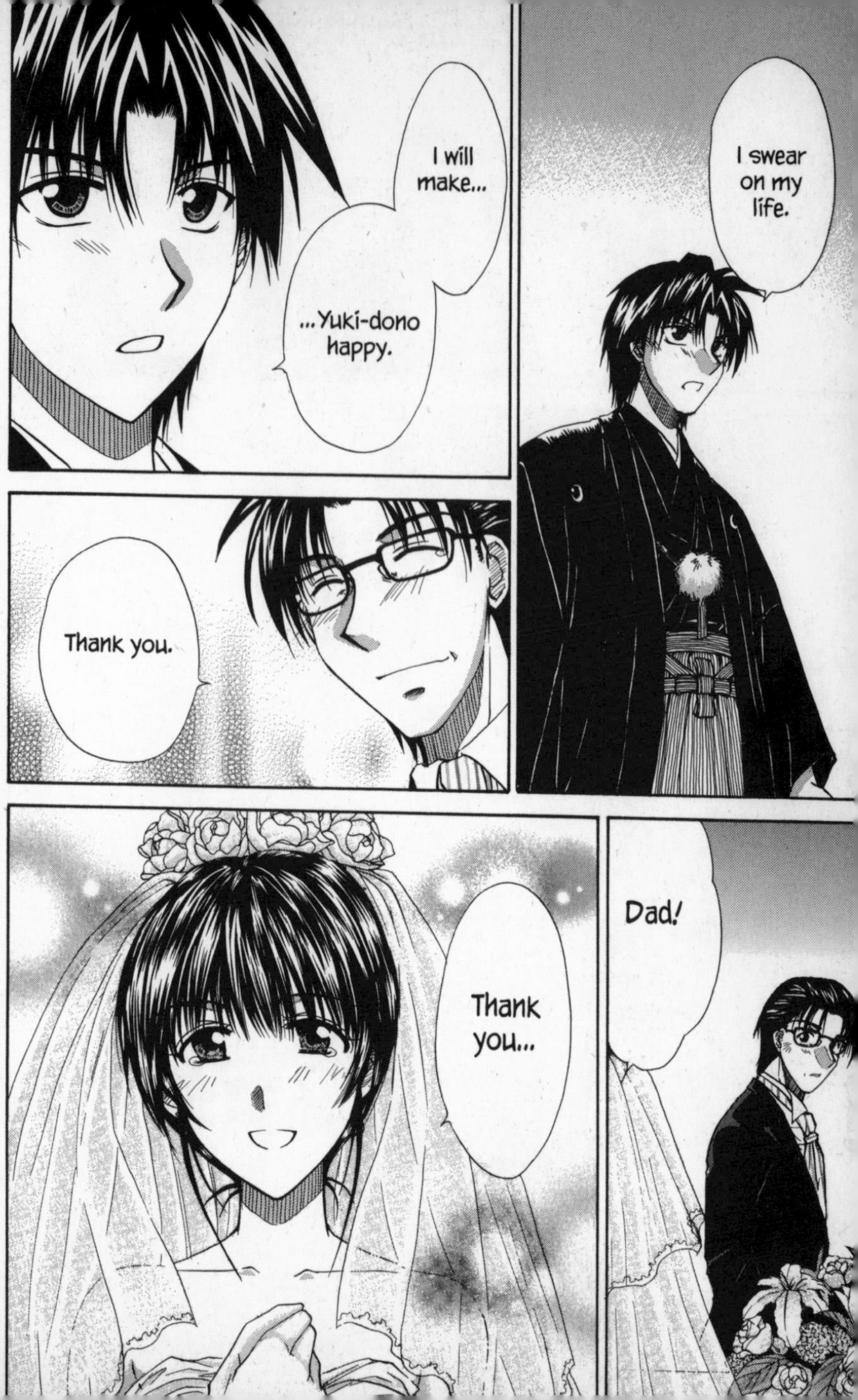
I swear on my life.
I will make...
...Yuki-dono happy.
Thank you.
Dad!
Thank you...

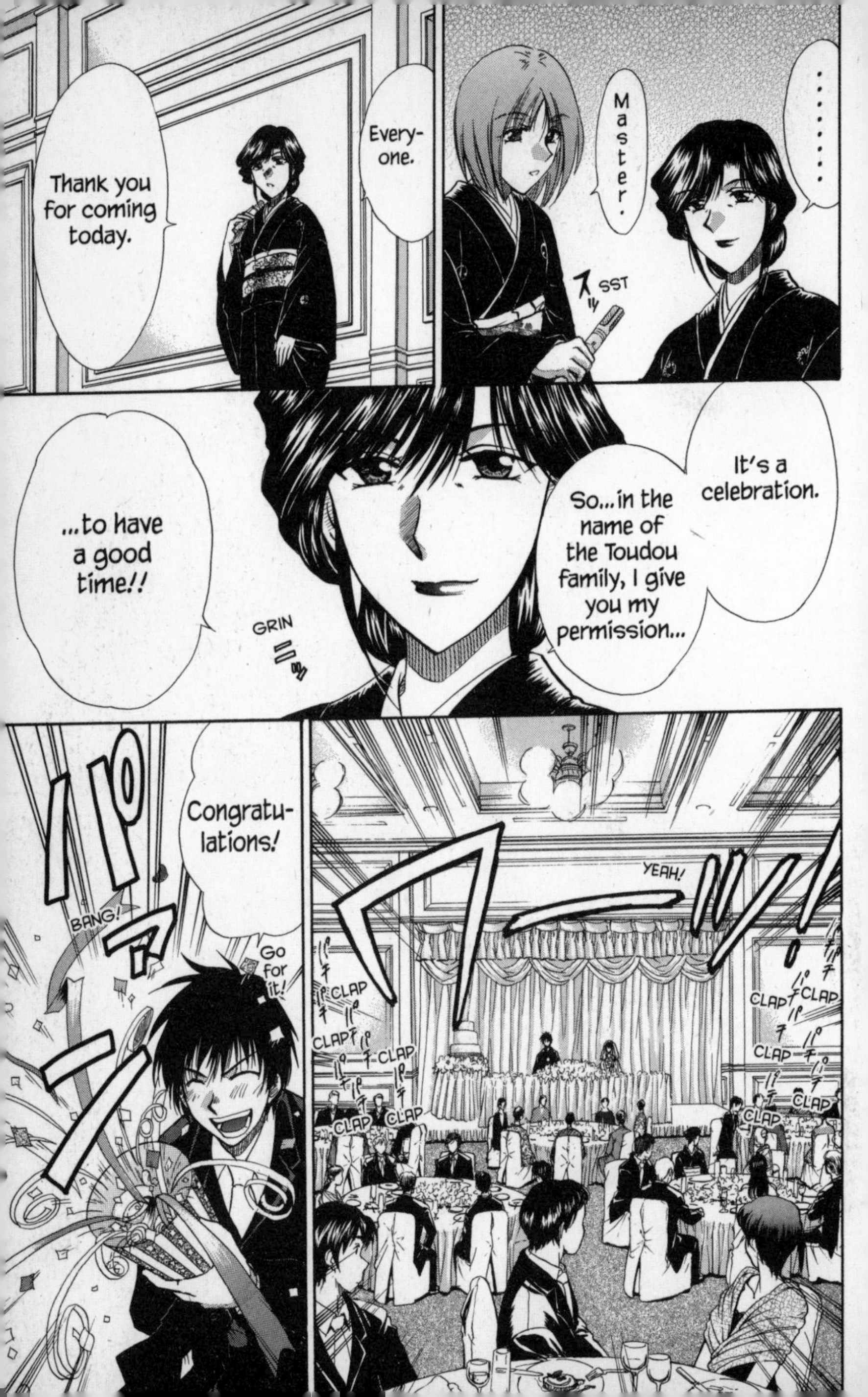

....
Master.
SST
Every-one.
Thank you for coming today.
It's a celebration.
So...in the name of the Toudou family, I give you my permission...
GRIN
...to have a good time!!
YEAH!
CLAP CLAP CLAP CLAP
CLAP CLAP CLAP CLAP CLAP CLAP
Congratu-lations!
BANG!
Go for it!

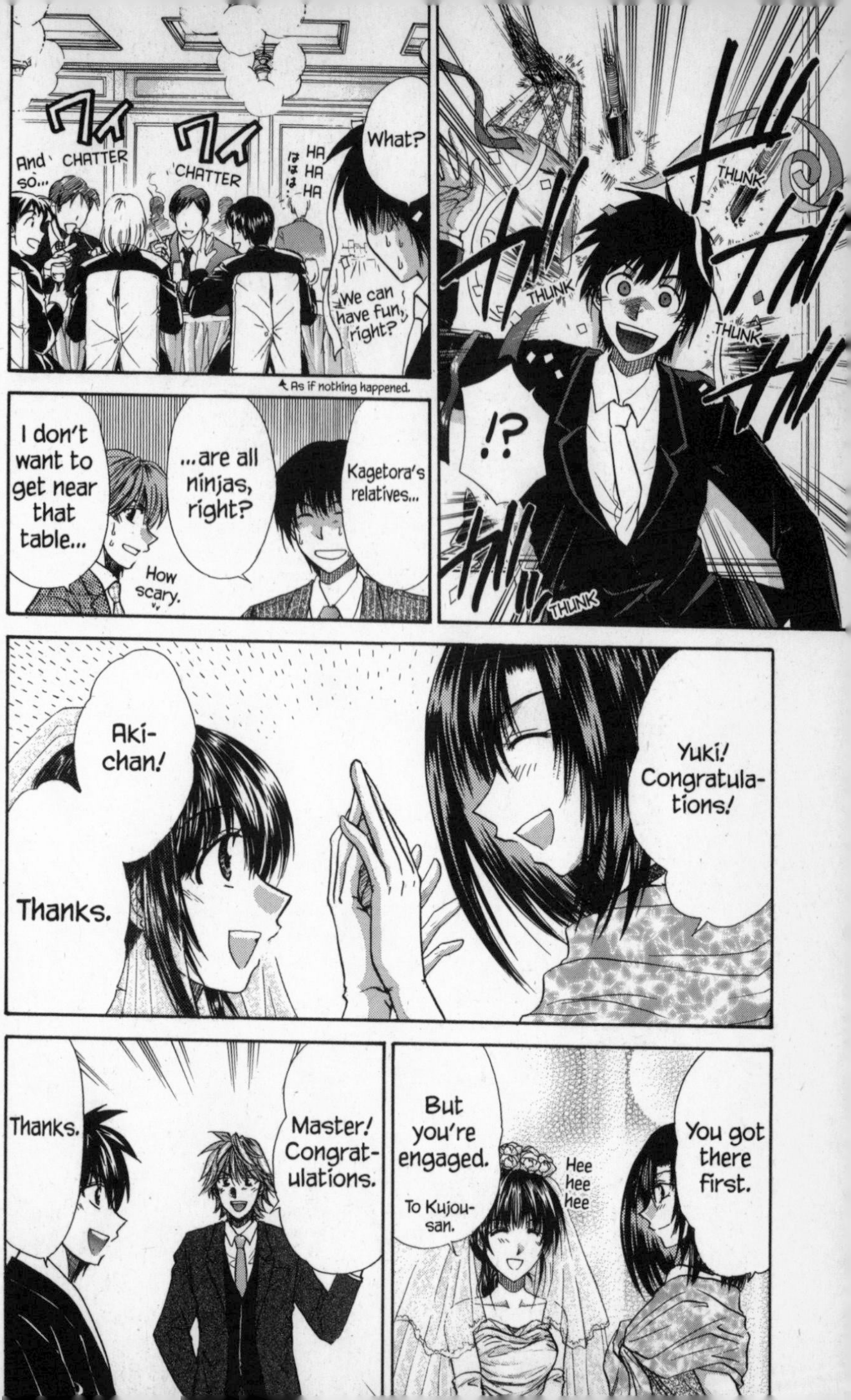
THUNK
THUNK
THUNK
!?
THUNK
What?
ははは HA HA HA
ワイ
ワイ
CHATTER
CHATTER
And so...
We can have fun, right?
As if nothing happened.
Kagetora's relatives...
...are all ninjas, right?
I don't want to get near that table...
How scary.
Yuki! Congratulations!
Aki-chan!
Thanks.
You got there first.
But you're engaged.
Hee hee hee
To Kujou-san.
Master! Congratulations.
Thanks.

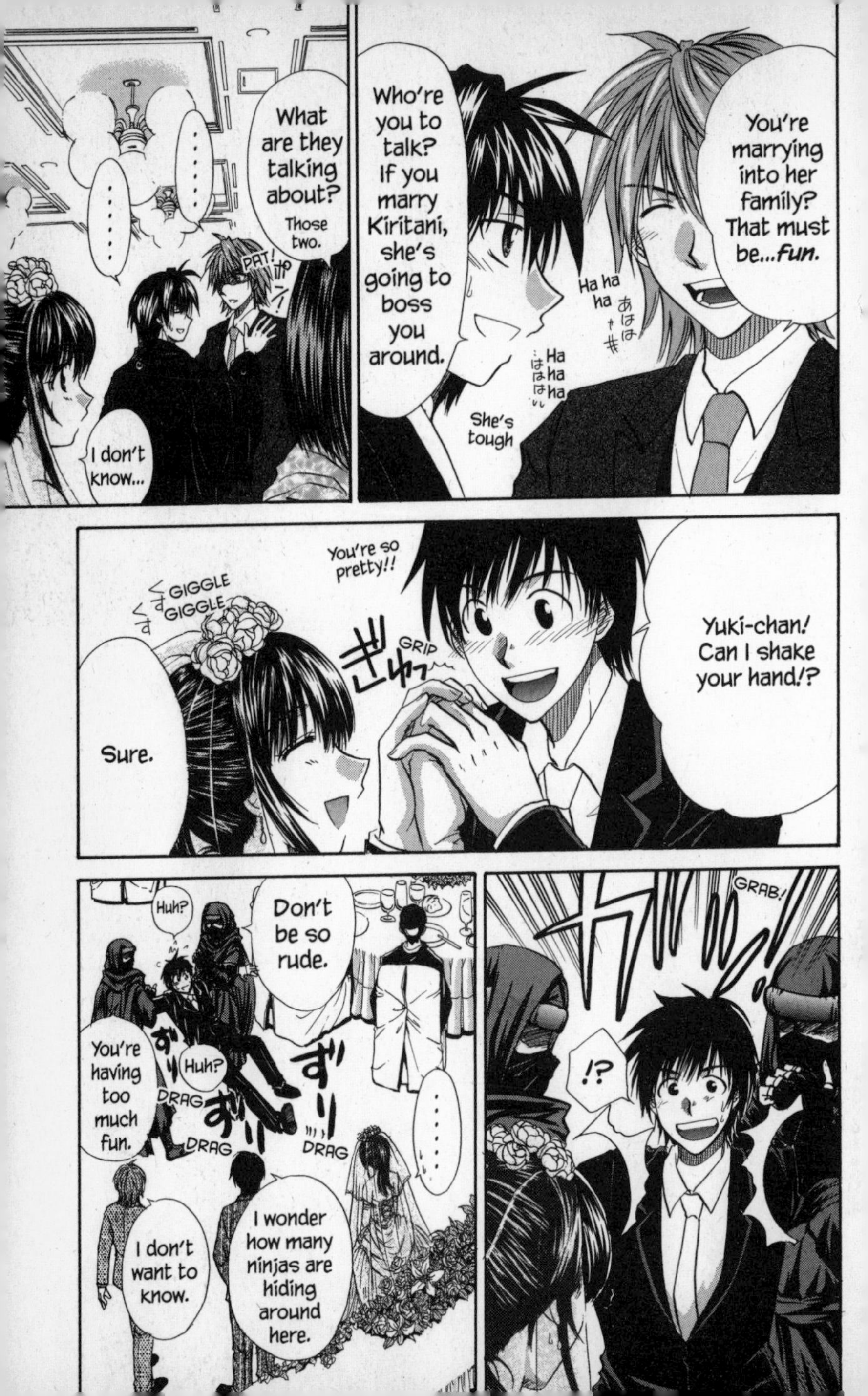
You're marrying into her family? That must be...*fun*.
Ha ha ha
あはは
Who're you to talk? If you marry Kiritani, she's going to boss you around.
Ha ha ha
ははは
She's tough
What are they talking about?
Those two.
PAT!
......
......
I don't know...
Yuki-chan! Can I shake your hand!?
You're so pretty!!
GRIP
ぎゅっ
GIGGLE GIGGLE
くすくす
Sure.
GRAB!
!?
Huh?
Don't be so rude.
You're having too much fun.
Huh?
ずり
DRAG
ずり
DRAG
ずり
DRAG
......
I wonder how many ninjas are hiding around here.
I don't want to know.

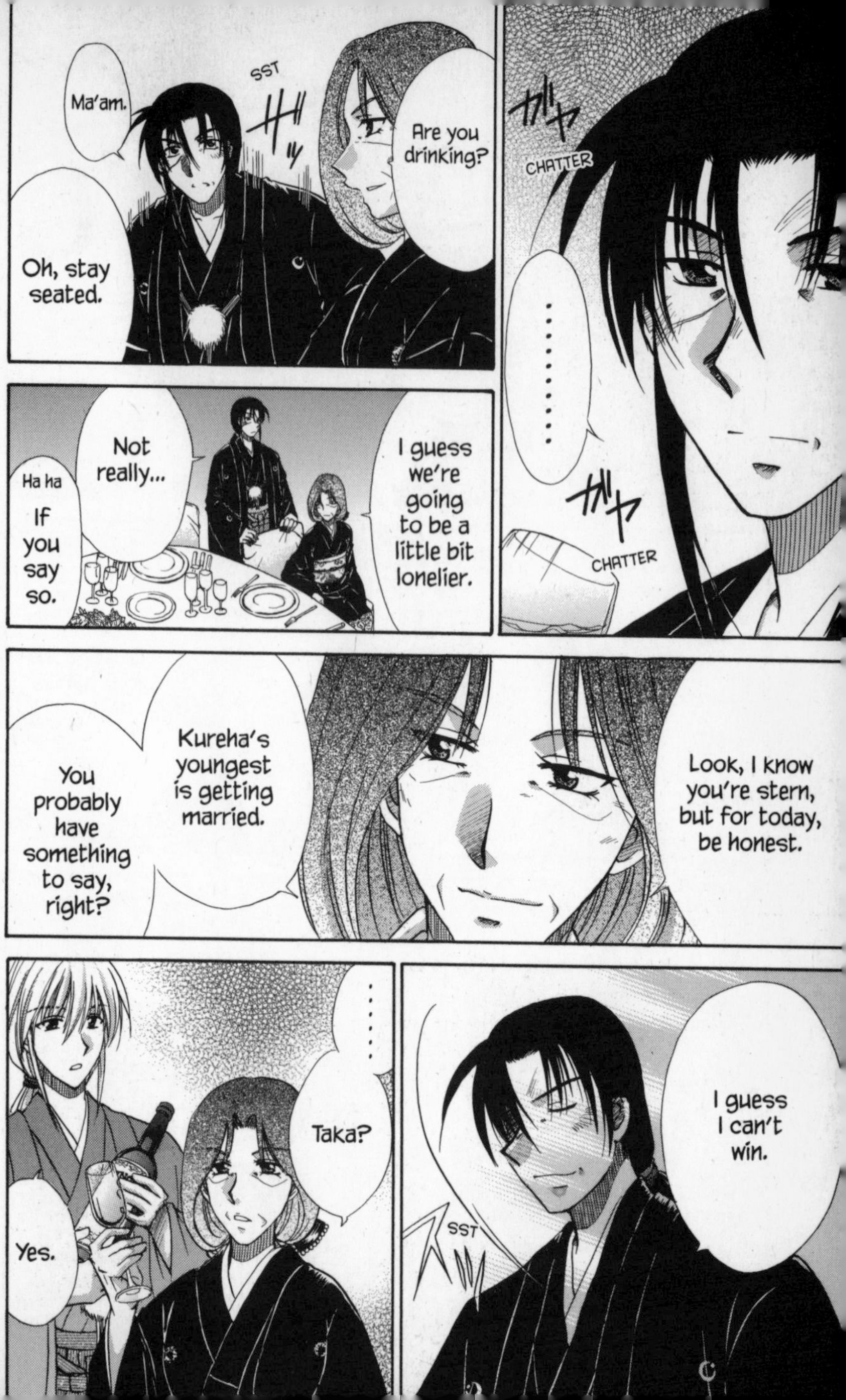

ガヤ
CHATTER
......
ガヤ
CHATTER
Are you drinking?
Ma'am.
SST
Oh, stay seated.
I guess we're going to be a little bit lonelier.
Not really...
Ha ha
If you say so.
Look, I know you're stern, but for today, be honest.
Kureha's youngest is getting married.
You probably have something to say, right?
I guess I can't win.
SST
......
Taka?
Yes.

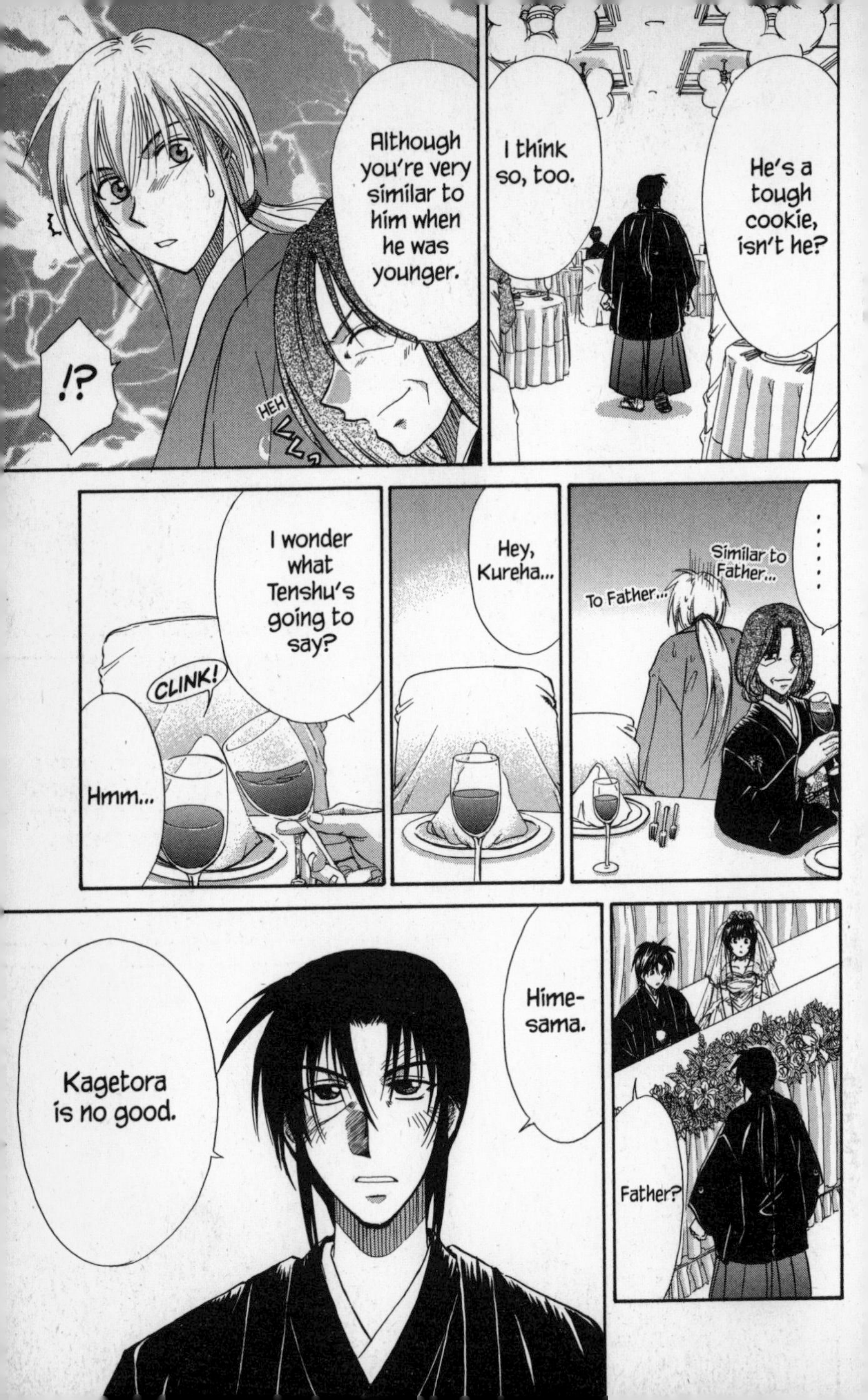
He's a tough cookie, isn't he?
I think so, too.
Although you're very similar to him when he was younger.
HEH
!?
......
Similar to Father...
To Father...
Hey, Kureha...
I wonder what Tenshu's going to say?
CLINK!
Hmm...
Father?
Hime-sama.
Kagetora is no good.

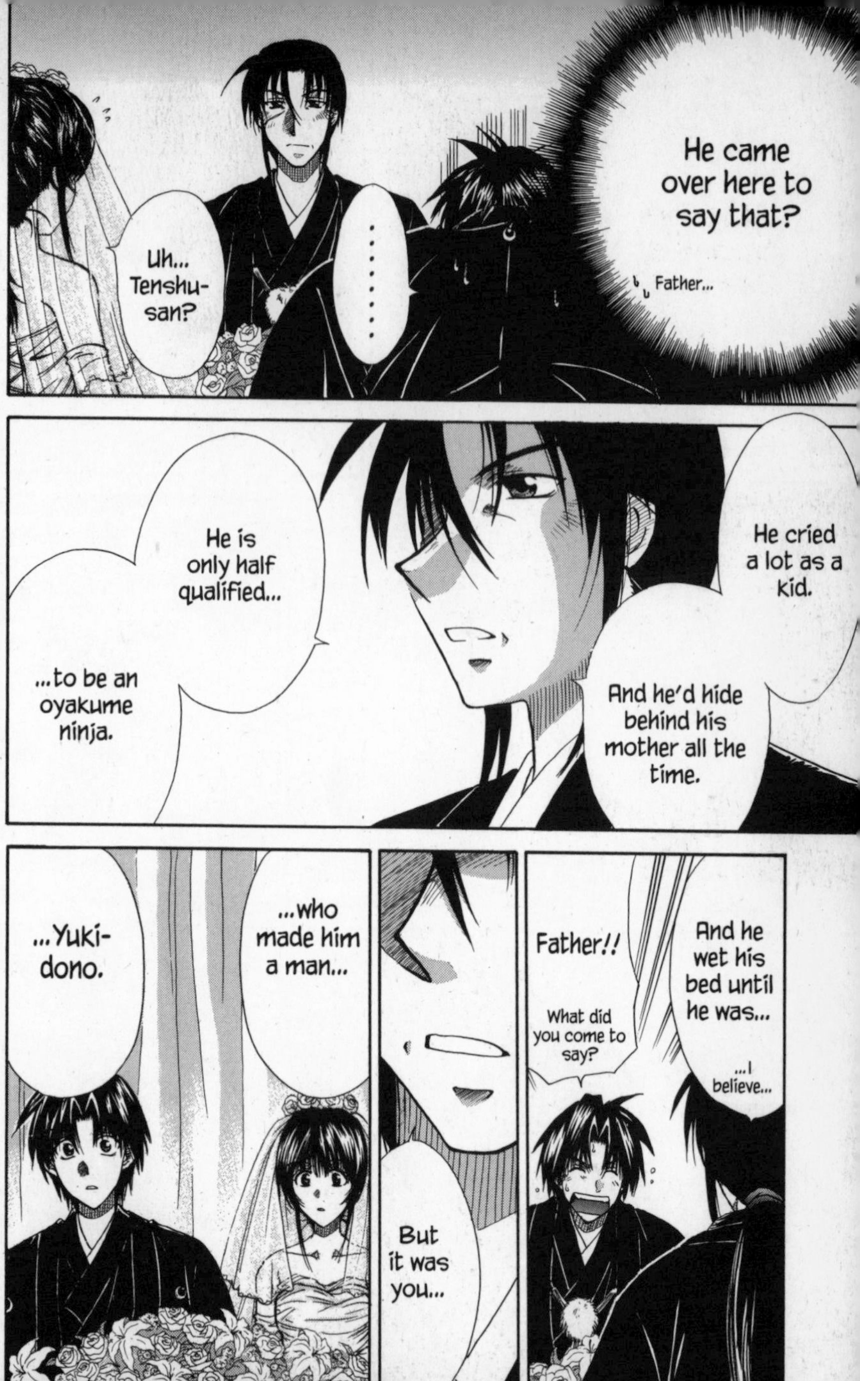
He came over here to say that?
Father...
......
Uh... Tenshu-san?
He cried a lot as a kid.
And he'd hide behind his mother all the time.
He is only half qualified...
...to be an oyakume ninja.
And he wet his bed until he was...
...I believe...
Father!!
What did you come to say?
But it was you...
...who made him a man...
...Yuki-dono.

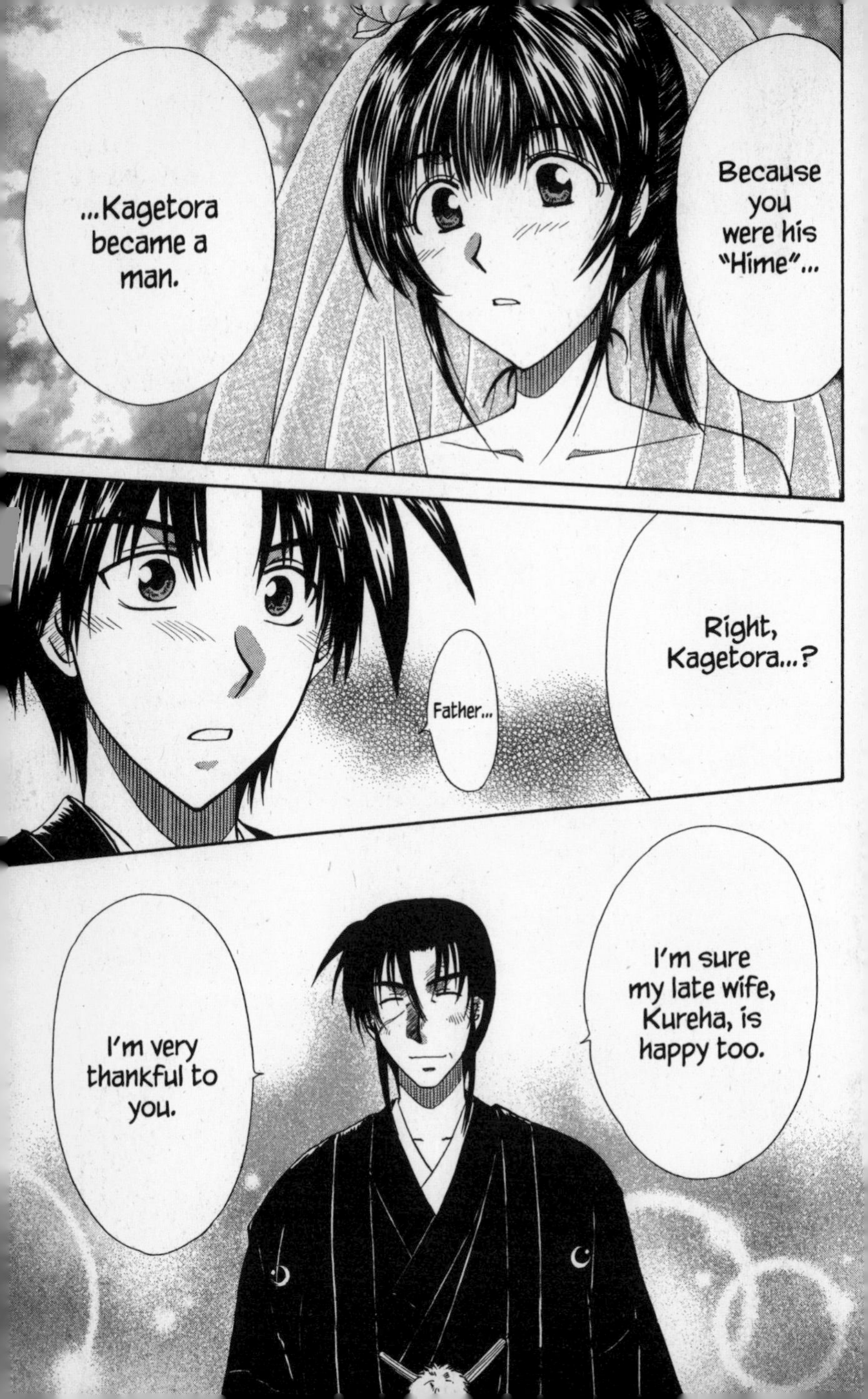
Because you were his "Hime"...
...Kagetora became a man.
Right, Kagetora...?
Father...
I'm sure my late wife, Kureha, is happy too.
I'm very thankful to you.

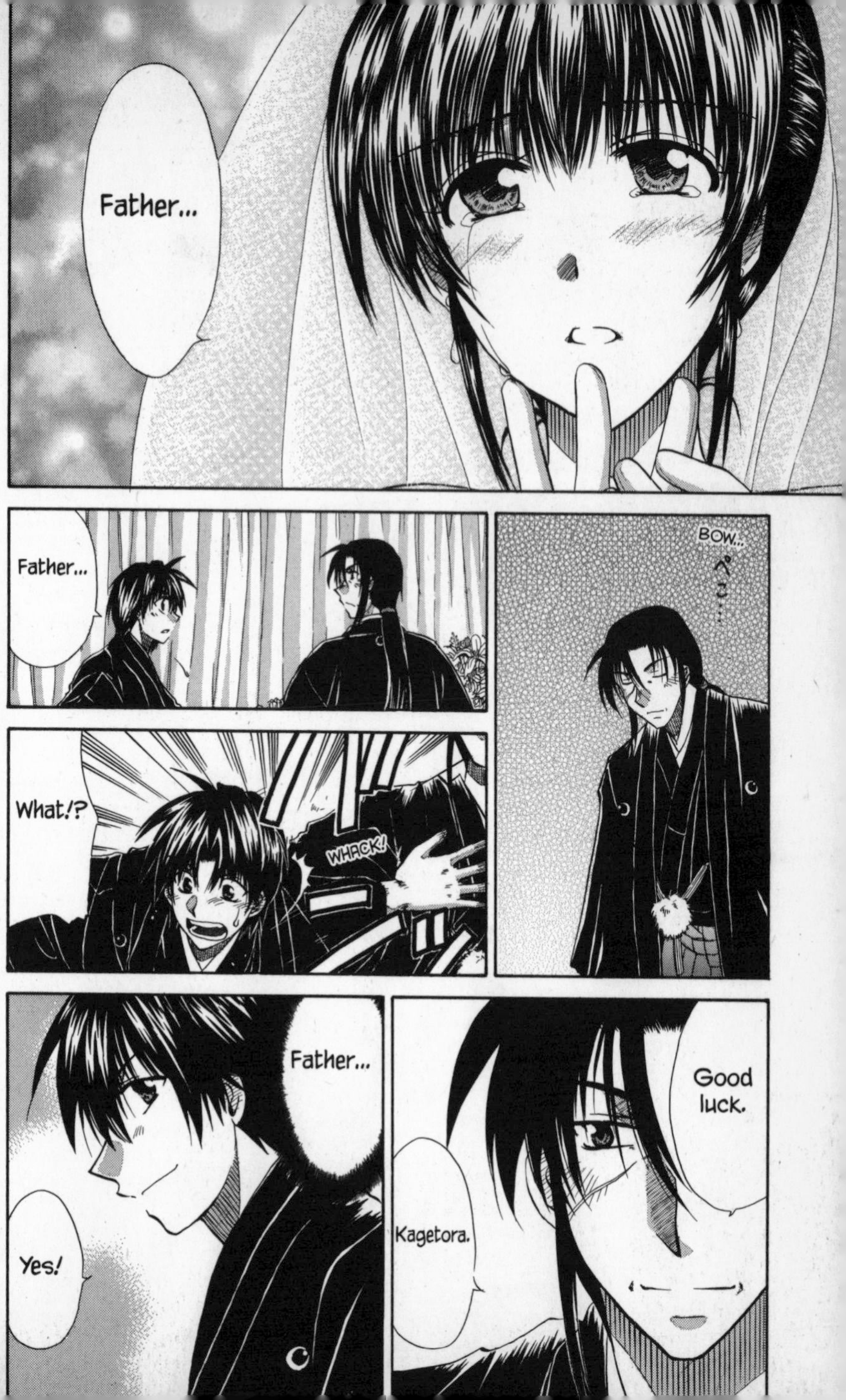
Father...
BOW...
ぺこ...
Father...
What!?
WHACK!
Good luck.
Kagetora.
Father...
Yes!

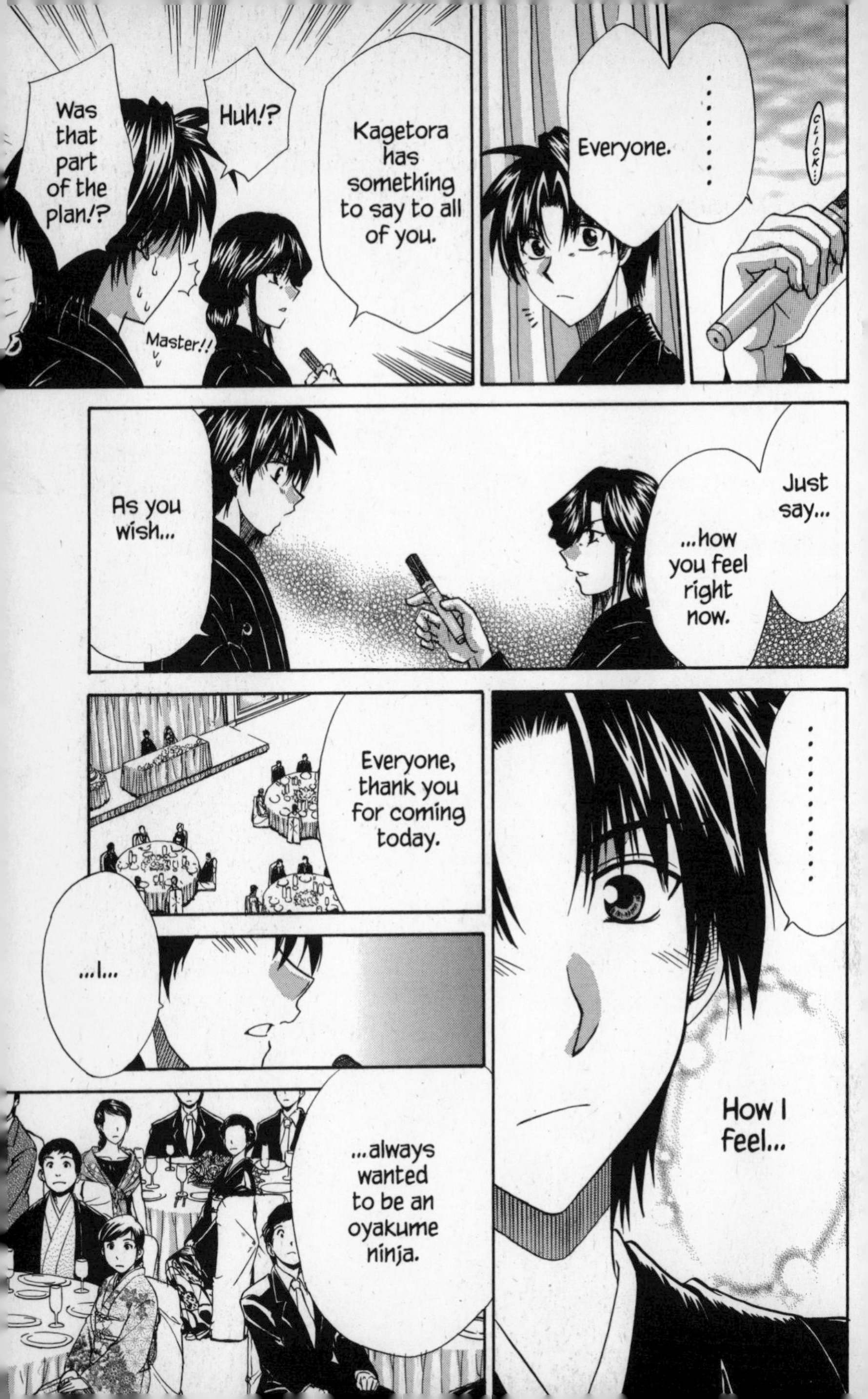
CLICK...
......
Everyone.
Kagetora has something to say to all of you.
Huh!?
Was that part of the plan!?
Master!!
Just say...
...how you feel right now.
As you wish...
....
How I feel...
Everyone, thank you for coming today.
...I...
...always wanted to be an oyakume ninja.

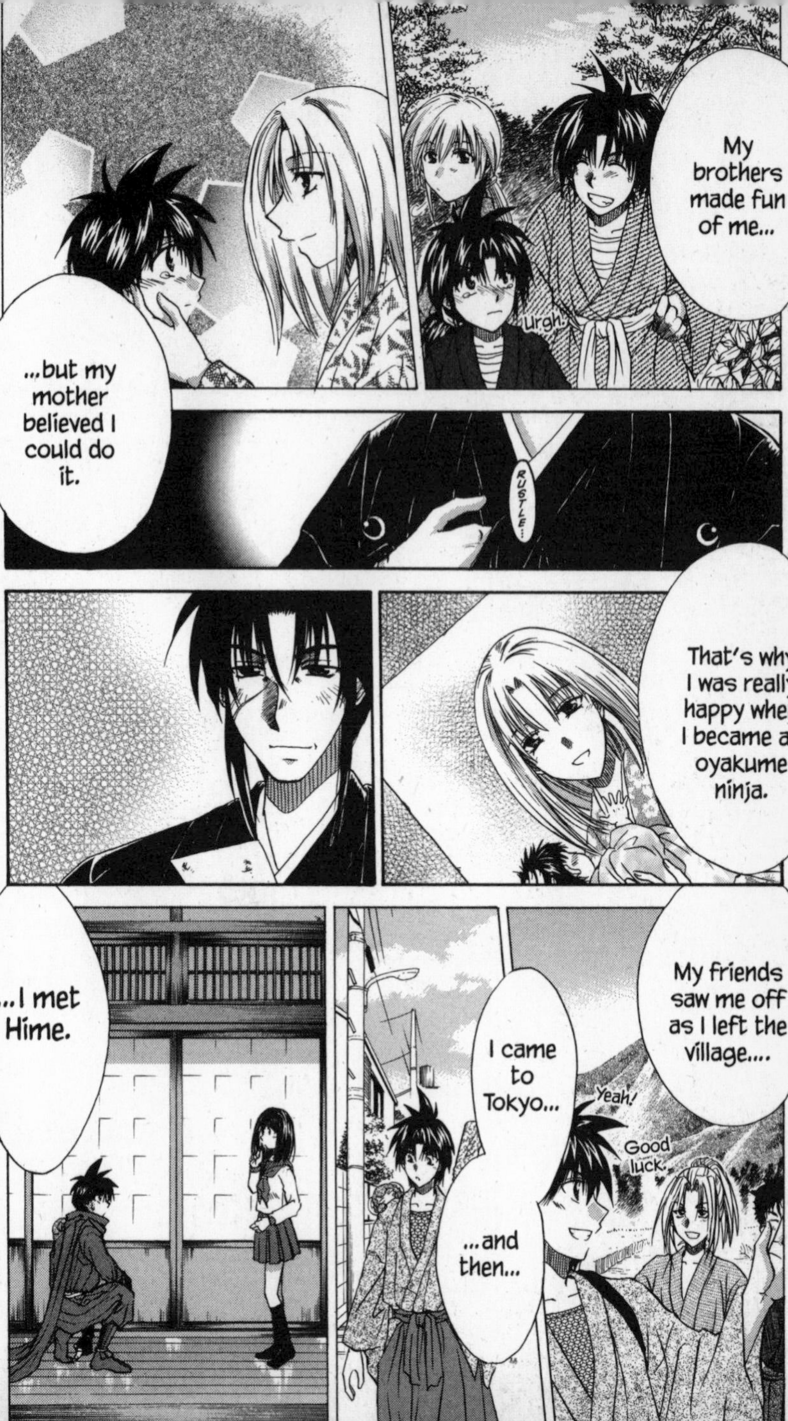
My brothers made fun of me...
Urgh!
...but my mother believed I could do it.
RUSTLE...
That's why I was really happy when I became an oyakume ninja.
My friends saw me off as I left the village....
Yeah!
Good luck.
I came to Tokyo...
...and then...
...I met Hime.

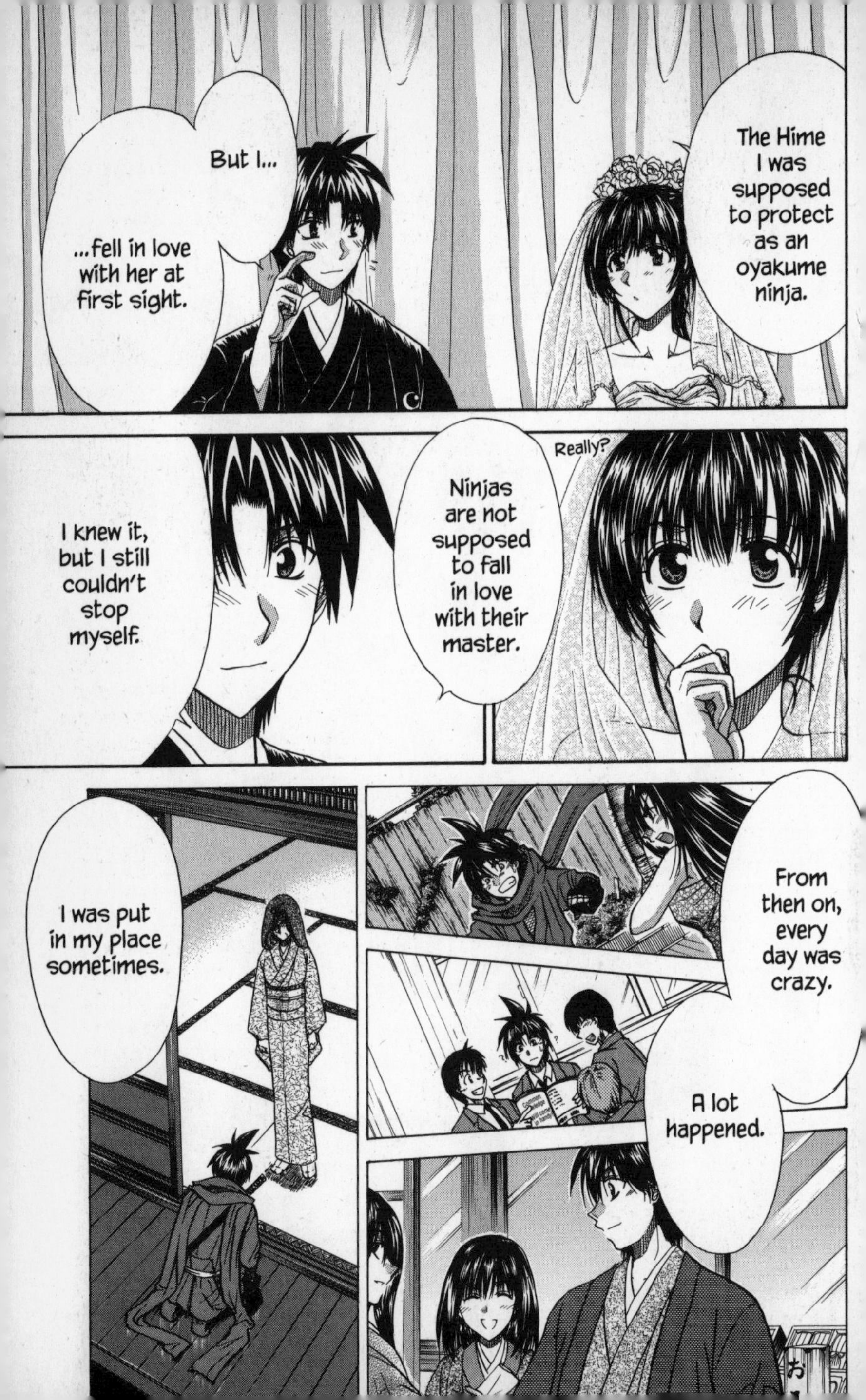
The Hime I was supposed to protect as an oyakume ninja.
But I...
...fell in love with her at first sight.
Really?
Ninjas are not supposed to fall in love with their master.
I knew it, but I still couldn't stop myself.
From then on, every day was crazy.
A lot happened.
I was put in my place sometimes.

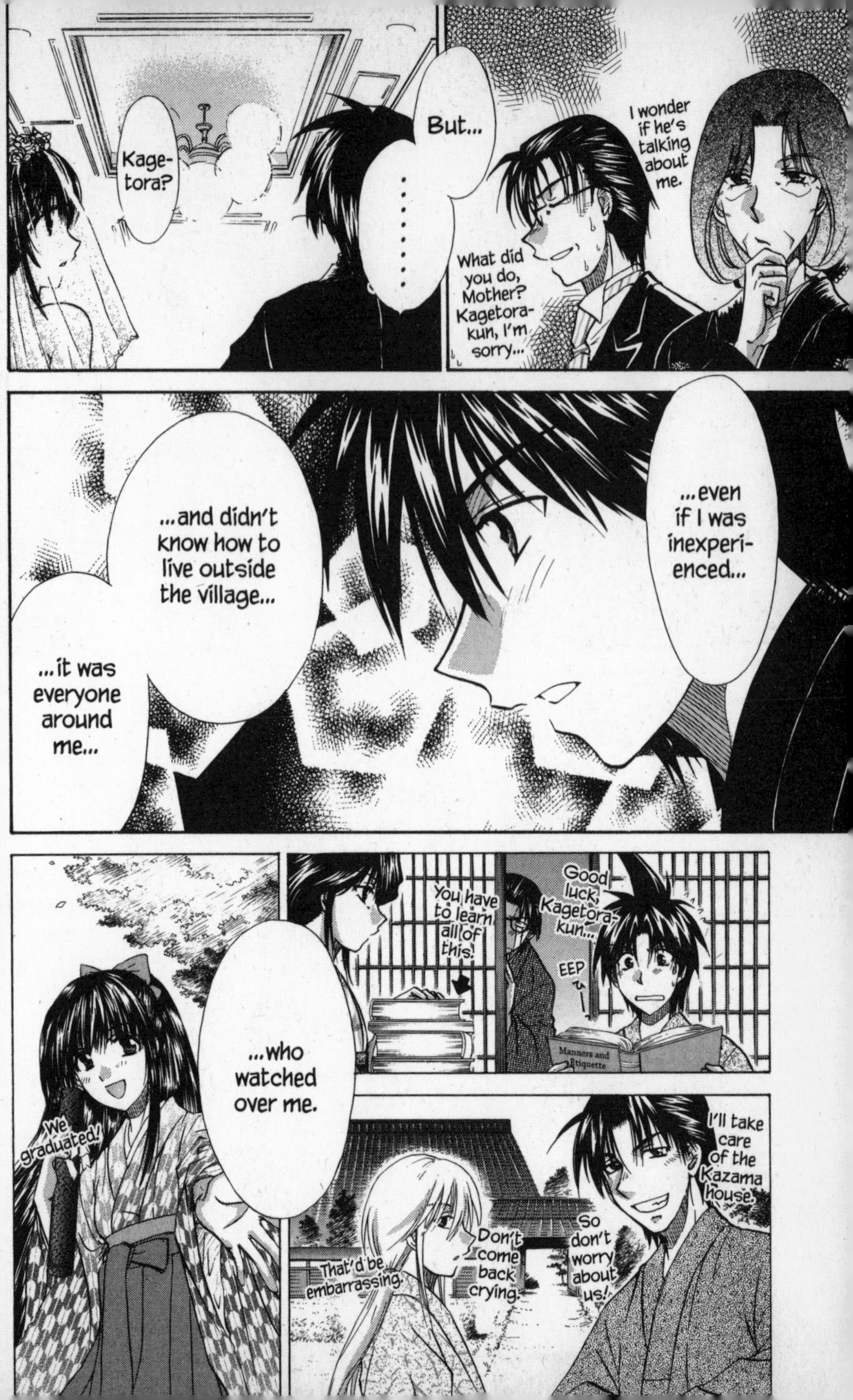
I wonder if he's talking about me.
What did you do, Mother? Kagetora-kun, I'm sorry...
But...
......
Kage-tora?
...even if I was inexperi-enced...
...and didn't know how to live outside the village...
...it was everyone around me...
Good luck, Kagetora-kun...
You have to learn all of this!
EEP
Manners and Etiquette
I'll take care of the Kazama house.
So don't worry about us!
Don't come back crying.
That'd be embarrassing.
...who watched over me.
We graduated!

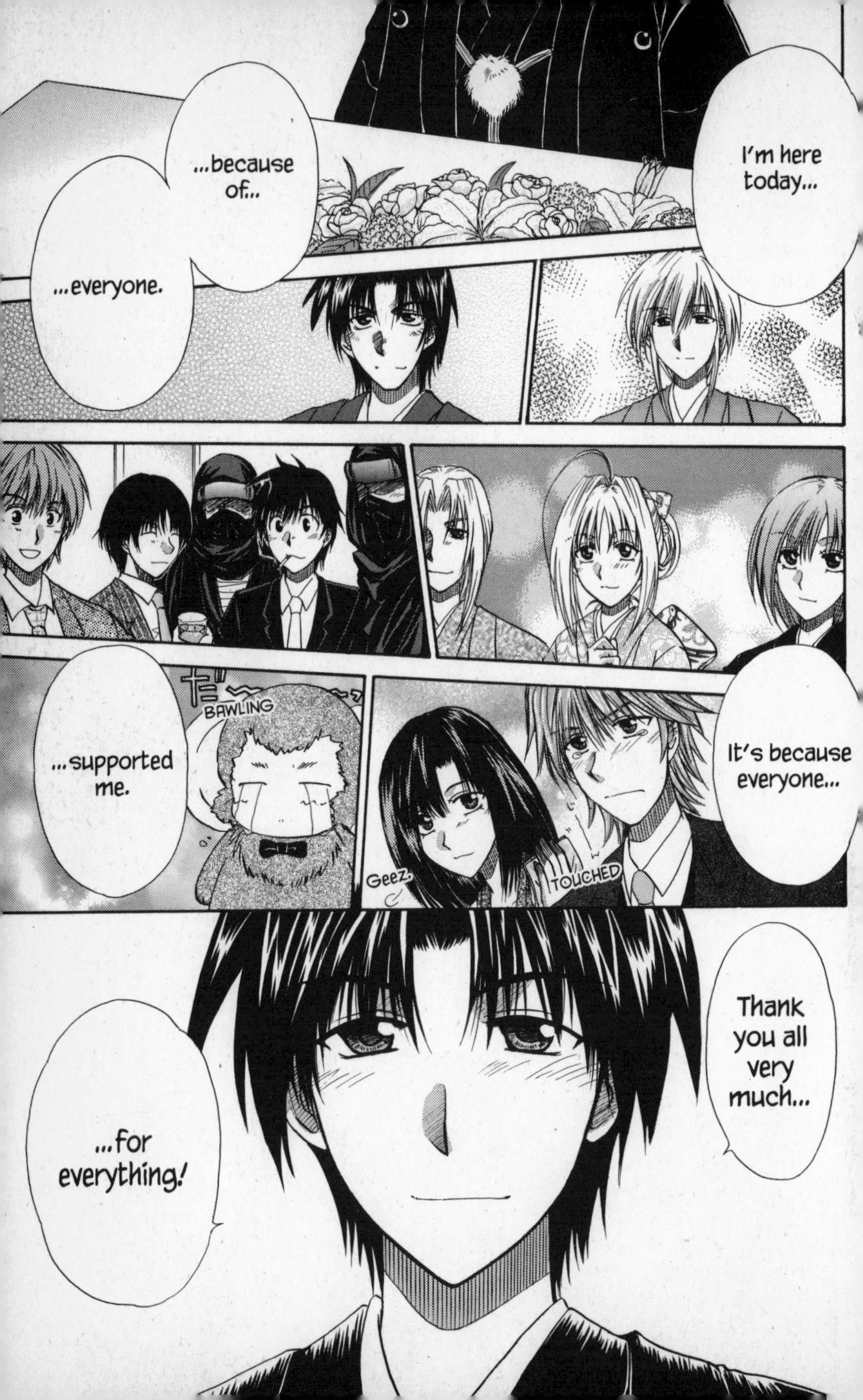
I'm here today...
...because of...
...everyone.
It's because everyone...
TOUCHED
Geez.
BAWLING
...supported me.
Thank you all very much...
...for everything!

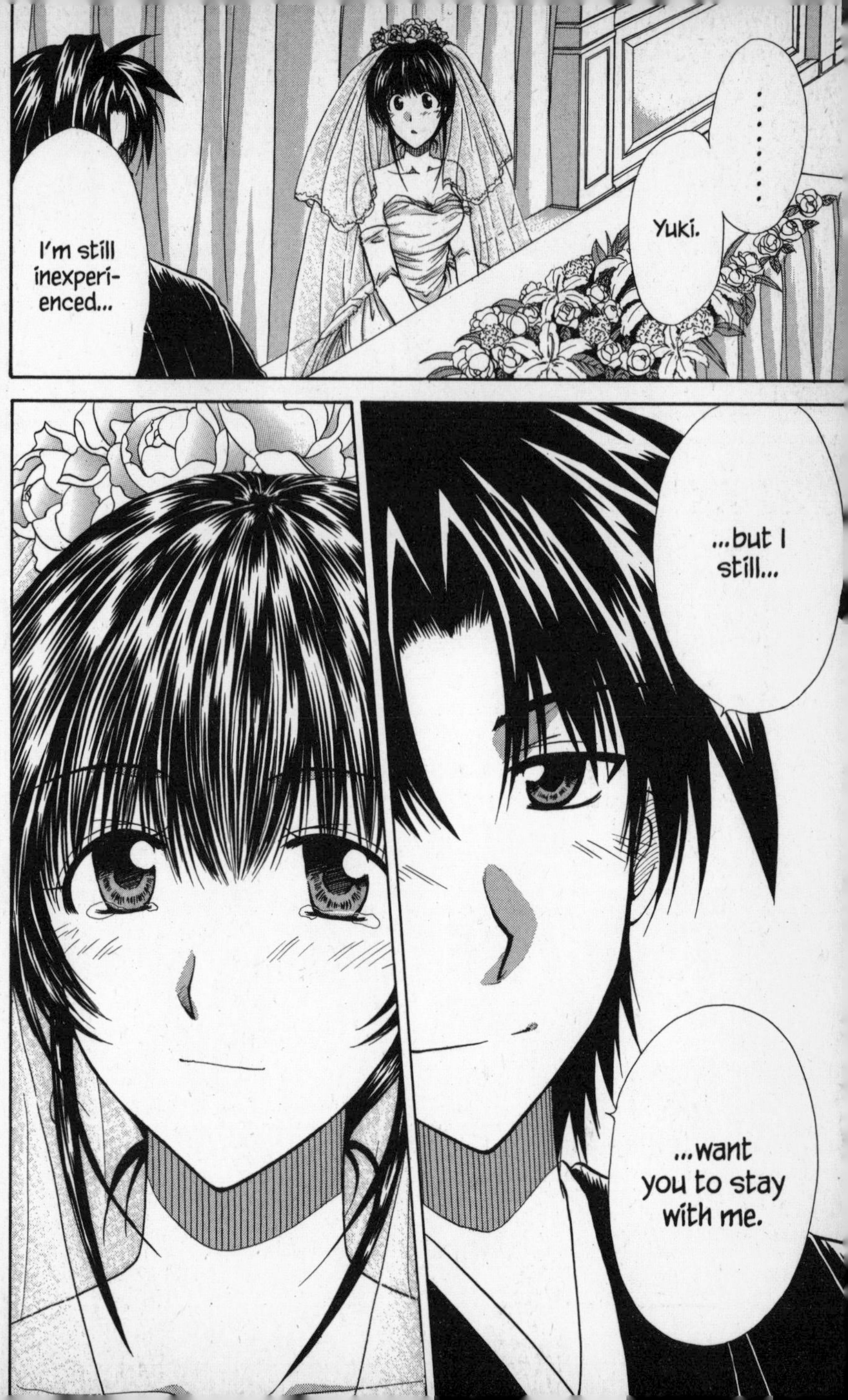
......
Yuki.
I'm still inexperienced...
...but I still...
...want you to stay with me.

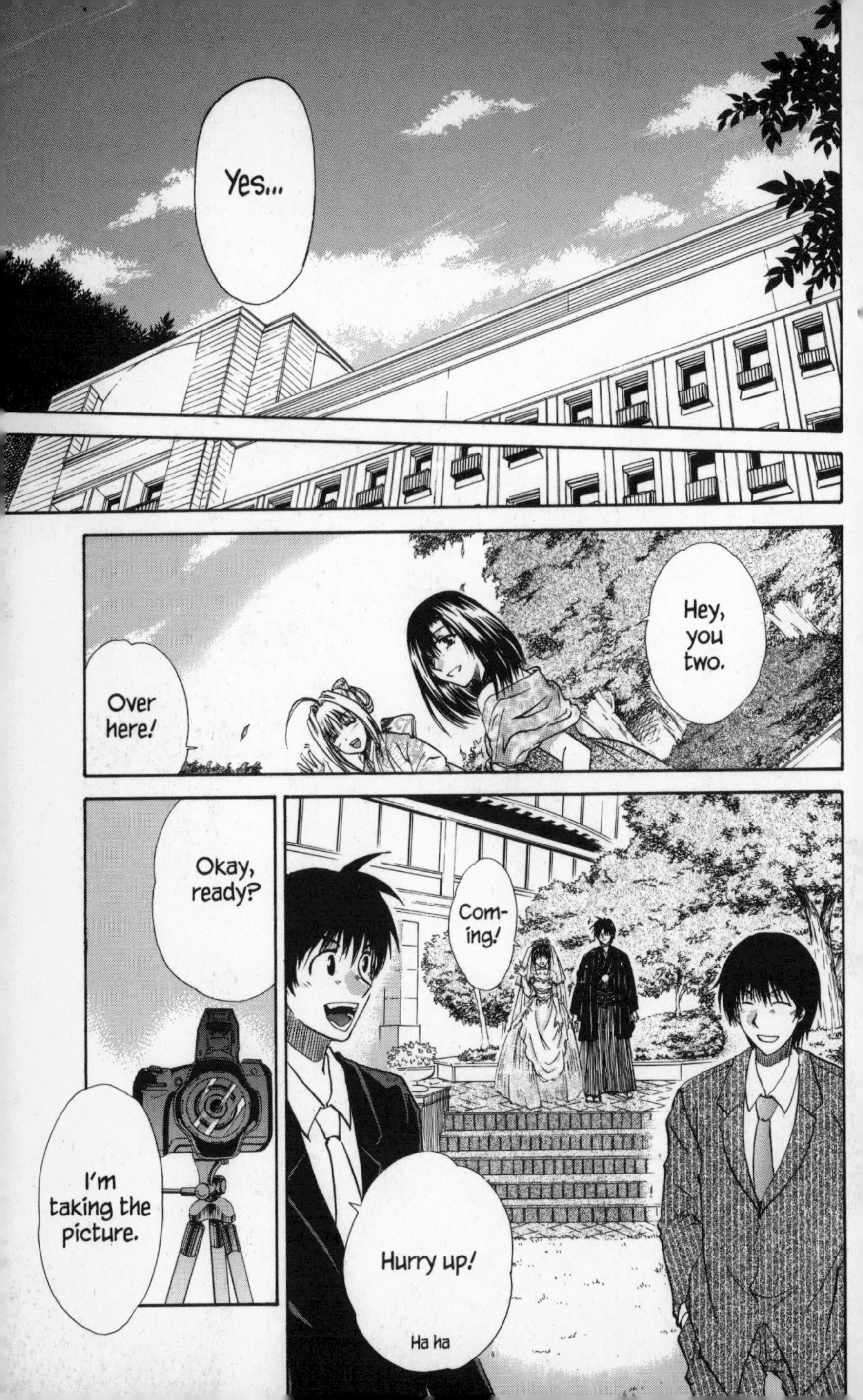
Yes...
Hey, you two.
Over here!
Com-ing!
Hurry up!
Ha ha
Okay, ready?
I'm taking the picture.

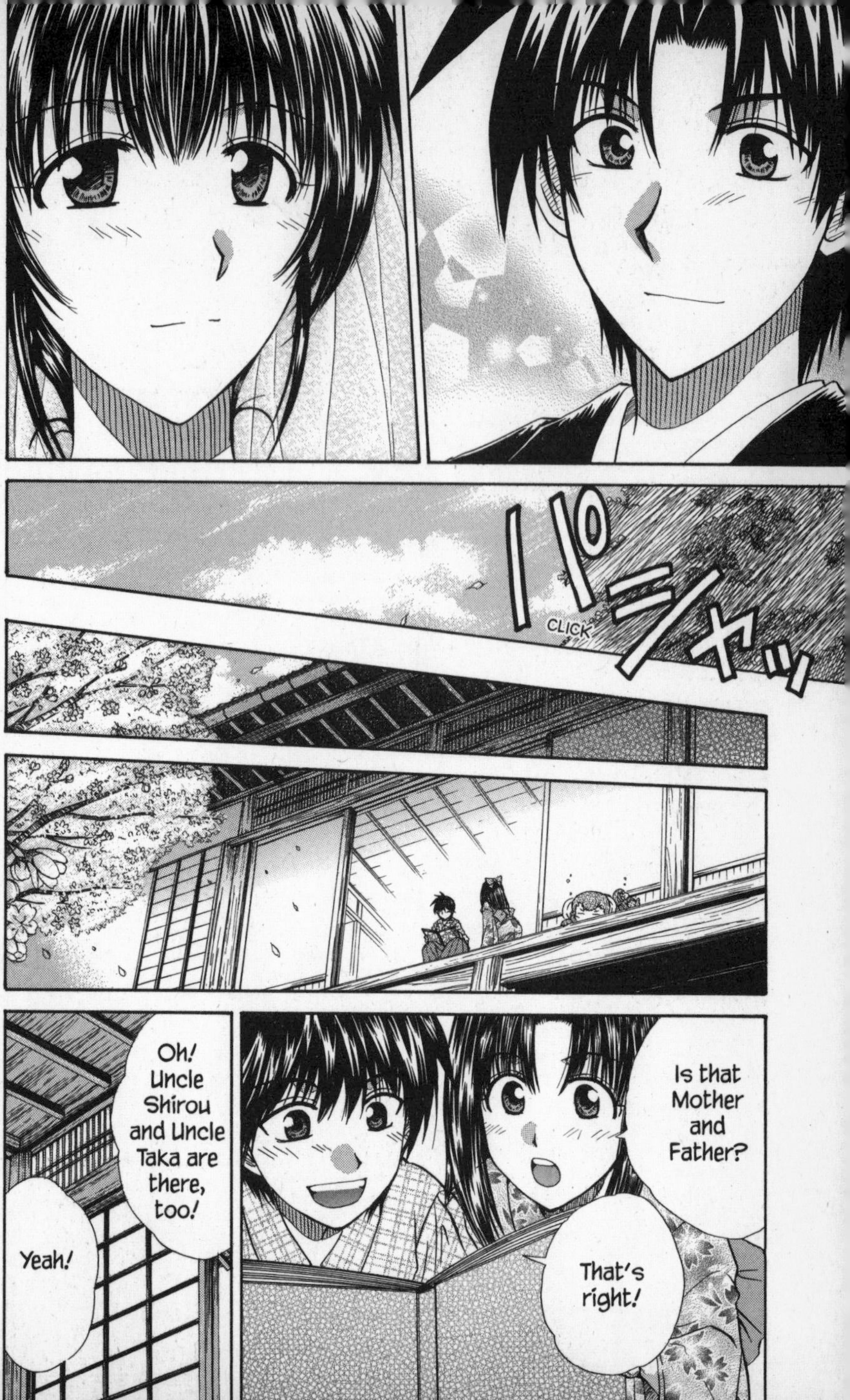

パシャッ
CLICK
Is that Mother and Father?
Oh! Uncle Shirou and Uncle Taka are there, too!
That's right!
Yeah!

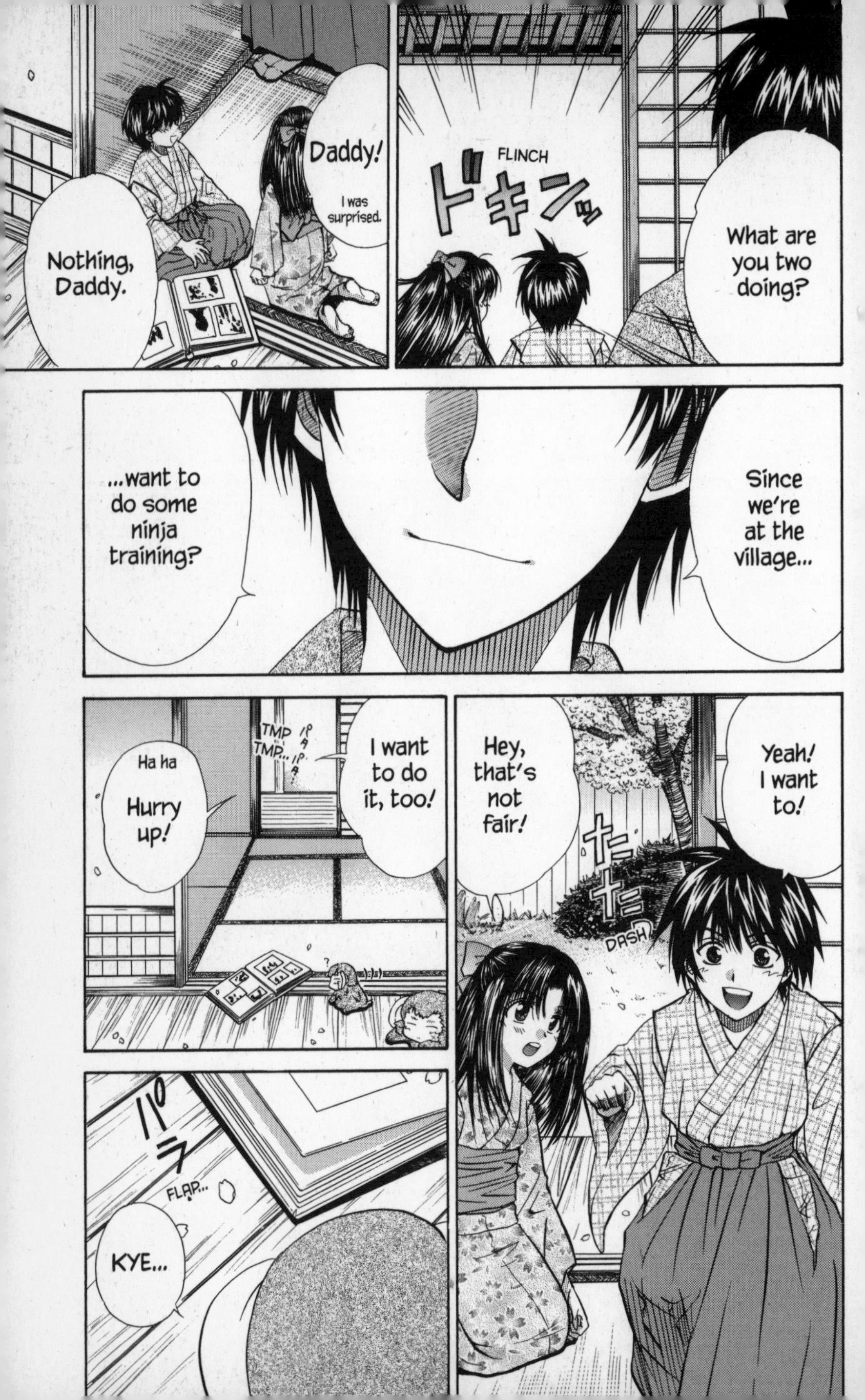
What are you two doing?
FLINCH
Daddy!
I was surprised.
Nothing, Daddy.
Since we're at the village...
...want to do some ninja training?
Yeah! I want to!
Hey, that's not fair!
DASH
I want to do it, too!
TMP TMP...
Ha ha
Hurry up!
FLAP...
KYE...

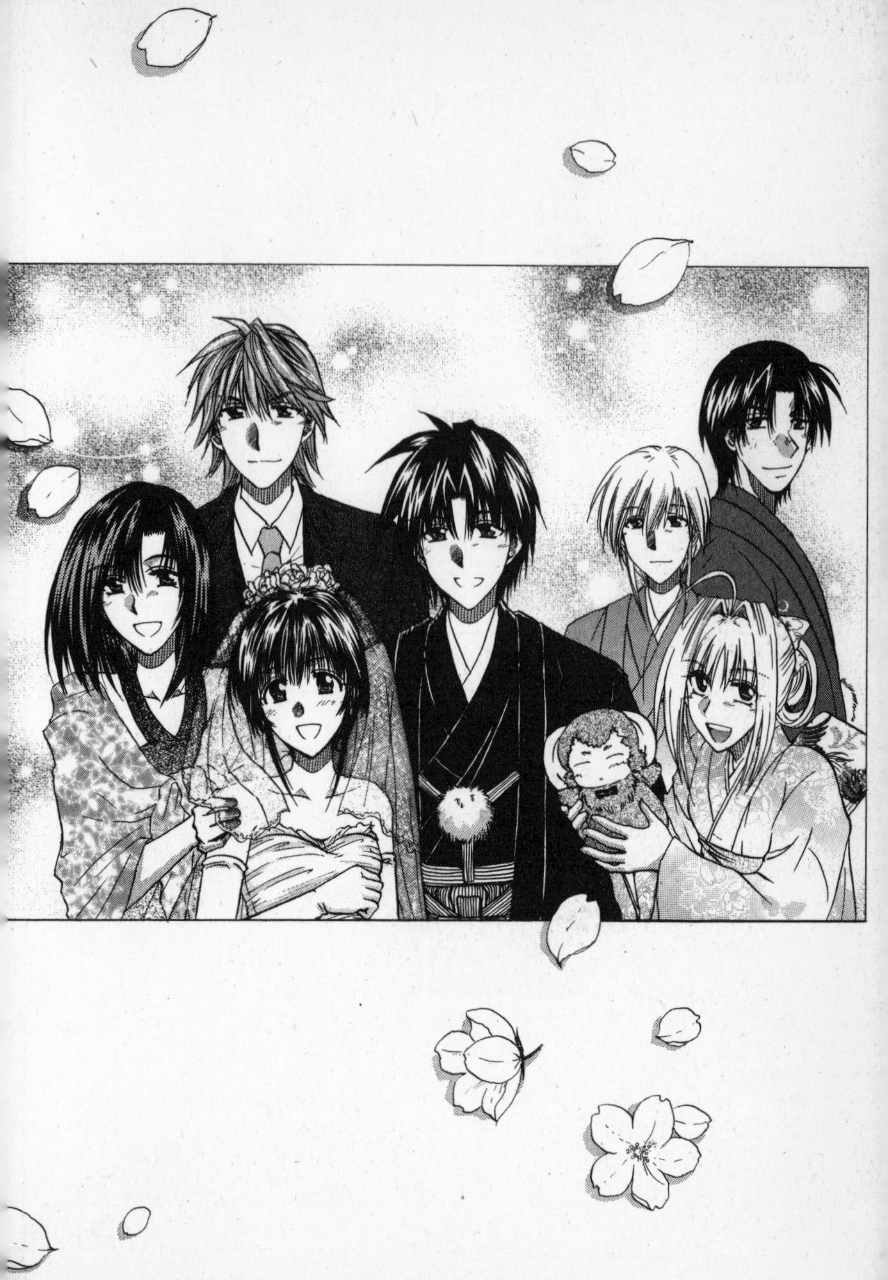

☆ The End ☆

This ends KAGETORA.
The following short story is the beta version I wrote before we started the KAGETORA series.
It's horrible (laugh) but if you can enjoy it, that would be great.
Kagetora is fine, but Yuki is pretty different... [face]

Segami

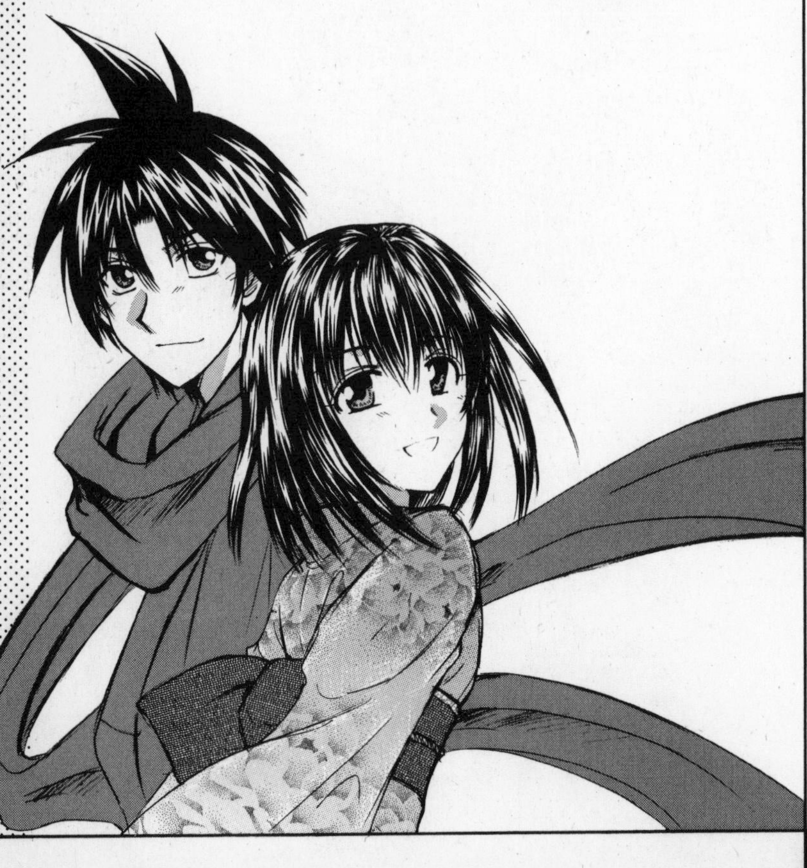

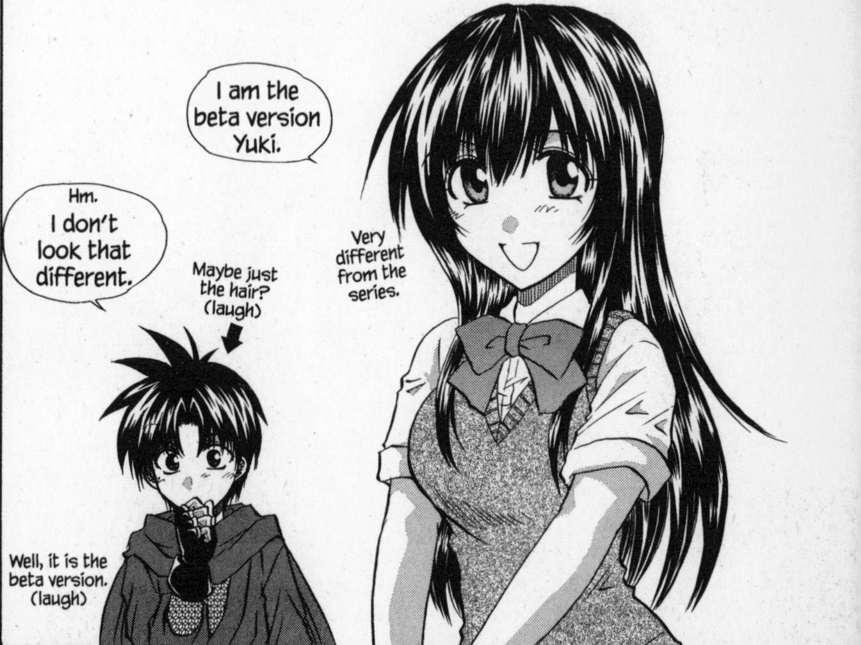
I am the beta version Yuki.
Very different from the series.
Maybe just the hair? (laugh)
Hm. I don't look that different.
Well, it is the beta version. (laugh)

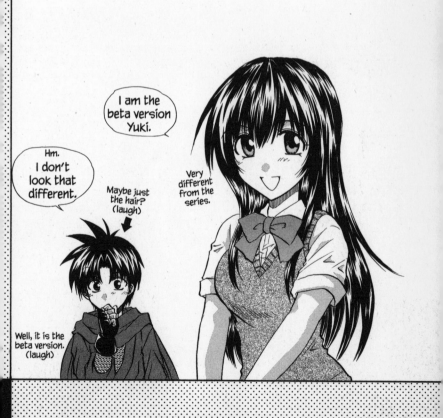

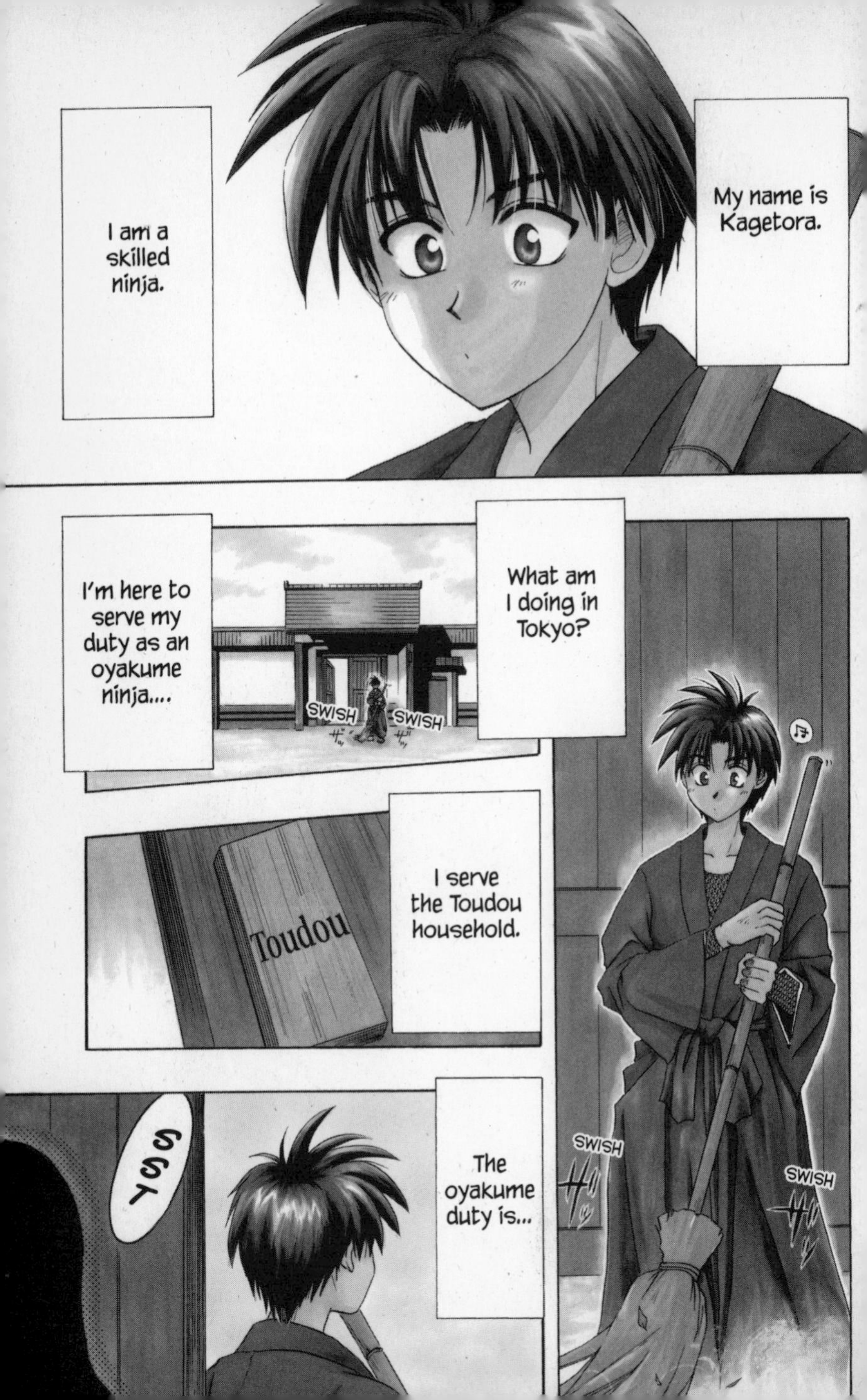
My name is Kagetora.
I am a skilled ninja.
What am I doing in Tokyo?
SWISH
SWISH
I'm here to serve my duty as an oyakume ninja....
SWISH
SWISH
Toudou
I serve the Toudou household.
The oyakume duty is...
SSST

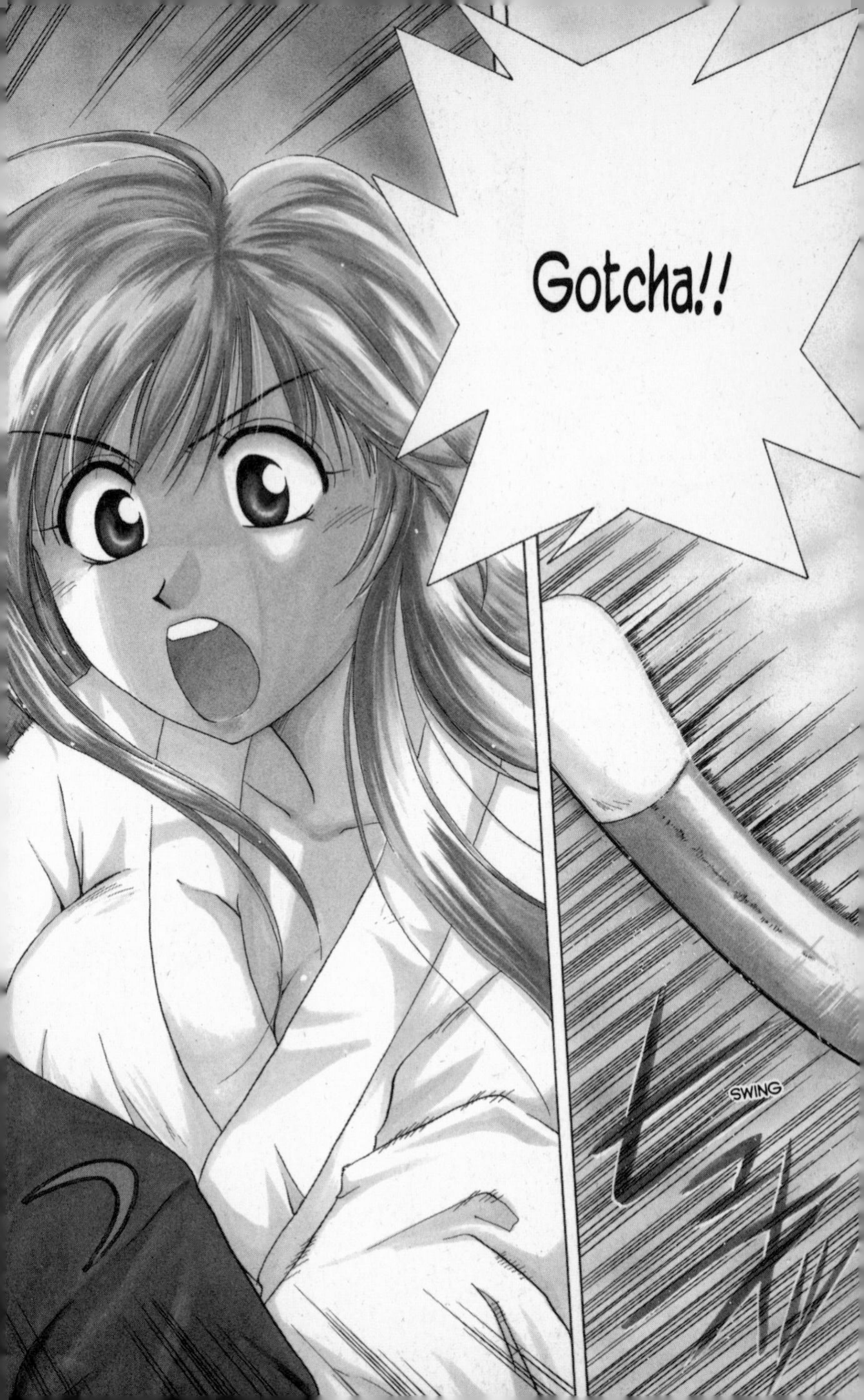
Gotcha!!
SWING

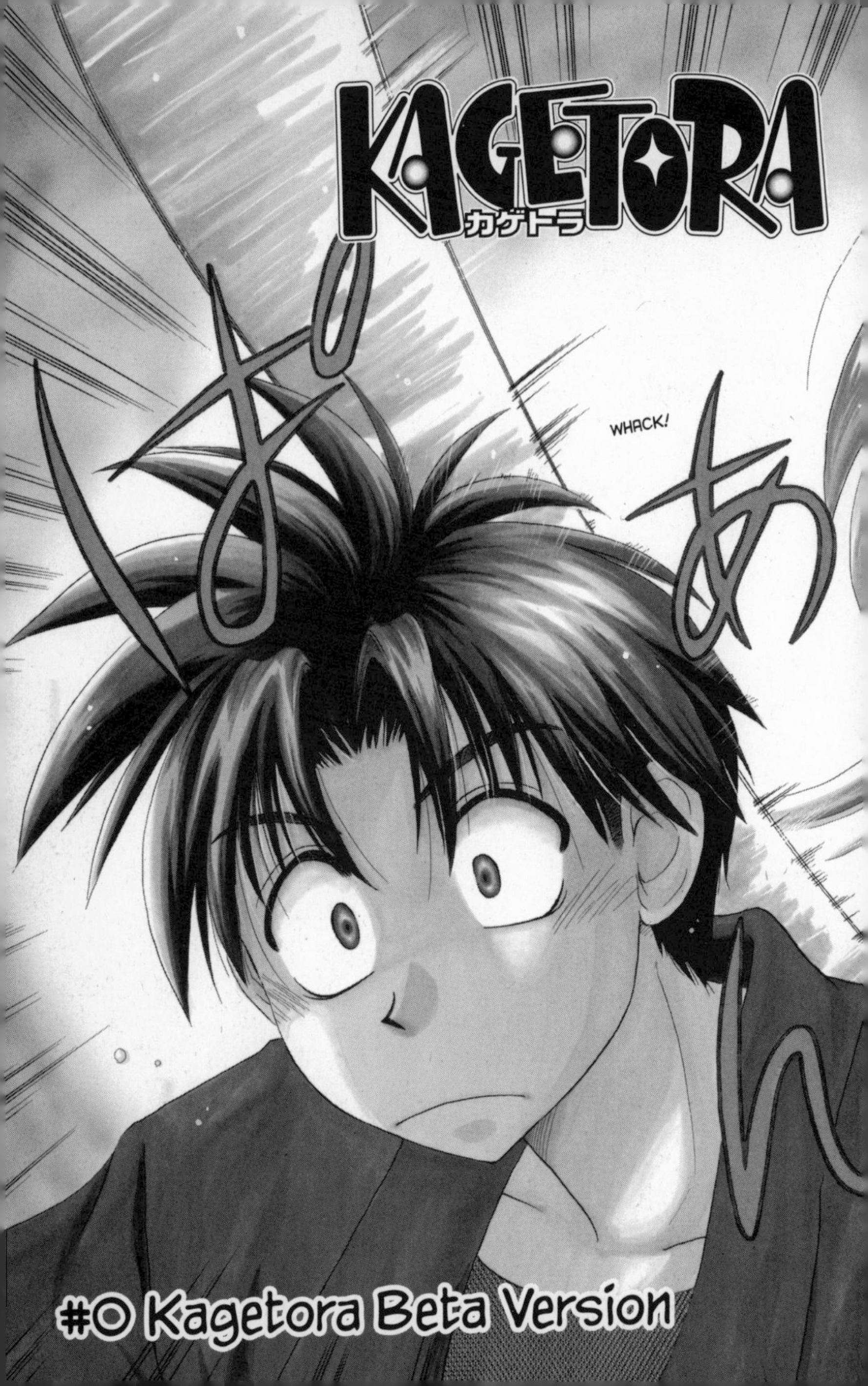
KAGETORA
カゲトラ
WHACK!
#0 Kagetora Beta Version

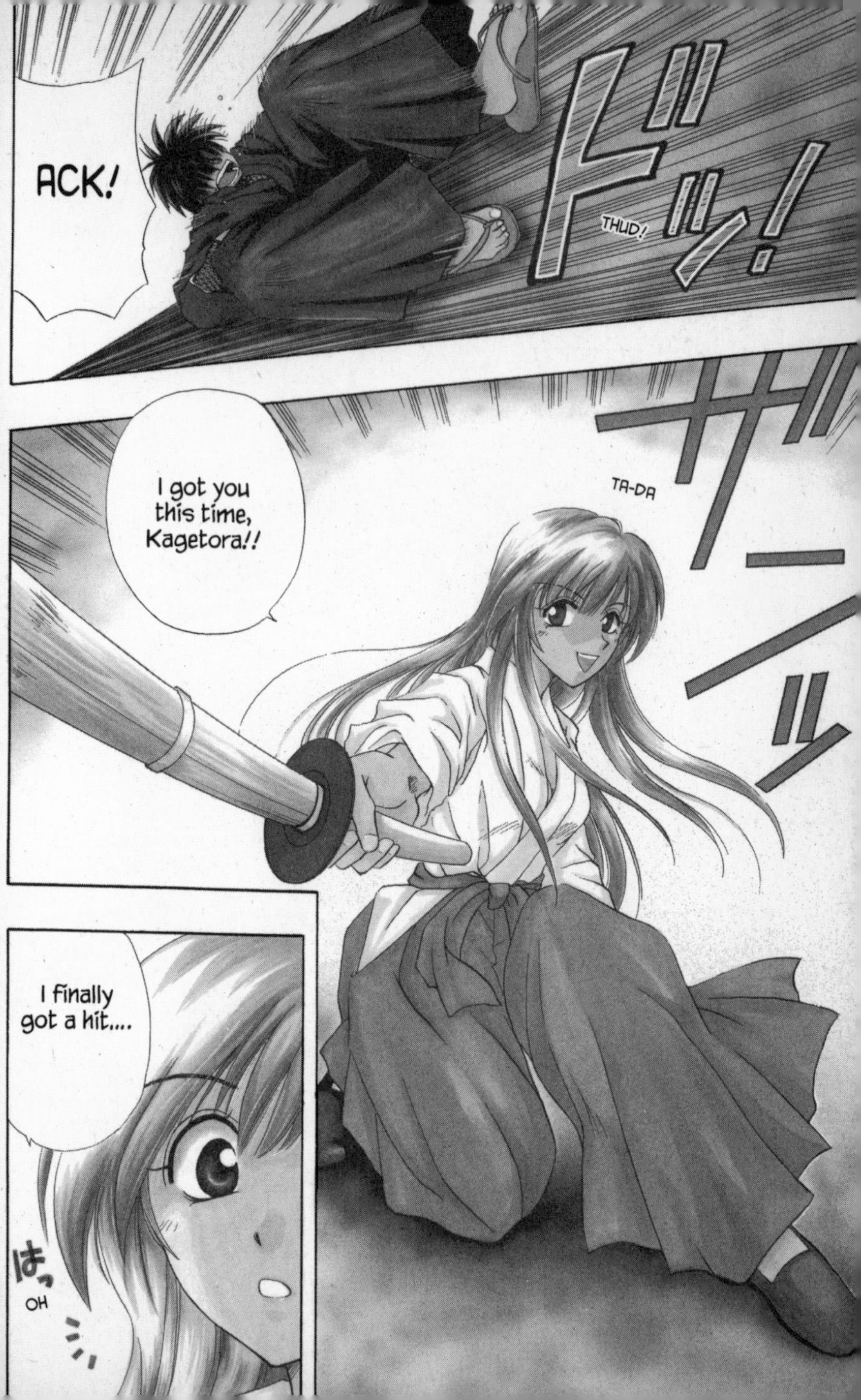
ドッ!
THUD!
ACK!
ザーッ
TA-DA
I got you this time, Kagetora!!
I finally got a hit....
はっ
OH

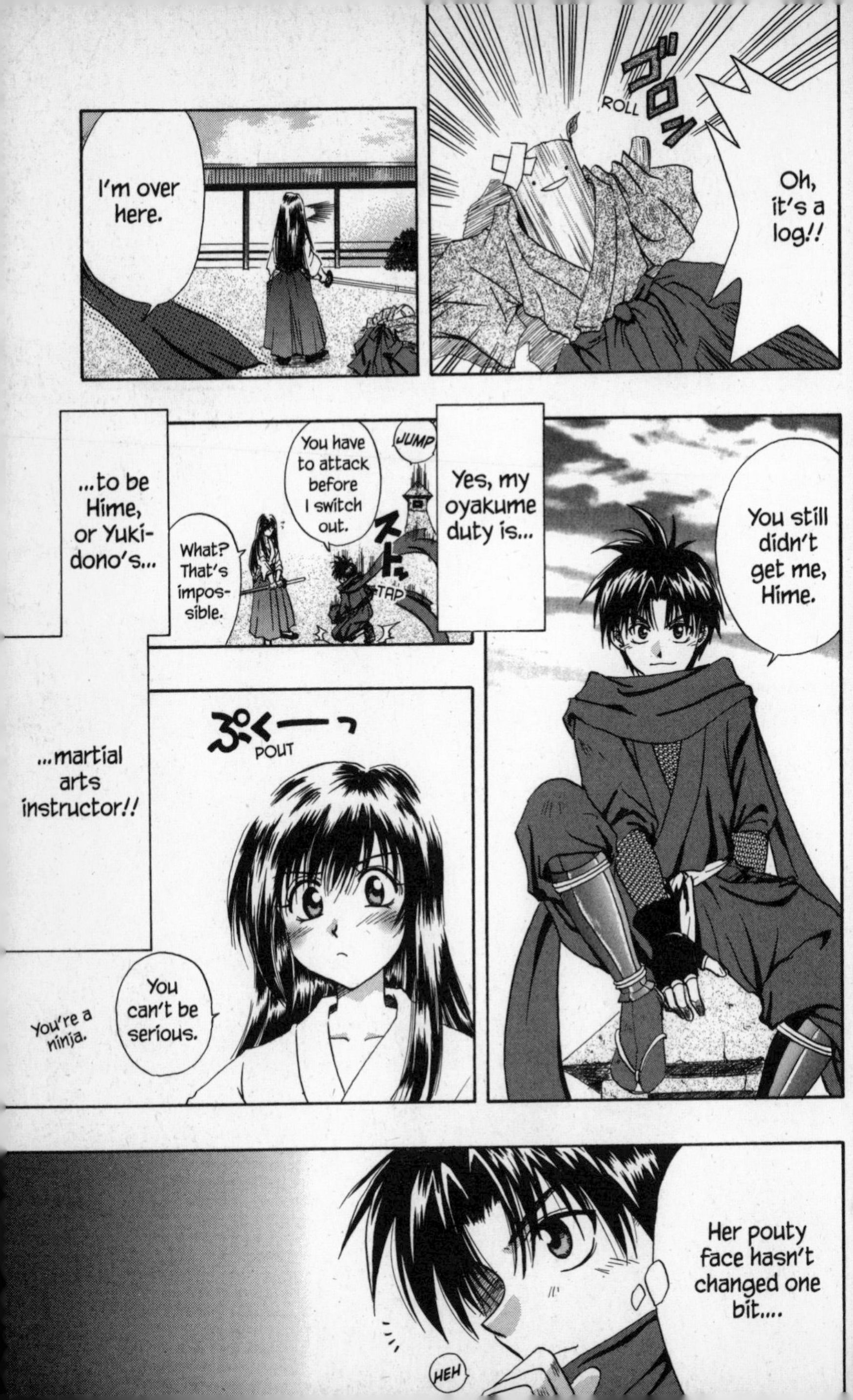
ゴロッ
ROLL
Oh, it's a log!!
I'm over here.
You still didn't get me, Hime.
Yes, my oyakume duty is...
JUMP
You have to attack before I switch out.
ストッ
TAP
What? That's impossible.
...to be Hime, or Yuki-dono's...
ぷくーっ
POUT
...martial arts instructor!!
You can't be serious.
You're a ninja.
Her pouty face hasn't changed one bit....
HEH

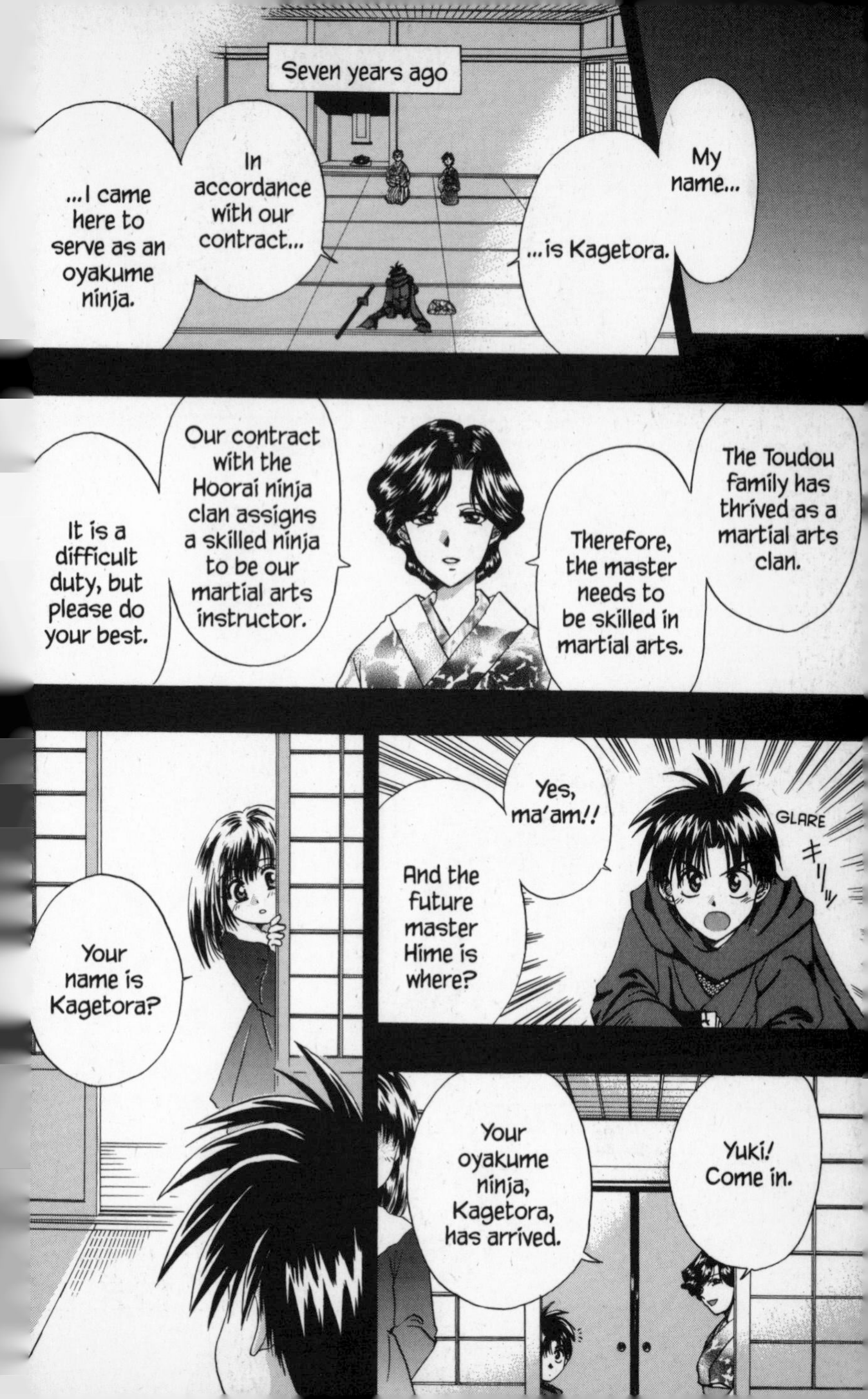
Seven years ago
My name...
...is Kagetora.
In accordance with our contract...
...I came here to serve as an oyakume ninja.
The Toudou family has thrived as a martial arts clan.
Therefore, the master needs to be skilled in martial arts.
Our contract with the Hoorai ninja clan assigns a skilled ninja to be our martial arts instructor.
It is a difficult duty, but please do your best.
Yes, ma'am!!
GLARE
キリッ
And the future master Hime is where?
Yuki! Come in.
Your oyakume ninja, Kagetora, has arrived.
Your name is Kagetora?

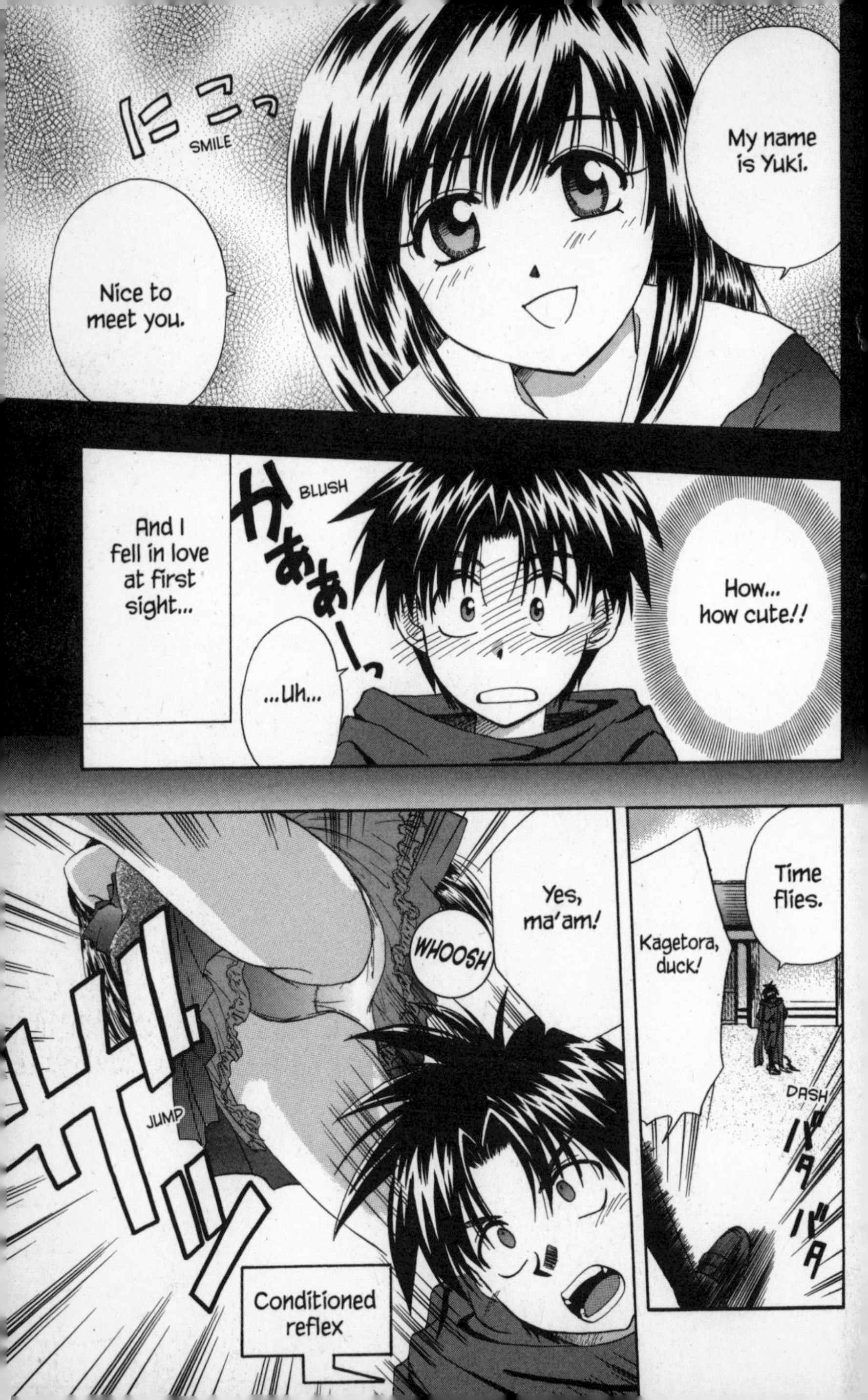
My name is Yuki.
にこっ
SMILE
Nice to meet you.
How... how cute!!
かあぁーっ
BLUSH
...uh...
And I fell in love at first sight...
Time flies.
Kagetora, duck!
DASH
パタパタ
Yes, ma'am!
WHOOSH
JUMP
Conditioned reflex

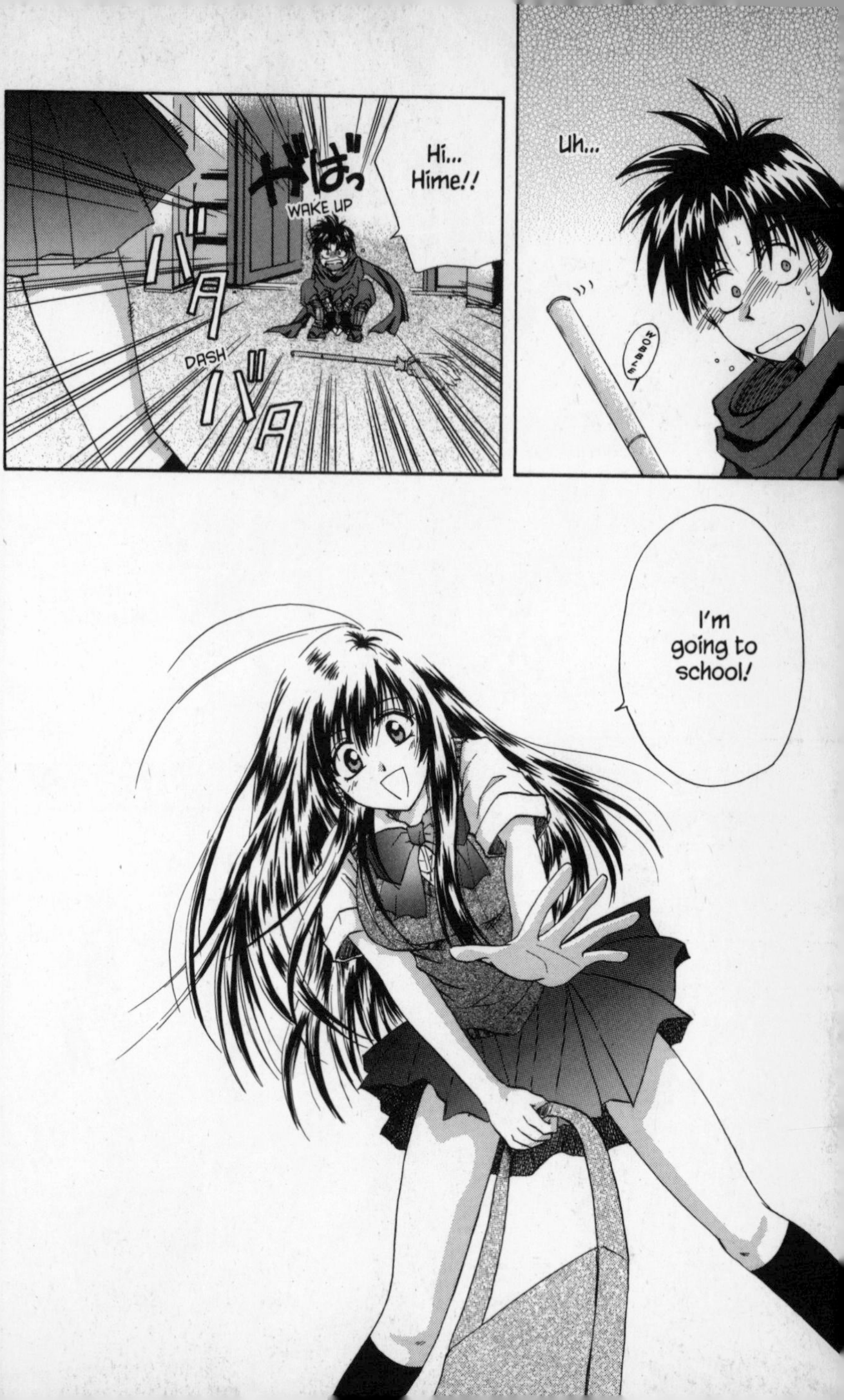
Uh...
WOBBLE
Hi... Hime!!
WAKE UP
DASH
I'm going to school!

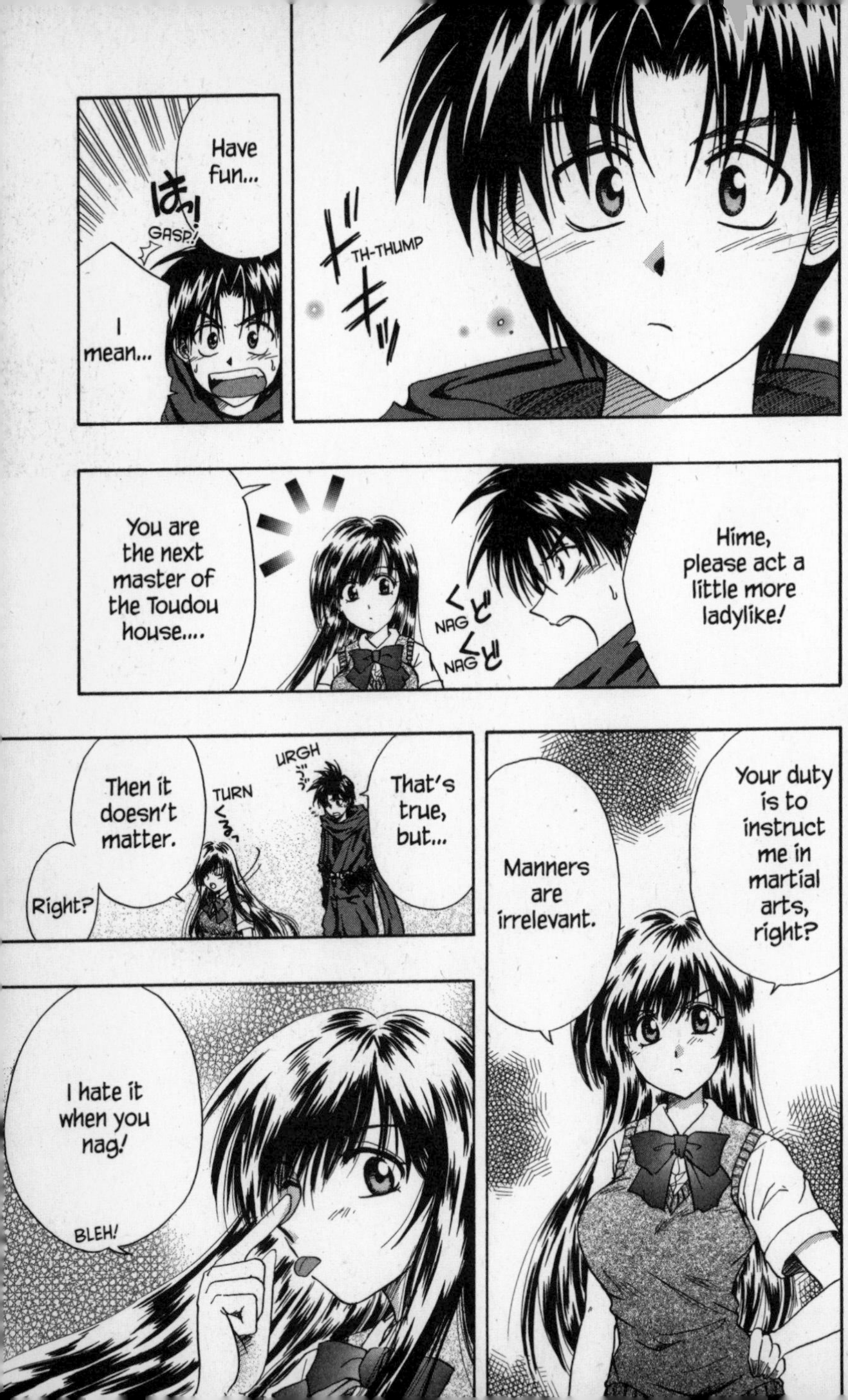
ドキッ
TH-THUMP
Have fun...
はっ!
GASP!
I mean...
Hime, please act a little more ladylike!
くど くど
NAG NAG
You are the next master of the Toudou house....
Your duty is to instruct me in martial arts, right?
Manners are irrelevant.
That's true, but...
URGH
TURN
Then it doesn't matter.
Right?
I hate it when you nag!
BLEH!

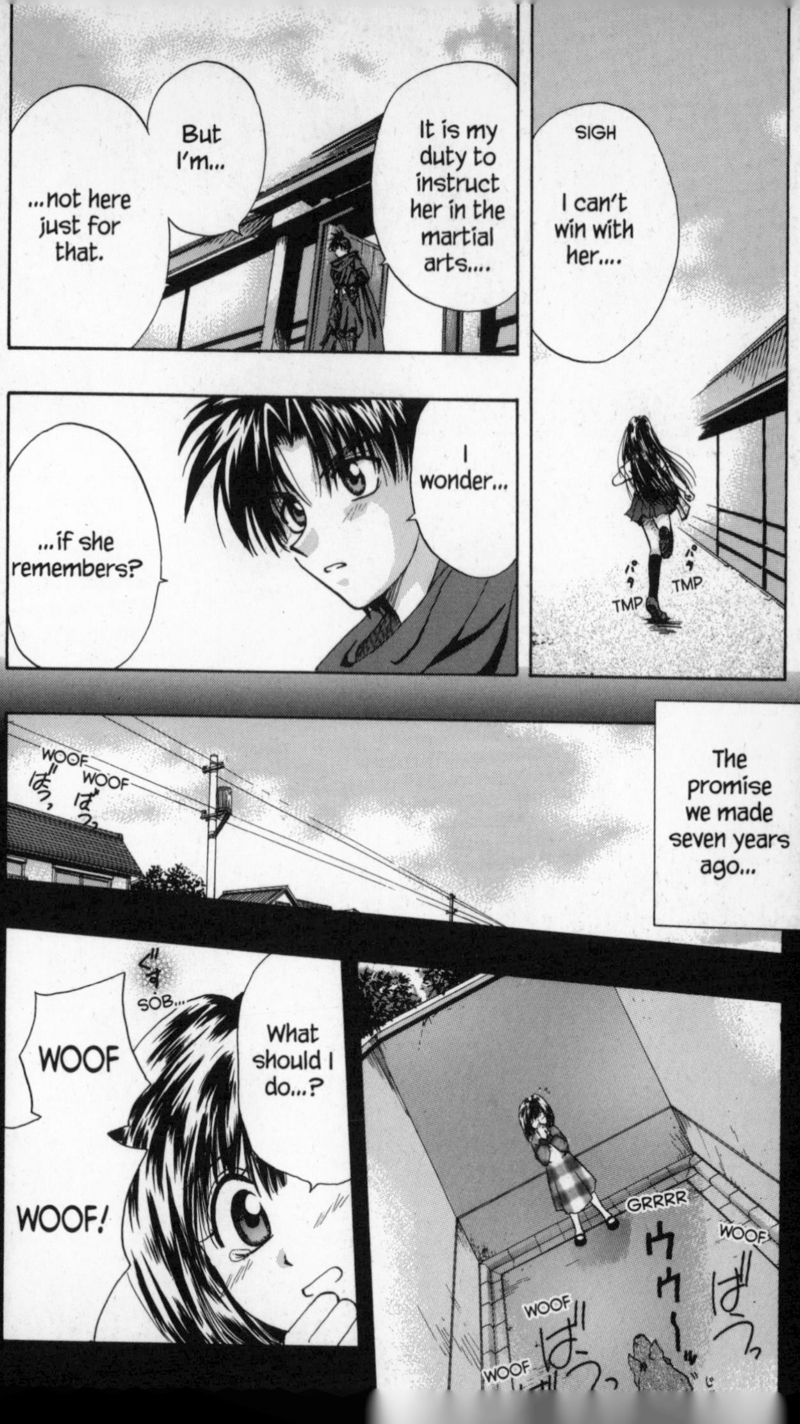
SIGH
I can't win with her....
TMP
TMP
It is my duty to instruct her in the martial arts....
But I'm...
...not here just for that.
I wonder...
...if she remembers?
The promise we made seven years ago...
WOOF
WOOF
GRRRR
WOOF
WOOF
WOOF
SOB...
What should I do...?
WOOF
WOOF!

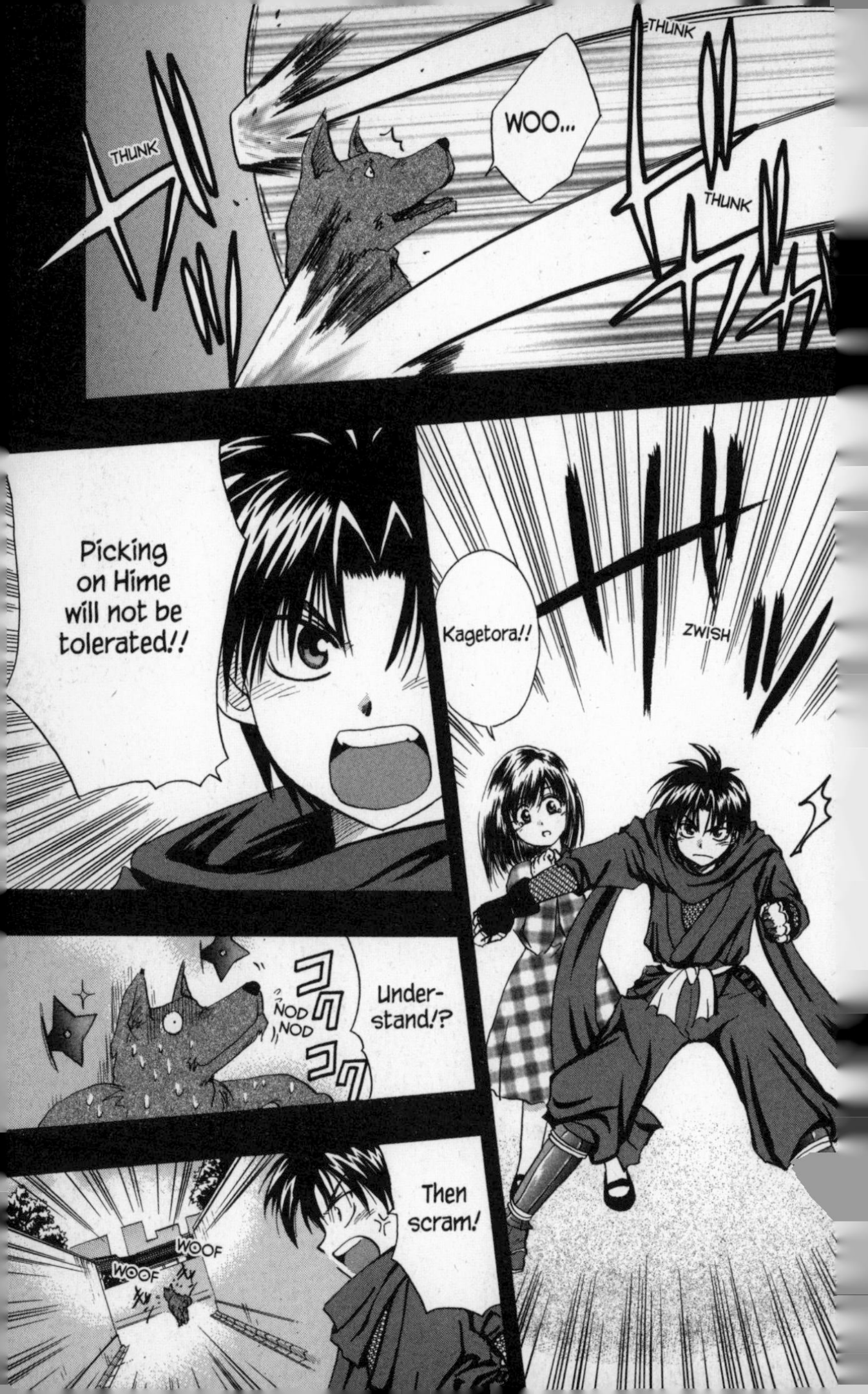
THUNK
WOO...
THUNK
THUNK
ZWISH
Kagetora!!
Picking on Hime will not be tolerated!!
Under-stand!?
NOD NOD
Then scram!
WOOF
WOOF

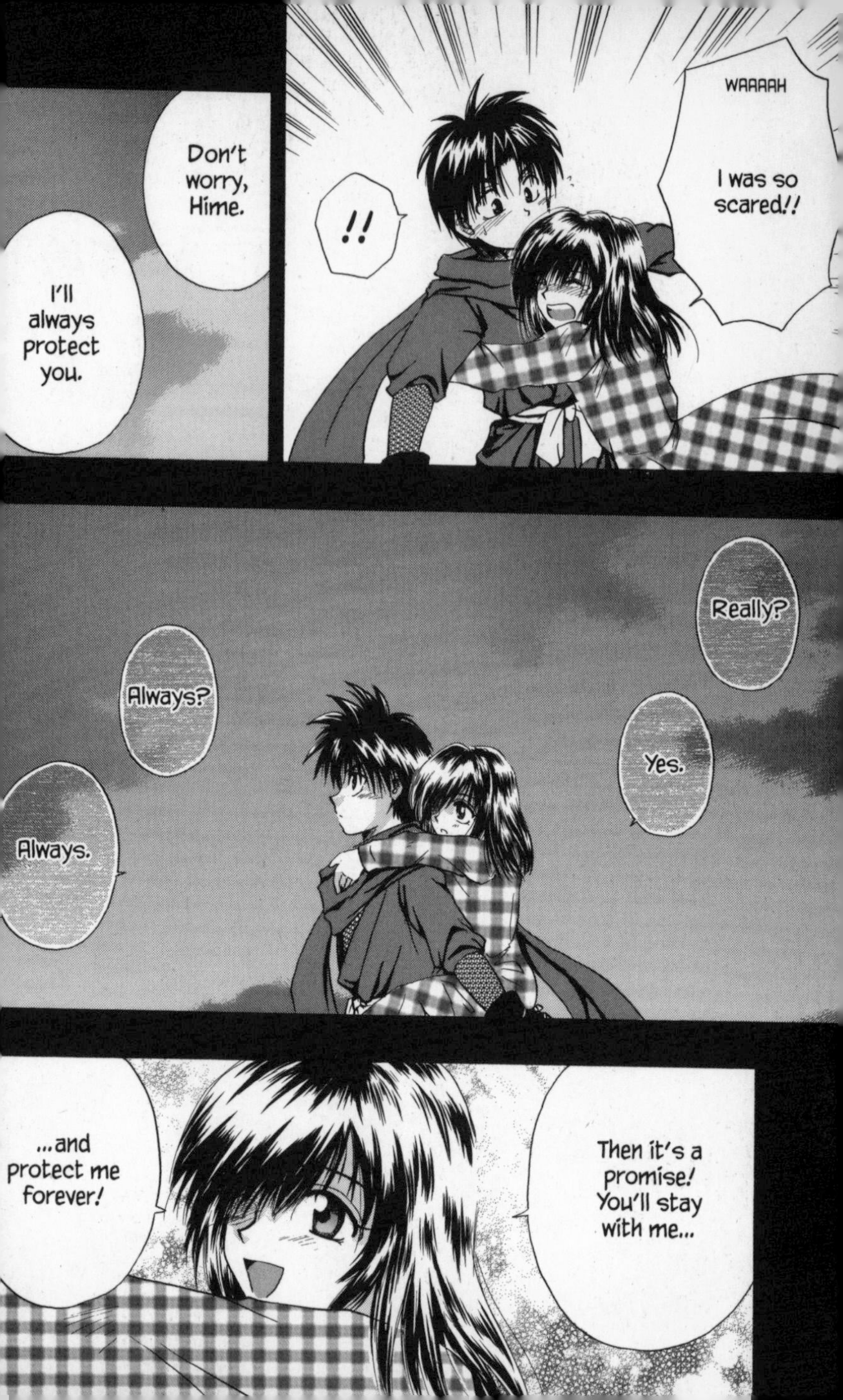
WAAAAH
I was so scared!!
!!
Don't worry, Hime.
I'll always protect you.
Really?
Yes.
Always?
Always.
Then it's a promise! You'll stay with me...
...and protect me forever!

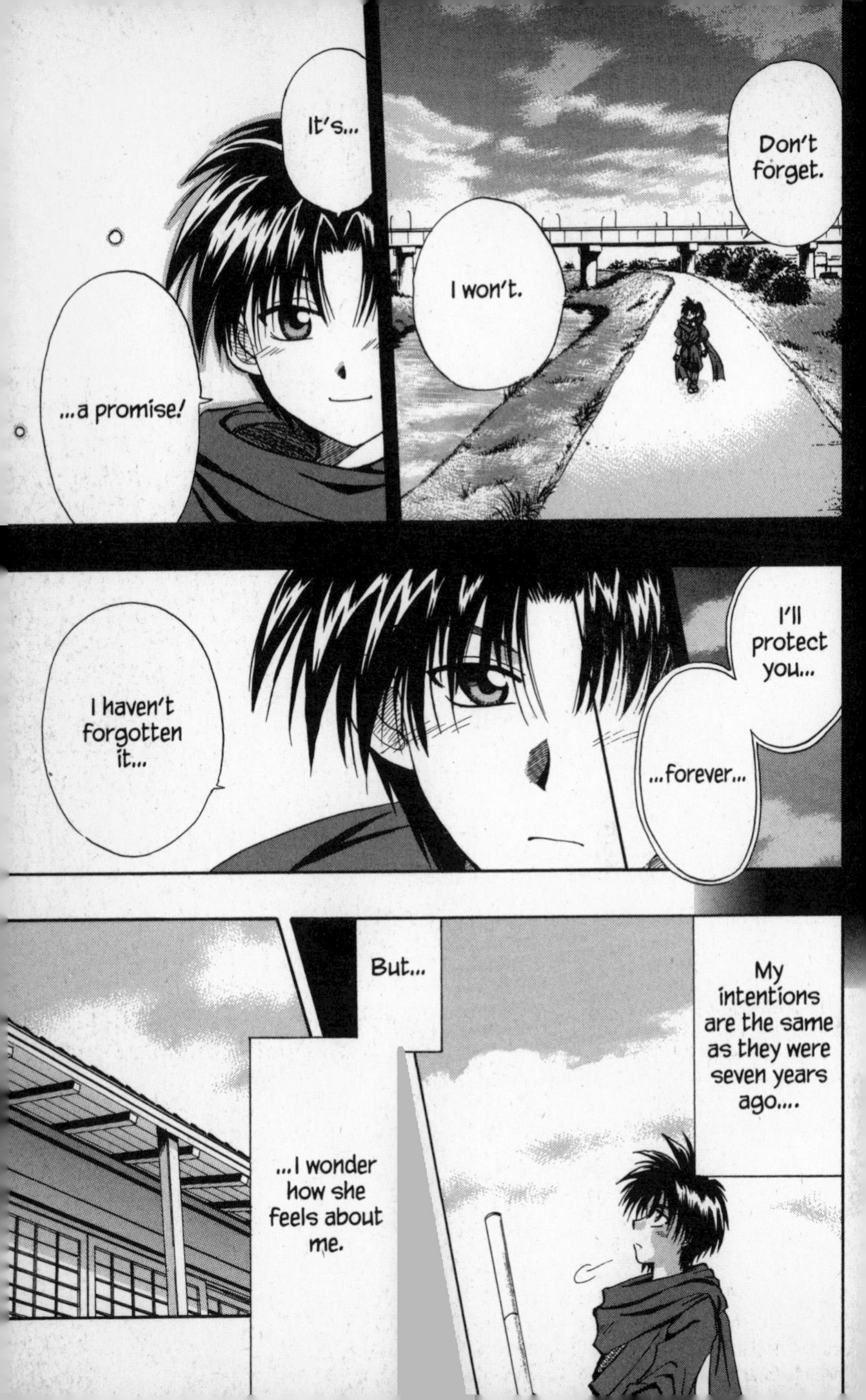
Don't forget.
I won't.
It's...
...a promise!
I'll protect you...
...forever...
I haven't forgotten it...
My intentions are the same as they were seven years ago....
But...
...I wonder how she feels about me.

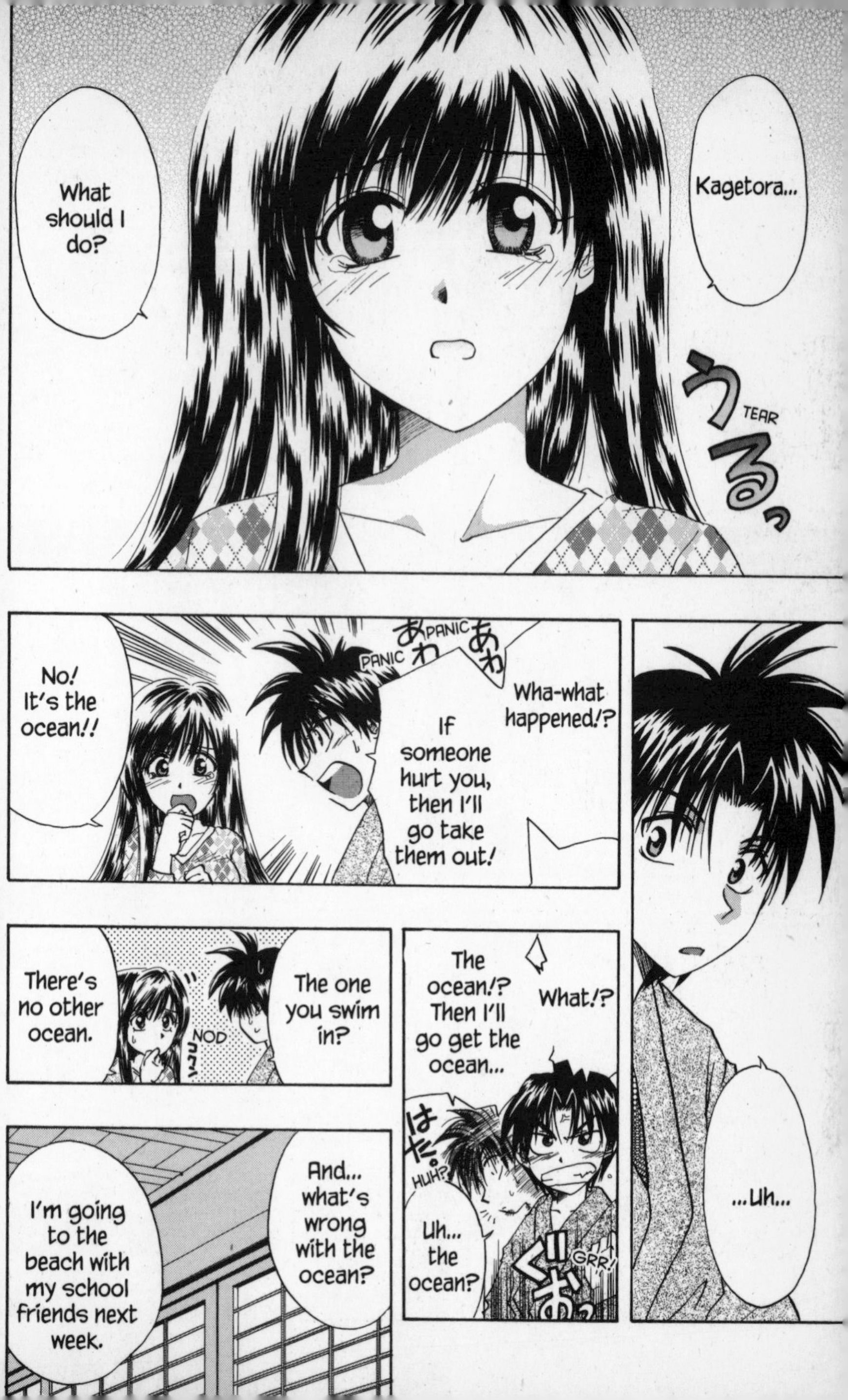
Kagetora...
うるっ
TEAR
What should I do?
...uh...
あわ
PANIC
あわ
PANIC
Wha-what happened!?
If someone hurt you, then I'll go take them out!
No! It's the ocean!!
What!?
The ocean!? Then I'll go get the ocean...
はっ
HUH?
Uh... the ocean?
ぐぉっ
GRR!
The one you swim in?
NOD
There's no other ocean.
And... what's wrong with the ocean?
I'm going to the beach with my school friends next week.

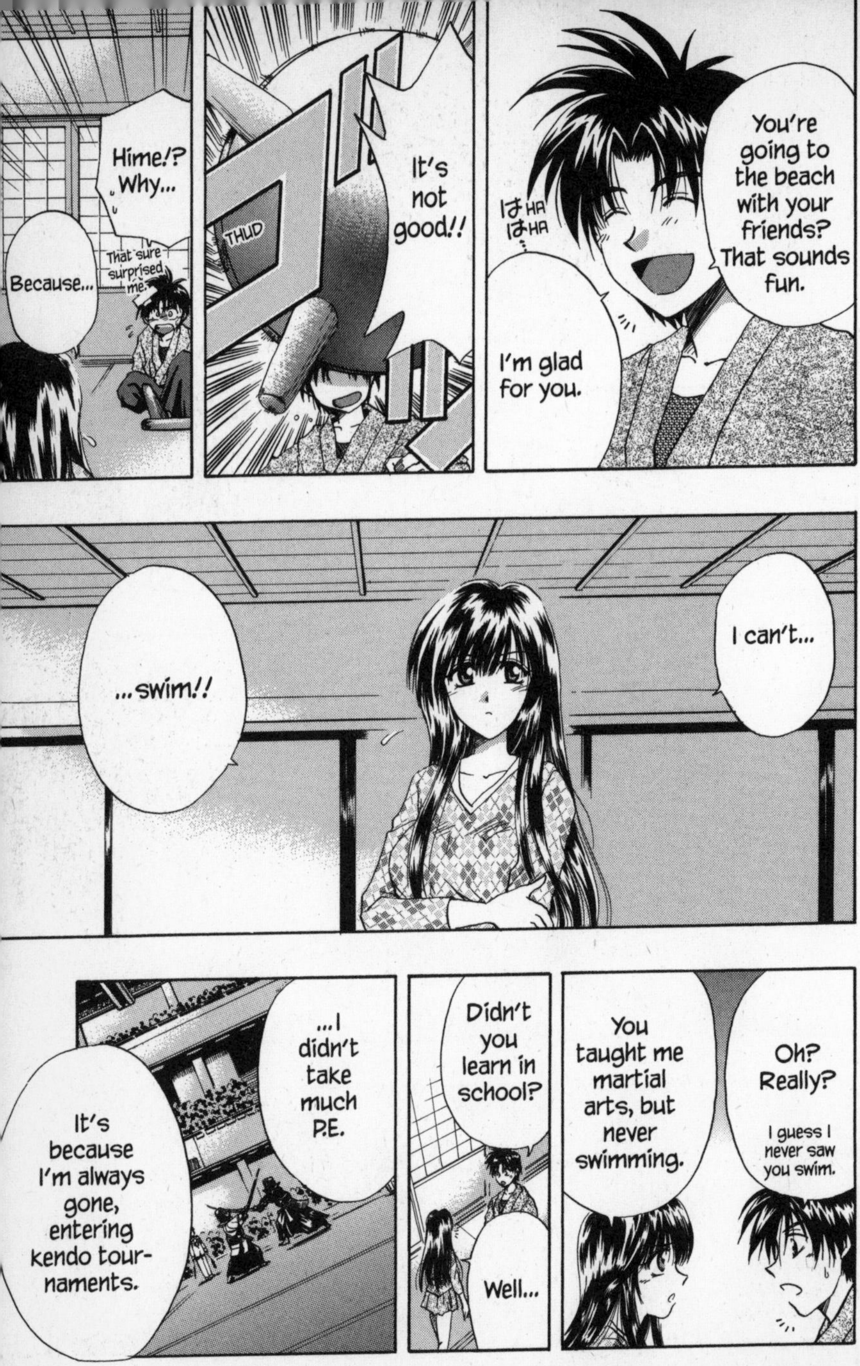
You're going to the beach with your friends? That sounds fun.
はHA はHA...
I'm glad for you.
THUD
It's not good!!
Hime!? Why...
That sure surprised me.
Because...
I can't...
...swim!!
Oh? Really?
I guess I never saw you swim.
You taught me martial arts, but never swimming.
Didn't you learn in school?
Well...
...I didn't take much P.E.
It's because I'm always gone, entering kendo tournaments.

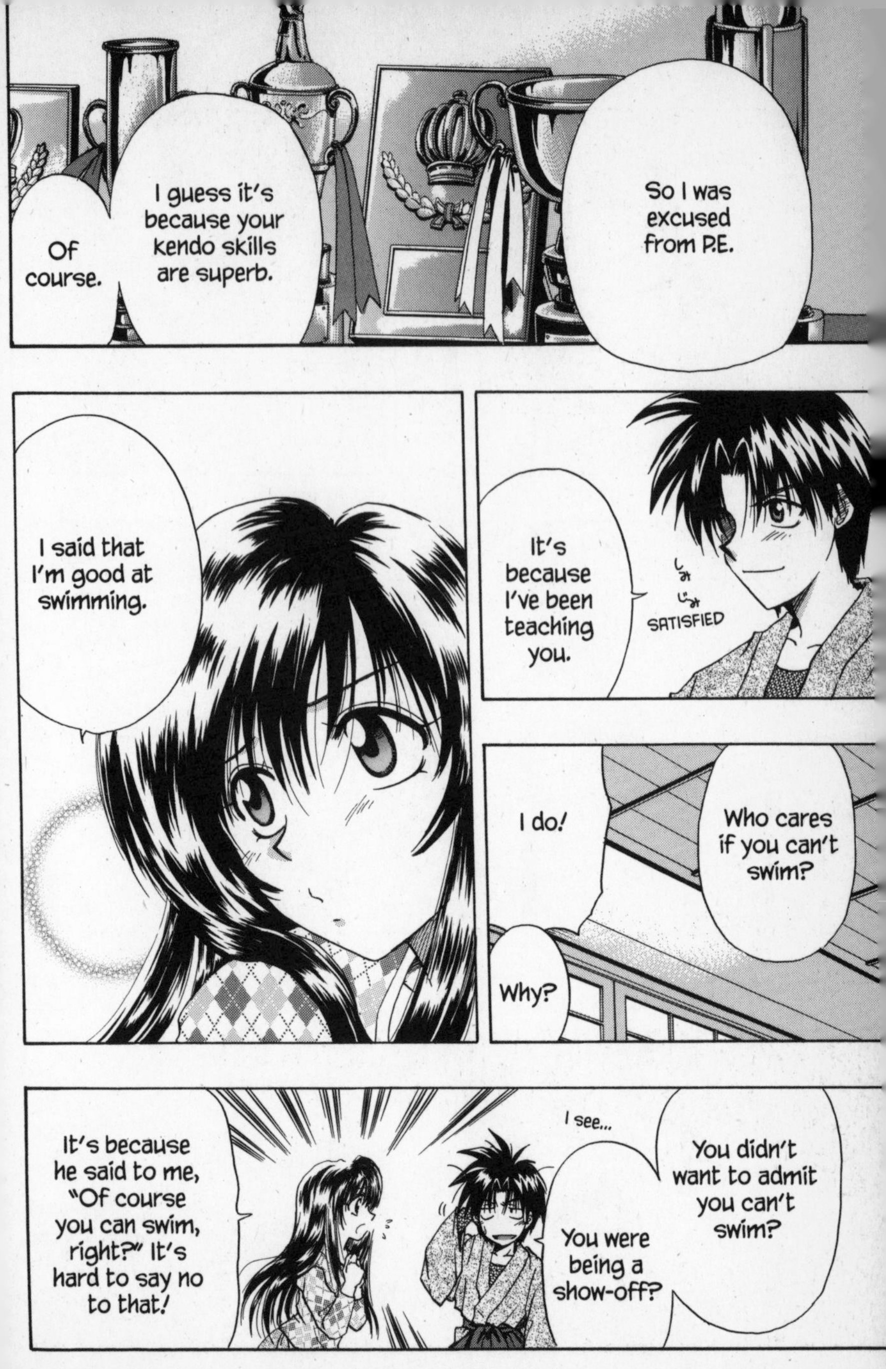
So I was excused from P.E.
I guess it's because your kendo skills are superb.
Of course.
It's because I've been teaching you.
しみじみ
SATISFIED
Who cares if you can't swim?
I do!
Why?
I said that I'm good at swimming.
You didn't want to admit you can't swim?
I see...
You were being a show-off?
It's because he said to me, "Of course you can swim, right?" It's hard to say no to that!

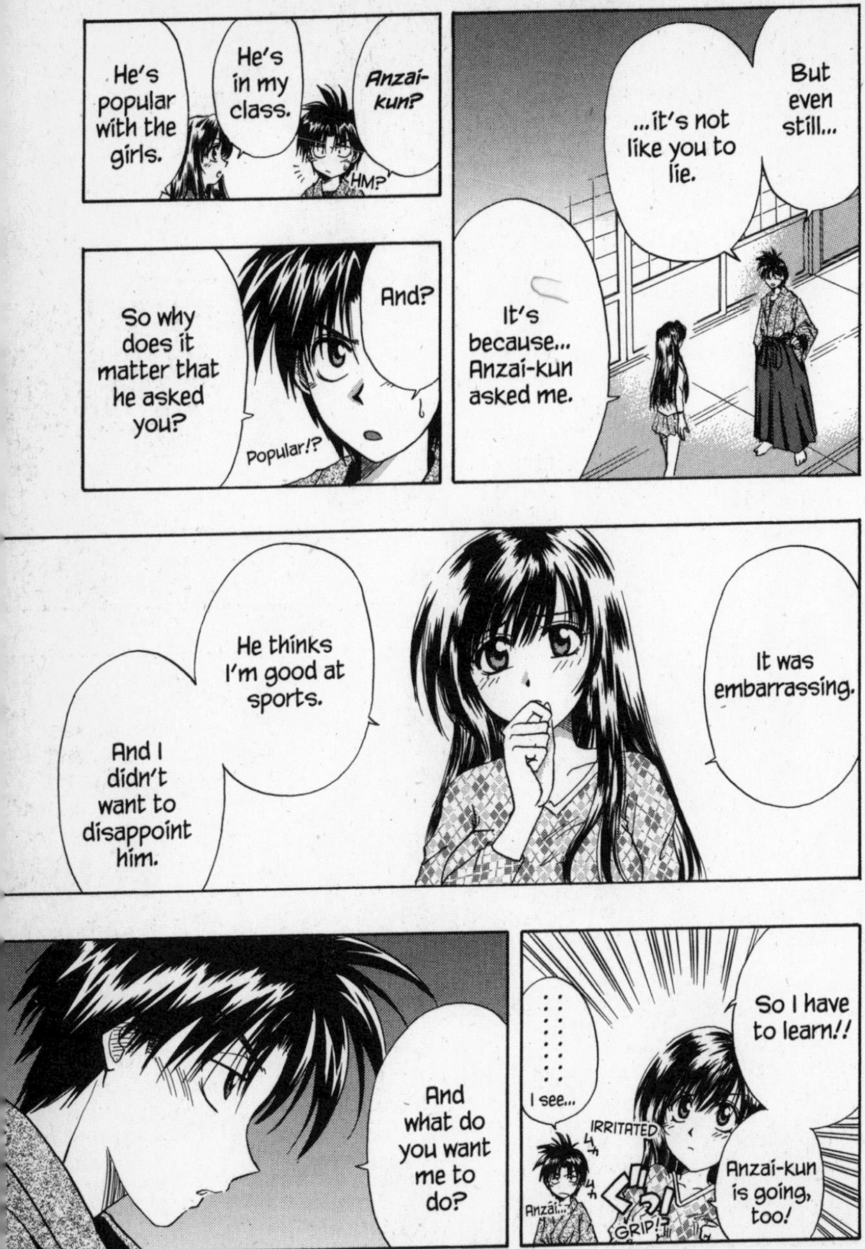

But even still...
...it's not like you to lie.
It's because... Anzai-kun asked me.
Anzai-kun?
HM?
He's in my class.
He's popular with the girls.
And?
Popular!?
So why does it matter that he asked you?
It was embarrassing.
He thinks I'm good at sports.
And I didn't want to disappoint him.
So I have to learn!!
Anzai-kun is going, too!
GRIP!?
IRRITATED
......
I see...
Anzai...
And what do you want me to do?

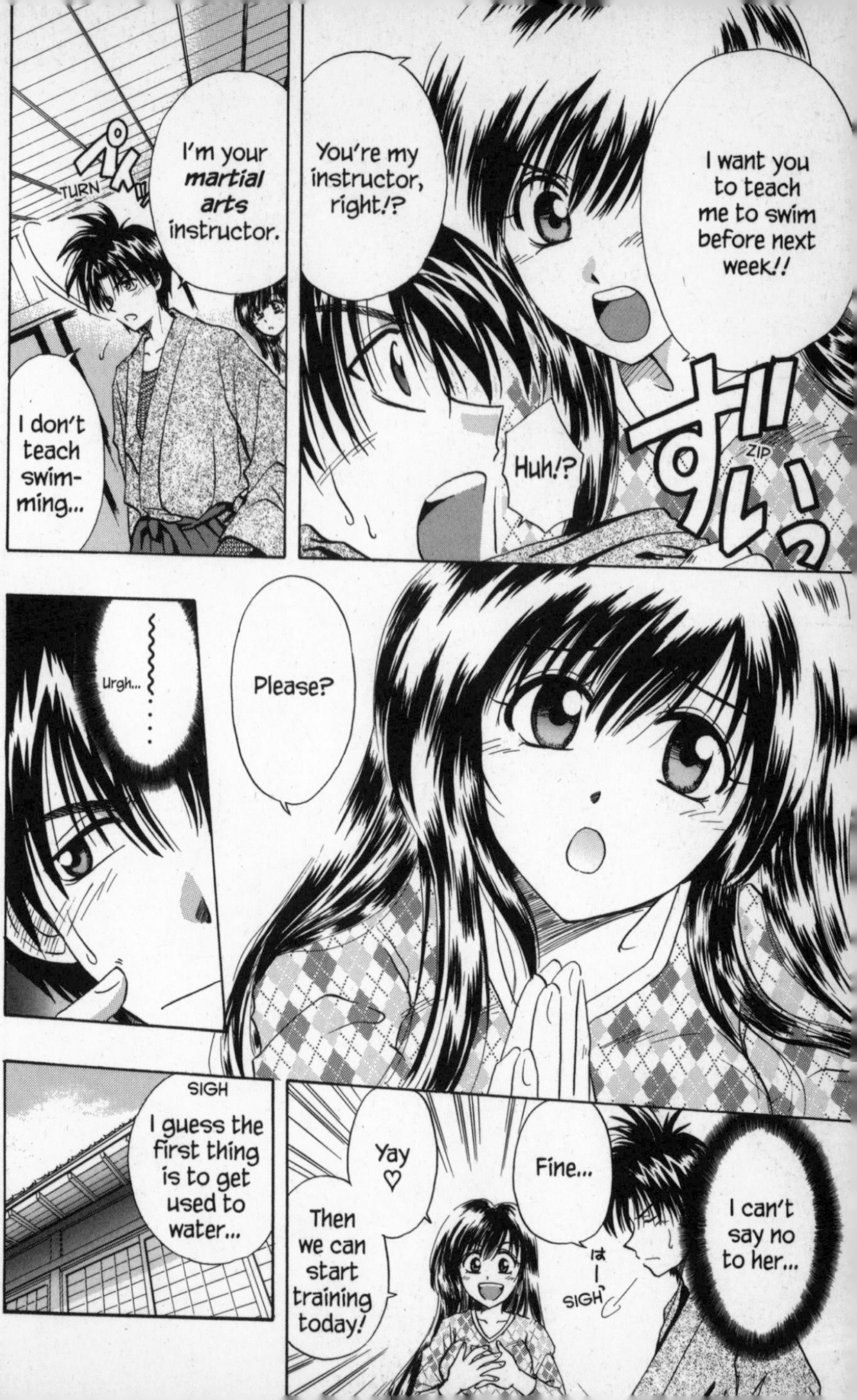
I want you to teach me to swim before next week!!
You're my instructor, right!?
ZIP
Huh!?
I'm your *martial arts* instructor.
TURN
I don't teach swimming...
Please?
Urgh......
I can't say no to her...
Fine...
SIGH
Yay ♡
Then we can start training today!
SIGH
I guess the first thing is to get used to water...

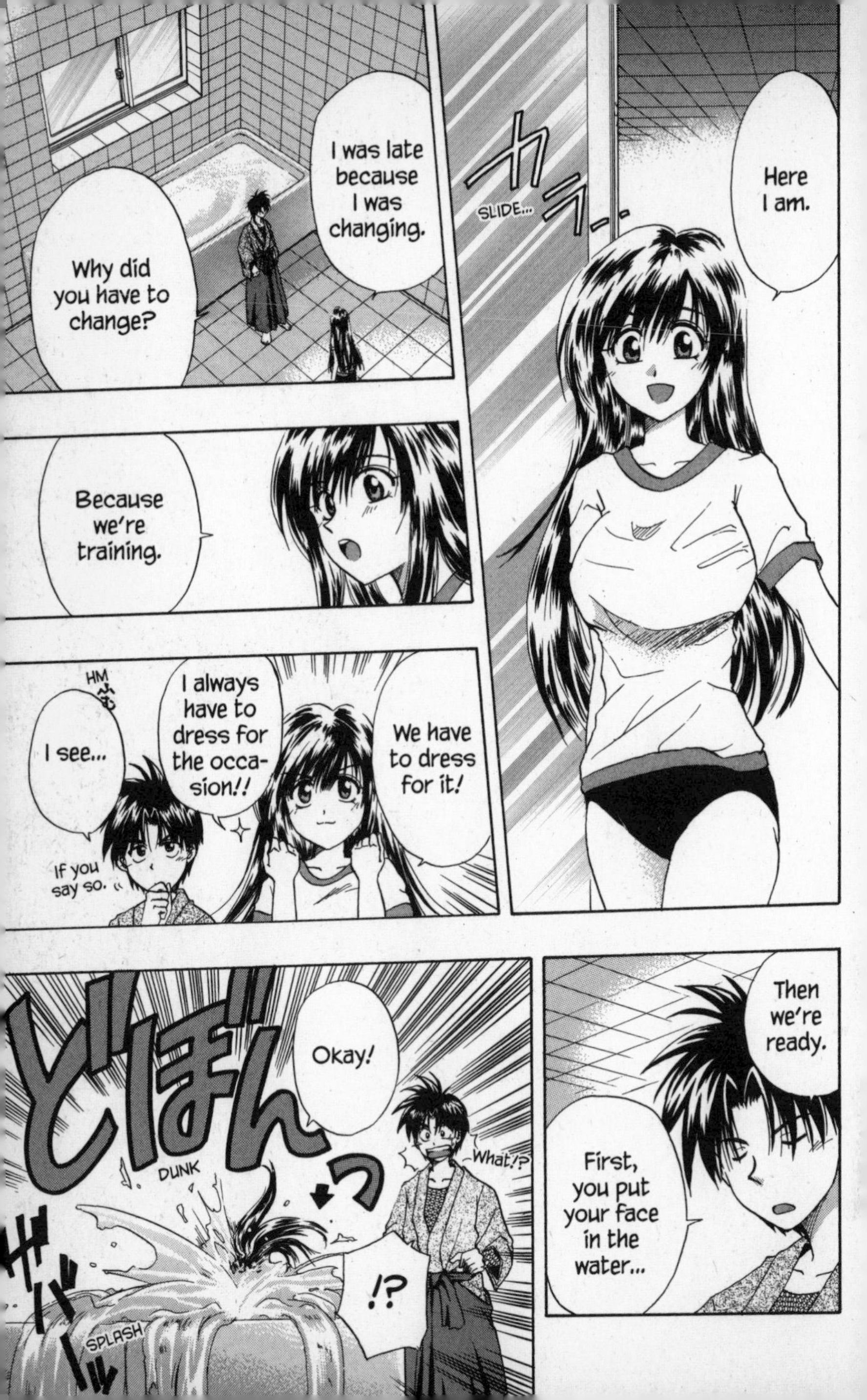
SLIDE...
Here I am.
I was late because I was changing.
Why did you have to change?
Because we're training.
We have to dress for it!
I always have to dress for the occasion!!
HM
I see...
If you say so.
Then we're ready.
First, you put your face in the water...
Okay!
What!?
DUNK
!?
SPLASH

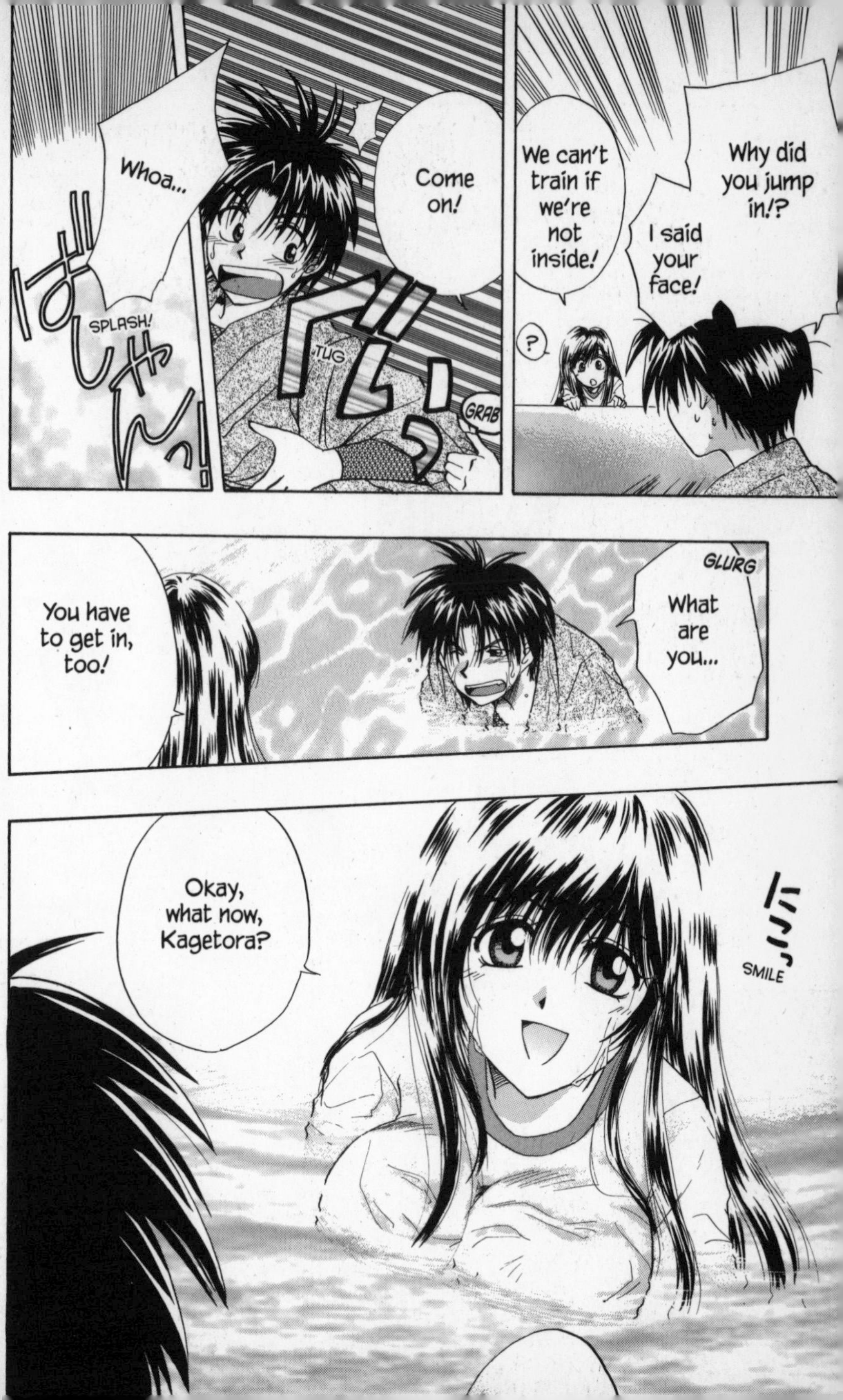
Why did you jump in!?
I said your face!
We can't train if we're not inside!
?
Come on!
Whoa...
TUG
GRAB
SPLASH!
GLURG
What are you...
You have to get in, too!
SMILE
Okay, what now, Kagetora?

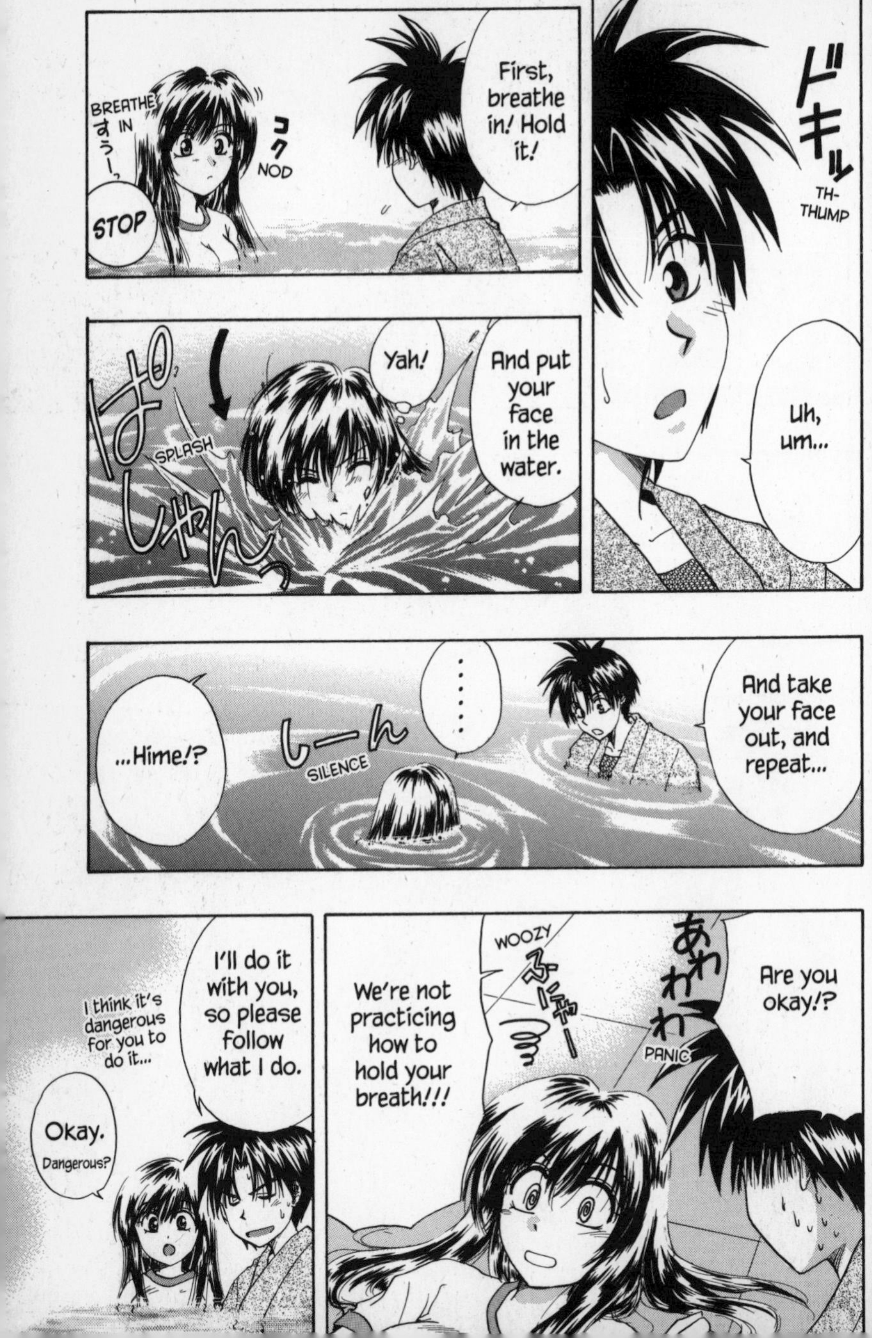

ドキッ
TH-THUMP
Uh, um...
First, breathe in! Hold it!
コク
NOD
BREATHE IN
すぅー
STOP
And put your face in the water.
Yah!
ぱしゃんっ
SPLASH
And take your face out, and repeat...
......
しーん
SILENCE
...Hime!?
Are you okay!?
あわわ
PANIC
WOOZY
ふにゃー
We're not practicing how to hold your breath!!!
I'll do it with you, so please follow what I do.
I think it's dangerous for you to do it...
Okay.
Dangerous?

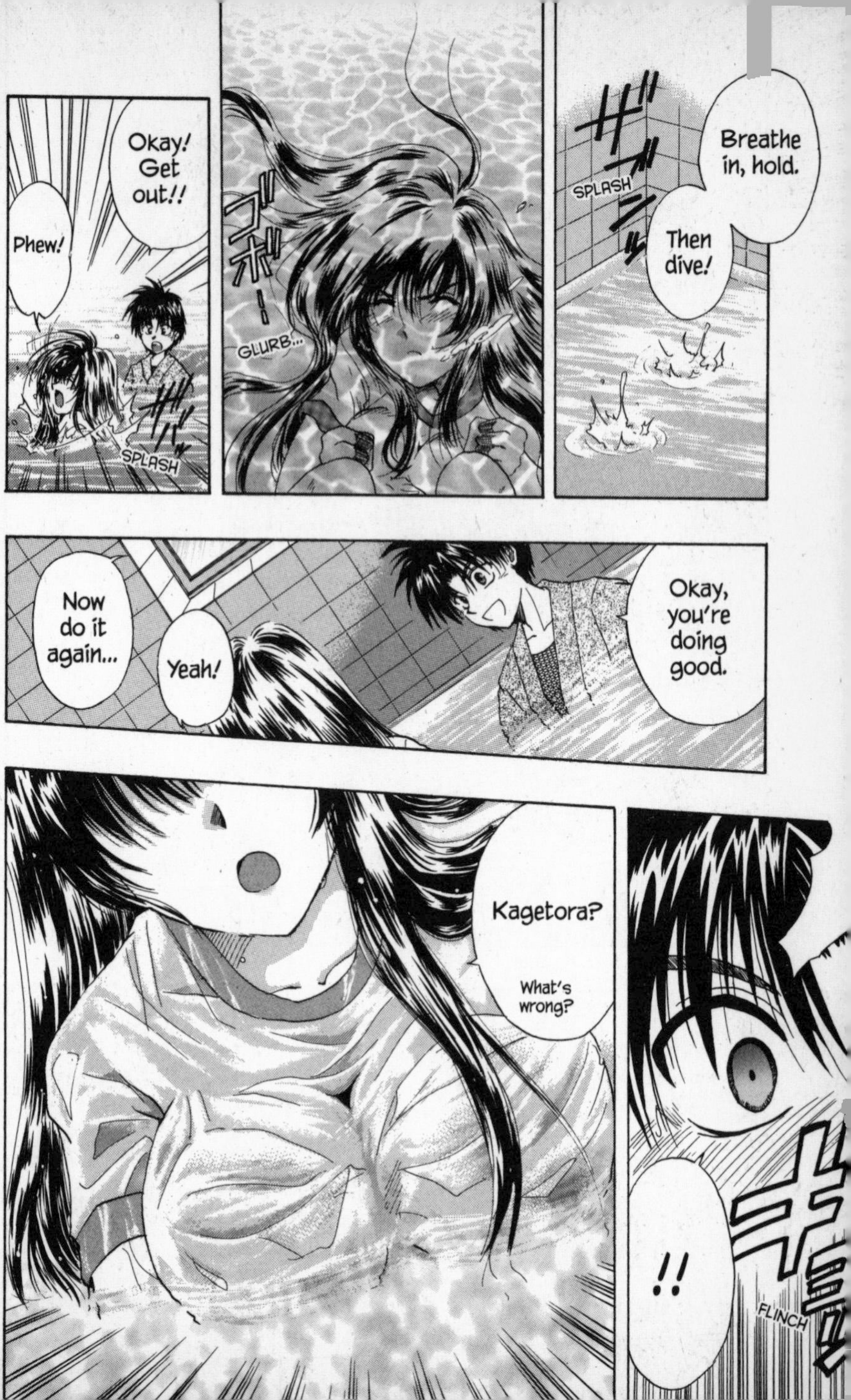

Breathe in, hold.
SPLASH
Then dive!
GLURB...
Okay! Get out!!
Phew!
SPLASH
Okay, you're doing good.
Yeah!
Now do it again...
!!
FLINCH
Kagetora?
What's wrong?

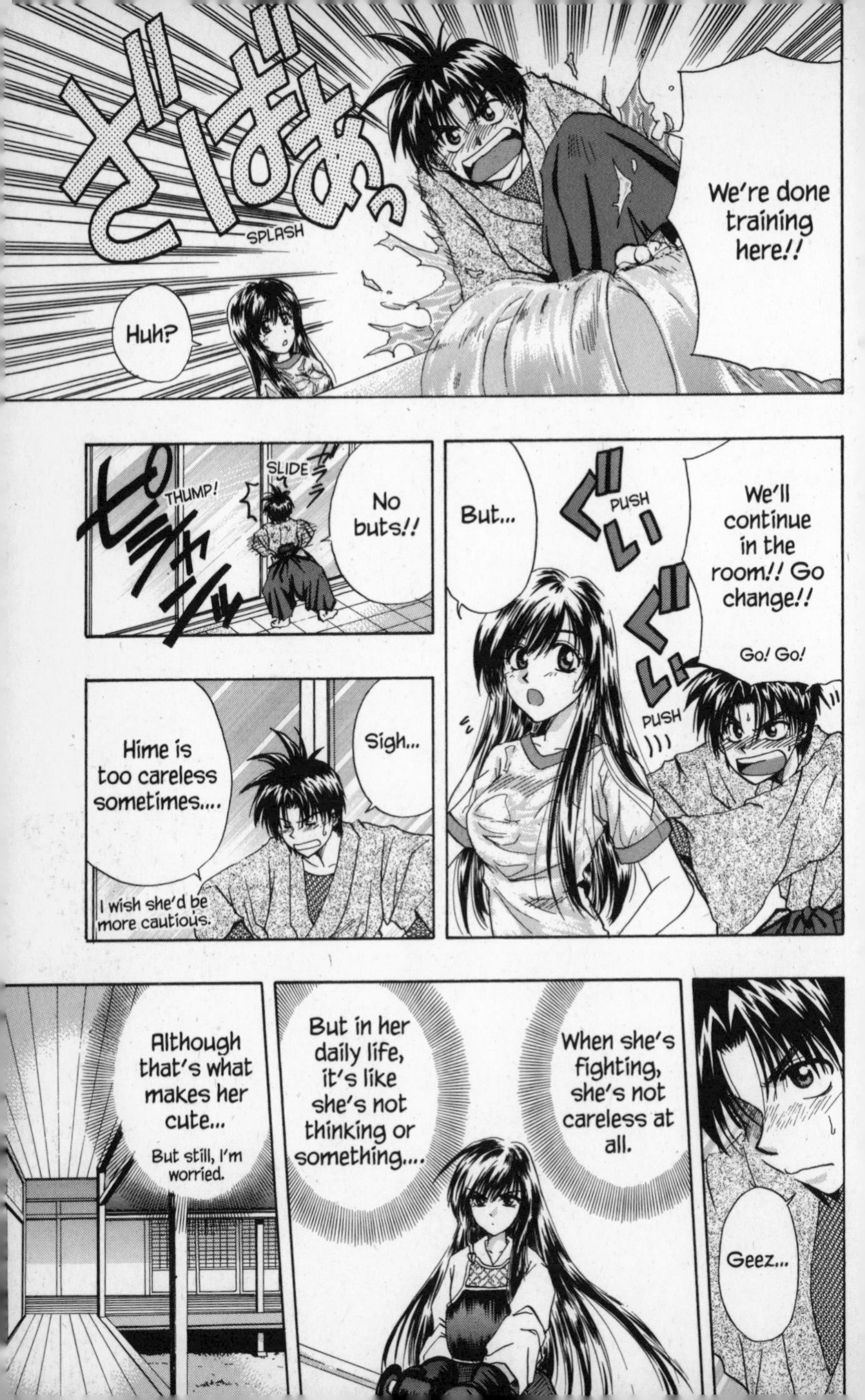
We're done training here!!
SPLASH
Huh?
We'll continue in the room!! Go change!!
PUSH
But...
Go! Go!
PUSH
No buts!!
SLIDE
THUMP!
Sigh...
Hime is too careless sometimes....
I wish she'd be more cautious.
Geez...
When she's fighting, she's not careless at all.
But in her daily life, it's like she's not thinking or something....
Although that's what makes her cute...
But still, I'm worried.

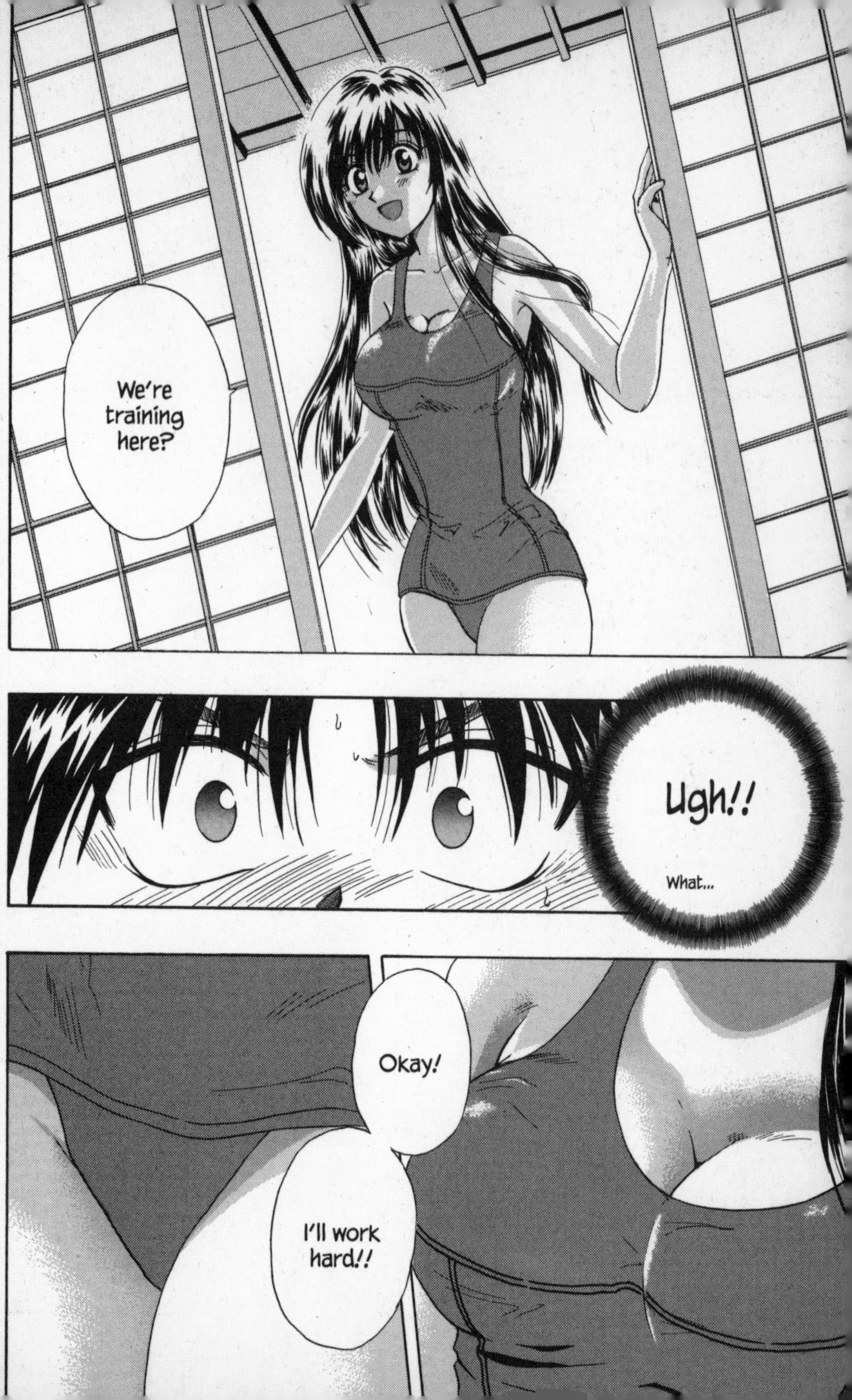
We're training here?
Ugh!!
What...
Okay!
I'll work hard!!

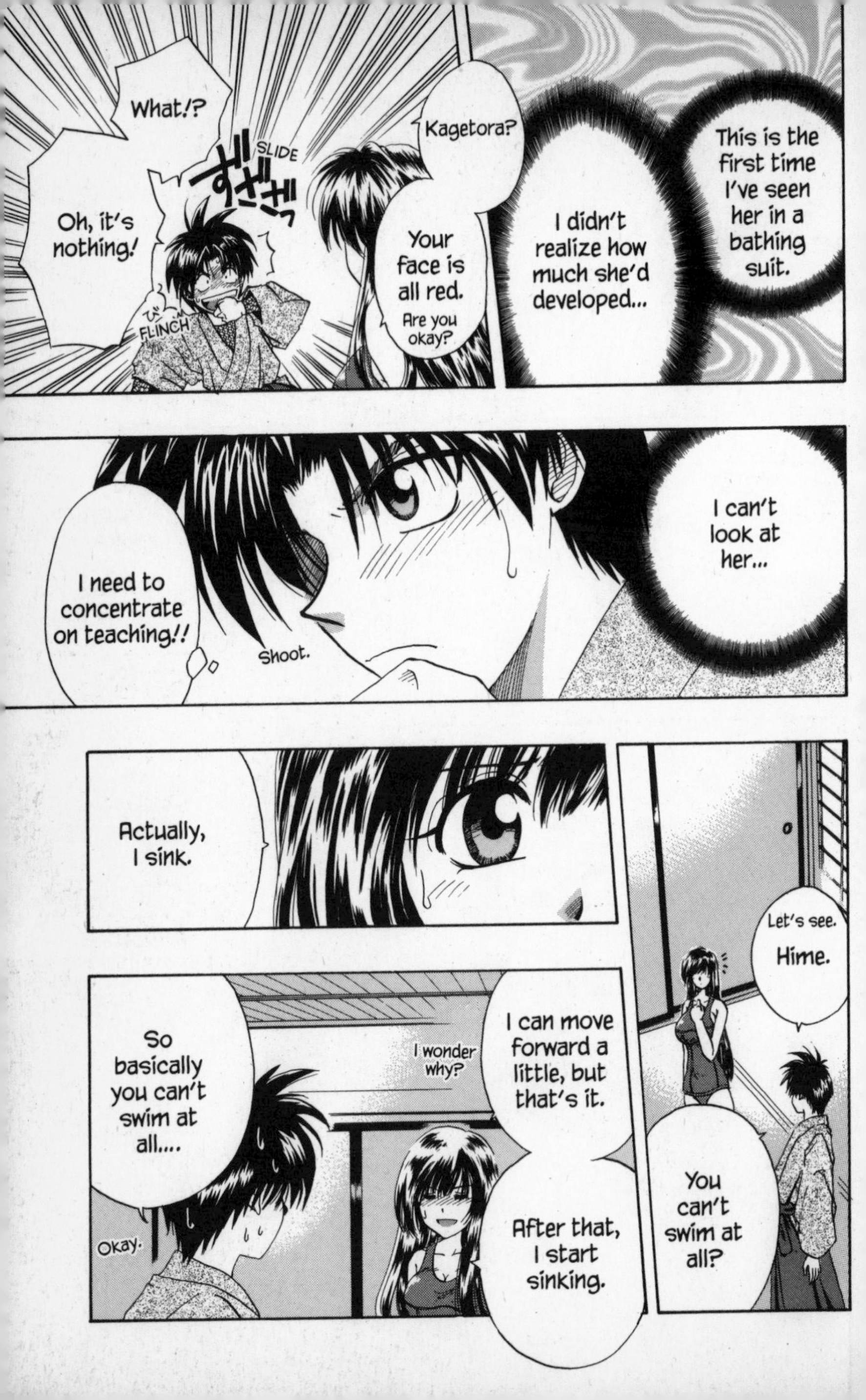
This is the first time I've seen her in a bathing suit.
I didn't realize how much she'd developed...
Kagetora?
Your face is all red.
Are you okay?
What!?
SLIDE
Oh, it's nothing!
FLINCH
I can't look at her...
Shoot.
I need to concentrate on teaching!!
Let's see.
Hime.
You can't swim at all?
Actually, I sink.
I can move forward a little, but that's it.
I wonder why?
After that, I start sinking.
So basically you can't swim at all....
Okay.

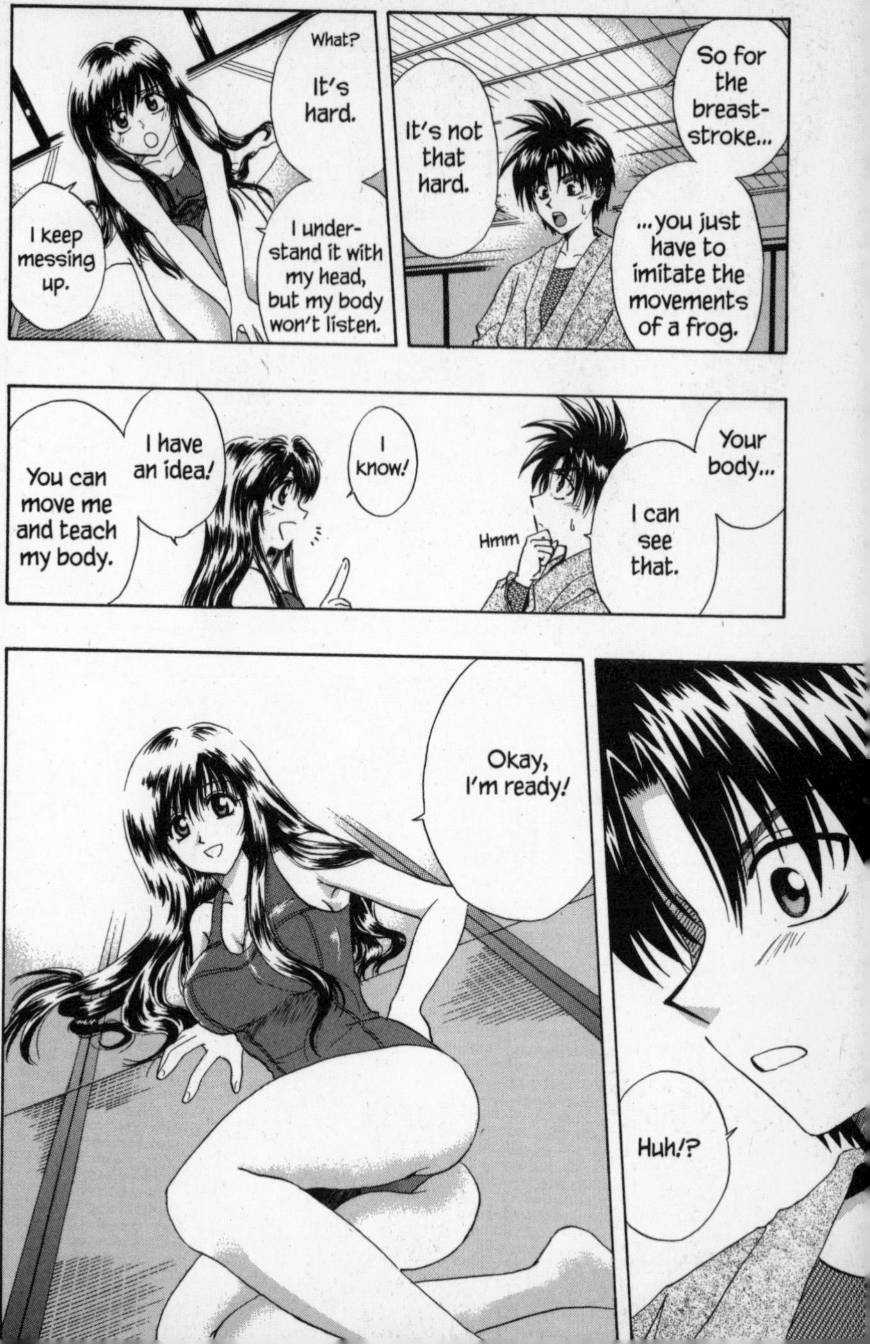
So for the breast-stroke...
...you just have to imitate the movements of a frog.
It's not that hard.
What?
It's hard.
I under-stand it with my head, but my body won't listen.
I keep messing up.
Your body...
I can see that.
Hmm
I know!
I have an idea!
You can move me and teach my body.
Huh!?
Okay, I'm ready!

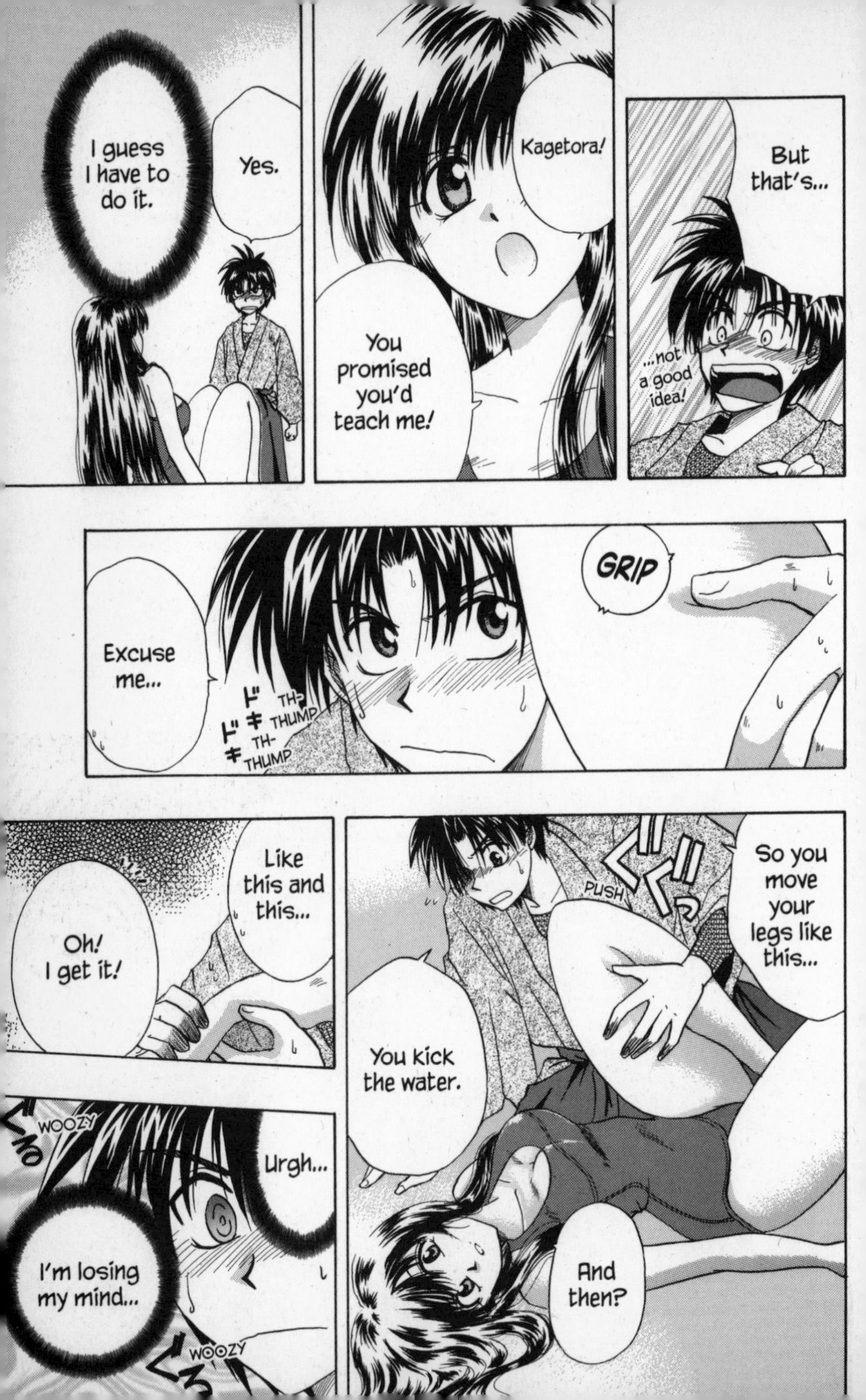

But that's...
...not a good idea!
Kagetora!
You promised you'd teach me!
Yes.
I guess I have to do it.
GRIP
Excuse me...
ドキドキ
TH-THUMP TH-THUMP
So you move your legs like this...
PUSH
You kick the water.
And then?
Like this and this...
Oh! I get it!
Urgh...
WOOZY
I'm losing my mind...
WOOZY

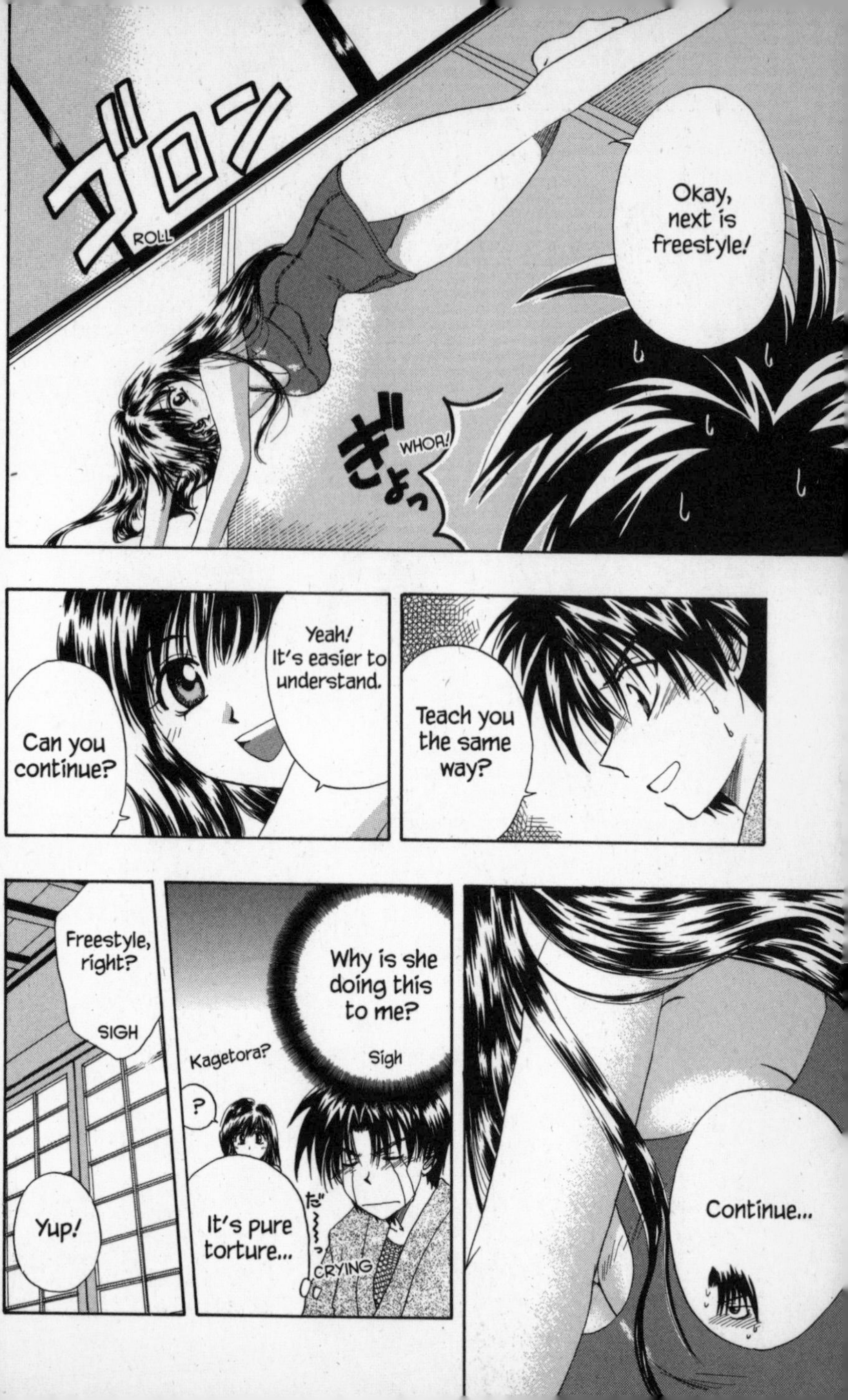
Okay, next is freestyle!
ゴロン
ROLL
ぎょっ
WHOA!
Teach you the same way?
Yeah! It's easier to understand.
Can you continue?
Continue...
Why is she doing this to me?
Sigh
Kagetora?
?
It's pure torture...
CRYING
Freestyle, right?
SIGH
Yup!

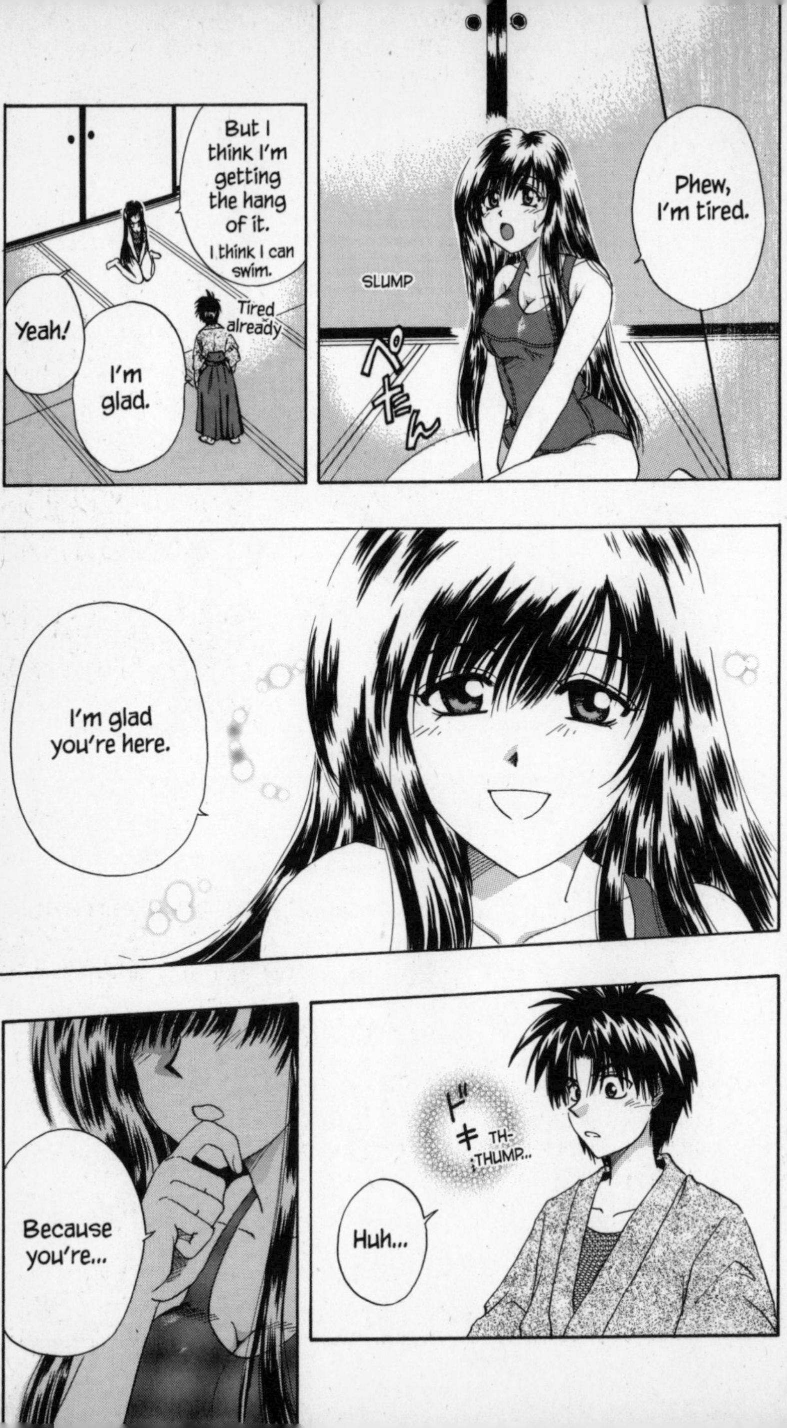
Phew, I'm tired.
SLUMP
ぺたん
But I think I'm getting the hang of it.
I think I can swim.
Tired already
I'm glad.
Yeah!
I'm glad you're here.
ドキ
TH-THUMP...
Huh...
Because you're...

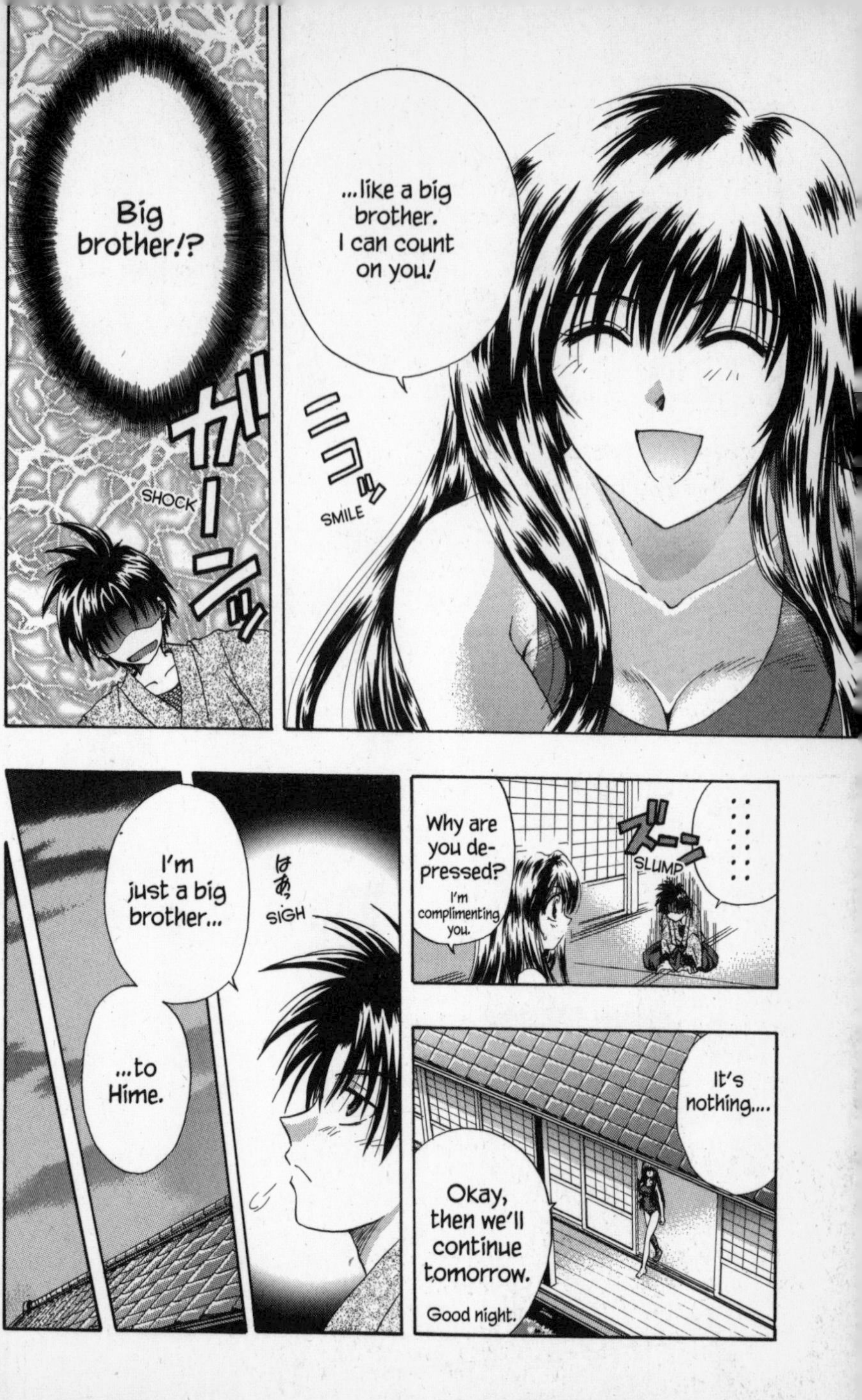
...like a big brother. I can count on you!
SMILE
Big brother!?
SHOCK
......
SLUMP
Why are you de-pressed?
I'm complimenting you.
It's nothing....
Okay, then we'll continue tomorrow.
Good night.
I'm just a big brother...
SIGH
...to Hime.

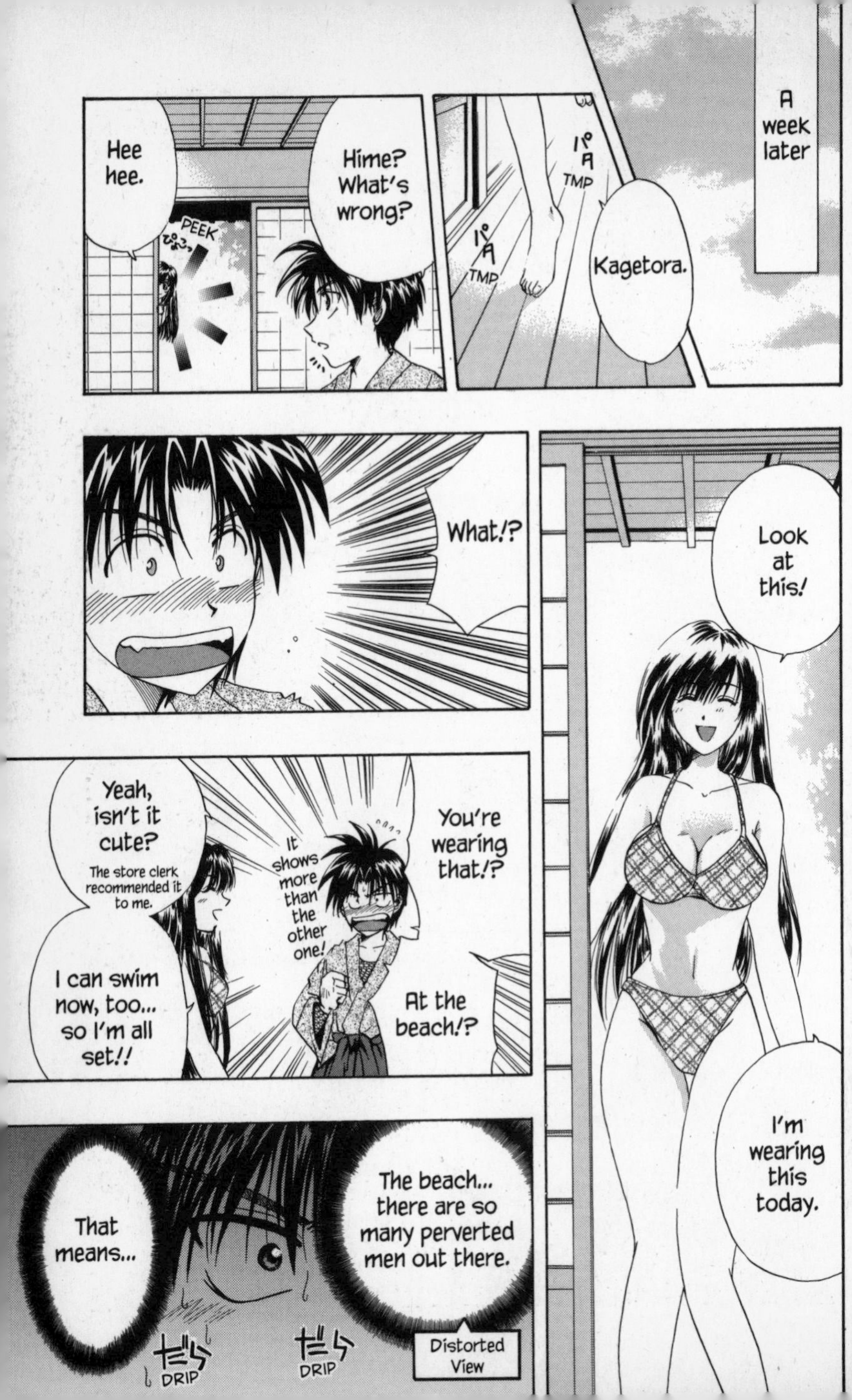
A week later
パ
TMP
パ
TMP
Kagetora.
Hime? What's wrong?
Hee hee.
PEEK
ぴょこっ
Look at this!
I'm wearing this today.
What!?
You're wearing that!?
At the beach!?
It shows more than the other one!
Yeah, isn't it cute?
The store clerk recommended it to me.
I can swim now, too... so I'm all set!!
The beach... there are so many perverted men out there.
That means...
だら
DRIP
だら
DRIP
Distorted View

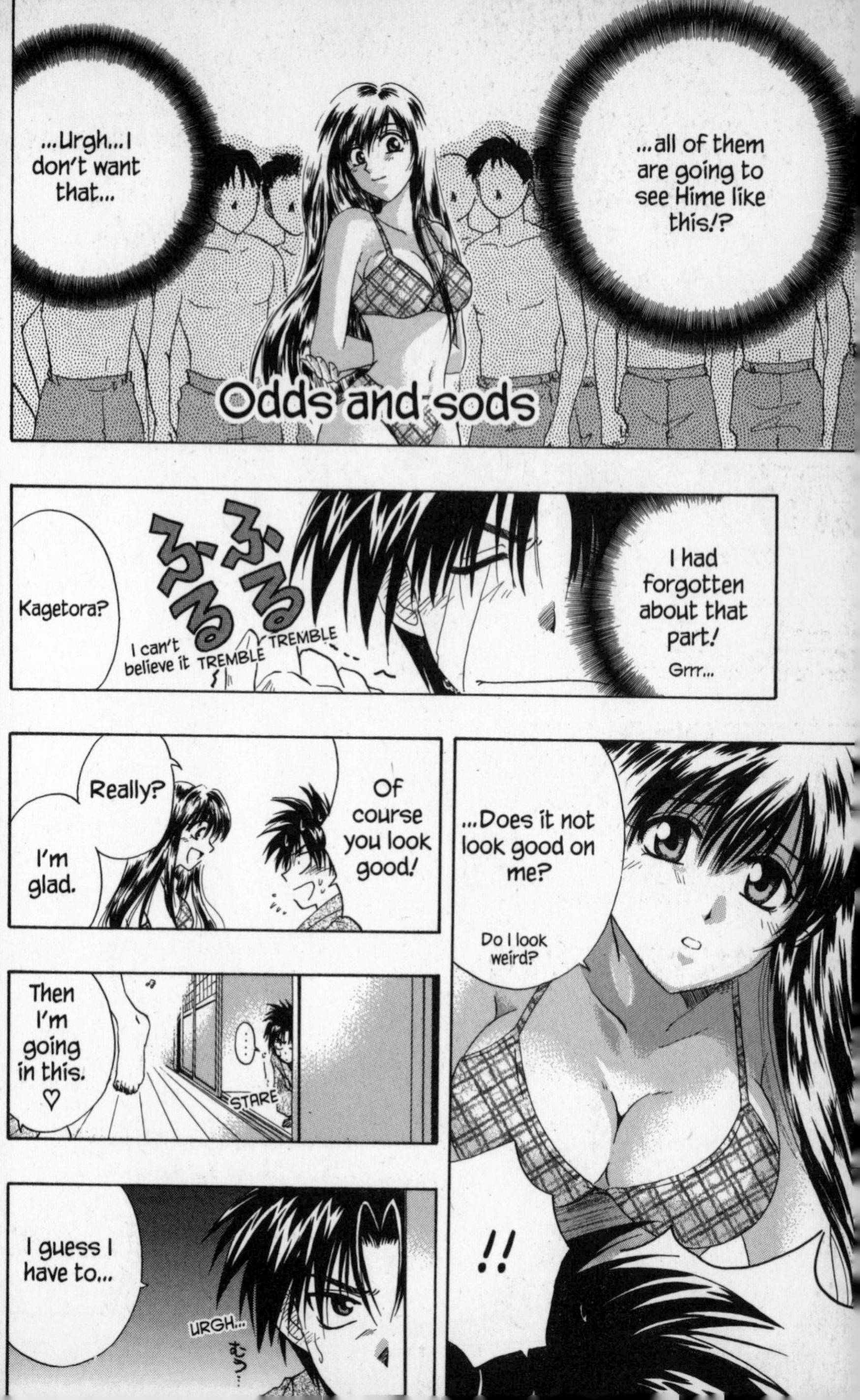

...all of them are going to see Hime like this!?
...Urgh...I don't want that...
Odds and sods
I had forgotten about that part!
Grrr...
ふるふる
TREMBLE TREMBLE
I can't believe it
Kagetora?
...Does it not look good on me?
Do I look weird?
!!
Of course you look good!
Really?
I'm glad.
Then I'm going in this. ♡
...
STARE
I guess I have to...
URGH...
むっ...

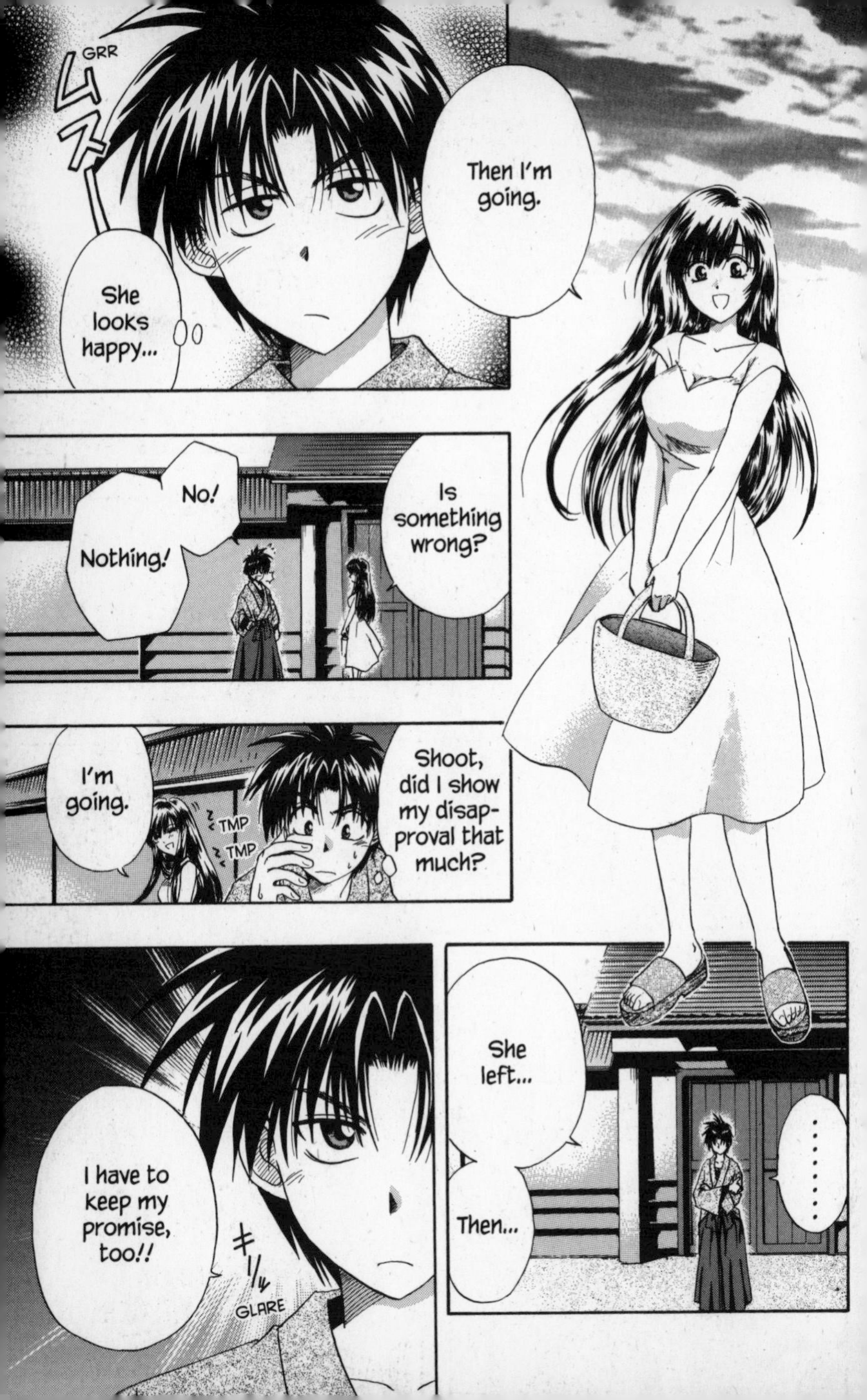
Then I'm going.
GRR
She looks happy...
Is something wrong?
No!
Nothing!
Shoot, did I show my disapproval that much?
TMP TMP
I'm going.
......
She left...
Then...
I have to keep my promise, too!!
GLARE

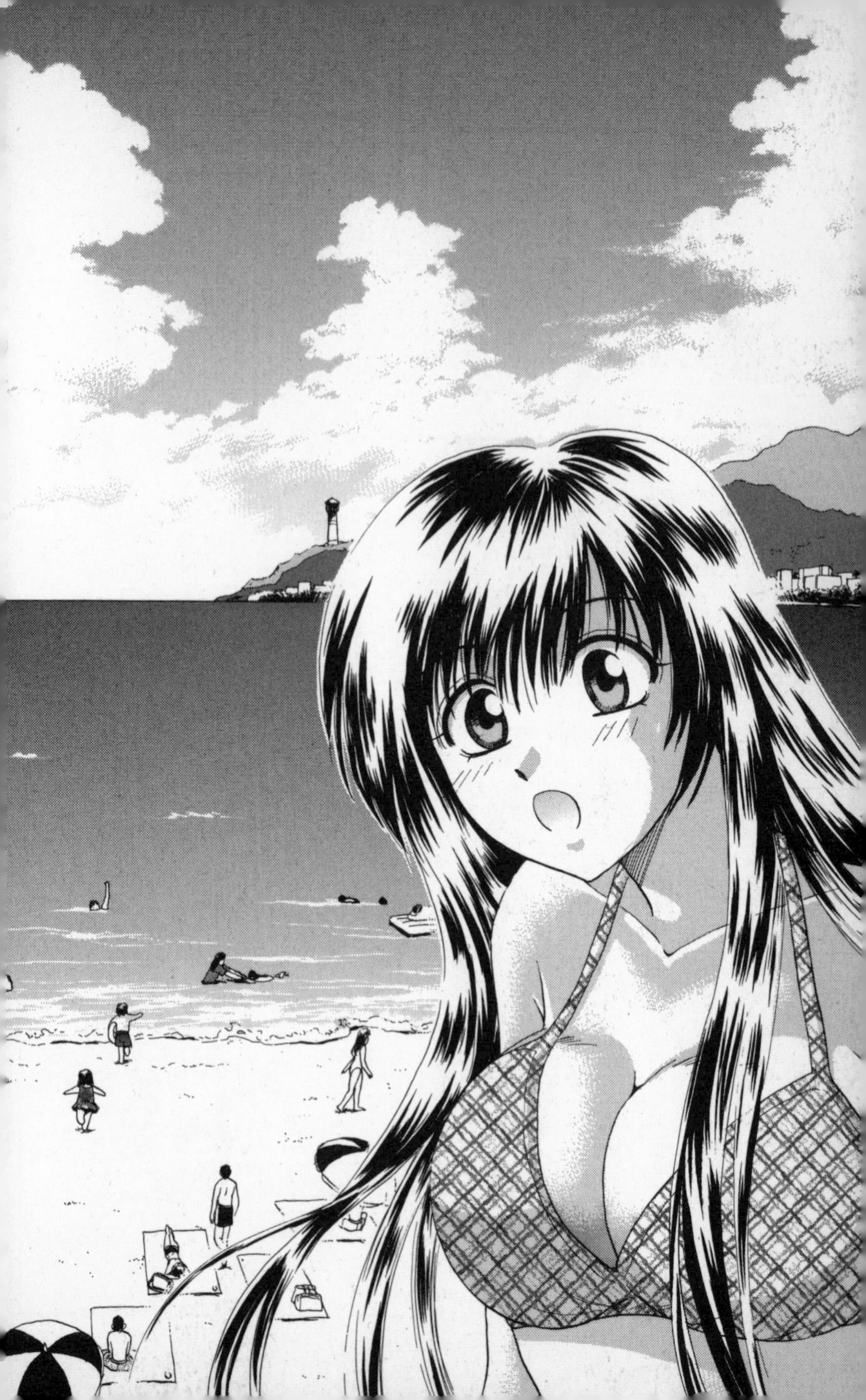

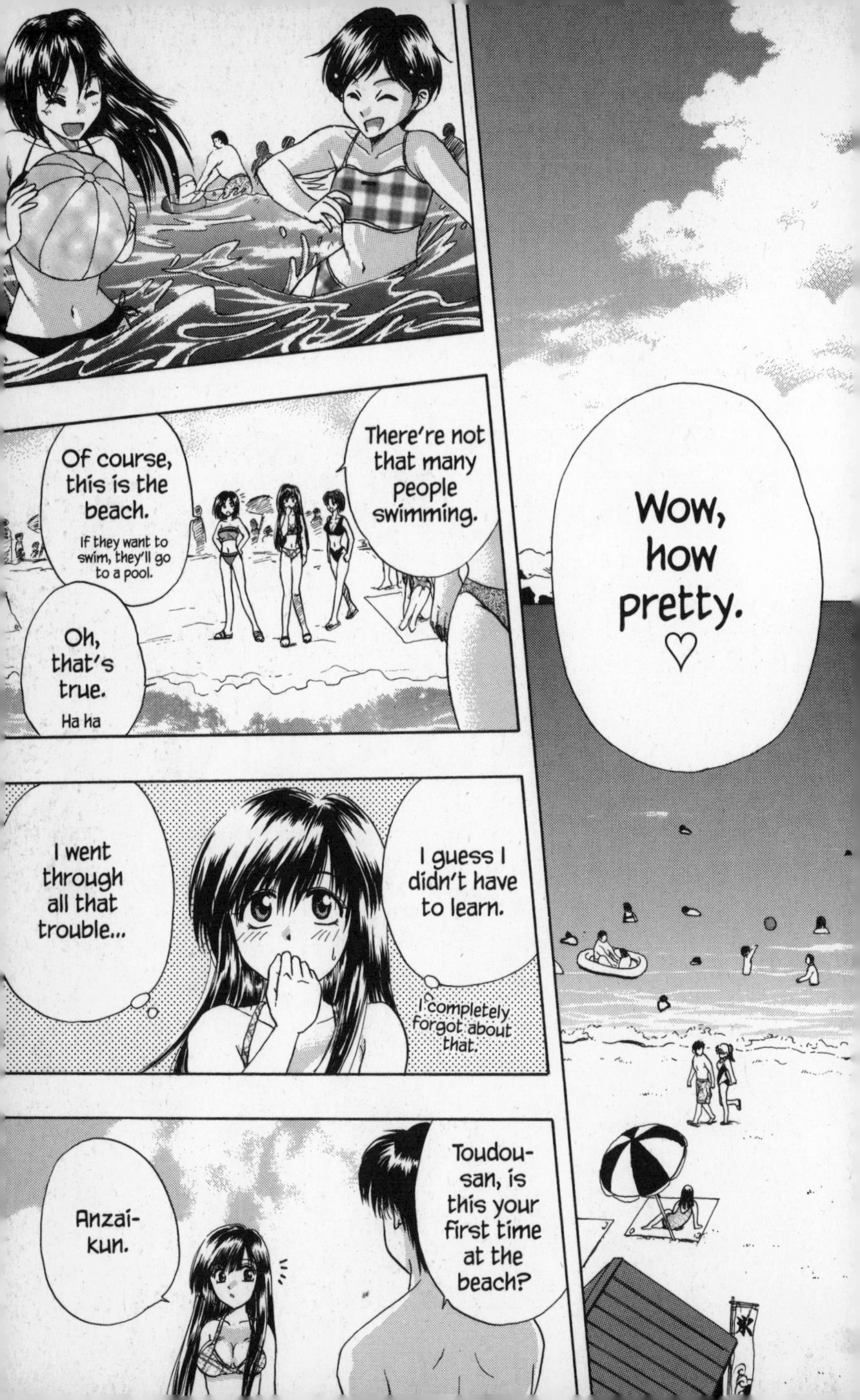

Wow, how pretty. ♡
There're not that many people swimming.
Of course, this is the beach.
If they want to swim, they'll go to a pool.
Oh, that's true.
Ha ha
I guess I didn't have to learn.
I completely forgot about that.
I went through all that trouble...
Toudou-san, is this your first time at the beach?
Anzai-kun.

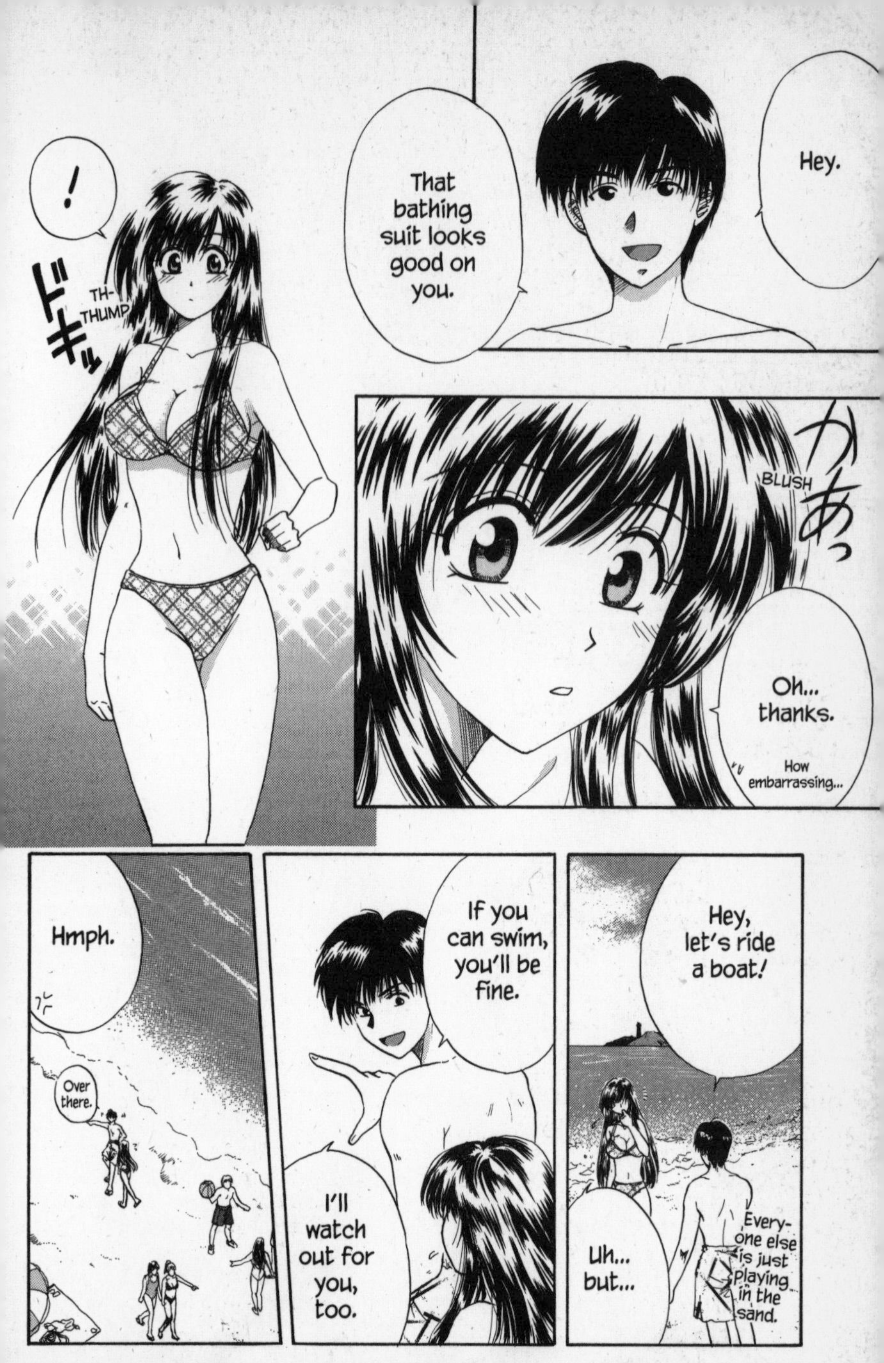
Hey.
That bathing suit looks good on you.
かあっ
BLUSH
Oh... thanks.
How embarrassing...
!
ドキッ
TH-THUMP
Hey, let's ride a boat!
Uh... but...
Everyone else is just playing in the sand.
If you can swim, you'll be fine.
I'll watch out for you, too.
Hmph.
Over there.

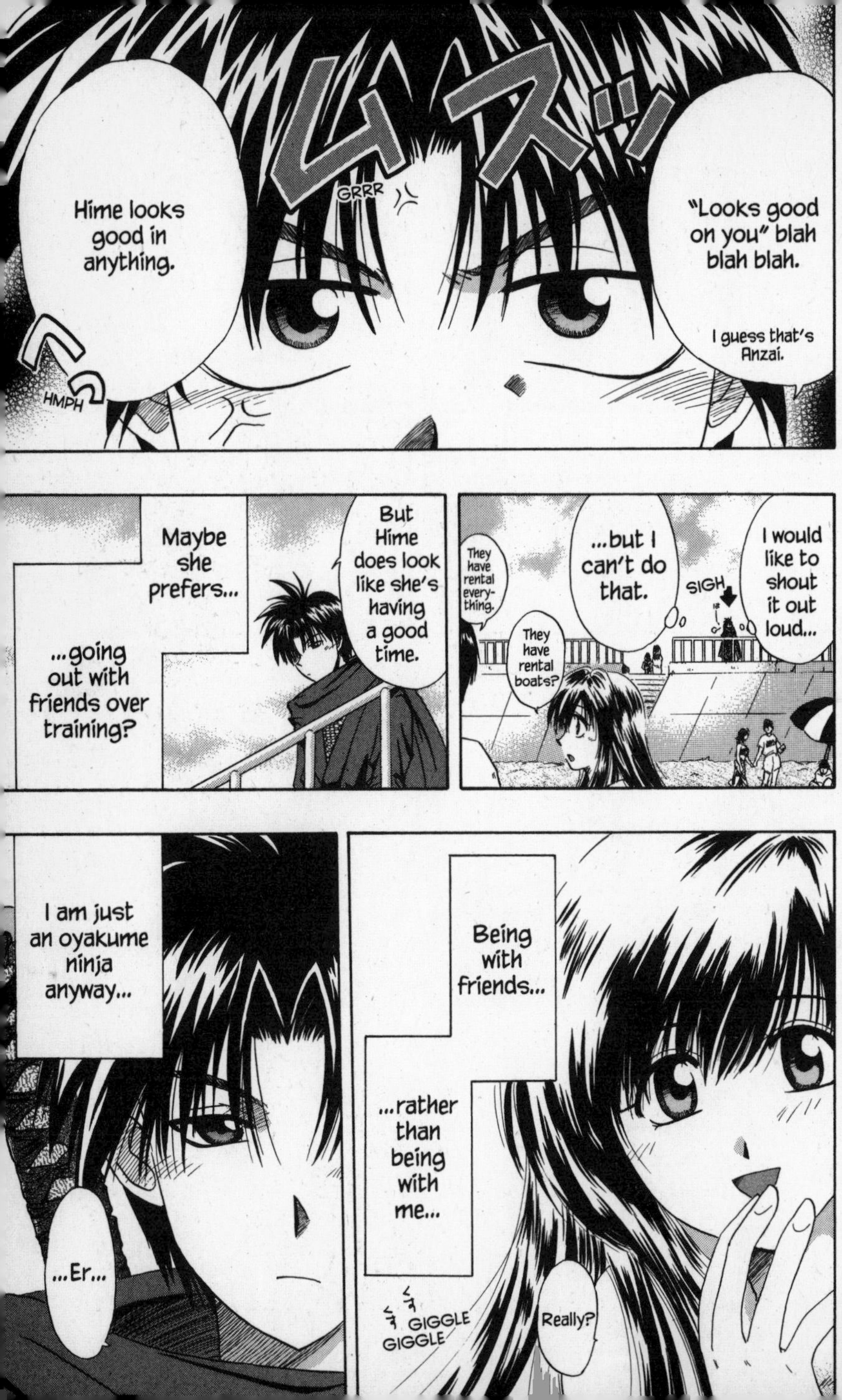
"Looks good on you" blah blah blah.
I guess that's Anzai.
ムズッ
GRRR
Hime looks good in anything.
HMPH
I would like to shout it out loud...
SIGH
...but I can't do that.
They have rental boats?
They have rental every-thing.
But Hime does look like she's having a good time.
Maybe she prefers...
...going out with friends over training?
Being with friends...
...rather than being with me...
Really?
GIGGLE GIGGLE
I am just an oyakume ninja anyway...
...Er...

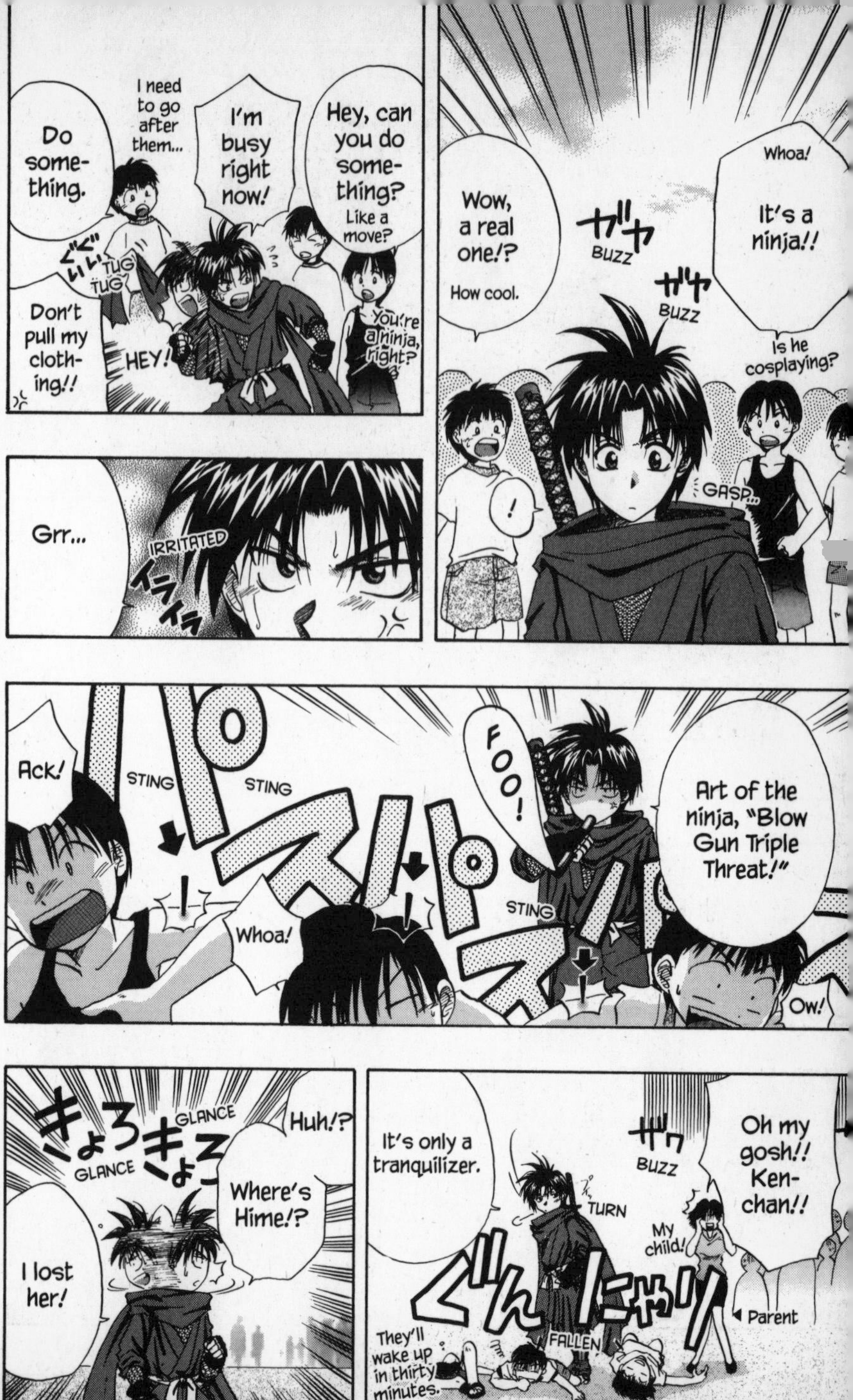
Whoa!
It's a ninja!!
ガヤ
BUZZ
Wow, a real one!?
How cool.
ガヤ
BUZZ
Is he cosplaying?
GASP...
!
Hey, can you do something?
Like a move?
I'm busy right now!
I need to go after them...
Do something.
You're a ninja, right?
ぐいぐい
TUG TUG
HEY!
Don't pull my clothing!!
IRRITATED
イライラ
Grr...
Art of the ninja, "Blow Gun Triple Threat!"
FOO!
Ow!
STING
Whoa!
STING
STING
Ack!
Oh my gosh!! Ken-chan!!
ザワ
BUZZ
My child!
TURN
Parent
It's only a tranquilizer.
ぐんにゃり
FALLEN
They'll wake up in thirty minutes.
Huh!?
きょろきょろ
GLANCE
GLANCE
Where's Hime!?
I lost her!

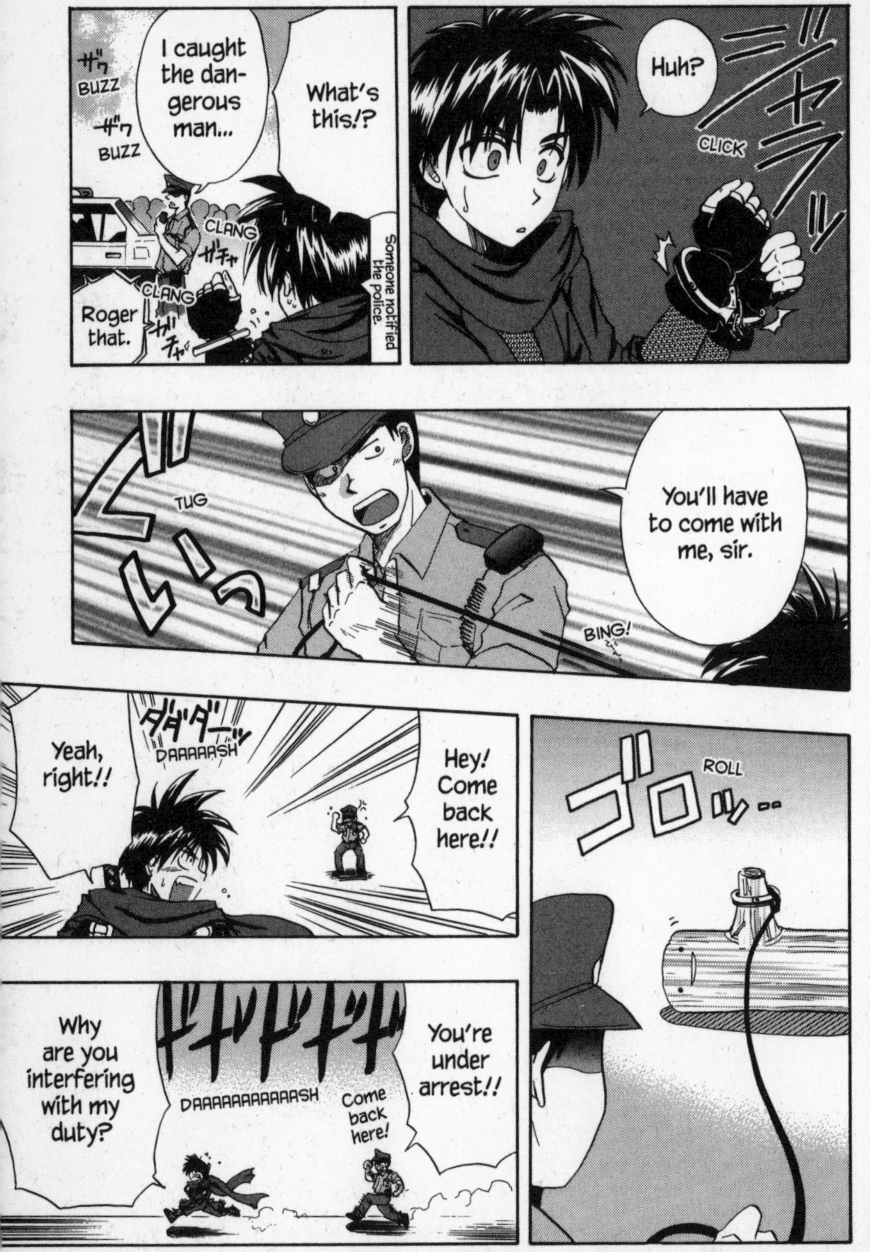

Huh?
CLICK
What's this!?
I caught the dangerous man...
Someone notified the police.
BUZZ
BUZZ
CLANG
CLANG
Roger that.
You'll have to come with me, sir.
TUG
BING!
ROLL
Hey! Come back here!!
DAAAAAASH
Yeah, right!!
You're under arrest!!
Come back here!
DAAAAAAAAAAAASH
Why are you interfering with my duty?

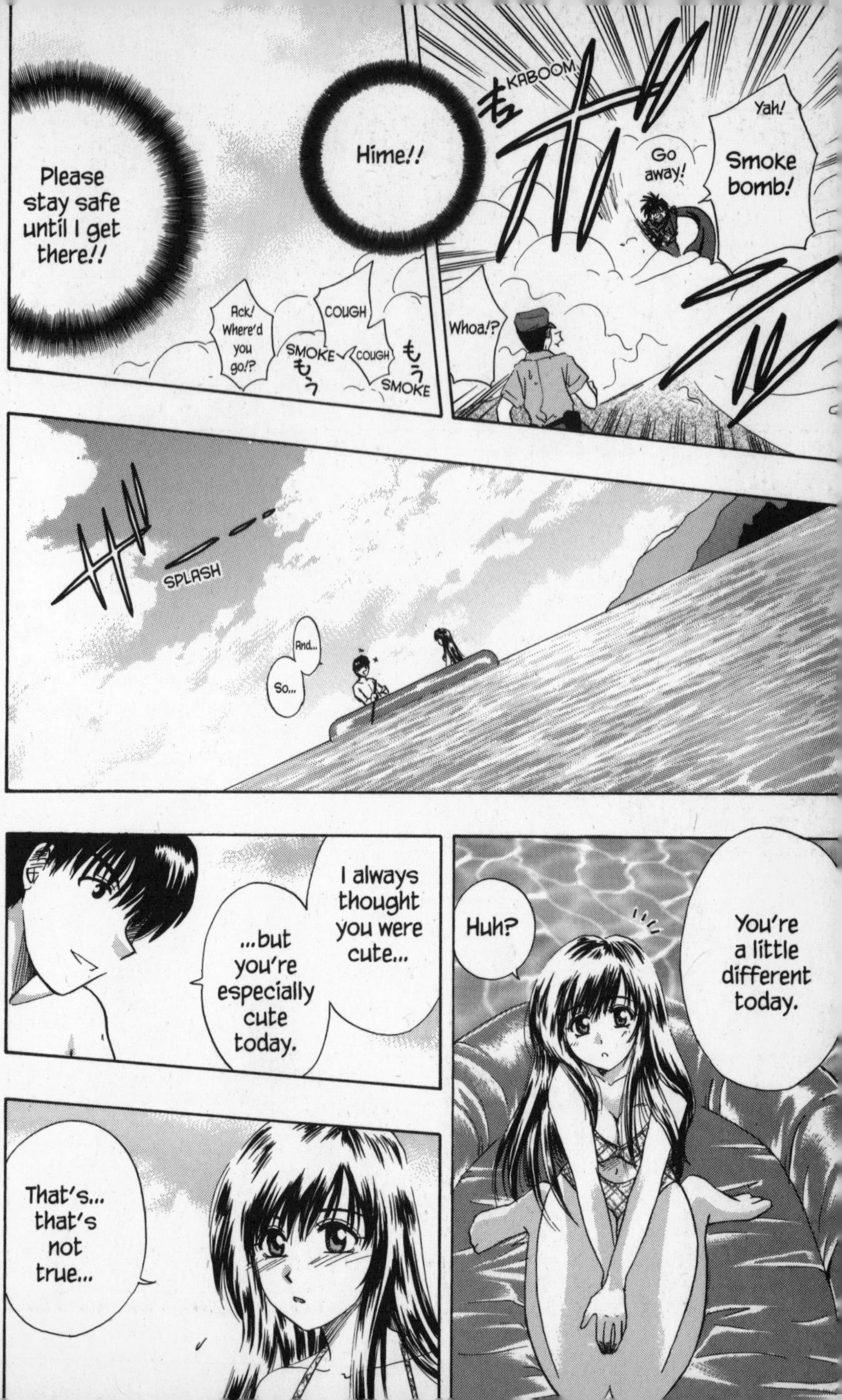
Yah!
Smoke bomb!
Go away!
KABOOM
Whoa!?
Hime!!
Please stay safe until I get there!!
COUGH
Ack! Where'd you go!?
SMOKE
COUGH
SMOKE
SPLASH
And...
So...
You're a little different today.
Huh?
I always thought you were cute...
...but you're especially cute today.
That's... that's not true...

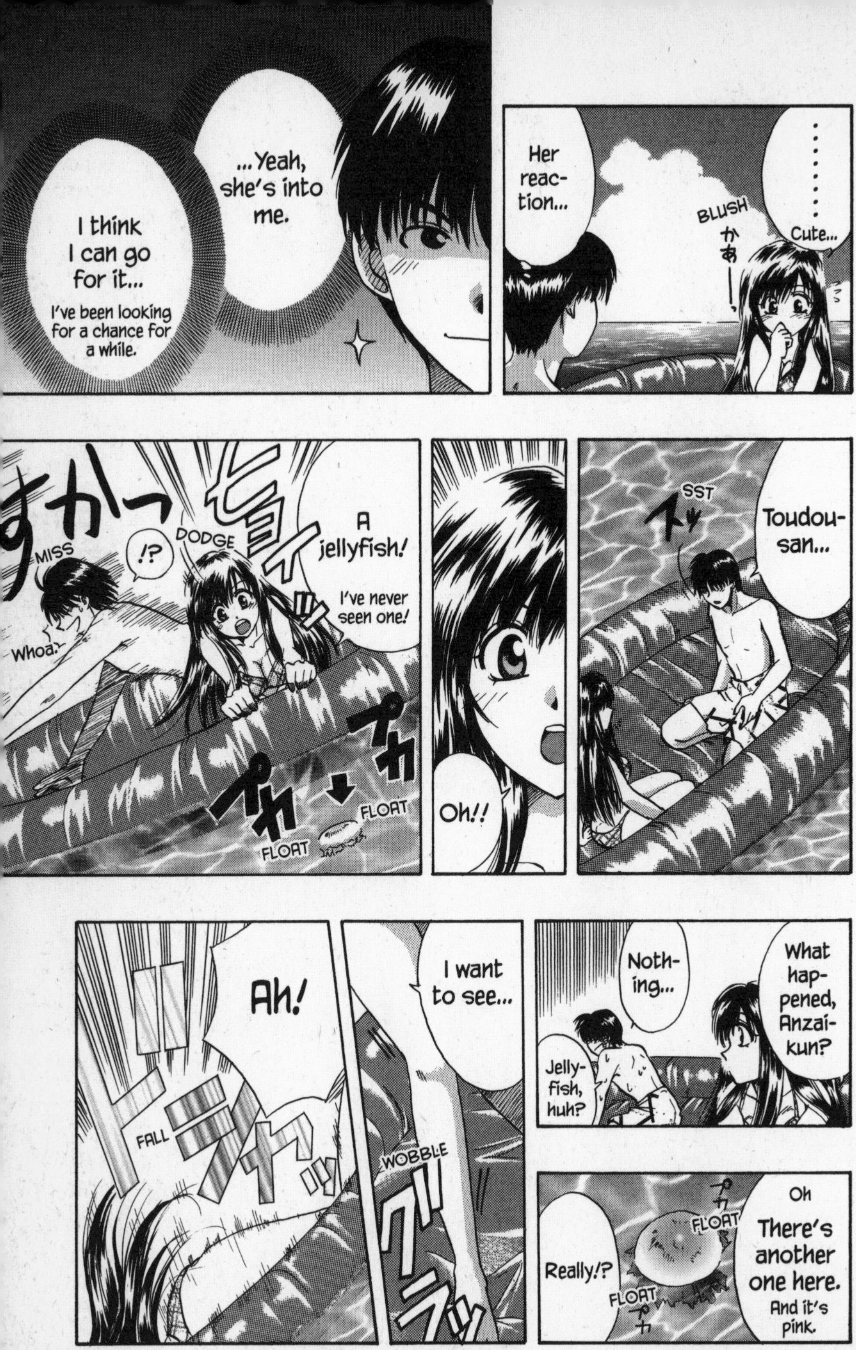

......
Cute...
BLUSH
かあー
Her reaction...
...Yeah, she's into me.
I think I can go for it...
I've been looking for a chance for a while.
SST
Toudou-san...
Oh!!
A jellyfish!
I've never seen one!
DODGE
!?
すかっ
MISS
Whoa.
FLOAT
FLOAT
What happened, Anzai-kun?
Nothing...
Jelly-fish, huh?
Oh
There's another one here.
And it's pink.
FLOAT
Really!?
FLOAT
I want to see...
WOBBLE
Ah!
FALL

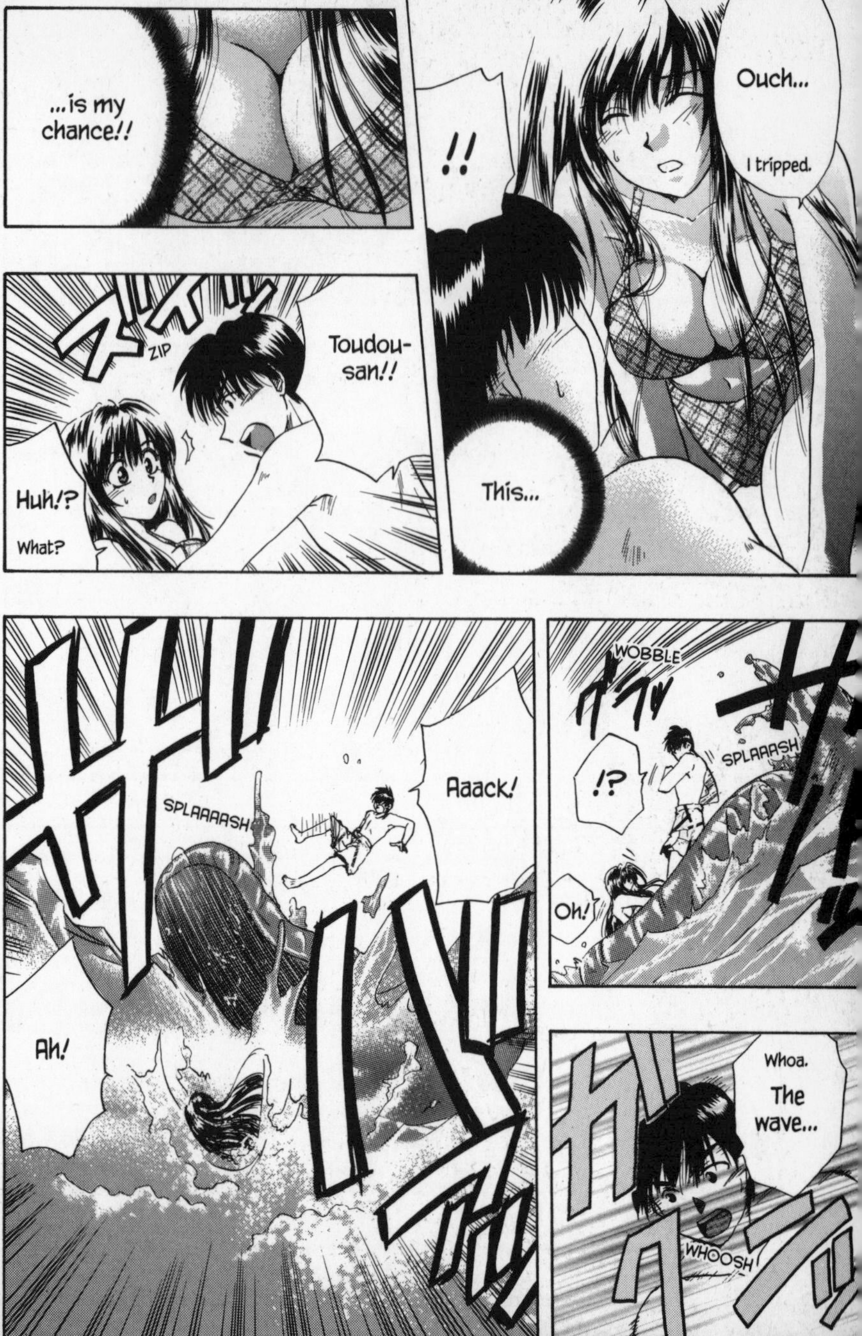
Ouch...
I tripped.
!!
This...
...is my chance!!
ZIP
Toudou-san!!
Huh!?
What?
WOBBLE
!?
SPLAAASH
Oh!
Whoa.
The wave...
WHOOSH
SPLAAAASH
Aaack!
Ah!

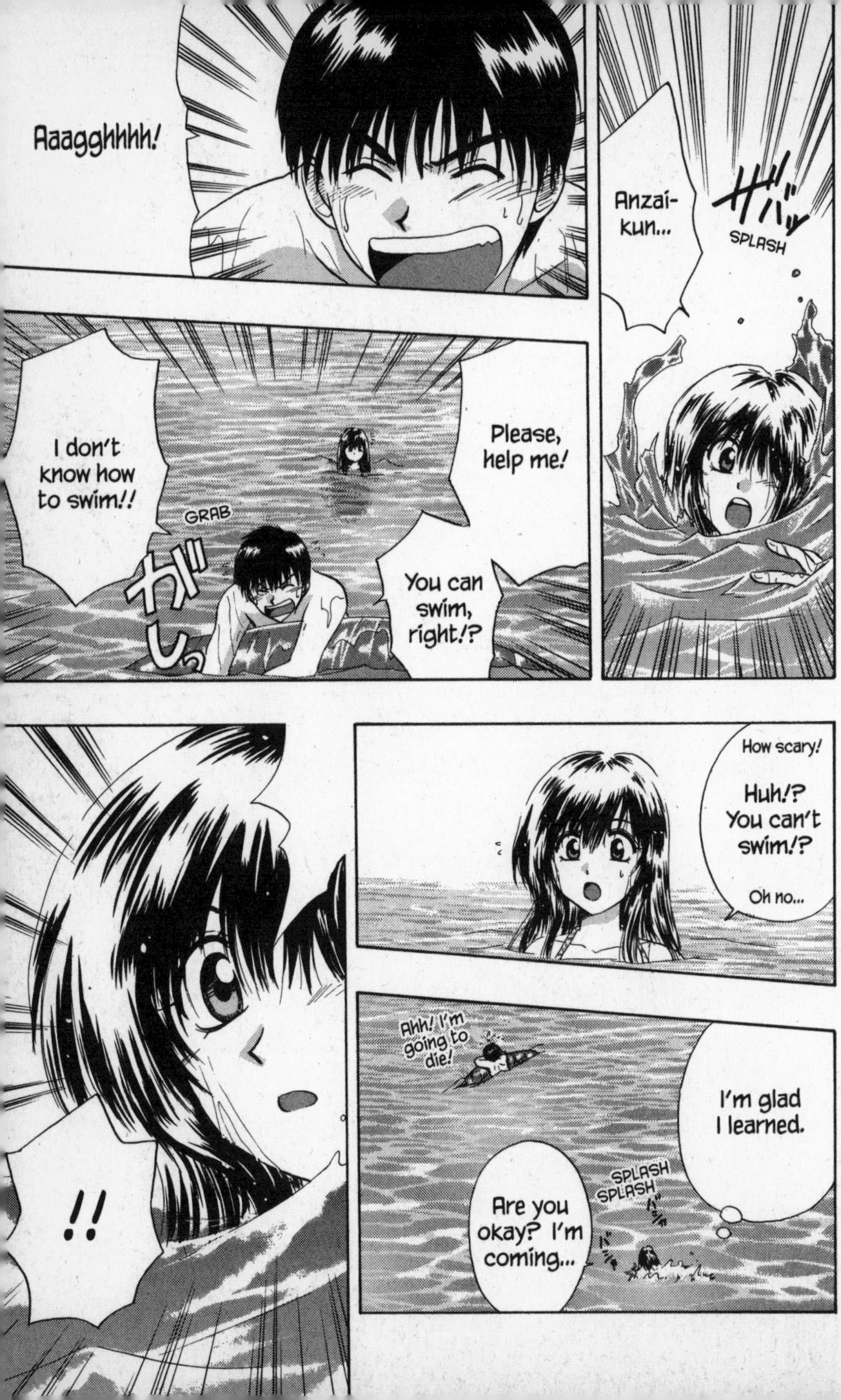
Anzai-kun...
ザバッ
SPLASH
Aaagghhhh!
Please, help me!
I don't know how to swim!!
GRAB
わしっ
You can swim, right!?
How scary!
Huh!? You can't swim!?
Oh no...
I'm glad I learned.
Ahh! I'm going to die!
SPLASH SPLASH
Are you okay? I'm coming...
!!

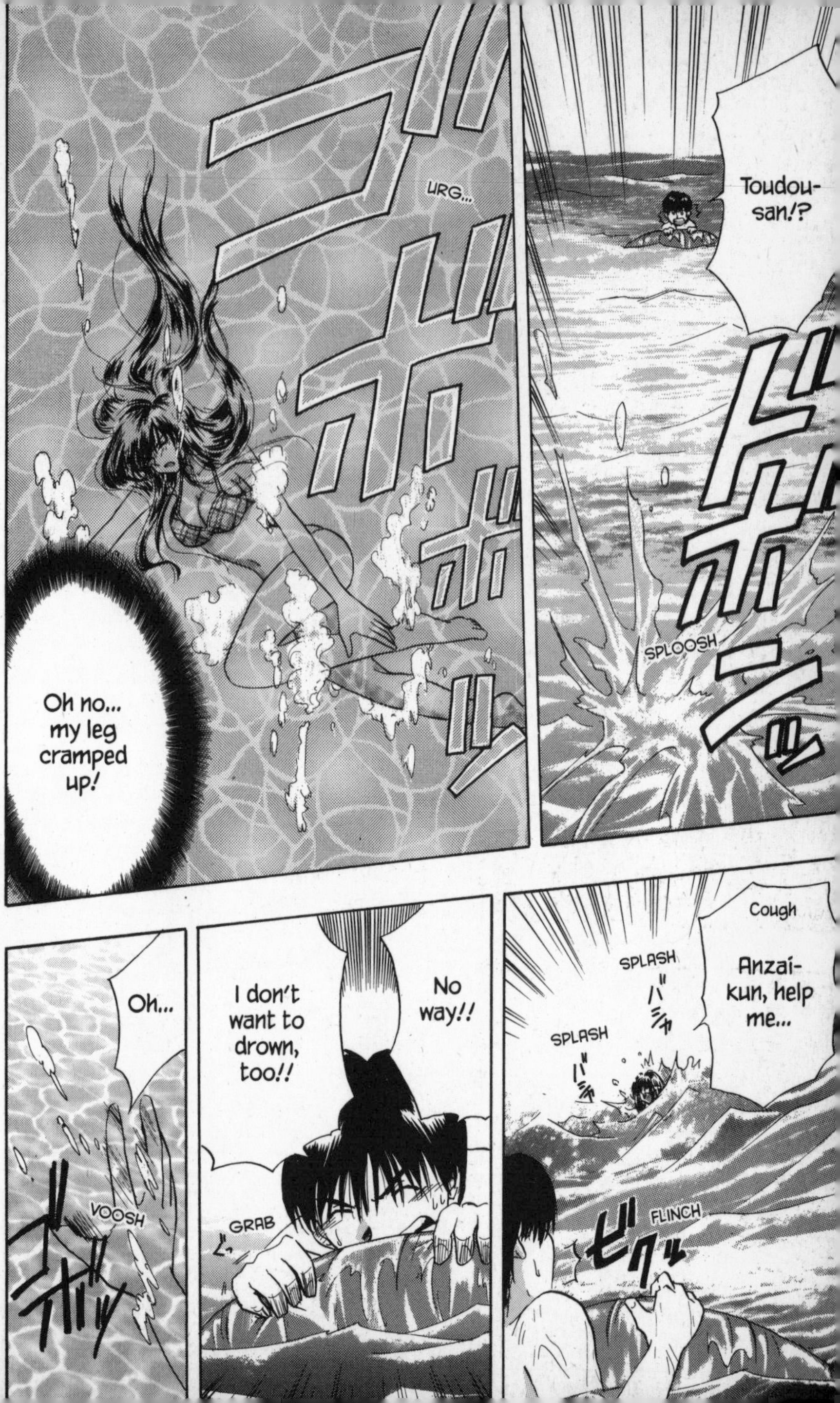
Toudou-
san!?
SPLOOSH
URG...
Oh no...
my leg
cramped
up!
Cough
Anzai-
kun, help
me...
SPLASH
SPLASH
FLINCH
No
way!!
I don't
want to
drown,
too!!
GRAB
Oh...
VOOSH

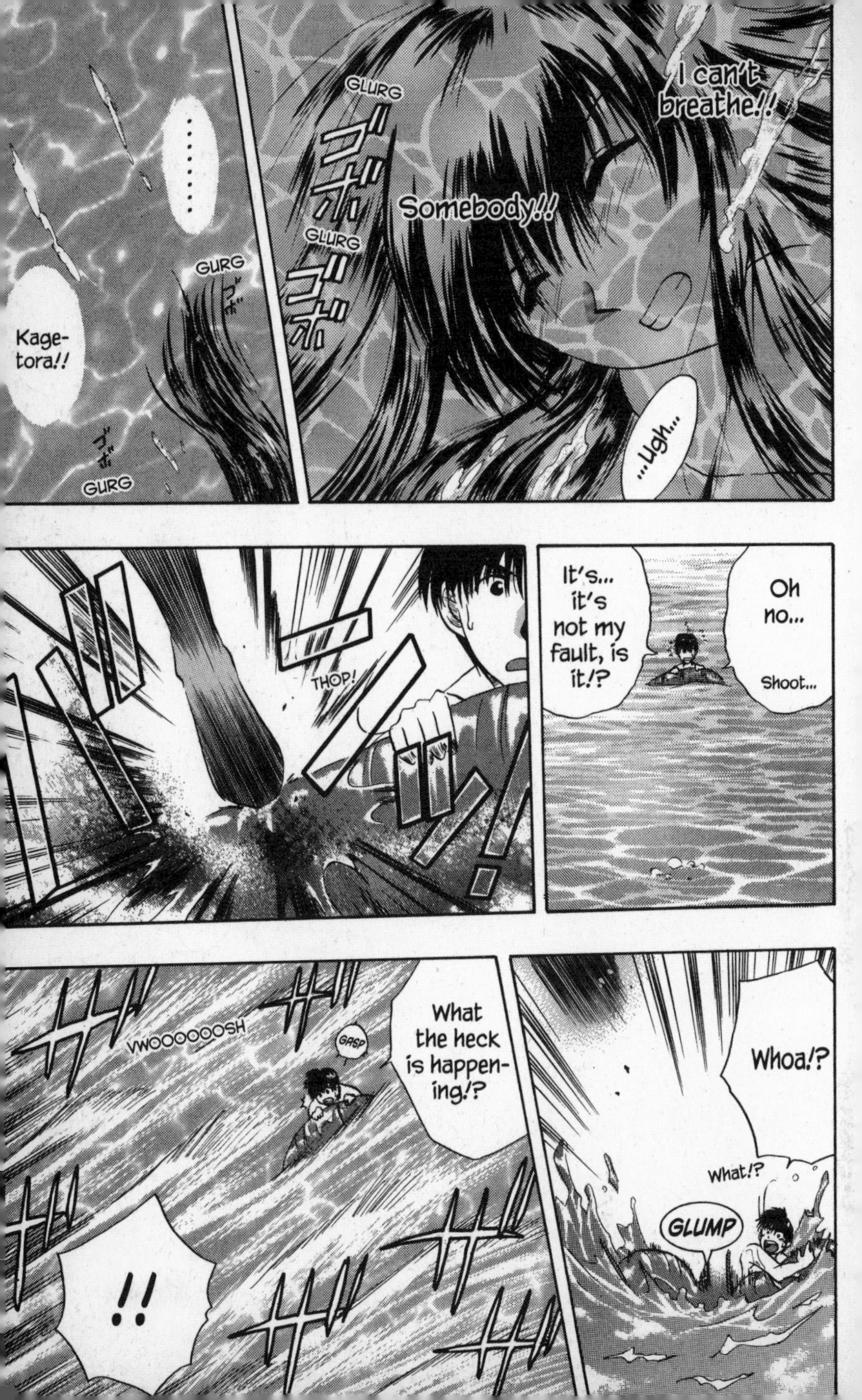
I can't breathe!!
GLURG
Somebody!!
GLURG
...Ugh...
......
GURG
Kage-tora!!
GURG
Oh no...
Shoot...
It's... it's not my fault, is it!?
THOP!
Whoa!?
What!?
GLUMP
What the heck is happening!?
VWOOOOOOOSH
GASP
!!

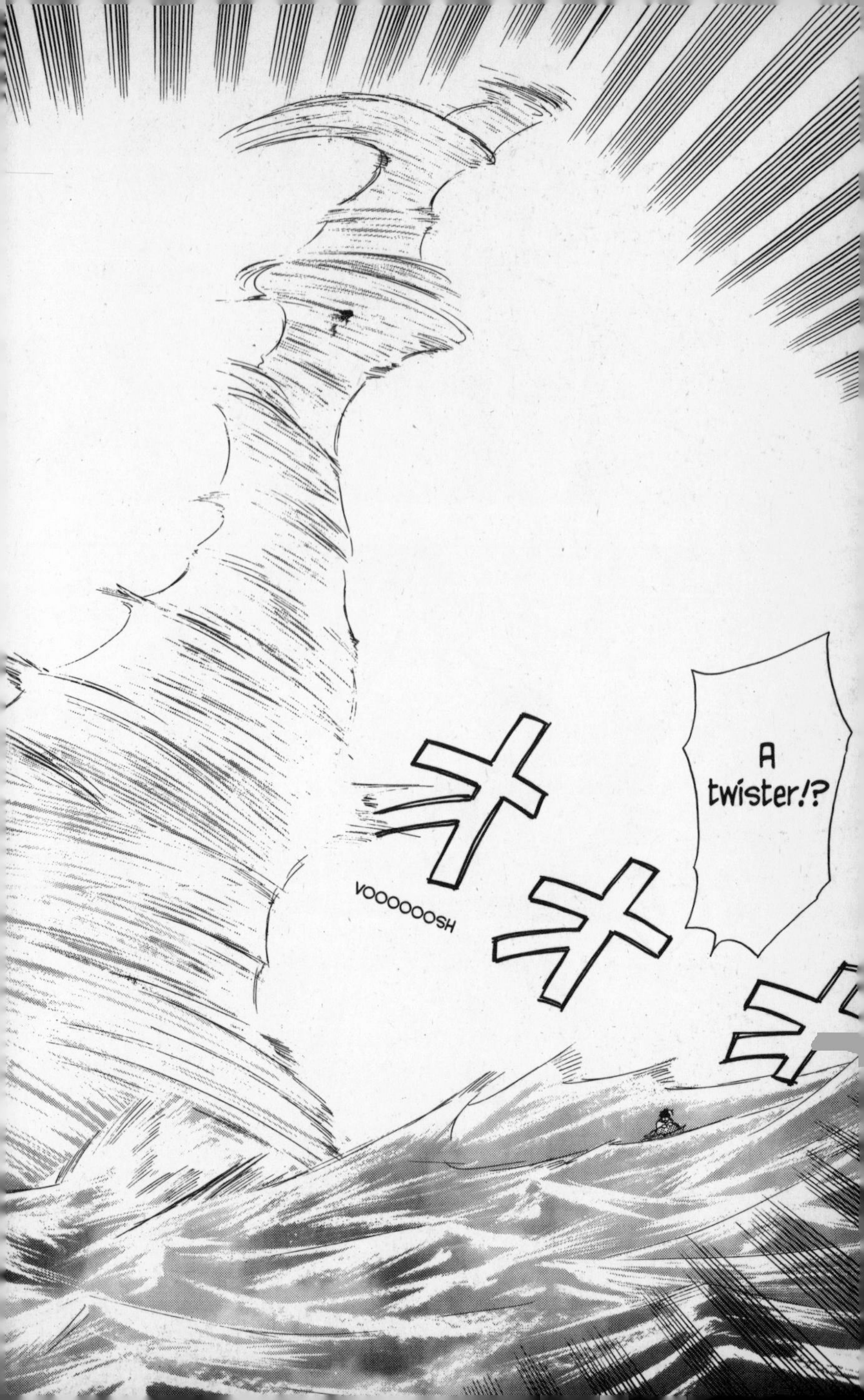
A twister!?
VOOOOOOSH

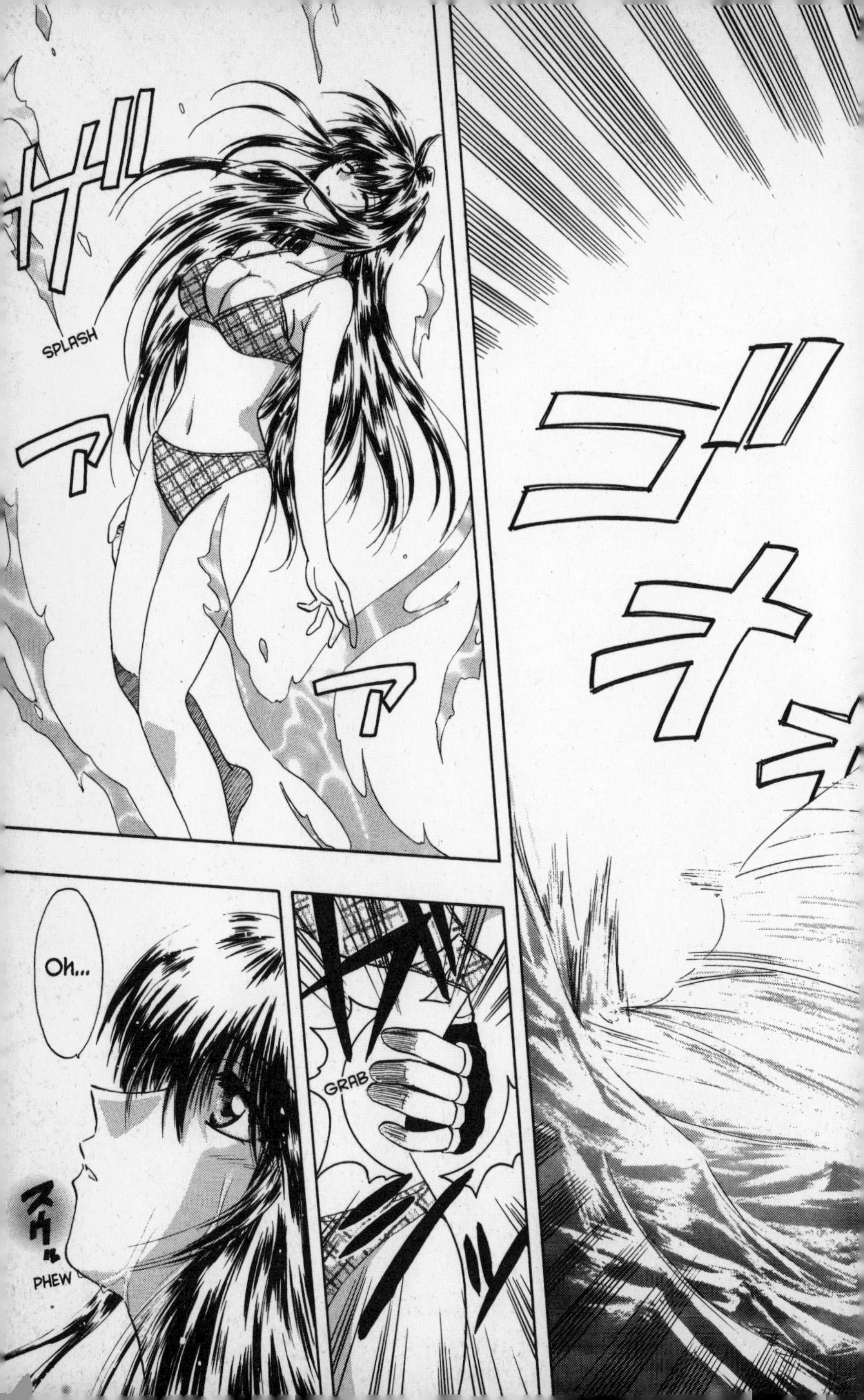
SPLASH
GRAB
Oh...
PHEW

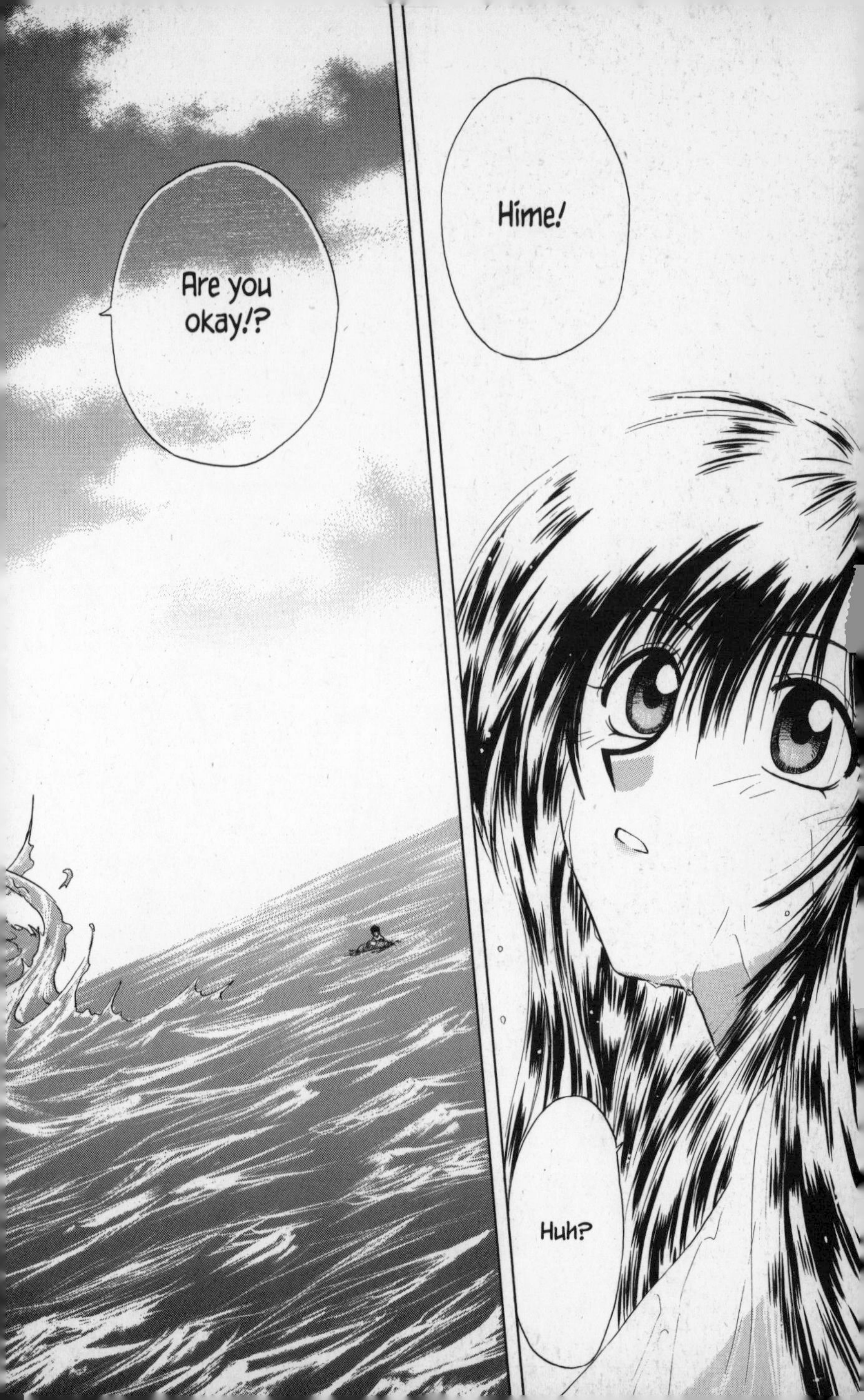
Hime!
Huh?
Are you okay!?

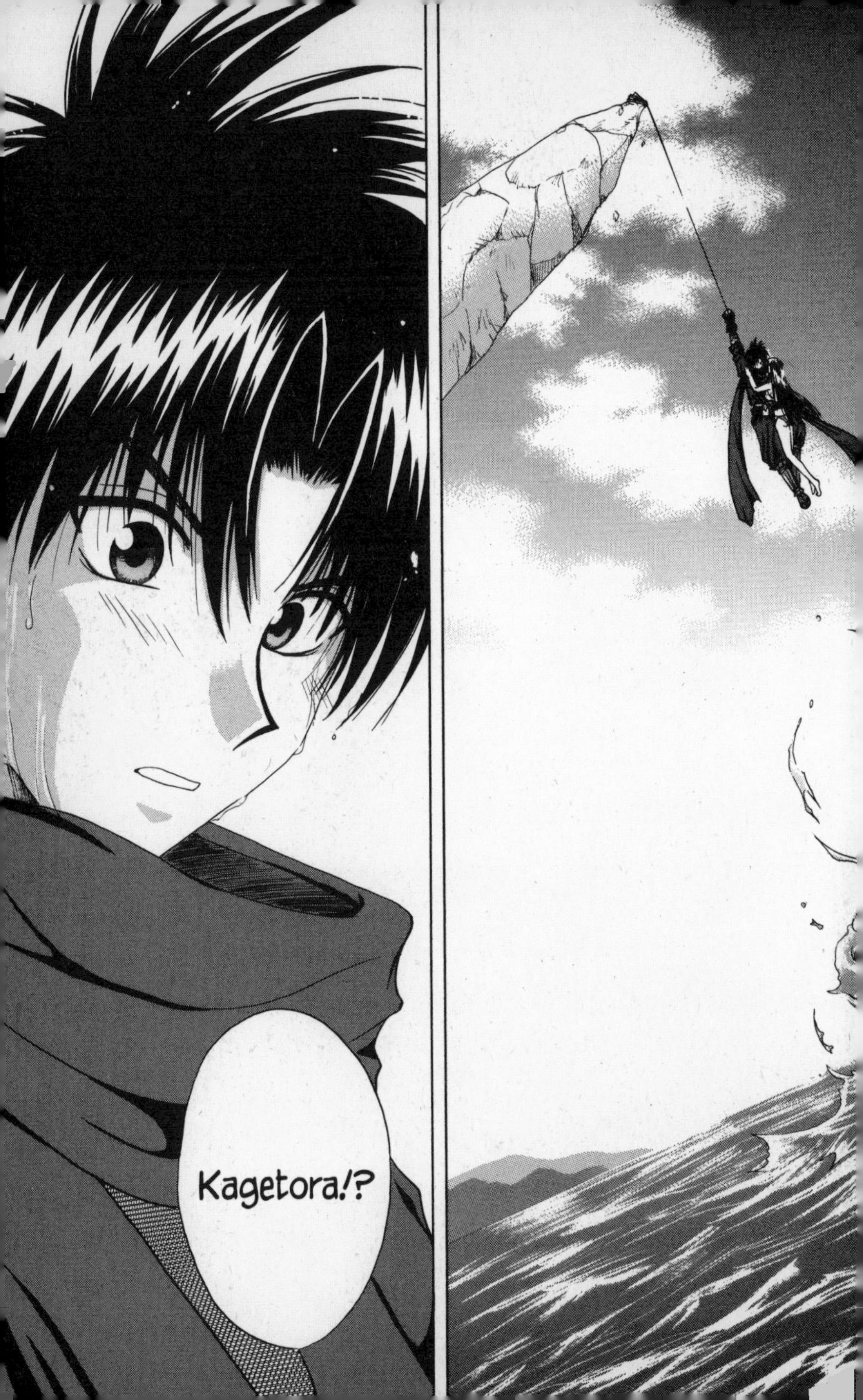
Kagetora!?

You're safe now!

Kagetora...

I'm sorry I was late...

A ninja!?

GAPE

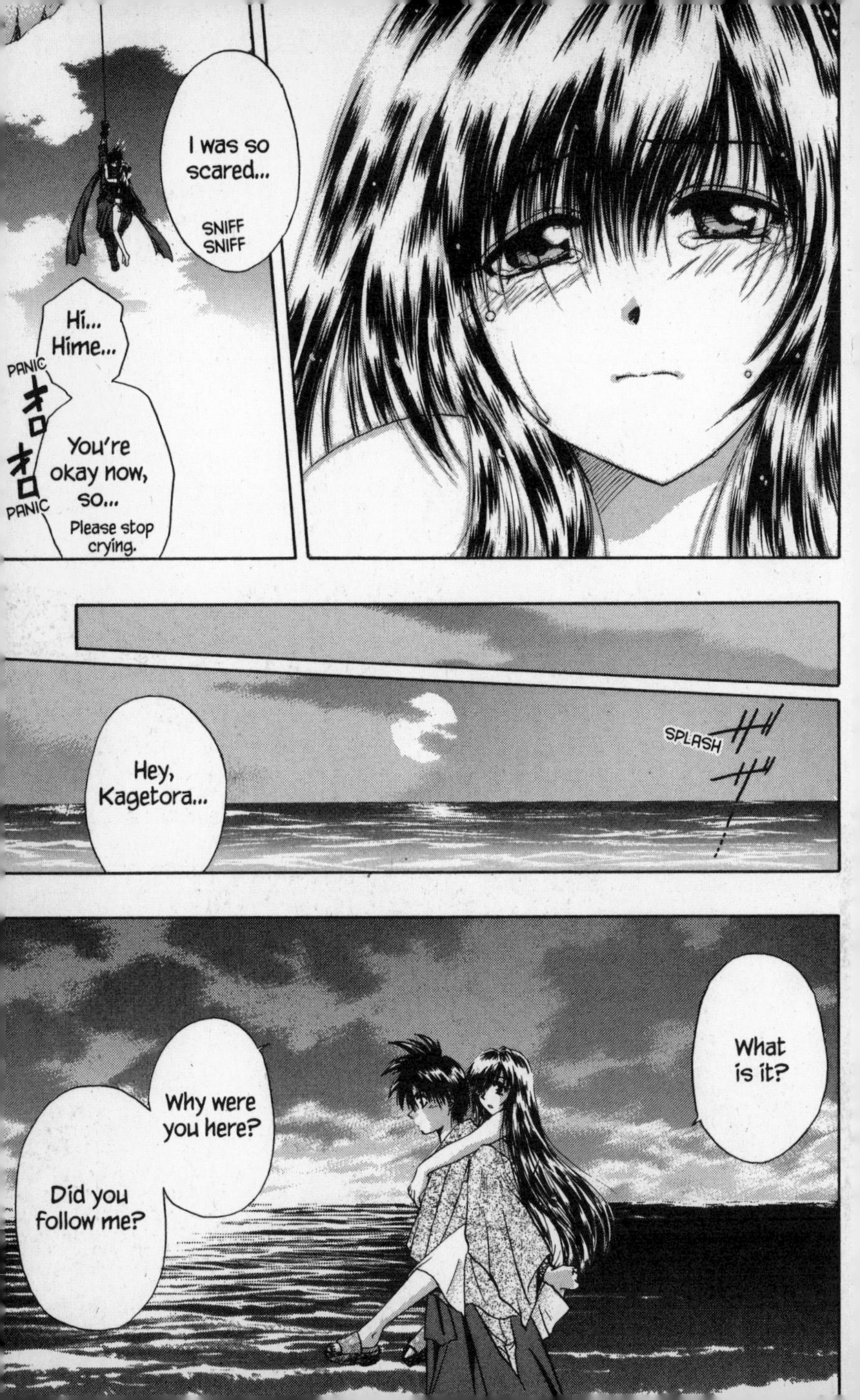
I was so scared...
SNIFF SNIFF
Hi... Hime...
PANIC
オロオロ
PANIC
You're okay now, so...
Please stop crying.
Hey, Kagetora...
SPLASH
ザザ
What is it?
Why were you here?
Did you follow me?

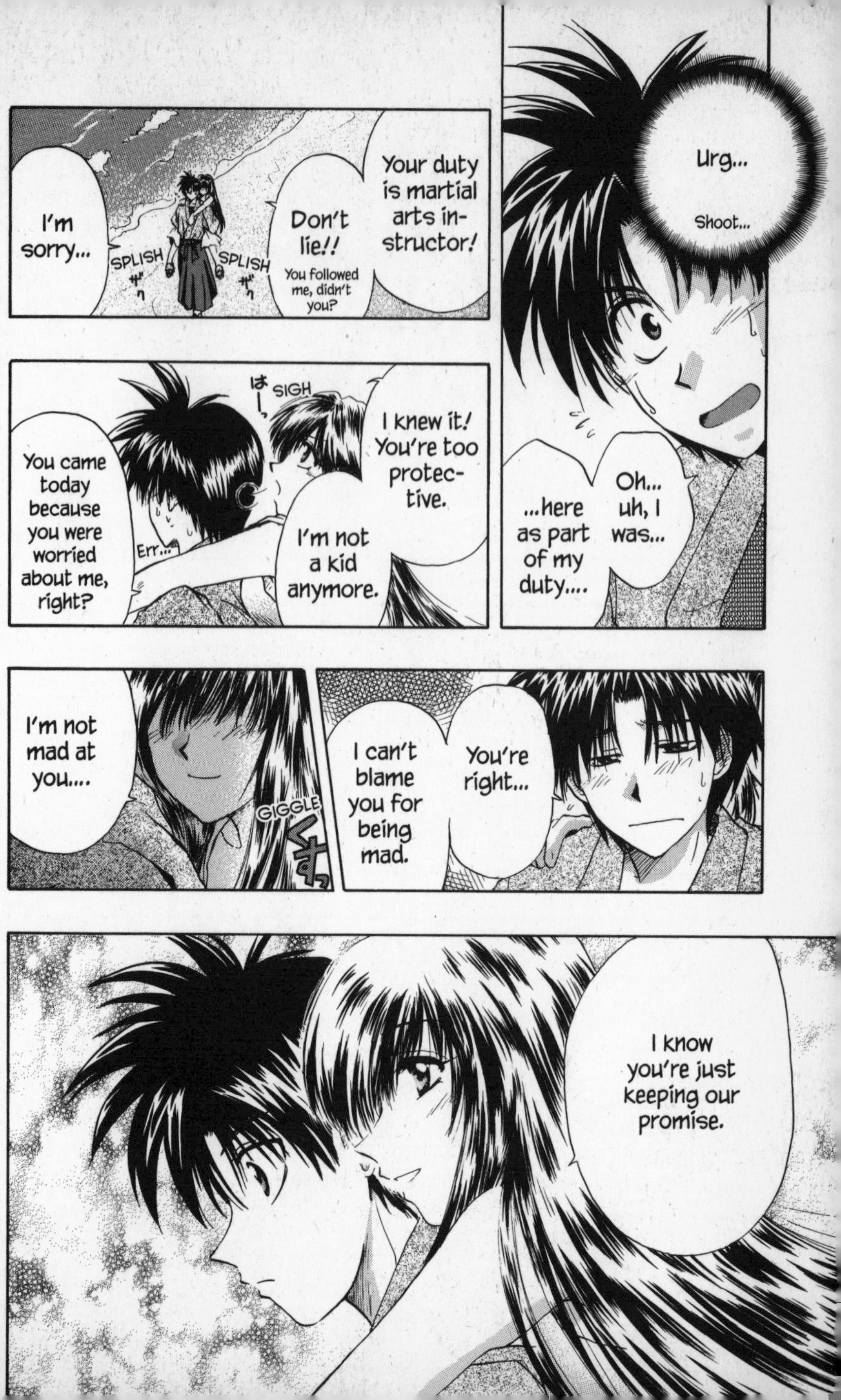
Urg...
Shoot...
Oh... uh, I was...
...here as part of my duty....
Your duty is martial arts instructor!
Don't lie!!
You followed me, didn't you?
SPLISH
SPLISH
I'm sorry...
I knew it! You're too protective.
SIGH
I'm not a kid anymore.
Err...
You came today because you were worried about me, right?
You're right...
I can't blame you for being mad.
GIGGLE
I'm not mad at you....
I know you're just keeping our promise.

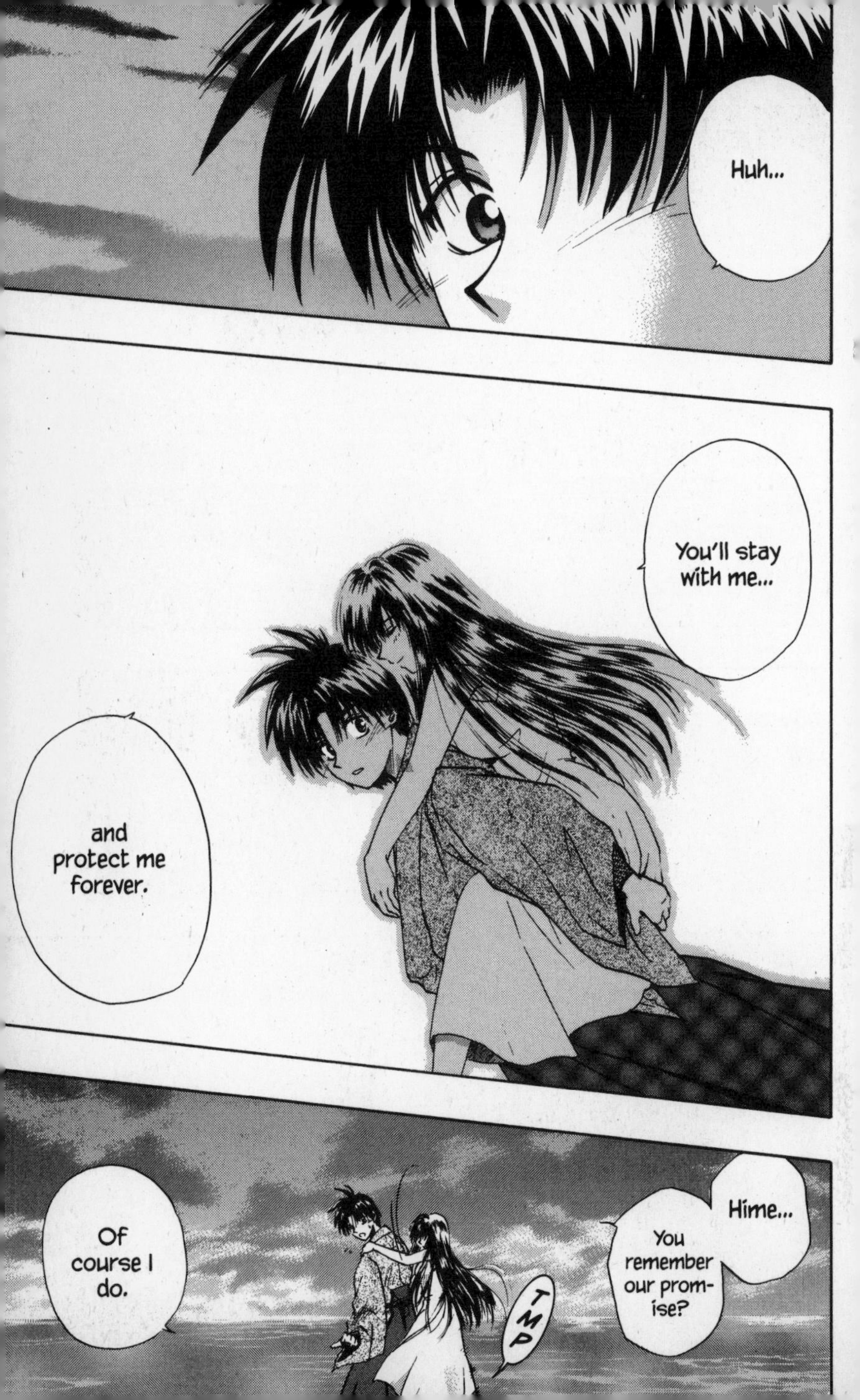
Huh...
You'll stay with me...
and protect me forever.
Hime...
You remember our prom-ise?
TMP
Of course I do.

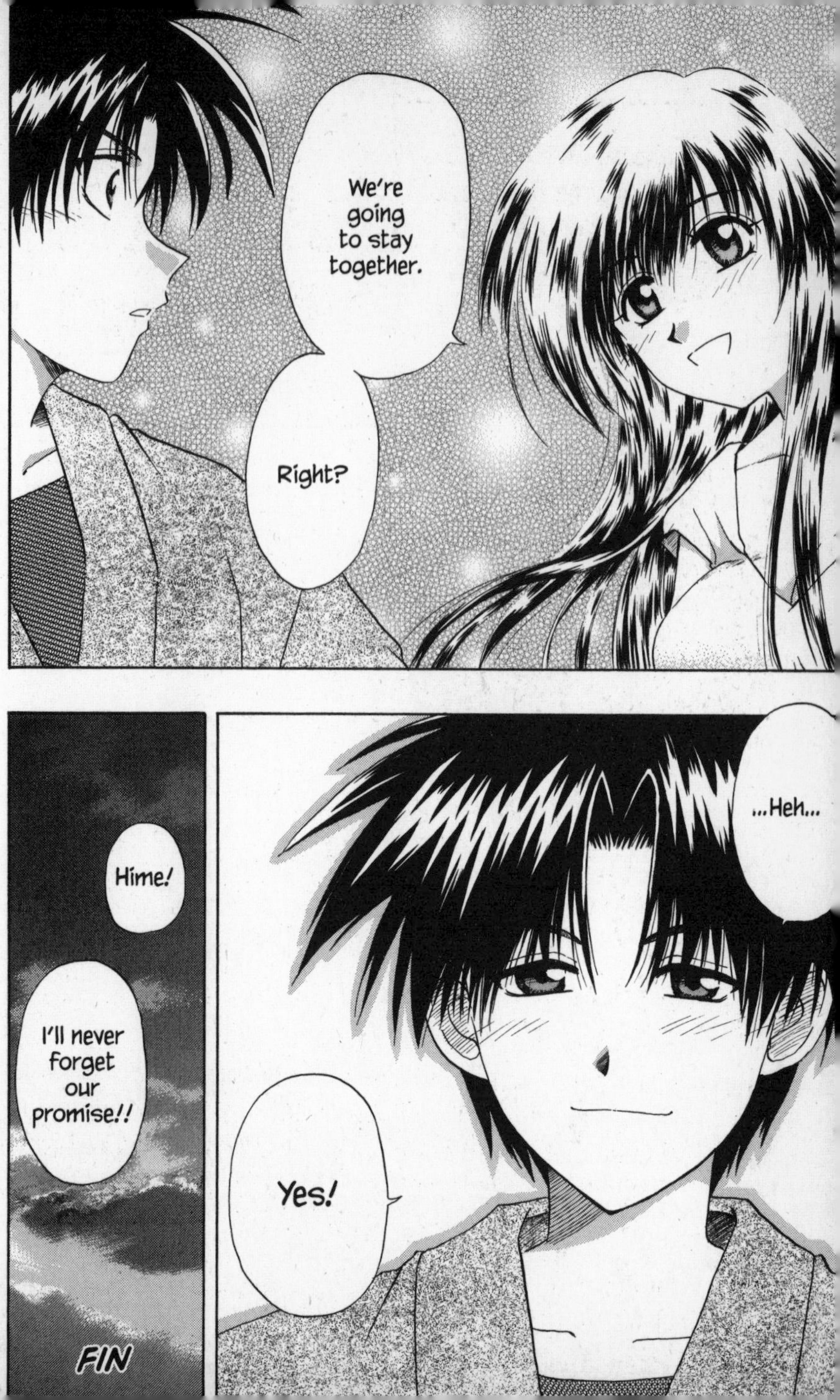
We're going to stay together.
Right?
...Heh...
Yes!
Hime!
I'll never forget our promise!!
FIN

Final Bonus Page!

This is Segami. It's finally Volume 11!! It's the final volume for "KAGETORA!!" I finally reached the ending! Thank you for sticking with me.

...Tears of joy.

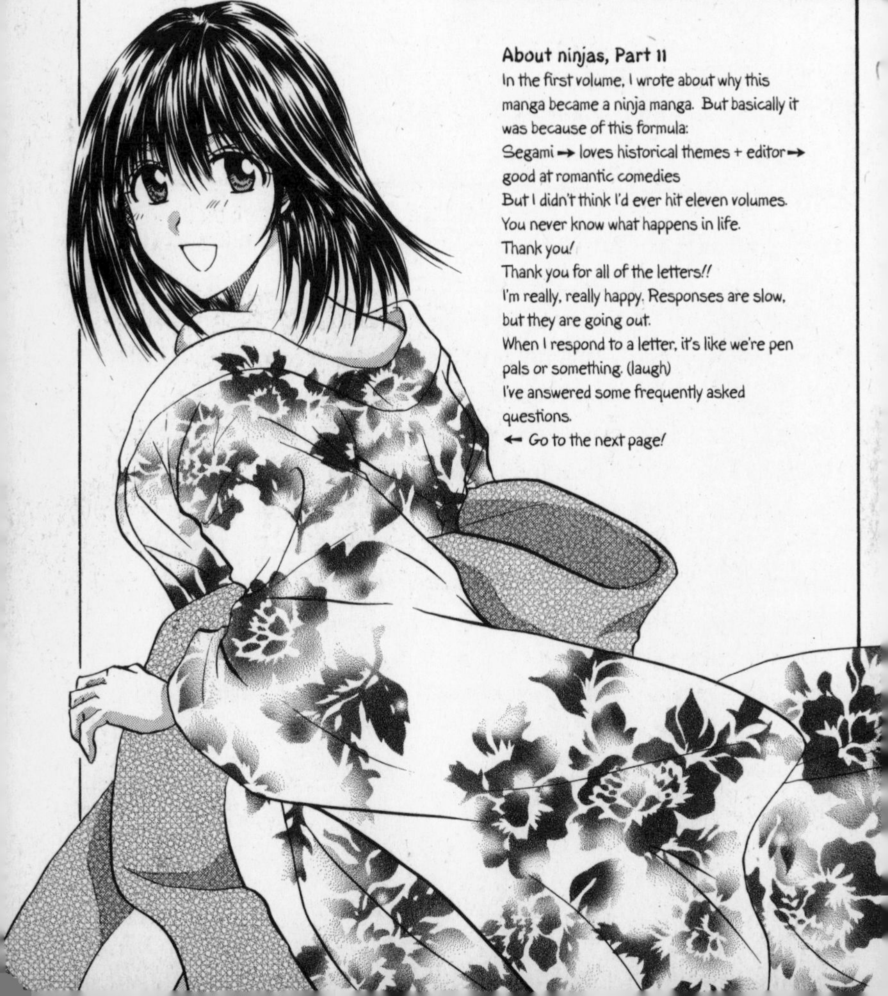

About ninjas, Part 11

In the first volume, I wrote about why this manga became a ninja manga. But basically it was because of this formula:

Segami → loves historical themes + editor → good at romantic comedies

But I didn't think I'd ever hit eleven volumes. You never know what happens in life.

Thank you!

Thank you for all of the letters!!

I'm really, really happy. Responses are slow, but they are going out.

When I respond to a letter, it's like we're pen pals or something. (laugh)

I've answered some frequently asked questions.

← Go to the next page!

Frequently Asked Questions

Q: What are the full names of Ono, Kamijou, and Ikoma?

A: Oops, I guess I never wrote them in the manga. (laugh) Sorry. Umm, it's "Hideaki Ono," "Hiroki Kamijou," and "Ryohei Ikoma."

Q: Is Grandma (Sagiri)'s husband a ninja?

A: Yes, he's a ninja. And he married into the Toudou family. (laugh)

Q: How did Yuki's parents meet?

A: Their houses were next door to each other and they were childhood friends.

There were other questions, but I'll leave them up to your imagination.

Well... KAGETORA finally reached its last volume. In the magazine, there was a countdown for the last three chapters ... It was interesting, but it also reminded me that KAGETORA was almost over. It's been five years (including the beta version), and a lot has happened. I've moved twice. I traveled and did research ... many times. (laugh) There were so many hectic deadlines ... But I was still able to do this, thanks to everybody!! KAGETORA was something I never could've done without the help of others. For me, someone who's bad at romantic comedies (laugh), to reach eleven volumes is a miracle! Although I was really worried at first ... slowly the characters started to develop and grow and move on their own (even if they went overboard sometimes). I feel like I grew with the characters ... and so I was able to reach the happy final chapter.

Maybe it's a cliché, but I think love stories should end happily!

So with that in mind, I drew the final chapter. I didn't think I could draw a wedding . . . but I'm happy I was able to end it like this. If the readers are satisfied, then I'll be the happiest manga artist in the world.

KAGETORA is over, but I hope I can draw an even better series in the future!!

To everyone involved in making KAGETORA and to all the readers who stayed with me until the end, I give my thanks and appreciation.

THANK YOU VERY MUCH!!

And please continue to root for me!!

2006. 瀬上あきら

SpecialThanks

Assistants: Ryoji Tanaka, Mayumi Oshima, Atsuko Takasou, Makoto Nishikawa, everyone else who helped
Editors: Makoto Morita, Masayuki Yonemura
My family, cat, friends, etc. . . .
And all of the readers!!

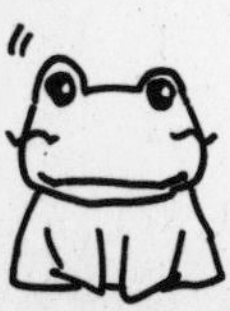

Then...let's see each other in my next series.

About the Author

Akira Segami's first manga was published by Shogakukan in 1996. He went on to do a few other small projects, including two short stories entitled "Kagetora" in 2001 and 2002. The character proved to be popular with fans, so Segami began his first ongoing series, *Kagetora*, with Kodansha in 2003. The series concluded with volume 11.

Translation Notes

Japanese is a tricky language for most Westerners, and translation is often more art than science. For your edification and reading pleasure, here are notes on some of the places where we could have gone in a different direction with our translation of the work, or where a Japanese cultural reference is used.

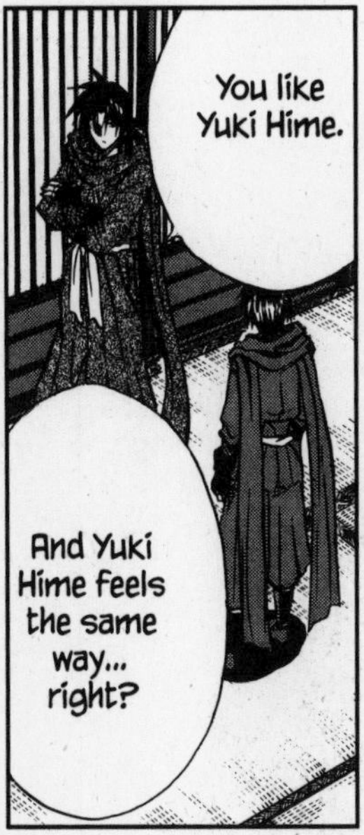
You like Yuki Hime.
And Yuki Hime feels the same way... right?

***Hime*, page 8**

The literal translation of the word *hime* is "princess" in Japanese. *Hime* can also be used as an honorific for a daughter of a high-class family. Generally, Kagetora refers to Yuki as a *hime*, as she's the daughter of a respected master of the martial arts, and from an honorable family. But in this panel, Shirou is specifically calling her Princess Yuki.

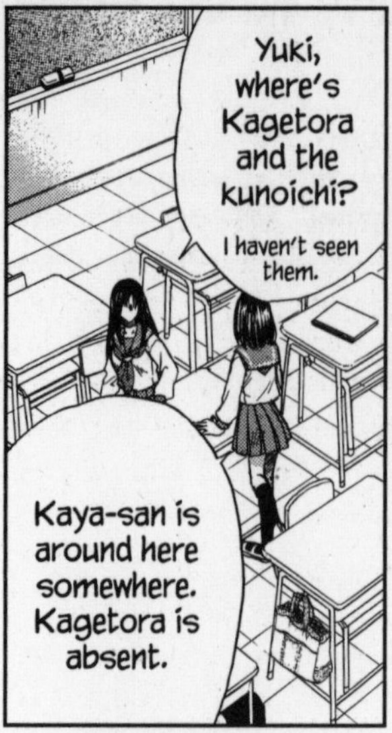
Yuki, where's Kagetora and the kunoichi?
I haven't seen them.
Kaya-san is around here somewhere. Kagetora is absent.

***Kunoichi*, page 13**

A *kunoichi* refers to a female ninja. Historically, *kunoichi* were trained in deception and seduction, designed to seduce men with political power. They were often disguised as dancers, geisha, and prostitutes. But in modern terminology, a *kunoichi* is simply a female ninja, trained in ninjutsu like their male counterparts.

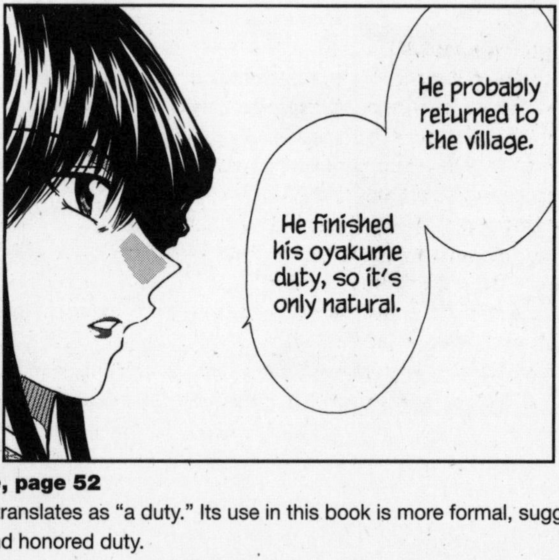
He probably returned to the village.
He finished his oyakume duty, so it's only natural.

***Oyakume*, page 52**

Oyakume translates as "a duty." Its use in this book is more formal, suggesting a specific and honored duty.

Hime wrote something before...

An ema...

Ema, page 68
Ema are wooden blocks found in shrines. They have a picture of a horse on them. Visitors to the shrine can buy an *ema* and write a wish or prayer on it and hang it at the shrine.

List of singers, page 98
Kobukuro is a duo of two male singers. They sing folk songs for the most part. They met while both were street musicians.

Angela Aki is a singer and songwriter. She grew up in the United States but decided to go back to Japan to pursue her music career. She is probably best known for her song "This Love" featured in "BLOOD+" anime, and "Kiss Me Good-bye" featured in the video game Final Fantasy XII.

Lyrico is a singer who was formerly known as Harumi Tsuyuzaki. After she married, she changed her name to Lyrico.

Emiko Shiratori is a singer, known for her great soprano voice. She covered "Amazing Grace" in 1987, which is one of the reasons why the song is well known in Japan. Among young people, she is best known for her song "Melodies of Life," which was featured in the video game Final Fantasy IX.

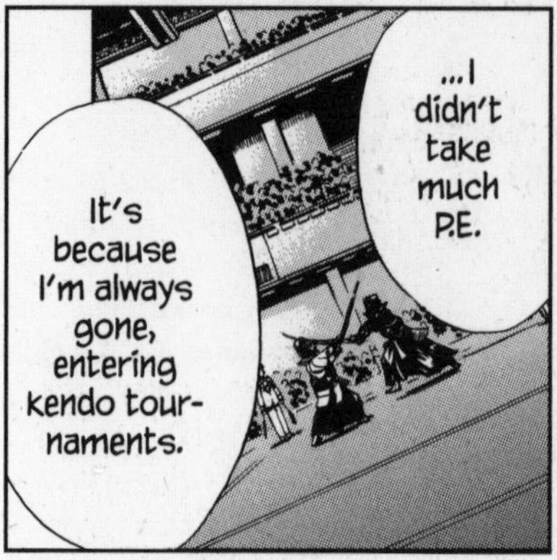
...I didn't take much P.E.
It's because I'm always gone, entering kendo tour-naments.

Kendo, page 149

Kendo, the way of the sword, is the art of Japanese swordsmanship and is similar to fencing. People use bamboo swords and wear protective gear. Its origin comes from *Budo*, the Martial way. *Kendo* is one of the most popular sports taught at Japanese schools, along with Judo.

Cosplay, page 172

Cosplay is short for Costume Play. Cosplay means dressing up as a character from manga, anime, and/or video games.

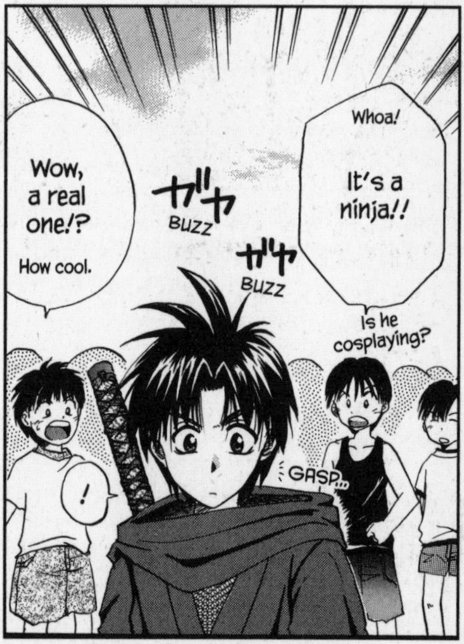
Whoa!
It's a ninja!!
Is he cosplaying?
ガヤ BUZZ
ガヤ BUZZ
Wow, a real one!?
How cool.
GASP...
!

BY MACHIKO SAKURAI

A LITTLE LIVING DOLL!

What would you do if your favorite toy came to life and became your best friend? Well, that's just what happens to Ame Oikawa, a shy schoolgirl. Nicori is a super-cute doll with a mind of its own—and a plan to make Ame's dreams come true!

Special extras in each volume! Read them all!

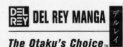

School Rumble

BY JIN KOBAYASHI

SUBTLETY IS FOR WIMPS!

She . . . is a second-year high school student with a single all-consuming question: Will the boy she likes ever really notice her?

He . . . is the school's most notorious juvenile delinquent, and he's suddenly come to a shocking realization: He's got a huge crush, and now he must tell her how he feels.

Life-changing obsessions, colossal foul-ups, grand schemes, deep-seated anxieties, and raging hormones—School Rumble portrays high school as it really is: over-the-top comedy!

Ages: 16 +

Special extras in each volume! Read them all!

BY YUKO OSADA

SEE THE WORLD WITH ME!

Kakashi is a small-town boy with a big dream: to travel around the world. He's so determined to leave his little island home behind that he stows away onboard a marvelous zeppelin—one that just happens to be loaded with treasure and a gang of ruthless criminals!

Special extras in each volume! Read them all!

VISIT WWW.DELREYMANGA.COM TO:
- Read sample pages
- View release date calendars for upcoming volumes
- Sign up for Del Rey's free manga e-newsletter
- Find out the latest about new Del Rey Manga series

RATING T AGES 13+

 **DEL REY MANGA** デルレイ

The Otaku's Choice™

You are going the wrong way!

Manga is a completely different
type of reading experience.

To start at the *beginning,* go to the *end!*

That's right! Authentic manga is read the traditional Japanese
way—from right to left. Exactly the *opposite* of how American
books are read. It's easy to follow: Just go to the other end of
the book, and read each page—and each panel—from right side
to left side, starting at the top right. Now you're experiencing
manga as it was meant to be.